ARTHUR ELLICOTT CASE
1894—1946

STUDIES IN THE LITERATURE
OF THE
AUGUSTAN AGE

Essays Collected in Honor of

ARTHUR ELLICOTT CASE

Edited by

Richard C. Boys

Distributed for the
AUGUSTAN REPRINT SOCIETY
by
THE GEORGE WAHR PUBLISHING CO.
Ann Arbor, Michigan
1952

CONTENTS

                          *   *   *   *   *

ARTHUR ELLICOTT CASE

INTRODUCTION

In 1938 the Editor, with Arthur Mizener, had an appointment to meet Arthur Case at a meeting of the Modern Language Association to discuss a new project in the field of the poetical miscellany. To the amazement of the two, whom Arthur Case had not known previously, they were presented with a suitcase full of invaluable notes. This act was typical of the generosity and friendliness of Arthur Case. Ever since his untimely death in 1946 some of his friends have contemplated a volume that would stand as a tribute to his kindness and scholarly achievement. The breadth of the present volume parallels his own wide range of interests; the enthusiasm with which our contributors offered their articles reflects the warmth these scholars felt toward Arthur Case.

Studies in the Literature of the Augustan Age grew out of the Editor's conferences with Moody E. Prior and Frederick W. Hilles, whose counsel and interest in the project played a large part in determining the direction the volume would take. Later the experience of Raymond D. Havens, Ronald S. Crane, Louis I. Bredvold, and Edward N. Hooker was drawn upon and the Studies was launched. Various kinds of festschriften were examined, the shortcomings analyzed and the virtues noted. The conclusions gave rise to the present volume, which presents, we believe, a new kind of scholarly contribution. As one guiding principle we adopted the idea that the volume should be useful to a large audience, to students just beginning research in the Augustan field and to scholars already at home amid the celandine and verdant greens of the Enlightenment. With a few exceptions all of the contributors were friends of Arthur Case; each was asked to suggest, in order of preference, a few of his own titles chosen along the lines laid out. From these were selected the pieces reprinted in the Studies. In some ways the volume, spanning as it does the period 1917-1951, is representative of much of the best scholarship of the last thirty five years. It was with regret that we had to pass over other excellent articles.

By reprinting contributions already in existence we have attempted to make available materials that in many cases are, for all practical purposes, not easily obtained. In some libraries these articles have literally been read into shreds and have had to be withdrawn from general use; furthermore, small and new libraries have often not been able to obtain copies of the older journals. We hope, too, that our volume will be a useful addition to the shelves of individual scholars.

To reach as wide an audience as possible we have lithoprinted Studies in the Literature of the Augustan Age, although we are fully aware of the problems such a reproduction presents. Aesthetically the reprinting of a series of articles in different kinds of type is offensive, but to have retyped or printed the lot would have doubled the cost of the volume. One small benefit we gain is the retention of the pagination of the original journal. The page numbers in parentheses are our own.

The editors of the following scholarly publications have graciously given their permission to reprint pieces: The Journal of English Literary History, the University of California Publications in English, Modern Philology, Studies in Philology, The Huntington Library Quarterly, Modern Language Notes, English Institute Essays. The Rice Institute Pamphlet, The Yale Review, The University of Toronto Quarterly, Modern Language Quarterly, The Art Bulletin. The Editor wishes to thank the editors and sponsors of these journals. To his colleagues Louis I. Bredvold and Arthur Eastman, and to his other consultants and contributors, especially to Moody E. Prior and Frederick W. Hilles, the Editor would like to express his gratitude.

All of us who have had a hand in the preparation of <u>Studies in the Litera-ture of the Augustan Age</u> offer it to Mrs. Arthur E. Case as a symbol of our admiration for Arthur E. Case, a fine scholar and a friend whom we miss.

Richard C. Boys

Ann Arbor
January, 1952

LOUIS I. BREDVOLD

A Note in Defence of Satire

from

A JOURNAL OF ENGLISH LITERARY HISTORY

Volume VII(1940), 253-64

ELH

A Journal of English Literary History

| VOLUME SEVEN | DECEMBER, 1940 | NUMBER FOUR |

A NOTE IN DEFENCE OF SATIRE

By LOUIS I. BREDVOLD

τὸ νεμεσᾶν interest τοῦ φθονεῖν.
Indignation is different from malice.
—Cicero, *Att.* V. xix.

The purpose of this paper is to reopen the question of the nature of satire and to make some suggestions towards the answer. In the current standard treatises on laughter and the comic spirit satire appears as the least attractive and the least defensible of the many manifestations of the comic spirit,—if, indeed, it can be defended at all. No one cares to champion anything so ignoble and ill-mannered and negative. And it is not difficult to understand why this should be so, in view of the orientation and general tendency of modern theory regarding the nature of the comic. The psychologists and estheticians who have studied laughter and the comic spirit have quite properly insisted that in their " pure " states they are innocent, even though they may be corrective; laughter is related to the play instinct, for instance, and the pure comic spirit is an enjoyable perception of mere incongruity, a free play of the intelligence without malice—as Meredith described it in his classic treatise. But in satire, they observe, the comic spirit is contaminated, if not obscured, by something foreign to its nature; in the place of hearty and wholesome laughter we get the sneer of malignity. Moreover, they derive conclusions distinctly unfavorable to

253

satire from their historical study both of the theories of the comic and of its manifestation in literature. The earlier theories assumed that laughter is derisive or vindictive, and the possibility of neutral or sympathetic laughter is a discovery of modern times. It is a commonplace also to observe that the scope of our humanitarian feelings has been greatly extended even since the Renaissance, and that we consequently no longer laugh at such unfortunates as cripples and idiots; and with this advance in civilization, which no one surely would sacrifice, the derisive laughter of some Renaissance comedy appears vulgar and brutal. Such a reflection naturally makes us rather uneasy regarding the ethics of satire. On the other hand, one of the most charming and civilizing developments in modern feeling is that of humor, which joins sentiment and sympathy with the comic spirit and thus reconciles it with humanitarianism; [1] this is admirable, this keep, the other banish. We can measure our progress against Hobbes' classic statement of the mistaken theory of derisive laughter:

Sudden glory is the passion which maketh those *Grimaces* called LAUGHTER, and is caused either by some sudden act of their own, that pleaseth them; or by the apprehension of some deformed thing in another, by comparison whereof they suddenly applaud themselves. And it is incident most to them, that are conscious of the fewest abilities in themselves; who are forced to keep themselves in their own favour, by observing the imperfections of other men. And therefore much laughter at the defects of others, is a signe of Pusillanimity. For of great minds, one of the proper workes is, to help and free others from scorn; and compare themselves onely with the most able. [2]

The modern theorist has an easy triumph over Hobbes, who could not understand the very common phenomenon of innocent laughter nor conceive of the pure comic spirit, and who so dogmatically asserted that all laughter is derisive. But perhaps the modern theorist goes wrong in turn in his assumption that,

---

[1] Max Eastman calls it the " discovery of benign humor." See his *Sense of Humor* (New York, 1922), Part 2, chap. 5.

[2] Eastman, *op. cit.*, p. 139. Eastman devotes a chapter to the illustration and refutation of the " derision theory." For other criticisms of it, see James Sully, *An Essay on the Theory of Laughter* (London, 1902), pp. 120 ff.; J. C. Gregory, *The Nature of Laughter* (New York, 1924), pp. 16 ff.; and Samuel S. Seward, Jr., *The Paradox of the Ludicrous* (Stanford, 1930), pp. 89-90.

in the course of his refutation of the derision theory, he has by implication dealt adequately with the nature of satire.

It is evident, however, that the lover of good satire is now put to it to defend his taste; new difficulties have arisen from an important group of historical and theoretical considerations which must in the main be accepted. For, although much great satire can probably be read only with a grave countenance and a pain in the heart, nevertheless all satire is related to laughter through the common element of the comic, and any sound theory of it must be adjusted to our theories of the comic and of laughter. The apologist must accordingly begin by acknowledging that derisive laughter is now regarded as a survival of our earlier barbarism which it is not honorable to cultivate. And if derisive laughter is no longer defensible, how can anyone extenuate the derision of satire, which, being of the same nature, must fall under the same condemnation? It is therefore not surprising that so little attention is given to satire in modern discussions of the comic spirit, and that this little is so unsympathetic.

It may be helpful at this point to sketch in outline the alternatives usually taken by modern theorists of satire. It is not easy, and perhaps sometimes not fair, to reduce their casual and often paradoxical comments to consistent systems, but it seems possible to distinguish three general types of theories either implicit or explicit in current discussion of the comic; the first is a direct condemnation of satire, and the second and third, which attempt to defend it, curiously begin by accepting uncritically the first.

According to the first of our theories, the pleasure we derive from satire may be explained frankly as a perversion of the emotions, an indulgence in cruelty, a *Schadenfreude*. Of course, if satire is a form of sadism, there is little to be said for it except that it is valuable clinical material for medical study. This unpleasant theory is not often expounded at length or pressed to its logical conclusion. It would involve us in the absurdity of condemning as corrupt a great body of literature which has been enjoyed by good men in all ages; it would be a ridiculous indictment of some of the Hebrew prophets and Dr. Johnson and Burke and Carlyle, as well as of Pope and Swift.

(4)

It usually lurks in the background, as an unexamined but indisputable axiom, its full enormity covered or softened by considerations of a more edifying character.

For it is the basic concession against which two other current theories attempt to erect the defence that satire is pardonable because it may be the instrument of moral and social reform. These theories begin by subscribing to the psychology of the *Schadenfreude*, of the laughter of derision, as the correct explanation of all shades of satire, from the light and gay to the malignantly bitter. The cruelty is admitted, but the application of whips and scorpions, it is added, is a necessary and wholesome corrective; like Hamlet, we must " be cruel only to be kind." On this fundamental principle one may proceed to vindicate satire in two ways.

A correction may be effected in the victim of the satire. This seems to be a very general hope, but a vague one, and plausible only if it is left vague. Although we frequently read about the satirist standing over the prostrate form of his victim, this picture seldom corresponds to any known historical fact. We have no evidence that corrupt politicians or hypocrites ever read the satires directed against them, or that, reading, their hearts are purified or their habits changed. The mere notion that literary satire accomplishes such a reformation is so preposterous as to be itself a specimen of the comic, and was so treated by Swift in a two-edged passage in that prefatory letter by Captain Gulliver which he added to the Faulkner edition of *Gulliver's Travels* in 1735:

I do in the next place complain of my own great want of judgement, in being prevailed upon by the entreaties and false reasonings of you and some others, very much against my own opinion, to suffer my travels to be published. Pray bring to your mind how often I desired you to consider, when you insisted on the motive of public good; that the Yahoos were a species of animals utterly incapable of amendment by precepts or examples: and so it hath proved; for instead of seeing a full stop put to all abuses and corruptions, at least in this little island, as I had reason to expect: behold, after above six months warning,[3] I cannot learn that my book hath produced one single effect according to my intentions. . . . And it must be owned that seven months were a sufficient time to correct

---

[3] Swift assigned to this letter the fictitious date of April 2, 1727.

every vice and folly to which Yahoos are subject, if their natures had been capable of the least disposition to virtue or wisdom.

We can all agree, and Swift doubtless would, that satire *ought* to accomplish more than it does; but Swift knew better than to expect in seven months to see " judges learned and honest; pleaders upright and modest, with some tincture of common sense; the young nobility's education entirely changed; the physicians banished; the female Yahoos abounding in virtue, honour, truth and good sense," and other such wholesale reforms. He had observed long before that satire is popular because every man applies it to his neighbor.

More credible is the second theory that satire is useful because it stirs up public opinion against malefactors, and thus prepares the way for effective social action against evils. This may be called the publicist function of satire. It would be easy to multiply evidence of its essential truth; revolutionists find " songs of hate " indispensable for their purpose; political satires, such as Swift's *Drapier's Letters,* have checked the courses of governments; poets, novelists, and artists have added momentum to many a great reform movement. But even with this element of truth in it, this theory is inadequate because it does not touch the heart of the problem; it is concerned with accidental effects rather than with the essential nature of satire; it is not even relevant to much great satire. Only an extraneous interest would impel a reader to hasten to historical works to discover whether Juvenal purified Rome and Dr. Johnson reformed London. We certainly read the satires of past ages, even those which had an influence on history, for some other reason than their historical or sociological importance.

The real weakness of both of these theories in defence of satire is that they are essentially sociological; they rely ultimately on some sort of statistical evidence—always a suspicious tendency in any theory of literary values. A theory of literature must first state with some precision the nature of the experience of the reader who enjoys it, and then inquire what implications of this experience appear necessary to the reader himself. If satire has any beneficent effects, they should be discoverable in this experience; and it is obvious enough that our enjoyment and our approval of satire are both integral parts of this experience, whereas all theories about the social utility of satire must in their very nature be derivative. We are therefore obliged to return to a further examination of the first theory we have described, the premise of the others.

As we have seen, satire is usually explained as that experience of the comic which is accompanied by a feeling of derision, of *Schadenfreude;* and it has been condoned, so far as possible, by the reflection that it often issues in social or moral reform. But the whole case is prejudicated by the iteration among our theorists of the word " derision," which is assumed to be the precise equivalent of satire. This term has not been a favorite with the satirists themselves; Juvenal did not say *fecit irrisio versum,* nor did Swift write in the epitaph he proposed for himself that he had gone *ubi saeva irrisio cor ulterius lacerare nequit.* The substitution debases them both; had they written so, they would have left us curious, but cold. The word they used was *indignatio,* which is nobler and touches deep sympathies within us. And the profound distinction between derision and indignation, which current theories either ignore or obscure, may be the clue to a more authentic explanation of our enjoyment of satire.

We must recognize that there are many kinds and shades of satire, and that some of these, lampoons for instance, may express nothing but derision. But personal abuse is satire of low order, unless neutralized by brilliant style and the gaiety of the comic spirit. Lampoons and libels are adequately explained by the derision theory, or, if they are witty enough, as Dryden suggested, to be enjoyed even by their victims, they would come under the theory of the *vis comica,* which need not be expounded again here. These ramifications of the subject have received abundant treatment elsewhere. We must limit our inquiry to the satire that arouses indignation, and to the possible alternative that it offers to the derision theory.

Derision and indignation cannot be absolutely opposed to one another; they are blended in our experience. Without disparagement there can be no satire. There is something like derision also in our indignation, but it is part of a larger complex and qualified by other elements; it may be better called contempt. On the other hand, what we usually call derision is

(7) .

incompatible with indignation. Derision is ridicule with an implication of our own superiority to its application; it is a cruel personal triumph, and deserves the condemnation it has received from Hobbes down to the present. Indignation is also directed against comic incongruities in our fellow-men, and implies, as truly as derision, a sense of our own superiority; but it includes also, by one of the marvels of our moral chemistry, a judgment which our moral integrity obliges us to make. We may laugh with mere derision at the failures of some incompetent bungler whose boasts may have bored or irritated us; but if we are worthy citizens we must feel a different kind of joy when an incompetent bungler is defeated for public office; we *must* rejoice at his defeat, lest we become unworthy in our own eyes. Derision, like envy, may be a mere personal feeling of a not very honorable kind; as it is essentially selfish, and unchecked by any ethical element, it may even turn brutally on victims of misfortune, such as a cripple or an old woman carrying a heavy burden. Indignation differs from derision in all these respects. It is an indictment, and as such appeals to some sort of categorical imperative, to what is right and just. It springs from some over-individual principle within us, not merely from our ego. Its harshness is not cruelty, but judgment against the avoidable errors, vices, and absurdities of life. We could feel indignation in the presence of a cripple only if we believed that his misfortune was the consequence of his own viciousness. For indignation is a judgment, not only *of* an individual, but *against* him. It is more than a perception of comic incongruity; it is a reproach addressed to some responsible individual who has deviated from a right and reasonable standard. Inanimate things and animals may be perceived as comic, but satire can be applied only to human beings, and only in situations for which they can be assumed responsible.

We often speak, too, of the anger and malice of the satirist. But we must distinguish between the simple and instinctive forms of these feelings and their very limited and specialized character when they become associated with indignation. The anger of the cheated horse-trader who vows revenge is one thing; the anger of a just God is another, and more likely to help us understand the nature of indignation. Irascibility and churlishness are not sufficient for satire, though théy may inspire mockery of a low kind. Malice and anger, like derision, may be either noble or ignoble, depending on the circumstances; and we must guard against the tendency of such words to carry over into our theory of satire certain meanings and connotations which, however applicable they may be in our other experience, are irreconcileable with the nature of indignation.

Indignation is distinguished from a merely personal feeling of resentment or desire for retaliation by the fact that its core is a judgment, an affirmation of some standard which we as good men cannot refuse to sustain. We must distinguish it on the other hand from the judgment involved in the pure comic, which is an intellectual perception of incongruity. All authorities seem to agree that laughter, whether derisive, neutral, or sympathetic, is a great corrective of human conduct; but its characteristic judgment is based on other than moral grounds, and its issue is merriment rather than condemnation. It may be the laughter of the mind at the incongruities of our civilization, as in Meredith; but Falstaff, the master comedian, is never more agreeably funny than when he mocks at old father antick the law. Laughter is a kind of play, which we may enjoy either by itself or in combination with a number of other feelings. Satiric indignation is aroused when we discover the incongruity of the comic in a situation which our moral judgment also condemns as unworthy, as *indignus*. It is this combination of the moral judgment with the comic experience which gives satire its distinctive character.

These propositions are of course not advanced here for the first time; they are in fact commonplaces. But they seem always to have been taken hold of by the wrong handle and their real significance discounted in favor of the derision theory. Max Eastman devotes a brief paragraph to one of the mistaken methods of " compensating for the inadequacy " of the " ungracious theory " of Hobbes; this method, he says, " was to mix a little feeling of the justice of one's scorn, a little moral complacence, into the comic emotion." [4] That is, in order to conceal the real cruelty of our derisive laughter, we mask it with hypocrisy. On this theory the satire of indignation would be doubly

[4] Eastman, *op. cit.*, p. 141.

vicious. Sully begins with a commendable concession regarding
the ethical element in satire, but as his exposition progresses it
deteriorates in the direction of a pure theory of derision.

> The distinguishing note of satire is the angry one of reproba-
tion. Here vices and follies are no longer set before us as a diverting spectacle, but emphasis is laid on their moral indignity. The
satirist is at the point of view of the moral judge; only, instead of
the calmness of the judge, he has something of the fierce attitude of
the prosecutor who aims at exposing and denouncing the turpitude
of an offence.
>
> This being so, we see that laughter enters into satire as an
expression of contempt and as an instrument of punishment. It
assumes its most pungent and most dreaded form, ridicule or
derision. . . . It is clear that the mirthful spirit when it thus lends
itself to the purpose of damaging attack becomes modified to the
point of transformation. To laugh with Juvenal or with Swift is to
feel more of a bitter malignity than of gaiety. We may say that
satire takes us back to the brutal laughter of the savage standing
over his prostrate foe. Or we may describe the laughter as a feeling
of " sudden glory " deeply tinged by the dominant angry attitude
of the laugher.[5]

It is instructive to observe how the " note of reprobation " here
changes into derision, thence into " bitter malignity," even as
the judge in the end turns out to be a brutal savage. Such a
conclusion is inevitable if we first accept the derision theory in
its usual form, as do Eastman and Sully, and assume that
derision is the same constant and unchanged component in the
satire of Juvenal and Swift as in the jubilation of the savage
victor or of Paris, who " laguhed sweetly " when he had pierced
the foot of Diomedes with an arrow.[6] In this assumption lies
the error. Against it we propose the theory that the derision of
good satire is qualified and modified by the moral judgment
which is combined with it in one act and one feeling, and that it
is thus transformed and elevated into indignation, a state of
mind of which the judge need not be ashamed and which is
certainly more characteristic of him than of the brutal savage.

We have said that the moral judgment in our experience of
indignation is felt as over-individual, as a categorical imperative; we are not thereby committed to any inference that there

[5] Sully, *op. cit.*, pp. 380-381.   [6] *Iliad*, 11, 378.

can be no wrong-headed satire, or that indignant men must be infallible. All men are liable to error in judgment, although this charge is not the one most frequently leveled against satirists. But such doubt and hesitancy is excluded from our enjoyment of satire; whatever we may think of the categorical imperative in our more reflective moments, we acknowledge its validity when we are indignant. We are indignant only because what actually is falls so far short of what it ought to be, and for the moment at least we are committed to an unreserved moral idealism. We have passed the weighing and balancing stage; our indignation only increases if anyone else begins to question our judgment. It is a popular *non sequitur* in our era to berate the wickedness of the world and then add in bitterness of spirit that there is no good. If we are seriously to believe in ethical " relativity " in its vulgar form, if we deny any imperative force to any moral principle, we must be more complacent; for how can we then berate wickedness, or how can it be judged to be wickedness? The *saeva indignatio* is a negation of such nega-tion. The whole art of satire rests on the assumption of the moral sympathy and agreement of the reader with the writer. For, as Hazlitt has said, ridicule " does not contain or attempt a formal proof " of truth,

but owes its power of conviction to the bare suggestion of it, so that if the thing when once hinted is not clear in itself, the satire fails of its effect and falls to the ground. . . . Before we can laugh at a thing, its absurdity must at least be open and palpable to common apprehension. Ridicule is necessarily built on certain supposed facts, whether true or false, and on their inconsistency with certain acknowledged maxims, whether right or wrong. It is, therefore, a fair test, if not of philosophical or abstract truth, at least of what is truth according to public opinion and common sense; for it can only expose to instantaneous contempt that which is condemned by public opinion, and is hostile to the common sense of mankind.[7]

Hazlitt's statement, however, does not cut deep enough; for though the satirist counts on the quick understanding and assent of the reader, even to the extent of saying the opposite of what he means, as in irony, his appeal is to a higher authority

---

[7] *English Comic Writers. Works,* ed. Waller and Glover (London, 1903), 8, 20.

than the court of public opinion. He is more than likely to believe that his readers are only a minority, a saving remnant; but he will never have peace of mind until all honest men are of his opinion.

It is after all the honest man, the man who is at least potentially reasonable—*rationis capax*—, who can read satire with any enjoyment; for him it is written, even when the rhetoric of direct address suggests the great improbability of wisdom crying out in the streets and iniquity patiently lending an ear. His goodness, which as things go in this world is in all likelihood normally languid, is activated through his sympathetic response to the innuendo of the satirist. And it is the nature of his enjoyment, rather than historical or sociological evidence that satire has actually been productive of good results, that must in the last analysis disclose whatever principles of justification may be advanced in defence of this genre. These principles we have sought for in the implications of indignation, the characteristic emotion which satire arouses in good men. And indignation, as we have seen, involves a moral judgment or condemnation; the writer and reader must have in common not only an antipathy towards the iniquity in question, but a conviction that there are valid universal principles upon which a condemnation may be based. Common parlance supports this contention. The expression " moral indignation," or " righteous indignation," comes readily to the lips of us all, not because there is need to distinguish one kind of indignation from another, but merely for emphasis. We mean to assert that our feelings are noble and impersonal; we are not merely yearning for retaliation,—we rather imply that we have no desire for retaliation; we are appealing to the eternal verities and on that basis demand the assent of our hearers to our judgment and their sympathetic participation in our anger. Those who hesitate must in their turn become the objects of our scorn; they betray the fact that they do not belong to the free-masonry of satire, the invisible church—not to speak it profanely—of good men. We may experience only a deferred satisfaction from the severity of the cleansing and cauterizing effect of satire—for, *pace* Swift, every man capable of honest confession must have had some smarting of that kind; but our immediate exhilaration comes from the tone-restoring exercise of our sluggish moral muscles. We are summoned from our indifference and quiescence; our latent energies awake and assume definite direction and character. We participate in the communion of those men —few though they may be—for whom things matter, and with them we share the faith in the validity of universal principles. The judgment at the core of the feeling of indignation involves a conviction regarding righteousness; indignation is the emotional realization of righteousness and all great satirists, as has always been observed, have been moralists. Though their picture of mankind has been anything but cheerful, they have not yielded to the ultimate cynicism, the derision which is directed against the very concept of the good. For in the true satirist, derision is limited and tempered by moral idealism.

University of Michigan

BERTRAND H. BRONSON

The Beggar's Opera

from

STUDIES IN THE COMIC

University of California Publications in English

Volume VIII, Number 2(1941), 197-231

Reprinted by permission of the University of

California Press

THE BEGGAR'S OPERA

BERTRAND H. BRONSON

ACCORDING to thrice-told report (a "most sweet robe of durance"), we owe it to Jonathan Swift's belief that a "Newgate pastoral" would make an "odd, pretty sort of thing" that *The Beggar's Opera* came into being. A more appropriate parentage could hardly be invented: the work is just what ought to have resulted from the impregnation of John Gay's somewhat feminine mind by the robust ironic intelligence of the Dean. That the union was brilliantly successful we do not need to be reminded. The play "was received with greater applause than was ever known.... The ladies carried about with them the favourite songs of it in fans, and houses were furnished with it in screens." For two hundred years and more it has given unceasing delight.

Reasons for this extraordinary success are not immediately apparent in the fable itself. A rascally thieftaker and receiver of stolen goods discovers that his daughter is married to a highwayman. Deliberation convinces him that he stands to win more by the reward for the highwayman's death than by what the latter may bring him if allowed to go free. Knowing that his son-in-law is promiscuously fond of women, he bribes two jades to put the man off his guard while constables rush in and arrest him. The highwayman is lodged in Newgate, but promptly gains his liberty through the Keeper's daughter, another sweetheart. Soon after escape, he is again betrayed by his fatal weakness, again confined, and condemned at once to be hanged. His last hours are disturbed by the wrangling of his two chief loves, the thieftaker's and the gaoler's daughters, both of whom get admittance to his cell. Their importunity reconciles him to the idea of dying, and his resolution is confirmed by the appearance of four more "wives," each with a child. At this point, in order that the piece

[197]

may not end unhappily, a reprieve is cried, and the play closes with a general dance.

On the face of it, there is nothing in this farcical plot—or no-plot—to bespeak consideration. How could such a scarecrow have been filled with vitality enough to last two centuries and to show every promise—if the world endure so long—of lasting for another, besides producing a numerous progeny, from *The Village Opera* of Charles Johnson to the Savoy Operas of Gilbert and Sullivan? Out of what textiles have the garments been woven that so miraculously cover this tawdry frame, and what is the magic that has kept them fresh?

It is not a facile formula that will account for such a wonder. From how many and what various fields Gay collected his elements, the careful investigations of several scholars in recent years have taught us.[1] French *Comédie en vaudevilles,* realistic Elizabethan comedy, the Italian tradition of Harlequin and Columbine, recent operatic fashions with both Italian features and elements of the English masque, contemporary news sheets and popular song—all these and more supplied Gay with the simples which his own genius enabled him to compound with such extraordinary felicity.

After so much patient research on *The Beggar's Opera,* it may well seem that the squirrel's granary is full and the harvest done. We must not be ambitious now to add anything considerable in the way of information to what scholarship has already amassed. Coming after those who have "led away the corn," we ought to be satisfied if, gleaning here and there, we may "find an ear of any goodly word that they have left." One or two aspects of the subject do await fuller illustration. But, in addition, reading the play in the light of all that is known about it, we may still feel that its continued popularity poses questions that invite further

[1] Cf. especially W. E. Schultz, *Gay's Beggar's Opera: Its Contents, History and Influence* (New Haven, 1923), and E. M. Gagey, *Ballad Opera* (New York, 1937).

scrutiny of its pages. Exploring once again the familiar configurations of character and scene, and meditating upon the way in which they exfoliate or, like concentric rings in water, are forced outward by some inner generative impulse into wider and wider areas, can we not press closer than heretofore toward the secret of their vitality? May we not, in considering afresh the appeals that evoked response when the play was young, as well as those which are still potent, sharpen our perception of its peculiar qualities, and, in so doing, enrich our understanding of the ways of the comic spirit? The effort is surely worth the cost.

I

Before passing to broader considerations of enduring value, our attention may reasonably be engaged by certain matters which were of importance to the play's first audiences but which now are generally overlooked or ignored. Without any pretense to an exhaustive summary of the findings of scholarship, we may at once note a few of the reasons why *The Beggar's Opera* should have captured the favor of its immediate public. We know that its political implications made part of its appeal. An audience that could interpret Addison's *Cato* as a tract for the times was not slow to catch the allusion to Walpole in a catalogue of thieves which included "*Robin* of *Bagshot, alias Gorgon,* alias *Bluff Bob,* alias *Carbuncle,* alias *Bob Booty.*" The First Minister's methods of political bribery, his success in amassing a private fortune, were easily read into an account of the tricks of gangsters. A recent quarrel with Townshend was perceived in the Peachum-Lockit dispute. Walpole's personal habits were understood in the remark, "He spends his life among women"; and Macheath's passion for the whole sex would have been interpreted in the same way even if Gay had not pointed it in that direction by transparent insinuation.

Then, too, the habitual Philistinism of the British attitude toward certain forms of art found cheap support in the gibes against the absurdities of opera. Gay asks to be forgiven for not making his own opera throughout unnatural, like those in vogue. He has omitted Recitative, he declares, but he has introduced all the favorite operatic similes: "the *Swallow,* the *Moth,* the *Bee,* the *Ship,* the *Flower"*; and in his avoidance of catastrophe he has followed good operatic tradition: "for you must allow, that in this kind of Drama, 'tis no matter how absurdly things are brought about," and an Opera "must end happily."

A matter not so frequently adverted to is the debt of *The Beggar's Opera* to Durfey's *Pills to Purge Melancholy* for some of its immediate popularity. Durfey's collection, in its third, six-volume, edition, had but recently appeared. It had gathered a vast quantity of songs from current and late Restoration plays, from single sheets and printed broadside ballads, incidentally including at least two-thirds of the sixty-nine tunes which Gay used in *The Beggar's Opera.* The *Pills* were familiar to most of the male part, at least, of Gay's audience. A large majority of the tunes he chose were associated with amorous words, and not infrequently Gay kept phrases, refrain lines or half lines, or followed the earlier verbal patterns, for his new lyrics. There is no doubt that he thus won the amused attention of all whose tastes had made them familiar with the originals. In the printed text of the play, the titles alone of many of the airs would suggest the content of the songs: "O Jenny, O Jenny, where hast thou been"; "Thomas, I cannot"; "When once I lay with another man's wife," and so on. He makes use of Congreve's familiar and wittily naughty song, "A Soldier and a Sailor," and keeps a line of the refrain of the catchy but obscene "Tom Tinker's my true-love": "This way, and that way, and which way I will." Similar play is made with the phrase "what I dare not name" in Mrs. Peachum's "If Love the virgin's heart invade," and, in other songs, with "Pretty Poll," "Over the hills and far away," and "How d'you do again." One of the best-loved songs in the play, Macheath's "If the heart of a man is deprest with Cares," is closely modeled on its original, a song in *The Modern Prophets,* the first stanza of which is as follows:

> Would you have a young Virgin of fifteen Years,
> You must tickle her Fancy with sweets and dears,
> Ever toying, and playing, and sweetly, sweetly,
> Sing a Love Sonnet, and charm her Ears:
>   Wittily, prettily talk her down,
>   Chase her, and praise her, if fair or brown,
>   Sooth her, and smooth her,
>   And teaze her, and please her,
> And touch but her Smicket, and all's your own.

A good deal subtler is the transformation of Durfey's song in *The Country Wake,* called "The Mouse Trap." Durfey bewails the hampering effect of marriage on a man's liberty. In contrast to the carefree frolics of bachelor days, he describes the married state in terms like the following:

> We're just like a Mouse in a Trap,
>   Or Vermin caught in a Gin:
> We Sweat and Fret, and try to Escape,
>   And Curse the sad Hour we came in.
>
> This was the worst Plague could ensue,
>   I'm Mew'd in a smoky House;
> I us'd to Tope a Bottle or two,
>   But now 'tis small Beer with my Spouse.

Remembrance of these words gives additional piquancy to Mrs. Peachum's praise of marriage. Only *after* a woman is married, she declares, does she win her freedom. Maidens are like unminted gold, with no currency: but

> A Wife's like a Guinea in Gold,
>   Stampt with the Name of her Spouse;
>   Now here, now there; is bought, or is sold;
>   And is current in every House.

(19)

There is a similar reversal, but in the opposite direction, in Polly's song, "Virgins are like the fair Flower." The words in *Dioclesian,* set to Purcell's exquisite melody, conclude as follows:

> In fair Aurelia's Arms, leáve me expiring,
>   To be Imbalm'd with the sweets of her Breath;
> To the last moment I'll still be desiring;
>   Never had Hero so glorious a Death.

Keeping this image in mind, listen to Polly's comment on the cropping of the fair flower.

> But, when once pluck'd, 'tis no longer alluring,
>   To *Covent-Garden* 'tis sent (as yet sweet,)
> There fades, and shrinks, and grows past all enduring,
>   Rots, stinks, and dies, and is trod under feet.

For the tune of "Our Polly is a sad Slut," no less than six sets of words, for the most part high-spirited and indecent, are to be found in Durfey's *Pills.* In all of them the idea of women "flinging themselves away" is not far to seek, so that the knowing ear would find a large allowance. Gay has not followed any of the six closely; the talk of Polly's fashionable apparel comes nearest to a song of a fashion called the Button'd Smock, in which occur the ensuing lines:

> For some will have the out-side fine,
>   To make the braver show;
> But she will have her *Holland* Smock
>   That's Button'd down below.

For a number of his other lyrics Gay has taken hints from the subject matter of the original songs. Macheath's disillusioned comment on the power of money, "If you at an Office solicit your Due," is based on two songs of worldly advice to the same tune in Durfey: "Advice to the Ladies" ("Ladies of *London,* both Wealthy and Fair") and "Advice to the Beaus" ("All Jolly Rakehells that Sup at the *Rose*"). "Come, Sweet Lass" begins with an identical line. With the substitution of "Polly" for "Shepherd," Polly's "When my Hero in Court appears" ends with the original four-line refrain:

> And alás poór Shépherd,
>   Alack and a welladay;
> Before I was in Love,
>   Oh every month was *May*.

Macheath's "But Valour the stronger grows, The stronger Liquor we're drinking" is set to the ancient drinking song of "Old Simon the King":

> For drinking will make a man Quaff,
>   Quaffing will make a man Sing;
> Singing will make a man Laugh,
> And laughing long life doth bring.

That universal favorite, "Fill ev'ry Glass," derives from a curious drinking song in Durfey celebrating Marlborough, Eugene, and d'Auverquerque, the words in French but accompanied with an English version. The song begins, "Que chacun remplisse son verre"; or, according to the Durfey translation, "Fill ev'ry glass"; its last stanza is particularly in the mood of Gay:

> Si nous a[i]mions autant la Gloire
> Que boire nous serions des Heros;
> Car parmi les verres [et] le[s] Pots,
> Nous sommes seurs [*sic*] de la victoire.

Lucy's confession to her father, "When young at the Bar," is a rare example of debasement by Gay of his original. Little remains of the charm of Purcell's song in *The Fairy Queen,* except subject and inviolably lovely melody, to which the words had been these:

> If Love's a sweet Passion, why does it Torment?
> If a bitter, oh tell me! whence comes my content;
> Since I suffer with Pleasure, why should I complain,
> Or grieve at my Fate, when I know 'tis in vain?
> Yet so pleasing the Pain is, so soft is the Dart,
> That at once it both wounds me, and tickles my Heart.

(21)

This song, incidentally, had gained a well-deserved popularity by the turn of the century. It appears on broadsides as well as in Durfey, and its title stands above many another ballad to designate the tune to which the new words should be sung.

Having brought his hero as it were to the foot of the gallows, Gay cast about for some piece of music that would rise to the needs of this important occasion. He found just what he wanted in Lewis Ramondon's "Hymn upon the Execution of two Criminals," a dirge in three-two time with appropriately lugubrious words, which may be seen in Durfey's final volume of the *Pills*. Its introductory stanzas will sufficiently display its character:

> All you that must take a leap in the Dark,
> Pity the Fate of *Lawson* and *Clark;*
> Cheated by Hope, by Mercy amus'd,
> Betray'd by the sinful ways we us'd:
> Cropp'd in our Prime of Strength and Youth,
> Who can but weep at so sad a Truth;
>   *Cropp'd in our Prime,* &c.

> Once we thought 'twould never be Night,
> But now alass 'twill never be light;
> Heavenly mercy shine on our Souls,
> Death draws near, hark, *Sepúlchres* Bell Toles:
> Nature is stronger in Youth than in Age,
> Grant us thy Spirit Lord Grief to asswage.
>   [*Grant us thy Spirit,* &c.]

These melancholy measures Gay divided for a grand trio between his three principals, Macheath, Polly, and Lucy, not neglecting the admirable hint of St. Sepulchre's bell for operatic effect: "But hark!" sings Macheath, "I hear the Toll of the Bell." Whereupon they all echo in chorus, "Tol de rol lol"!

II

In the course of the opera Gay has introduced among the arias sundry duettos in the proper contemporary operatic manner, to

(22)

vary the entertainment and underline the burlesque. Polly and her mother share one, Polly and Macheath three, and Polly and Lucy another three. There is likewise due use of a chorus at several points, and, for an echo of operatic ballet, three dances are introduced, including Macheath's cotillion of ladies and the grotesque dance of prisoners in chains. Thus most of the musical elements of real opera are used by Gay, in his fashion. To introduce recitative he would have had to employ the services of a composer. What he does, instead, is to suggest a parody of recitative in Macheath's meditations in the condemned hold. The Ladies, as the Beggar announces in the Introduction, always reckon a Prison Scene "charmingly pathetick"; and in this affecting passage it would not do to allow his hero to express himself in ordinary fashion. Here Gay constructs a medley, linking phrases out of nine familiar melodies (including one from Purcell's *Bonduca,* Farinel's *Ground,* Carey's *Sally,* the popular "Why are mine Eyes still flowing," and *Chevy Chase* and other ballad tunes) and rising to *Greensleeves* by way of closing aria. The fun of this sequence was considerably lessened in the late Hammersmith production (otherwise admirable) by the omission of more than half the excerpts. The omissions unfortunately resulted also in obscuring Gay's equating of his hero's courage with the amount of liquor he contained at the moment. Macheath tugs at the bottle after nearly every phrase. Raising his spirits with a brimmer, he boldly chants (to Purcell's air of "Britons, strike home"),

> Since I must swing,—I scorn, I scorn to wince or whine;

but his next words are,

> But now again my Spirits sink,

and he promptly endeavors to "raise them high with wine." After another phrase or two, he turns to brandy for further assistance.

Thus he ascends by degrees to his ironic aria (omitted at Hammersmith):

> Since Laws were made for ev'ry Degree,
> To curb Vice in others, as well as me,
> I wonder we han't better Company,
> Upon *Tyburn* Tree!

But the effect soon wears off: "O Leave me to Thought!" he entreats Polly and Lucy in the trio which follows:

> I fear! I doubt!
> I tremble! I droop!—See, my Courage is out,
> *[Turns up the empty Bottle.*

POLLY.　No token of Love?
MACHEATH.　　　　　　　　See, my Courage is out.
　　　　　　　　　　　　　[Turns up the empty Pot.

The whole scene is treated as the most extravagant burlesque, and it is time to pursue the hint which Gay has dropped earlier about pathetic prison scenes, and inquire whether anything in particular lies behind the burlesque here.

Considering the amount of minute investigation accorded *The Beggar's Opera,* one wonders that no student appears to have examined the contemporary operas of Händel, Buononcini, and Ariosti, to learn whether general parody anywhere becomes specific. For if the search has been made, the results of it, whether positive or negative, have nowhere been announced in print. Schultz, indeed, has noted Sir John Hawkins' observation, that "possibly Macheath's appearance in Newgate fetters might be supposed to ridicule the prison scene in *Coriolanus,* performed a few years before."[2] But Hawkins flouted the notion generally of burlesque in Gay's play, and Schultz did not—or could not— verify his suggestion here. F. W. Bateson, in a recent edition of *The Beggar's Opera,*[3] converted "possibly" into "probably" and amplified the note: "a hit probably at the prison scene in Attilio Ariosti's opera, *Caius Marius Coriolanus,* produced in 1723." A glance at Burney's History supplies the fuller reference and the

---

[2] Schultz, *op. cit.,* p. 143.　　　[3] London, 1934.

date. *Marcius* has been miscopied *Marius;* but the fact is irrelevant, for the opera was doubtless known simply as *Coriolano.* Suggestion of any specific parody in this direction thus rests where Hawkins left it in 1776.

Schultz has caught one other allusion in the Beggar's preliminary statement: "I have observ'd such a nice Impartiality to our two Ladies, that it is impossible for either of them to take Offence." "This," Schultz observes, "seems to have no bearing on Polly and Lucy"; and he continues with the correct explanation, though vaguely expressed: "it is clearly a reference to the quarrel between two rival singers, Cuzzoni and Faustina, in 1727, over the leading part in an Italian opera." Now this quarrel was the most notorious event in the annals of the operatic stage during the two years preceding the appearance of Gay's work. Faustina Bordoni was imported in the spring of 1726 at the fabulous salary of £2500. Cuzzoni, already established, was receiving £2000. Cuzzoni, in spite of what Burney calls her "native warble" and "a perfect shake," was dumpy and singularly unattractive in personality. Faustina seems to have been an appealing creature, and pleasing to the eye, as well as the possessor of an equally miraculous voice. Fashionable London at once took sides. Lampoons were published on both parts in the papers, and the friends of the two singers met in the theater to hiss their enemies off the stage in turn, until the universal clamor broke up the performance. Matters came to a hysterical climax when, in a performance of Buononcini's *Astyanax,* in the spring of 1727, the rivals actually resorted to mutual scratching and hair pulling on the stage. Nobody could possibly have remained ignorant of this notorious dispute. Gay's allusion to it goes much beyond an introductory reference. The rivalry of Polly and Lucy, in this view, takes on added comic significance:

> LUCY. If you are determin'd, Madam, to raise a Disturbance in the Prison, I shall be oblig'd to send for the Turnkey to show you the Door. I am sorry, Madam, you force me to be so ill-bred.

POLLY. Give me leave to tell you, Madam: These forward Airs don't become you in the least, Madam ...

[Then a song:]

LUCY.   Why how now, Madam Flirt?
                         If you thus must chatter;
                    And are for flinging Dirt,
                         Let's try who best can spatter;
                              Madam *Flirt!*

POLLY.   Why how now, saucy Jade;
                         Sure the Wench is tipsy;
                    How can you see me made   [*To him.*
                         The Scoff of such a Gipsy?
                              Saucy Jade!   [*To her.*

In this song, the monosyllable *Dirt* occupies a running passage nearly three bars long, in true bravura style, and in strong contrast to the usual note-for-syllable habit of the settings. The quarrel subsequently works toward a fateful climax. "I could murder that impudent happy Strumpet," cries Lucy; and she proceeds to make the attempt. In a speech which is the exact counterpart in English of contemporary Italian operatic recitative, she declares: "Jealousy, Rage, Love and Fear are at once tearing me to pieces. How am I weather-beaten, and shatter'd with distresses!" This launches her naturally upon her next aria, built on the figure of the Ship ("I'm like a Skiff on the Ocean tost"), and rising to its climax:

Revenge, Revenge, Revenge,
Shall appease my restless Sprite.

In the right operatic tradition, she has prepared a poison draught against Polly's arrival; and, dropping to speech again, she says:

I have the Rats-bane ready.—I run no Risque; for I can lay her Death upon the Ginn [this of Cuzzoni!].—But say, I were to be hang'd—I never could be hang'd for any thing that would give me greater Comfort, than the poysoning that Slut.

(26)

Polly enters, and there is pretense of a reconciliation, Lucy recommending—pleasantly enough, in the light of her intentions—a "quieting Draught." "I wish," she says pointedly, "I wish all our Quarrels might have so comfortable a Reconciliation"—a patent allusion to matter outside the play.

But Faustina and Cuzzoni will take us yet further. When Faustina arrived early in 1726, the very first task which Händel set himself was to write an opera in which both stars could sing, and in which neither could claim that the other's role was better than her own. The job seems to have taken him nearly a month! and a handsome piece of work it was, in which the arias were shaped as by the hand of an expert *couturier* to display the special excellences of each voice. The recitatives were evenly divided, and the duets so artfully contrived that now Faustina and now Cuzzoni had the foremost part. Each lady had as well a duet with the leading man. The opera was *Alessandro*. It opened on May 5, and proved so popular that, instead of the usual twice, it was performed thrice a week for the rest of the season. The plot is very largely taken up with the rivalry of Rossane and Lisaura for the love of Alessandro, who, outwardly at least, vacillates deplorably between them, inclining to the nearer, and not fixing upon Rossane until the last possible moment. "How happy could [he] be with either, Were t'other dear charmer away!" Throughout the three' acts of the opera, the ladies consequently live upon the rack, singing all the while of their pains and doubts and jealousy. "How sweet love would be," sings Lisaura, "were it not for jealousy with its icy poison." There is no close parody in *The Beggar's Opera* of any particular scene in *Alessandro,* but a kind of condensed parody occurs here and there of broader vistas. Thus, in

---

[4] Schultz credits Gay with breaking the five-act theatrical tradition. "Gay's three acts," he declares, "among the very first to stand alone, furnished a pleasing contrast to the five acts of the majority of comedies; and ... exerted a real influence, if we may judge by later work ... [which took up] the battle for a shorter dramatic scale" (*op. cit.,* p. 281). But Gay was merely following the established operatic tradition in this matter.

Alessandro, there is a scene in which the hero comes back from
martial exploits to his two loves. Alessandro greets Rossane with
a loving embrace, and is well received, whilst Lisaura watches
with inward rage. Then he turns to Lisaura with the words: "Delightful Lisaura, no less gladly do I return to thee." Thereupon,
Rossane starts away in jealous wrath. Alessandro follows her, and
Lisaura exclaims that she cannot longer endure this unworthy
treatment: "More unstable is this inconstant one than the wave,
more easily set in motion than a leaf." So in balder fashion do
Polly and Lucy bid for Macheath's notice:

> POLLY. Hither, dear Husband, turn your Eyes.
> LUCY.   Bestow one glance to cheer me.
> POLLY. Think with that Look, thy *Polly* dyes.
> LUCY.   O shun me not—but hear me.
> POLLY. 'Tis *Polly* sues.
> LUCY.   —'Tis *Lucy* speaks.
> POLLY.   Is thus true Love requited?
> LUCY. My Heart is bursting.
> POLLY.   —Mine too breaks.
> LUCY.   Must I
> POLLY.   —Must I be slighted?

Again, in the third act of Händel's opera, the women meet by
themselves to take stock of the situation. "Let us leave jealousy,
deceit, and trickery, fair Lisaura," says Rossane; "let us both
equally love the conqueror of the world, and let Alessandro's
heart fall to her who shall have the better hap in true loving constancy." "In vain you try to put me down with your fine boast-
ing," replies Lisaura; "as for me, I would imitate the fair flower
which turns toward the sun's brightness, and finds solace in admiring his beauty. Yet I differ in that I long for what consumes
me, whilst the flower only follows that which gives it life." Similarly, Gay's ladies meet to discuss their mutual unhappiness. "Ah,
Polly! Polly!" cries Lucy; "'tis I am the unhappy Wife; and he
loves you as if you were only his Mistress." "Sure, Madam," Polly

(28)

answers, "you cannot think me so happy as to be the Object of your Jealousy.—A Man is always afraid of a Woman who loves him too well—so that I must expect to be neglected and avoided." "Then," says Lucy, "our Cases, my dear *Polly,* are exactly alike. Both of us indeed have been too fond." Rossane, however, has premonitions of felicity, and in a brilliant aria she describes her feelings in images comparable to those in which Lucy earlier expresses Polly's good fortune. While like the rudderless skiff, cries Lucy, "I lye rolling and tossing all Night, That *Polly* lyes sporting on Seas of Delight!" "Si nella calma azurro," sings Rossane, "brilla il mar, se splende il sole, e i rai fan tremolar tranquilla l'onda."

All this makes something of an Alexander out of Macheath, and indeed the two heroes have significant traits in common. Both have attained their greatest successes in the same manner— by force of arms—and both tower above their associates in magnanimity. The parallel is hinted by Swift in a letter to Gay. "I wish," Swift writes, "Macheath, when he was going to be hanged, had imitated Alexander the Great when he was dying. I would have had his fellow-rogues desire his commands about a successor, and he to answer, Let it be the most worthy, etc." (March 28, 1728). But Alexander's death was not in the opera. What was in the opera was Alessandro's passion for the sex, and his reluctance to say no to a pretty face. He comes upon the sleeping Rossane and thinks to obtain a kiss. But Lisaura is on the watch and promptly comes forward. When Alessandro perceives her, "Come," he says, "beautiful Lisaura, and console the distresses of a sorrowful heart." Rossane awakes at that moment, but feigns continued slumber. Mockingly, Lisaura repeats the words she has just heard him use to her rival: "Let me kiss you, lovely rubies"; and departs with disdain. Alessandro turns back to Rossane for solace of his pains. She in turn picks up the words he has just addressed to Lisaura, pointing them against him with scorn: "Proud eyes beloved, let me no longer languish,"—and mockingly abandons him. "What honor," he exclaims ironically, "is given to the world's conqueror! Alexander made a mock by two stubborn women!" So, at a great remove, sings Macheath:

> One wife is too much for most husbands to hear,
> But two at a time there's no mortal can bear.
> This way, and that way, and which way I will,
> What would comfort the one, t'other wife would take ill.

Until someone can make a careful examination of the whole file of Italian operas that were produced in London before 1728, it will not be possible to draw up an exact account of Gay's use of them. The operas of Ariosti and Buononcini have not been accessible to the present writer, but a cursory inspection of Händel's operas alone is enough to reveal a good many interesting parallels. Thus, in several of them the poisoned cup appears. *Flavio* (1723) has a scene of quarreling fathers. *Ottone* (1723) has a pirate, a daring, resourceful, wild fellow, who might almost have given hints for Macheath. *Ottone* was very popular, its phrases, according to Burney, passing current among musical people almost as the *bons mots* of a wit circulate in society. In *Giulio Cesare* (1724) there is a scene in a seraglio in which the tyrant Ptolemy gets into a genial frame, forgets his mistrust, and lays aside his sword, whereupon, at a sign from Cornelia, Sextus rushes in and attempts to stab him. In outline, this is close to the capture of Macheath.

Hawkins may have had a special reason for suggesting *Coriolano* as the original of the prison scene in *The Beggar's Opera*. But he could have pointed equally to several of Händel's operas for prison scenes that the ladies might have considered "charmingly pathetick." *Silla* (1714) has an affecting one; *Tamerlano* (1724), a fine and popular opera, of which the favorite songs were separately published by Walsh, has another, involving a cup of poison. Radamisto, in the opera of that name (1720), is condemned to

(30)

death by the tyrant Tiridate. Zenobia, Radamisto's love, is given the choice of marrying Tiridate or of carrying death to her lover. She enters the prison with the poisoned bowl and, as she approaches Radamisto, tries to drink it herself. Unable to move because of his shackles, he can do nothing to prevent her. But the cup is dashed to the ground by Tiridate, who enters just in time. A nearly identical scene is worked out in *Floridante* (1721)— sufficient testimony to its theatrical appeal. *Rodelinda* (1725) contains an equally telling prison scene, which has recently been favorably compared (by Hugo Leichtentritt) to the famous one in Beethoven's *Fidelio,* with which, indeed, it has striking features of resemblance. *Alessandro* itself has a prison scene, though one not so affecting as the preceding; and, speaking generally, there is hardly an opera in which someone does not suffer duress for a time, and later make his escape by force or stratagem.

Of all the operas mentioned, *Floridante* seems most likely to have contributed elements to *The Beggar's Opera,* not only in the prison scene, but also in two noteworthy parting scenes between the hero and his love. Floridante, meditating in his dungeon, displays fine courage without any of the fortifying draughts which Macheath found so necessary under similar circumstances. Chained to a pillar, he sings defiantly: "These shackles and this horror cause no fear in my breast. My torment is welcome to me." He greets as his deliverer the cup of death which his love comes to bring him. "Oh cara soave morte!" he cries to Elmira: "oh troppo a te crudele, troppo pietoso a me, fiero tiranno! candida man, lascia ch'io stempri in baci su te il cor mio! tu dolce puoi far morte." Polly and Lucy only wish that they might suffer in Macheath's place; but Elmira attempts to exhibit "l'ultima prova d'un amor fedele" by drinking the poison herself, in this intensely dramatic and memorable scene.

The parting between Polly and Macheath at the end of Act I is obviously patterned on the fervent protestations and lingering

(31)

farewells of high romance. "Is there any Power, any Force," asks Macheath, "that could tear me from thee?" And they sing together the well-known duet, "Were I laid on *Greenland's* Coast— Were I sold on *Indian* Soil." "But oh!" says Polly, "we must part." And she sings the plaintive "O what Pain it is to part!" concluding, with perhaps a little admixture of Juliet: "One Kiss and then—one Kiss—begone—farewell . . . A few Weeks, perhaps, may reconcile us all . . . MACHEATH. Must I then go? POLLY. And will not Absence change your Love? . . . O how I fear!—How I tremble." And they sing a final song as they part, "looking back at each other with fondness; he at one Door, she at the other." With all this it is interesting to compare the conclusion of Act I of *Floridante:*

FLORIDANTE. Ch'io parta? ELMIRA. Ch'io ti perda? Anima mia! In van l'invidia rea lo spera. FL. In vano me'l prefigge il destin, se non m'uccide. Solo partir? ELM. Sola restar? FL. Lasciarti? ELM. Più non vederti? Oh Dei! Non so. FL. Non vo'. ELM. Troppo amo. FL. Troppo adoro. Ahi! che a pensarlo sol, sento che moro.

Elmira then sings an aria, not about Greenland's coast, but to the following similar effect: "I shall sooner see the stars plunge into the sea than abandon my dear love. Thou art my life, my fate." To this, Floridante replies in similarly impassioned style, and a little later both join in a duet which prettily rings the changes on the same theme:

> FL.   Ah mia cara, se tu resti,
>   infelice a morte io vo.
> ELM. Ah mio caro, se tu parti,
> FL.   se tu resti,
> ELM.   se tu parti,
> { FL.   infelice a morte io vo.
> { ELM. per l'affanno io morirò.
> ELM. Altra spene
> FL.   altro bene
> ELM. senza te, cor mio, non ho.
> FL.   senza te, cor mio, non ho.

(32)

If this was not the scene which Gay had in mind, it will, under submission, do well enough.

It does not appear to have been Gay's method to paraphrase the actual songs or scenes of his originals. Rather, he re-created, so that while many of the images reappear so sharply that we cannot doubt a reminiscence, yet it is hard to convince ourselves that a specific passage is the unquestionable original of one in Gay. For example, is or is not Lucy's "I'm like a skiff on the ocean tossed, Now high now low with each billow borne" indebted to the air of Berenice in *Scipione?*—

> Com' onda incalza altr' onda,
> pena sù pena abbonda,
> sommersa al fin è l'alma in mar d'affano.

In general, all Gay's similes except the ones which are obviously ludicrous, like the housewife's rat, may be suspected of operatic parentage. The following parallel, however, seems to be more than fortuitous. Polly, toward the end of Act II, has a song—set, it is amusing to note, to an air by Sandoni, Cuzzoni's own husband—which reads as follows:

> Thus when the Swallow, seeking Prey,
>   Within the Sash is closely pent,
> His Consort, with bemoaning Lay,
>   Without sits pining for th' Event.
> Her chatt'ring Lovers all around her skim;
> She heeds them not (poor Bird!) her Soul's with him.

In the opera *Scipione,* produced a year and a half before *The Beggar's Opera,* Berenice, a prisoner of war, is followed by her lover, who sings this aria:

> Lamentando mi corro a volo,
> qual colombo che solo,
> và cercando la sua diletta
> involata dal casciator;
> E poi misero innamorato
> prigionero le resta stato;
> mà la gabbia pur lo alletta,
> perchè restaci col suo amor.

(33)

It may be objected that we have been assuming a rather intimate acquaintance on Gay's part with the particulars of Italian opera. Not more intimate, in my opinion, than the probabilities warrant. That Gay was himself musical admits of no dispute. All his life he wrote ballads and lyrics to be sung, and from first to last his works display a wide familiarity with popular song. (That Pepusch, as Burney suggests, selected the tunes for *The Beggar's Opera* and *Polly* is pure nonsense, not worth a moment's consideration. If the internal evidence of the lyrics did not disprove the suggestion, the list of popular songs at the end of Gay's *Shepherd's Week,* 1714, would by itself be enough to resolve any doubts.) He himself is known to have played the flute. He moved in a fashionable set that would as a matter of course have interested itself in opera, just as people of fashion today, whether or not they love music, attend the opera for social reasons. But Gay had a better reason, for he was even professionally connected with it. He wrote the libretto of *Acis and Galatea,* which, in 1719 or 1720, Händel set to music that puts this work among the composer's masterpieces. There is little probability that Gay intended a serious attack upon Italian opera, and he may even have been somewhat appalled at the amount of damage caused by his play. For his ridicule does not go beyond poking affectionate fun at conventions which, like most conventions objectively regarded, have their ludicrous side. Händel had the sense to see this truth, and there is no evidence that *The Beggar's Opera* ever caused a rift between the two men. Years before *Acis and Galatea,* Händel had set a lyric for Gay's early play, *The What D'Ye Call It.* (Gay used the tune again in his opera.) And in 1732, after *The Beggar's Opera* and *Polly* had done their worst, Händel returned to *Acis and Galatea* in order to rework it. Intrinsically, there is nothing in *The Beggar's Opera* which even approaches significant criticism of serious opera; and Professor Dent,[5] in contrast to most

---

[5] E. J. Dent, *Händel* (London, 1934, p. 77).

who have written on the subject, has sound sense on his side when he declares: "The Italian opera was killed, not so much by the fact that *The Beggar's Opera* made its conventions ridiculous (for its conventions could at that time have been ridiculous only to quite unmusical people), as by the incontestable attraction of the new work itself."[6] Everything considered, *The Beggar's Opera* may more properly be regarded as a testimonial to the strength of opera's appeal to John Gay's imagination than as a deliberate attempt to ridicule it out of existence.

Further evidence of Gay's serious musical taste lies closer at hand. So much has been made of the popular character of the melodies in *The Beggar's Opera* that it will probably surprise most readers to learn that nearly a third of the airs employed are by known composers; for none, I believe, of the editions of the play, nor of its songs, takes the trouble to point out the fact, although students have traced nearly every one of the tunes to earlier sources. We have hardly noticed how amply Gay laid under contribution the most reputable composers of his age. Purcell leads the list, in number as in excellence. But Händel follows him close; and among other composers who make an appearance are Buononcini, Sandoni, Akeroyde, Leveridge, and Eccles. Nevertheless, Gay had a sure ear for a good tune, whether or not it bore the distinction of a famous name; and it cannot be said that the anonymous airs which he selected are noticeably inferior, as a class, to the others.

III

What has neither been forgotten nor ignored is the poet's ability to devise excellent lyrics for his tunes. In approaching this aspect of the play, we move at once from the ephemeral causes of its

---

[6] Neither, though the point is hardly worth defending, does Gay's epigrammatic motto for *Muzio Scævola* sound like the word of a man who despised the class to which this work belonged:

> Who here blames words, or verses, songs, or singers,
> Like *Mutius Scævola* will burn his fingers.

popularity to grounds which have permanent validity. Gay's easy grace, his power of being witty whilst remaining fluent and sing-able, have never been touched unless by poets who have written with a tune in mind. Even Burns—who did so write,—though his emotional range was much wider and deeper, seldom hit the level of Gay's succinct wit in song, but generally resorted to ampler forms for his most pungent expression. In mere singing quality, few English lyric poets have surpassed Gay at any time since Elizabethan days, and probably none save Burns since his own day. Everyone has his own favorites in *The Beggar's Opera,* and it is almost an impertinence to single out for quotation things so familiar and beloved. But Gay's special flavor, his ironic wit, his perfect sense of how to match a tune with words, are brilliantly displayed in Macheath's sardonic meditation upon experience:

> Man may escape from Rope and Gun;
>   Nay, some have out-liv'd the Doctor's Pill;
> Who takes a Woman must be undone,
>   That Basilisk is sure to kill.
> The Fly that sips Treacle is lost in the Sweets,
>   So he that tastes Woman, Woman, Woman,
> He that tastes Woman, Ruin meets.

More typical, perhaps, of Gay's performance is the Gilbertian verve and speed of the following:

> If you at an Office solicit your Due,
>   And would not have Matters neglected;
> You must quicken the Clerk with the Perquisite too,
>   To do what his Duty directed.
> Or would you the Frowns of a Lady prevent,
>   She too has this palpable Failing,
> The Perquisite softens her into Consent;
>   That Reason with all is prevailing.

(36)

In quite another category stand the lines of the cotillion in Act II—a silvery Augustan echo of the golden chime of the Renaissance:

> Let us drink and sport to-day,
>   Ours is not to-morrow.
> Love with Youth flies swift away,
>   Age is nought but Sorrow.
>   Dance and sing,
>   Tíme's on the Wing,
>   Lífe never knóws the return of Spring.
> CHORUS. Let us drink &c.

The note of that stanza, though it exactly expresses the nostalgic quality of much of Purcell's music, is very rare in Gay's work.

The scrupulous ear that so nicely adjusted the phrases of the lyrics has exerted the same felicitous control over the dialogue. Not enough praise has been accorded to Gay's prose. The wit of his epigrams, to be sure, has received applause. But the perspicuous timing of his cadences, even in passages devoid of epigrammatic pointing, is worthy of careful study. He never taxes the ear. The ease and polish of his phrases is perfectly calculated for oral delivery. It is self-conscious, but not insistent; and it has just the right amount of emphasis to gratify the listener. Take for example a passage which eschews the advantages of aphorism, the quarrel of Peachum and Lockit—a delightful and conscious parody[7] of the familiar scene between Brutus and Cassius in *Julius Caesar,* as well as a fling at the differences between the brothers-in-law, Walpole and Townshend:

PEACHUM. Here's poor *Ned Clincher*'s Name, I see. Sure, Brother *Lockit,* there was a little unfair Proceeding in *Ned*'s case: for he told me in the Condemn'd Hold, that for Value receiv'd, you had promis'd him a Session or two longer without Molestation.

LOCKIT. Mr. *Peachum*—this is the first time my Honour was ever call'd in Question.

PEACHUM. Business is at an end—if once we act dishonourably.

[7] Cf. Swift to Gay, March 28, 1728: "I did not understand that the scene of Lockit and Peachum's quarrel was an imitation of one between Brutus and Cassius, till I was told it."

LOCKIT. Who accuses me?

PEACHUM. You are warm, Brother.

LOCKIT. He that attacks my Honour, attacks my Livelihood.—And this Usage—Sir—is not to be borne.

PEACHUM. Since you provoke me to speak—I must tell you too, that Mrs. *Coaxer* charges you with defrauding her of her Information-Money, for the apprehending of curl-pated *Hugh*. Indeed, indeed, Brother, we must punctually pay our Spies, or we shall have no Information.

LOCKIT. Is this Language to me, Sirrah,—who have sav'd you from the Gallows, Sirrah!

[*Collaring each other.*

PEACHUM. If I am hang'd, it shall be for ridding the World of an arrant Rascal.

LOCKIT. This Hand shall do the Office of the Halter you deserve, and throttle you—you Dog!—

PEACHUM. Brother, Brother—We are both in the Wrong—We shall be both Losers in the Dispute—for you know we have it in our Power to hang each other. You should not be so passionate.

LOCKIT. Nor you so provoking.

PEACHUM. 'Tis our mutual Interest; 'tis for the Interest of the World we should agree. If I said any thing, Brother, to the Prejudice of your Character, I ask pardon.

LOCKIT. Brother *Peachum*—I can forgive as well as resent.—Give me your Hand. Suspicion does not become a Friend.

PEACHUM. I only meant to give you Occasion to justify yourself.

When he heightens the dialogue by the addition of epigrammatic statement, Gay comes very near the level of Congreve himself. What he lacks of the Congrevean brilliance, he compensates for by never giving more at a time than ordinary attention will sustain without conscious effort. He seldom allows himself Congreve's length of phrase. It is illuminating to compare the pace of the two:

FAINALL. You are a gallant man, Mirabell; and though you may have cruelty enough not to satisfy a lady's longing, you have too much generosity not to be tender of her honour. Yet you speak with an indifference which seems to be affected, and confesses you are conscious of a negligence.

(38)

MIRABELL. You pursue the argument with a distrust that seems to be unaffected, and confesses you are conscious of a concern for which the lady is more indebted to you than is your wife.

Gay's tempo is more rapid: his cadences beach themselves much sooner, with an impact that is less impressive to watch, but more immediately felt:

PEACHUM. Dear Wife, be a little pacified. Don't let your Passion run away with your Senses. *Polly,* I grant you hath done a rash thing.

Mrs. PEACHUM. If she had had only an Intrigue with the Fellow, why the very best Families have excus'd and huddled up a Frailty of that sort. 'Tis Marriage, Husband, that makes it a blemish.

PEACHUM. But Money, Wife, is the true Fuller's Earth for Reputations, there is not a Spot or a Stain but what it can take out. A rich Rogue now-a-days is fit Company for any Gentleman; and the World, my Dear, hath not such a Contempt for Roguery as you imagine.

For the most part, Gay's epigrams do not bear lifting out of their contexts so well as do Congreve's; but Congreve would have found it difficult to better the aphorism of Macheath:

Do all we can, Women will believe us; for they look upon a Promise as an Excuse for following their own Inclinations.

IV

Gay has invented for us a vivid group of people, with an appeal that is hard to resist. They are so delightful, and, in the discrepancy between their reprehensible ends and the self-righteousness with which they pursue them, so ludicrous that we may miss the richer significance of the satire in our mere spontaneous enjoyment. The matter is treated with so light a hand that we incline to ignore its serious implications. It is important, therefore, to remind ourselves of the actual weight of these persons, for without this solid underpinning Gay could hardly have made his play carry the considerable cargo of its deeper meaning,—could hardly have made it a social commentary which, for all its surface playfulness, fulfills some of the profoundest ends of comedy.

(39)

Each of the leading characters is a positive force. Let us hold in abeyance for the moment our amused perception of their real worth, while they parade before us in the favoring light of their own self-regard. Peachum is a man of responsibility who has constantly to make decisions affecting the welfare and the lives of many people. He has to weigh the importance of particular cases, adjudicate conflicting claims, and issue commands. And his orders are not lightly disobeyed. His wife has a proper sense of her husband's importance in their world, and of her own position. She shares his counsels, but respects his authority and does not abuse her privilege. Her solicitude for her family's reputation is keen, her maternal sense is well developed. She does not lightly give way to emotion, but, on a sufficient occasion, her passions are impressive. Polly is neither feather-brained nor impulsive, but basically prudent and steady. She accepts, and respects, her parents' values, and her single point of difference with them is rationally grounded though admittedly in significant accord with her inclinations. Filch, the servant, recognizes that his own interests are identified with his masters', and is accordingly trusted and accepted almost as one of the family. He is a boy of the brightest parts, quick and apt, ready to give his best efforts to the discharge of his varied responsibilities. Lockit is another, but lesser, Peachum, with a philosophy equally well developed though not quite so fully uttered, and with a visible satisfaction in the power he wields. His daughter Lucy is a Salvator Rosa set over against the Claude of Polly. In her tempestuous nature we can trace Ercles' vein:

> The raging rocks
> And shivering shocks
> Shall break the locks
> Of prison gates.

She has a streak of tenderness, but in anger she is terrible and dangerous. She is crafty and determined in pursuit of revenge,

(40)

and does not flinch from the possible consequences. As for Macheath, his sangfroid, dash, and prodigality of purse and person make him a favorite with both sexes. He is not easily cast down, and he knows that there are things worse than death in the human lot. Hazlitt calls him "one of God Almighty's gentlemen." His gallantry and good breeding rise, declares Hazlitt, "from impulse, not from rule; not from the trammels of education, but from a soul generous, courageous, good-natured, aspiring, amourous. The class of the character is very difficult to hit. It is something between gusto and slang, like port-wine and brandy mixed."[8]

None of these persons appears to be suffering from a sense of inferiority. Their words give proper dignity to their ideas, and their conduct proceeds in accordance with principles to which they have given a good deal of thought. Without in the least minimizing the pleasure of their company, one may assert that, with the possible exception of Polly, they all have a better opinion of themselves than we do. For we are not taken in: we know them for the immoral rogues that they are. They are the most immediate objects of Gay's satire. However loftily they bear themselves, the human reality of their lives is sordid and contemptible. Remembering the dreariness of many of the products of "realism" in later days, we may well be grateful for an occasional example of the mock heroic, which subjects to the purposes of humor the matter generally reserved for "realistic" treatment. The flair for this inverted kind of burlesque has, for reasons which might elsewhere be significantly pursued, been all but lost in our time. It is enough to note here that, in our recognition of Gay's burlesquing of the highflown manners and sentiments of operatic romance, we ought not to lose sight of the fact that he is simultaneously ridiculing a low society by decking them in all this borrowed finery. For burlesque has a two-edged blade,

---

[8] *On the English Stage*, July 27, 1816, quoted by Schultz, *op. cit.*, p. 274.

though both edges need not be equally sharp. "Had the Play remain'd, as I at first intended," says Gay in the person of the Beggar, with glancing irony, "it would have carried a most excellent Moral. 'Twould have shown that the lower Sort of People have their Vices in a degree as well as the Rich: And that they are punish'd for them."

The characters in the play are aware of our low opinion of them, and stand on the defensive against us. Offspring of corruption as they are, feeding on sin and death, what are their bulwarks, that so magnificently shore up their self-respect?

It is not by maintaining that the bases of our criticism are unsound that they are able to repel our attack. Truth and falsehood, good and evil, right and wrong are for them fundamentally the same as they are for us. Peachum, for example, accepts the conventional morality, and can even afford to make gestures of kindliness when they do not interfere with more important considerations. He delights "to let Women scape." "Make haste to *Newgate,* Boy," he commands Filch, "and let my Friends know what I intend; for I love to make them easy one way or other." And Filch, in the orotund fashion of sentimental drama, replies, "I'll away, for 'tis a Pleasure to be the Messenger of Comfort to Friends in Affliction." Neither Filch nor Mrs. Peachum is a stranger to feelings of gratitude and good will. Peachum, moreover, is above petty animosities. When Polly recoils from the idea of having Macheath impeached, protesting that her blood freezes at the thought of murdering her husband, Peachum replies:

Fye, *Polly!* What hath Murder to do in the Affair? Since the thing sooner or later must happen, I dare say, the Captain himself would like that we should get the Reward for his Death sooner than a Stranger. Why, *Polly,* the Captain knows, that as 'tis his Employment to rob, so 'tis ours to take Robbers, every Man in his Business. So that there is no Malice in the Case.

Clearly, these are no devils. Evil is not their good.

Rather, they stand us off by admitting the justice of our cause and then diverting our attack all along the line to their betters. Gay himself is easily deflected and we follow him in full cry. Here we reach the second degree of his satire, and it is on this level that the main attack is launched. People in the honorable walks of life—men of great business, ladies of fashion, lawyers, courtiers, statesmen—it is these who come in for the hottest fire. "Murder," declares Peachum, "is as fashionable a Crime as a Man can be guilty of.... No Gentleman is ever look'd upon the worse for killing a Man in his own Defence." If Macheath cannot do well at the gaming tables, the fault lies in his education: "The Man that proposes to get Money by Play should have the Education of a fine Gentleman, and be train'd up to it from his Youth." "Really," replies Mrs. Peachum to her husband, "I am sorry upon *Polly's* Account the Captain hath not more Discretion. What business hath he to keep Company with Lords and Gentlemen? he should leave them to prey upon one another." Society is a casino. Both sexes play; and since the only purpose that motivates their play is the desire of gain, it follows that very few persons are above sharp practice. "Most Ladies take a delight in cheating, when they can do it with Safety," declares Mrs. Trapes. Gamesters are the vilest of Mechanics, but "many of the Quality are of the Profession," and they have admittance to the politest circles. "I wonder," remarks Matt of the Mint, "I wonder *we* are not more respected."

> Thus Gamesters united in Friendship are found,
> Though they know that their Industry all is a Cheat;
> They flock to their Prey at the Dice-Box's Sound,
> And join to promote one another's Deceit.
>   But if by mishap
>   They fail of a Chap,
> To keep in their Hands, they each other entrap.
> Like Pikes, lank with Hunger, who miss of their Ends,
> They bite their Companions, and prey on their Friends.

(43)

Money will do anything in this fashionable world. Ladies marry in hopes of soon being widows with a jointure. When Polly announces that she has married for love, her mother is horrified: "Love him! I thought the Girl had been better bred." And to marry a highwayman: "Why, thou foolish Jade, thou wilt be as ill us'd, and as much neglected, as if thou hadst married a Lord!" But Polly herself knows—at least in her own opinion—"as well as any of the fine Ladies how to make the most of my self and of my Man too."

No love is lost in those exalted spheres. And even friendship proceeds merely upon the foot of interest. "Those that act otherwise are their own Bubbles." Promises are plentiful, but a court friend was never known to give anything else. Quite the contrary: "In one respect," says Peachum, "our Employment may be reckon'd dishonest, because, like great Statesmen, we encourage those who betray their Friends." But again: "Can it be expected that we should hang our Acquaintance for nothing, when our Betters will hardly save theirs without being paid for it?" And think of the legal profession. Robbery may be common elsewhere, but beside the wholesale robbery of the law it is nothing at all. "Gold from Law can take out the Sting," but, on the other side,

> It ever was decreed, Sir,
> If Lawyer's Hand is fee'd, Sir,
> He steals your whole Estate.

It appears, then, that if the Newgate people are culpable, they are merely imitating their betters, who must be charged with equal blame. But grant so much, and we must grant more. The criminals press their advantage by suggesting that guilt is proportional to the amount of harm done, which in turn depends on the degree of power to execute it. There is no question where the power resides. The statesman may think his "trade" as honest as Peachum's, but logic will say him no. Thinking of our own

days, we shall have little heart to contradict logic. Then, sings
Macheath unanswerably:

> Since Laws were made for ev'ry Degree,
> To curb Vice in others, as well as me,
> I wonder we han't better Company,
>   Upon *Tyburn* Tree!
>
> But Gold from Law can take out the Sting;
> And if rich Men like us were to swing,
> 'Twould thin the Land, such Numbers to string
>   Upon *Tyburn* Tree!

Moreover, Macheath and his gang have one more shaft to shoot,
for what it is worth. They can set an example of loyalty and generosity and honor among themselves. "Who is there here," cries
Nimming Ned, "that would not dye for his Friend?" "Who is
there here," adds Harry Padington, "that would betray him for
his Interest?" "Show me a Gang of Courtiers," says Matt of the
Mint, "that can say as much." Macheath prides himself upon
being a man of his word and no court friend. "We, Gentlemen,"
he declares, "have still Honour enough to break through the Corruptions of the World.—And while I can serve you, you may
command me."

Here the defense rests its case. The ground has been occupied
before, and will be again. The abuse of power, the chasm between
profession and practice in high place, the constant defeat of principles by wealth, the oppression of desert born a beggar, "the
spurns that patient merit of the unworthy takes," the immorality
and selfishness of privileged society—all these themes are the
stock-in-trade of satirists, familiar to our ears as household words.
This is the habitual level of Swift, whose way is to show how
much more reprehensible those are whom the world admires
than those whom the world despises.

But Gay's satire does not stop at this point. There are hints in
The Beggar's Opera of a more revolutionary doctrine. If we really

believe in truth and justice and the general welfare, doubtless we should all be glad to see temporary violations of these principles set right. We should welcome, should we not, a fairer distribution of this world's goods, juster apportionment of the right to life, liberty, and the pursuit of happiness? But do we not, on the contrary, resist by all the means in our power any attempts at readjustment? Are not Macheath and his fellows more active laborers for the general good than we? We adopt the principles but obstruct their realization. The Newgate gentry adopt them and work for the cause:

BEN BUDGE. We are for a just Partition of the World, for every Man hath a Right to enjoy Life.

MATT OF THE MINT. We retrench the Superfluities of Mankind. The World is avaritious, and I hate Avarice. A covetous fellow, like a Jack-daw, steals what he was never made to enjoy, for the sake of hiding it. These are the Robbers of Mankind, for Money was made for the Free-hearted and Generous.

Who, then, are the true friends of man? Are they not the so-called enemies of society? Is it possible to be actively a friend of mankind without being a revolutionary? The established order is radically iniquitous: how can we defend the *status quo* and remain true to the principles to which we profess allegiance?

Thus it becomes clear that *The Beggar's Opera,* half a century before Figaro burst upon the world, foreshadowed in significant ways the point of view which Beaumarchais was to develop with such devastating results.[9] That the political and social implications of the earlier work did not explode with equal violence is in large measure due, of course, to the different temper of society

---

[9] "Mais il y a un jour où se remassent dans une explosion unique tous les sentiments de toute nature, moraux, politique, sociaux, que l'œuvre des philosophes avait développés dans les cœurs, joie de vivre, avidité de jouir, intense excitation de l'intelligence, hains et mépris du présent, des abus, des traditions, espoir et besoin d'*autre chose:* ce jour de folie intellectuelle où toute la société de l'ancien régime applaudit aux idées dont elle va périr, c'est la première représentation du *Mariage de Figaro* (27 avril 1784)."—Lanson, *Hist. de la Litt. Française,* p. 807.

at the time. But equally it is due to the broader base of Gay's satire. Figaro, besides being the spokesman of democratic defiance against rank and privilege, is basically the wholesome representative of those conventional virtues that popular sentiment judged worthy of perpetuation. He is therefore a revolutionary symbol to which generous souls could pay sympathetic homage.

There is no comparable figure in the earlier play. For the Newgate knaves, however they may color their actions, are only masquerading. When their conduct is scrutinized, it is obvious that self-interest is at the bottom of everything they do. It is shot through with bad faith and disloyalty even to their own class. Jealousy and suspicion are the rule here as elsewhere. In the end, Macheath is forced to draw the inevitable conclusion from his experience: "That *Jemmy Twitcher* should peach me, I own surpriz'd me!—'Tis a plain Proof that the World is all alike, and that even our Gang can no more trust one another than other People."

The world is all alike! That is the final lesson of Gay's satire. We laughed at the obvious reversal of accepted values which runs through the play. We laughed to hear Black Moll's industry commended, knowing that that industry was actively expended upon thievery and playing the whore. Laziness is a vice, and it was refreshing to see sloth in the performance of crime meet with its due punishment. But, *mutatis mutandis,* were we not laughing at ourselves? As Peachum told his wife, "The World, my Dear, hath not such a Contempt for Roguery as you imagine." We are all cheats, paying lip service to one set of principles and motivated in actual truth by another. Every man presents to the world an idealized dream picture as his authentic and veracious self-portrait. The institutions of society, which we pretend are so solidly established, rest on a fiction that has no external actuality. The ideals we profess are impossible to live by in this world, for they are undermined both from within and without. Private interest

(47)

seldom coincides with public good, and private interest has the controlling hand, whether in the political, the social, the commercial, or the sexual sphere. Of this truth we are reminded in the play. "Now, *Peachum,*" soliloquizes Lockit, "you and I, like honest Tradesmen, are to have a fair Tryal which of us two can overreach the other." "All men," reflects Mrs. Peachum, "are thieves in love, and like a woman the better for being another's property." "Of all Animals of Prey," says Lockit, again, "Man is the only sociable one. Every one of us preys upon his Neighbour, and yet we herd together." "Well, Polly," sighs Mrs. Peachum, "as far as one Woman can forgive another, I forgive thee." The opposition of class against class, youth against age, sex against sex, individual against individual, is both inevitable and involuntary. We are predatory by the mere physiological premises of our common humanity. Under the conditions of existence, idealism is a merely relative term. "Oh, gentlemen," cried Hotspur before he died,

> the time of life is short;
> To spend that shortness basely were too long
> If life did ride upon a dial's point,
> Still ending at the arrival of an hour.

The irony is that, paying homage all our lives to these principles, it would hardly be possible to point to a single hour in which we lived in entire accordance with them. This is the doom of man, and each of us postures as if it were reversed for him, condemning others for what he excuses in himself, and generally playing such fantastic tricks before high heaven as are enough to make immortals laugh themselves to death. Fixed in this dance of plastic circumstance, we persist in declaring that we are the captains of our souls. Existence itself is the ultimate irony.

To go on breathing in the utter vacuum of this realization is impossible, and most of us are able to enter it only at rare moments. Acceptance of the pessimistic view may generate reactions which are diametrical opposites. The picture may be seen as comedy, or it may be seen as tragedy. To the romantic vision, speaking generally, it will appear tragic; to the classical, comic. The romantic attitude, being chiefly concerned with the individual ego, finds this spectacle of a divided self all but intolerable, and, to restore inner consistency, may take refuge in the Byronic pose. If I cannot be true to the ideals I profess, let me overturn those ideals and set up others that will be valid, and in accordance with the facts of my existence. "Evil, be thou my good!" Thus, in solitary grandeur, the diabolist may enjoy the luxury of integrity. For man in society, however, such an escape is hardly possible. The eighteenth century was not an age of solitaries; its characteristic orientations concerned man as a social being. It took little pleasure in exploring the orbit of the lonely soul through infinite space; it derived strength and assurance from solidarity. The contradictions of life become once again endurable when shared with one's brother men, and it is possible to be objective in contemplating the universal lot. Thus the age of Gay tended to see the irony of existence as fundamentally comic. For Swift, indeed, who had to watch the comedy through eighteenth-century eyes but with the passionate emotions and gigantic ego of a romantic, the spectacle turned bitter. Gay's good-humored view of it, as seen in *The Beggar's Opera,* is essentially characteristic both of his age and of himself. It was Gay who devised for his own epitaph the well-known lines:

> Life is a jest; and all things show it.
> I thought so once; but now I know it.

(49)

JAMES L. CLIFFORD

The Authenticity of Anna Seward's Published

Correspondence

from

MODERN PHILOLOGY

Volume XXXIX(1941-2), 113-22

Reprinted by permission of The University of

Chicago Press

Reprinted for private circulation from
MODERN PHILOLOGY, Vol. XXXIX, No. 2, November, 1941
PRINTED IN THE U.S.A.

MODERN PHILOLOGY

VOLUME XXXIX   *November 1941*   NUMBER 2

THE AUTHENTICITY OF ANNA SEWARD'S PUBLISHED CORRESPONDENCE

JAMES L. CLIFFORD

IN THE year 1811, two years after the death of Anna Seward, the "Swan of Lichfield," the publisher Constable in Edinburgh brought out a six-volume edition of her letters. Since that time these rather pretentious epistles have been used, along with the comments of Boswell and Horace Walpole, as genuine contemporary evidence concerning the social and literary life of the late eighteenth century. They have been quoted extensively by competent scholars and critics. Now it seems certain that they do not represent what Anna Seward originally wrote but rather what she decided in late life would better enhance her reputation. The published letters are late revisions, made from copies of the originals, and as such cannot be trusted as evidence in controversial matters.

Before conclusive evidence is presented to support this claim, a short account should be given of the circumstances attending the 1811 publication. For a large part of her life, certainly after 1784, Miss Seward kept rough copies of every important letter she wrote. Convinced that she was a remarkable person, she did not wish to allow chance alone to determine whether her brilliant correspondence should one day see the light of day. She even tried to find a celebrated editor to insure a favorable reception of the work. Sir Walter Scott was her choice, but, though he did finally agree to edit her poetry, Scott refused to put his name to the edition of her letters. As he wrote on

March 18, 1810, to Joanna Baillie, he had "declined on principle having a particular aversion at perpetuating that sort of gossip."[1]

Balked in her attempt to get Scott as an editor, Anna Seward instead left at her death the following letter to Constable:

> In a Will, made and executed since I had the pleasure of seeing you in April last, I have left you the exclusive copy-right of Twelve Volumes quarto, half-bound. They contain copies of letters, or of parts of letters, that, after I had written them, appeared to me worth the attention of the public. Voluminous as is the collection, it does not include a twelfth part of my epistolary writing from the time it commences, viz. from the year 1784, to the present day.
>
> I wish you to publish two volumes annually; and by no means to follow the late absurd custom of classing letters to separate correspondents, but suffer them to succeed each other in the order of time, as you find them transcribed. . . . .[2]

In his three-volume edition of *The poetical works of Anna Seward*, in 1810, Scott published in the preface a selection from her early letters (October, 1762—January, 1768).[3] Perhaps he took this means of easing his conscience over his refusal to be responsible for the rest, or possibly these few were intended to serve as an advertisement of the forthcoming larger edition. It might even be that Scott, besides disliking the style of the later letters, suspected their authenticity and printed only a few early ones which he felt certain were genuine. Whatever the reason, Scott had no official connection with Constable's printing in 1811.[4]

In this six-volume edition not all of Miss Seward's copies were included. Constable stated in his Advertisement that he had omitted some letters referring to persons then living and some critical discussions which appeared too long and detailed.[5] Moreover, the request that the volumes be issued two at a time was not followed. In general, however, the publisher presented what he believed to be accurate copies of letters actually sent through the post. And most readers have accepted the versions as genuine.

---

[1] *The letters of Sir Walter Scott*, ed. H. J. C. Grierson (London, 1932), II, 315.

[2] *Letters of Anna Seward* (Edinburgh, 1811), I, v–vi.   [3] Pp. xliii–ccvi.

[4] All Scott did was to read through the manuscript copies and cut out numerous references to himself (see J. G. Lockhart, *Memoirs of the life of Sir Walter Scott, Bart.* [2d ed.; Edinburgh and London, 1839], III, 298).

[5] *Letters of Anna Seward*, I, x.

To anyone who chanced to compare original letters with the printed versions, on the other hand, the result was very disillusioning. Thus in 1863 the Rev. Hill Wickham, when publishing the correspondence of Thomas Sedgewick Whalley, D.D., wrote of finding the manuscripts of Anna Seward's letters "often varying from the printed copy";[6] but he obligingly refused to give the lady away further and printed in his volumes only letters not re-written. Yet evidently few other people took the trouble, or were able, to make such comparisons. Only today, when more of Anna Seward's genuine letters have become available for study, are we able to estimate the nature and number of her changes.

In the John Rylands Library there are twelve holograph letters from Anna Seward to Mrs. Piozzi, seven of which represent the originals of versions printed in 1811. An examination of one letter having to do with Mrs. Piozzi's publication of correspondence with Dr. Johnson will show the nature of the changes.

ORIGINAL LETTER (JOHN RYLANDS LIBRARY, ENG. MS 565, 5)	PUBLISHED VERSION (1811 ED., II, 39–46)
LICHFIELD March 14.th 1788	LICHFIELD, March 7, 1788

MY DEAR MADAM

I am honored, & obliged by the kind present of your last entertaining, & valuable Publication. It shews the great man in an infinitely more *benign*, tho' less *resplendent* point of view than any other of his writings, or than any veritable record of his conversation cou'd possibly place him. Letter-writing however appears to me not to have been his talent, whatever scatterings we find in these his epistles of the Johnsonian fire. He, whose eloquence in his *Essays* has unrivalled *grace*, as well as force, seems but an unwieldy Trifler, tho' it is amusing to see him gambol

This kind present, your last entertaining and valuable publication of the Goliah's Epistles, at once obliges and does me honour. They shew him in a more benign, though less resplendent point of view, than, perhaps, any other of his writings, or than he could appear from any veritable records of his conversation, since you have, doubtless, expunged the malignant passages, from your benevolent attention to the feelings of many.

Letter-writing, however, appears not to have been his talent, though, in the course of these epistles, we find

---

[6] *Journals and correspondence of Thomas Sedgewick Whalley, D.D.*, ed. H. Wickham (London, 1863), I, 15.

with Taylor's great Bull. His general playfulness wants the elegance, his wit the brilliance, & his style that polished ease, which adorn the letters of Gray, & give *them* a superiority so decided. We here see *that* collection pronounced a *dull Work*, thro' Johnson's prejudice against the Genius which had outshone him in more ways than one.

Ah! my dear Madam, how much more charming are your letters than your Philosopher's!—*gems* of the collection! gems of the *first* water! A transcendence so incontrovertible shall, in spite of sexual jealousy, oblige the justice of the English to emulate that of the Theban Literati, &, in this display of epistolary talent, decree to *you* the palm which crowned the lyre of Corinna in her contest with Pindar.

. . . .

Doc[r] Johnson seems to me most himself in the letters from Scotland. It is charming to observe him carelessly sketching out those Scenes, of which his Tour presents us with so sublime a picture.

M[r] Boswell will be gratified to find here, in Doc[r] Johnson's approbation of his Anecdotes, a full acquittal of treachery to the confidence, & to the fame of his Friend; a charge so loudly brought against him by Dullness, & by Malice—

Your translation of the latin Poem. . . . .

. . . .

frequently scattered rays of Johnsonian fire. He, whose eloquence has, in his essays, unrivalled majesty and force, seems an unwieldly trifler. When he will gambol, he gambols best with Dr. Taylor's great bull, a sort of cousin-german of his in strength and surliness.

His playfulness wants the elegance, his wit the brilliance, and his style the polished ease of Gray's Letters; which, as letters, are very superior indeed to Johnson's, though he pronounces them a dull work; but that was from envy.

Your epistles in this collection outshine your preceptor's, and are the gems of the volume. A transcendence so decided, must surely oblige the English to imitate the justice of the Theban literati, and, in this mutual display of epistolary powers, decree that palm to you which crowned the lyre of Corinna in her contest with Pindar.

. . . .

Johnson, as a writer, is most himself in his letters from Scotland. We are delighted to observe him familiarly sketching out those scenes, of which his Tour presents so sublime a picture. Mr Boswell will be gratified to find here, in Dr Johnson's approbation of his anecdotes, a full acquittal of his imputed treachery to the confidence and fame of his friend. Those who brought that accusation against Mr Boswell, evinced that they little understood Johnson's character. He said nothing to any one in confidence. Far from wishing to hide, he gloried in his malignity, and in the trust that it would be recorded. He had none of those "compunctious visitings of nature," which make softer dispositions scrupulous of wounding the feelings of others. I have heard him say, that distinguished people know that their colloquial opinions will be recorded, and their letters published.

Your translation of his Latin verses. . . . .

. . . .

Since I see so many Lichfield People often mentioned, whose visits were not much more frequent than mine, & whose talents wou'd not attract his notice, there is no great vanity in supposing he w^d *not* pass *me* over in total silence. It is therefore that I sincerely *thank* you for your suppressions.

I cannot imagine what anonymous Poem that was, w^h he was solicited to read *here* in the year 81, or who it was that cou'd make such a request. Not a single soul of them, whose names are *frequent* in his letters, cou'd be interested about a *Poem*, whatever excellence it might possess. I never shewed, or asked his opinion of a line of mine, & always had an horror at the idea of any body else doing it. To me he constantly spoke with strong dislike over the idea of female Readers, & Writers. As I so carefully avoided every thing which cou'd lead to the subject of *my* compositions, it was the only method in which he cou'd decently insinuate his dislike of them—yet once he said a very handsome thing to me of my Elegy on Cook. I blushed, curtsied, & turned the conversation into another channel . . . .

Since I see so many Lichfield people mentioned in these letters, whose visits were not much more frequent than mine, and whose talents had no sort of claim to lettered attention, there can be no great vanity in believing that he would not pass me over in total silence. Therefore is it that I thank you for your suppressions. I must have been pained by the consciousness of going down to posterity with the envenomed arrows of Johnson's malevolence sticking about me; though I am well aware, from the recording spirit of his less benevolent biographers, that it is the fate of numbers to bear them, whose virtues and abilities are superior to mine.

I cannot imagine what anonymous poem it could be, which it appears, from these letters, that he was solicited to read on one of his visits to Lichfield in 1781. Not a creature among the number of his visitors, whom he mentions, are capable of being enough interested about any poetic effort to have requested his attention to it. I never shewed him, or asked his opinion about a single line of mine, either in print or manuscript, nor of any unpublished work of others. To me he almost invari-

ably spoke with strong dislike of all
our celebrated female writers, except
yourself. As I so carefully avoided
all conversation that could lead to
the subject of my compositions, it
was the only way he had of imparting
that mortification to my literary self-
love, which it was the first joy of his
gloomy spirit to impart to every person, at times.

That any human being, male or female, could endeavour to draw Johnson's attention to their own writings,
is to me astonishing. How little insight into character must they, who
made the rash, the vain attempt,
have possessed!

Once, however—perhaps as a reward for the unobtrusive disposition
of my muse, he paid an high compliment, in my presence, to my Elegy on
Cook. He was speaking favourably
of the Columbia of Madame Bocage,
and added, "she describes many
things well, but nothing so well as
you have described the seas, and
shores, round the South Pole." I
blushed, curtsied, and instantly
turned the conversation into a different channel. . . . .

Three observations can be made: the dates of the two letters do not
coincide; the phraseology throughout has been materially altered; and
long passages containing new ideas or amplifying old opinions have
been added. More will be said later concerning the matter of dating.
The changes of wording can almost all be explained as efforts to better
the literary style, to suit the taste of the aging bluestocking. Of greater
importance are the definite additions and obvious changes in meaning.

It must be remembered that the original letter was written before
the appearance of Boswell's *Life of Johnson*, but there can be little
doubt that the published version was composed some time after its

appearance. Nor can the printed version have possibly been an earlier rough draft from which the transmitted letter was fashioned. Definite proof may be found in the account, near the end, of Johnson's remarks about the "Elegy on Cook." In the original letter Anna Seward only casually referred to the incident; but Boswell in the *Life* had given a more detailed account, actually quoting the Doctor's remark about Mme Bocage.[7] Reading this passage, Miss Seward was forcibly reminded of the conversation and decided to include the complimentary reference in the later revision of her letter to Mrs. Piozzi. Thus the re-writing of this particular letter must almost certainly have occurred after 1791, and from other evidence it was probably much later.

At the time of the publication of the *Life* Boswell was on fairly good terms with Miss Seward, but a bitter quarrel in 1793, over one of Johnson's minor verses,[8] forced a breach in their friendship. Miss Seward's remark about "the recording spirit of his less benevolent biographers" would seem to mirror her resentment and would therefore indicate that the passage had been written later than 1793. All in all, the probability is that the revision took place after 1800, although no conclusive evidence can be brought forward to prove the assertion.

The changes of chief interest to us today concern Dr. Johnson. "The Swan of Lichfield" had never been one of the Doctor's real admirers; but before the appearance of Boswell's *Life*, and especially when writing to Johnson's former intimate friend, Mrs. Piozzi, Miss Seward did not show her true feelings. In the later revision, however, there was no reason to hold back, and as a result she speaks of "malignant passages" in Johnson's letters, of "his malignity," and again of his "malevolence." This was to be her revenge for real or fancied slights received at Johnson's hands. But it certainly does not represent what she was willing to write to Mrs. Piozzi in 1788.

Enough has been given, perhaps, to show the character of the changes made in letters addressed to Mrs. Piozzi. Those to other correspondents, at least the ones so far examined, show similar alterations in phraseology. In the Huntington Library may be found the originals

[7] *Boswell's Life of Johnson*, ed. G. B. Hill, revised by L. F. Powell (Oxford, 1934), IV, 331.

[8] *Ibid.*, pp. 331–32; F. A. Pottle, *The literary career of James Boswell, Esq.* (Oxford, 1929), p. 234.

of Miss Seward's letters to the flamboyant Edward Jerningham.[9] The opening sentences from one of the letters follow:

HUNTINGTON JERNINGHAM MSS UNCATALOGUED	PUBLISHED VERSION (1811 ED., V, 290–95)
	LICHFIELD, June 23, 1800
Thank you for your interesting volume, your attention to my health, your friendly council. Silence has made me seem negligent of all this goodness. I was at Buxton when your letter & book, arrived here; the former followed me thither, but the Coach, w.h passes thro' that place, is so careless of small parcels, that I always order *those* to wait my return. I waited to read you in print before I answered you in manuscript. Arriving a few days back, it was only yesterday that the slightest portion of seclusion cou'd be obtained, & it was devoted to your new Publication. The prefatory Essay.	Thank you for your interesting volume, your attention to my health, your friendly counsel. I was at Buxton when these testimonies of friendship arrived at Lichfield. Your letter followed me thither; your book waited my return. I staid to read you in print, ere I answered you in manuscript. Your prefatory essay. . . . .
LICHFIELD, June 24, 1800	

Several pages at the end of the original letter were omitted in the printed version.

That her letters to Boswell were also re-written is evident from one short quotation included in C. C. Abbott's *Catalogue of papers relating to Boswell, Johnson & Sir William Forbes found at Fettercairn House* (Oxford, 1936). On March 7, 1786, Miss Seward wrote to Boswell about his *Tour to the Hebrides:* that she had recommended it to her literary friends in "the warmest Spirit of encomium" for its "characteristic strength, gay benevolence, scenic graces, & biographic fidelity."[10] Then followed an account of how Lucy Porter had left her fortune and some description of her character. In the printed version, dated "March 25, —," but placed in 1786,[11] the recommendation is phrased

---

[9] I am indebted to Professor W. Powell Jones for all information about the Huntington Library Jerningham manuscripts. He has kindly supplied me with copies of some of the letters and data about the remainder.

[10] *Fettercairn catalogue*, p. 121.   [11] I, 129–33.

"in a spirit of warm encomium upon the gay benevolence, character-istic traits, scenic graces, and biographic fidelity which adorn its pages." No reference whatsoever to Lucy Porter is included.

We come now to a much more puzzling problem than the mere re-wording of the published versions: the startling discovery that none of the original letters examined bears the same date as its correspond-ing printed version. The genuine letters sent to Boswell, Jerningham, and Mrs. Piozzi all vary slightly in dating from the established ver-sions. For instance, the seven to Mrs. Piozzi are dated:

MS	Postmark	Published Version
March 14, 1788	Blurred, but after MR 10, since the 1 is visible	March 7, 1788 (II, 39–46)
March 26, 1788	MR 28, 88	March 13, 1788 (II, 53–58)
Feb. 15, 1789	FE 16, 89	Feb. 13, 1789 (II, 242–46)
April 15, 1789	AP 17, 89	April 11, 1789 (II, 260–62)
Dec. 31 [1789]	JA 6, 90	Dec. 21 [1789] (II, 336–42)
Feb. 23, 1790	Blurred	Feb. 20, 1790 (II, 374–80)
No date or address	None	April 15, 1790 (III, 3–7)

It will be noted that the intervals between the dates of the original manuscripts and the stamped postmarks vary between one and six days—about what we should expect, since we now believe that it was the eighteenth-century practice to place the postmark on a letter upon its arrival in London rather than at the provincial place of posting. But intervals as great as fifteen and sixteen days are much too long. Thus it seems almost certain that the printed dates are spurious or at least only approximately correct.

Proof of another sort indicates that the date of the printed letter of March 7, 1788, is wrong. As we have seen, Miss Seward thanked Mrs. Piozzi for a presentation copy of *Letters to and from the late Samuel Johnson, LL.D.* But this work was not published until March 8, 1788,[12] and in this instance it is unlikely that the volumes would have been sent to Miss Seward before the day of publication. The date on the original letter of March 14—six days after the appearance of the work—is much more credible.

Additional evidence of the changing of dates in other series of letters comes in Miss Seward's account of her first meeting with Mrs. Piozzi

---

[12] The *Morning post* and other London newspapers of that day.

in the summer of 1787. In her printed correspondence she writes on October 6 both to Whalley and to the poet William Hayley, rhapsodizing over her first meeting with the Piozzis.[13] Consequently, scholars have always assumed that the meeting must have occurred late in September or early in October, 1787; and most books on the Johnsonian circle have repeated this error. Unquestioned evidence now shows that the Piozzis were in Lichfield on August 22 and 23;[14] and an original letter of Miss Seward's to Mrs. Piozzi, dated August 24, referring to the visit has been discovered.[15] Furthermore, since in her letter to Whalley, Miss Seward explains her inability to introduce Mr. Saville to the Piozzis because he had been "last week at Birmingham," the conclusion becomes obvious that the original letter must have been posted late in August or early in September. The published date is therefore at least a month off, and probably more.

What could have been Miss Seward's motive in consistently altering all the dates in her re-written correspondence? Did she believe that by making the change she was absolving herself from the guilt of re-writing? Did she somehow believe that, if the dates were different, anyone making a comparison with the original letters would assume that there was no connection? Or is it possible that in keeping copies of her correspondence she failed to put a definite date on them, retaining only the month and the year, and later was forced to guess at the actual days? We may only surmise; but certainly the last assumption seems the most likely. As she progressed with her revisions, the thought may have occurred to her that for published letters a precise date was preferable. And, being an ingenious lady, she promptly supplied the missing figures.

In conclusion, it must be admitted that, until all the originals of Miss Seward's correspondence can be compared with the published material, no conclusive statement can be made; yet the evidence presented here would seem to be sufficient to show that the 1811 edition cannot be implicitly trusted for facts or contemporary opinions and not even for a strict chronology of the period.

Lehigh University

[13] I, 335–40.
[14] See my *Hester Lynch Piozzi* (*Mrs. Thrale*) (Oxford, 1941), p. 306.
[15] John Rylands Library, Eng. MS 892.

RONALD S. CRANE

Suggestions toward a Genealogy of
'The Man of Feeling'

from

A JOURNAL OF ENGLISH LITERARY HISTORY

Volume I(1934), 205-30

SUGGESTIONS TOWARD A GENEALOGY OF THE "MAN OF FEELING"[1]

By R. S. CRANE

We may take, as a convenient starting-point for our inquiry, two passages from works published respectively in 1754 and 1755. In the first of these the Scottish moralist David Fordyce is attempting to enumerate the emotional satisfactions peculiar to the benevolent man:

> His Enjoyments [he writes] are more numerous, or, if less numerous, yet more intense than those of bad Men; for he shares in the Joys of others by Rebound; and every Increase of *general* or *particular* Happiness is a real Addition to his own. It is true, his friendly *Sympathy* with others subjects him to some Pains which the hard-hearted Wretch does not feel; yet to give a loose to it is a kind of agreeable Discharge. It is such a Sorrow as he loves to indulge; a sort of pleasing Anguish, that sweetly melts the Mind, and terminates in a Self-approving Joy. Though the good Man may want Means to execute, or be disappointed in the Success of his benevolent Purposes, yet . . . he is still conscious of good Affections, and that Consciousness is an Enjoyment of a more delightful Savour than the greatest Triumphs of successful Vice.[2]

In the other passage an anonymous essayist writes in a somewhat similar vein on the subject of " moral weeping ":

••

---

[1] This paper was prepared for presentation before the Language and Literature Club of the University of Wisconsin in April, 1934. I have inserted many additional references, but have not otherwise greatly altered the exposition. It goes without saying that I have not attempted an exhaustive study of any aspect of the subject.

[2] *The Elements of Moral Philosophy*, 1754, pp. 263-4.

Moral weeping is the sign of so noble a passion, that it may be questioned whether those are properly men, who never weep upon any occasion. They may pretend to be as heroical as they please, and pride themselves in a stoical insensibility; but this will never pass for virtue with the true judges of human nature. What can be more nobly human than to have a tender sentimental feeling of our own and other's [sic] misfortunes? This degree of sensibility every man ought to wish to have for his own sake, as it disposes him to, and renders him more capable of practising all the virtues that promote his own welfare and happiness.[3]

That these two passages sum up fairly well between them the peculiar moral doctrine which lay back of the mid-eighteenth-century cult of the " man of feeling " no one familiar with the popular literature of that period will be disposed to deny. The identification of virtue with acts of benevolence and still more with the feelings of universal good-will which inspire and accompany these acts; the assumption that such " good Affections " are the natural and spontaneous growth of the heart of man uncorrupted by habits of vice; the anti-stoical praise of sensibility—" it may be questioned whether those are properly men, who never weep upon any occasion "; the complacent emphasis on the " pleasing Anguish, that sweetly melts the Mind, and terminates in a Self-approving Joy ": these, it will be readily granted, were the distinguishing " notes " of the philosophy which found expression, between the seventeen-thirties and the seventeen-nineties, in the sentimental heroes and heroines of countless English novels, plays, and poems.

We may leave to others the task, still far from completed, of tracing the fortunes of this philosophy in the days of its triumph and especially of describing the varied forms of opposition which it provoked and the reaction which set in against it in the closing decades of the century. Our immediate concern in this paper is rather with the question how it ever came to triumph at all. For it was not a philosophy which the eighteenth century could have derived full fledged, as it derived its primitivism, for example, from ancient or Renaissance tradition. It was something new in the world—a doctrine, or rather a complex of doctrines, which a hundred years before 1750 would have been frowned upon, had it ever been presented

[3] *Man*, No. 43, October 22, 1755 (in a letter signed "A. B.").

to them, by representatives of every school of ethical or religious thought. Neither in antiquity, nor in the Middle Ages, nor in the sixteenth century, nor in the England of the Puritans and Cavaliers had the " man of feeling " ever been a popular type.

It is true that a solution of the problem has been offered us— a solution which in recent years has won wide acceptance among students of English literature. It has been observed that most if not all of the distinctive elements of the sentimental benevolism of the mid-eighteenth century already existed at the beginning of the century in the writings of the third Earl of Shaftesbury, and it has been noted that the aristocratic author of the *Characteristics*, for all the suspicions which could be cast on his religious orthodoxy, enjoyed a very considerable vogue in intellectual circles during the four or five decades following his death; from these facts the conclusion has been drawn that it was mainly from Shaftesbury and his immediate disciples that the impulses came which affected both the literary creators of the " man of feeling " and his admirers among the public.[4]

The chief difficulty with this explanation is that it begins too late. If we wish to understand the origins and the widespread diffusion in the eighteenth century of the ideas which issued in the cult of sensibility, we must look, I believe, to a period considerably earlier than that in which Shaftesbury wrote and take into account the propaganda of a group of persons whose opportunities for moulding the thoughts of ordinary Englishmen were much greater than those of even the most aristocratic of deists. What I would suggest, in short, is that the key to the popular triumph of " sentimentalism " toward 1750 is to be sought, not so much in the teaching of individual lay moralists after 1700, as in the combined influence of numerous Anglican divines of the Latitudinarian tradition who from the Restoration onward into the eighteenth century had preached to their congregations and, through their books, to the larger public essentially the same ethics of benevolence, " good nature," and

---

[4] The best statement of the case for Shaftesbury is still that of C. A. Moore in *PMLA* 31 (1916). 264-325. Cf. also W. E. Alderman, *ibid.* 46 (1931). 1087-94, and *Transactions of the Wisconsin Academy of Sciences, Arts and Letters* 26 (1931). 137-59.

" tender sentimental feeling " as was expressed in the passages from Fordyce and his anonymous contemporary quoted at the beginning of this paper.[5]

In order to make this clear it will be necessary to consider somewhat at length four principal aspects of the ethical and psychological propaganda of these divines during the period from about 1660 to about 1725.

1. *Virtue as universal benevolence.*—That the teaching of the Latitudinarian clergy should have assumed from the first a strongly humanitarian bent is not surprizing in the light of the purposes which animated the earliest leaders of the movement. Along with other aims which need not concern us here, it was the fervent hope of the " Latitude-men " that they might succeed in freeing the religion of the English people from those errors concerning the nature of God and the value of human works which had been spread by the Puritans. Their characteristic views on both these questions were clearly summarized by Joseph Glanvill, himself an adherent of the party, in an essay published in 1676.

They took notice [he wrote], what *unworthy* and *dishonourable Opinions* were publish'd abroad concerning *God*, to the disparagement of all his Attributes, and discouragement of vertuous Endeavours, and great trouble and dejection of many pious Minds; and therefore here they appear'd also to *assert* and *vindicate* the Divine Goodness and *love of Men* in its *freedom* and *extent,* against those Doctrines, that made his *Love, Fondness;* and his *Justice, Cruelty,* and represented God, as the Eternal Hater of the far greatest part of his reasonable Creatures, and the designer of their Ruine, for the exaltation of *meer Power,* and *arbitrary Will:* Against these sowr and dismal Opinions They stood up stoutly, in a time when the Assertors of the Divine Purity and Goodness, were persecuted bitterly with nicknames of Reproach, and popular Hatred. . . . They shew'd continually how impossible it was that *Infinite Goodness* should *design* or delight in the misery of his *Creatures:* . . . That

---

[5] I have brought together some of the evidence in the *Philological Quarterly* 11 (1932). 204-06. See also Rae Blanchard, *The Christian Hero, by Richard Steele,* Oxford, 1932, pp. xvii-xxv, and Lois Whitney, *Primitivism and the Idea of Progress in English Popular Literature of the Eighteenth Century,* Baltimore, 1934, pp. 21-6. Shortly before his death my friend, the late F. B. Kaye, had projected a study of the question which, had he lived to complete it, would have made the present essay superfluous. Though my own conclusions differ in some particulars from his, I am heavily indebted to him both for interpretative suggestions and for materials.

Goodness is the Fountain of all his Communications and Actions *ad extra:* That to *glorifie* God, is rightly to apprehend and celebrate his Perfections, by our Words, and by our Actions: That *Goodness* is the *chief* moral Perfection: That *Power* without Goodness is *Tyranny;* and *Wisdom* without it, is but *Craft* and *Subtilty;* and *Justice, Cruelty,* when *destitute* of Goodness: . . .

By *such* Principles as *These,* which are wonderfully fertile, and big of many great Truths, they undermined, and from the bottom overthrew the fierce and churlish *Reprobatarian Doctrines.* . . .[6]

Nor were they any less hostile, Glanvill goes on to say, to the Puritan dogma of justification solely by faith in the imputed righteousness of Christ, with its corollary of the worthlessness of " our *Good Works* and Christian *Vertues* ":

And because *Morality* was despised by those elevated Fantasticks, that talked so much of *Imputed Righteousness,* in the false sense; and accounted by them, as a *dull,* and *low* thing; therefore those Divines labour'd in the asserting and vindicating of this: Teaching the *necessity* of *Moral* Vertues; That *Christianity* is the *highest improvement* of them; . . . That the *power* of it consists in subduing *self-will,* and ruling our *passions,* and moderating our *appetites,* and *doing* the *works* of real Righteousness towards God, and our Neighbour.[7]

For this reason, Glanvill further tells us, what chiefly distinguished their teaching was its practical temper and aim. Vigorous upholders of the rights of human reason in matters of religion, they nevertheless attached much more importance to the moral ends of Christianity than to the speculative content of its theology. " Their main Design was, to make Men *good,* not *notional,* and knowing; and therefore, though they *conceal'd* no *practical* Verities that were proper and seasonable, yet they were sparing in their *Speculations,* except where they tended to the necessary vindication of the *Honour* of *God,* or the directing the Lives of Men. . . ."[8] " They cared for no mans *wit,* that wanted *goodness;* and despis'd no mans *weakness,* that had it." [9]

And finally, as a consequence both of their faith in God's impartial benevolence toward all men and of their belief in the primacy of practice over doctrine, they set themselves to break

[6] *Essays on Several Important Subjects in Philosophy and Religion,* 1676, Essay 7, pp. 21-2. The essay purports to be a continuation of Bacon's *New Atlantis.*
[7] *Ibid.,* pp. 24-5.   [8] *Ibid.,* p. 15. Cf. pp. 26, 30, 45.   [9] *Ibid.,* p. 51.

down sectarian prejudices and to proclaim the Catholic principle of "*universal* Charity, and Union," holding, as Glanvill
again expressed it, that "the *Church* consists of all those that
agree in the profession, and acknowledgment of the Scripture,
and the *first* comprehensive, *plain Creeds*, however scatter'd
through the World, and distinguish'd by names of Nations and
Parties, under various degrees of light, and divers particular
models, and forms of Worship, as to circumstance, and order:
That every lover of God, and of the Lord Jesus Christ in sincerity, who lives according to the few, great acknowledg'd
Doctrines, and Rules of a vertuous and holy life, is a *true
Christian*, and will be happy; though he be ignorant of many
points that some reckon for Articles of Faith, and err in *some*,
which others account *sacred*, and *fundamental*. . . ." [10]

The purposes and doctrines which Glanvill here attributes
to the original "Latitude-men" met with increasingly wide
acceptance, in the years following the Restoration, among the
more influential clergy of the Establishment, especially, it would
seem, among those who had been educated at Cambridge. We
may trace them in the sermons and other writings of prominent
divines like Isaac Barrow, Robert South, John Tillotson, Richard Cumberland, Samuel Parker, Hezekiah Burton, Richard
Kidder, John Scott, Edward Pelling, William Sherlock, Gilbert
Burnet, Richard Bentley, Samuel Clarke, as well as in the discourses of many lesser men who yet occupied important livings
in the days of the later Stuarts and the early Hanoverians.
Whatever differences there may have been among these clergymen, they were all united in their detestation of the darker
aspects of the Puritan creed, in their insistence on the religious
value of human works, in their exaltation of "goodness" over
doctrine, in their zeal for "universal Charity and Union." [11]

---

[10] *Ibid.*, p. 31. A characterization of the Latitudinarians similar on most points
to Glanvill's is given in Edward Fowler's *The Principles and Practices of Certain
Moderate Divines of the Church of England Abusively Called Latitudinarians*, 1670.
See the 2d ed., 1671, pp. 18, 115, 117, 120, 126, 129, 194, 199, 228, 234-7, 347.

[11] Cf., e. g., Isaac Barrow, *Theological Works*, 1830, 6. 541: "It is a peculiar
excellency of our religion, that it doth not much employ men's care, pains, and
time about matters of ceremonial observance; but doth chiefly (and in a manner
wholly) exercise them in the works of substantial duty, agreeable to reason, per-
fective of man's nature, productive of true glory to God, and solid benefit to men";
Robert South, *Sermons*, Philadelphia, 1844, 1. 462: "Believing without doing good

With this general outlook, it was natural that they should become great preachers of the social virtues. And few things, indeed, were more characteristic of these Latitudinarian divines than the assiduity with which they exhorted their hearers and readers to benevolent feelings and acts as the best means at once of actualizing the beneficent designs of God for man and of realizing the aim of religion to perfect human nature. Charity was one of their favorite themes: not the charity which was primarily love of God; not charity merely to the parish poor or to fellow Christians, but a " general kindness " to all men because they are men, an active desire to relieve their sufferings, if not to alter the social conditions in which they live; the kind of charity best described by the words—more common in the eighteenth century, but already coming into use—" humanity," " good nature," " universal benevolence."

Of this strain in their preaching numerous illustrations could be given from the Restoration onward. The sermons of Isaac Barrow (d. 1677) were particularly rich in expressions of the theme, and his discourse on *The Duty and Reward of Bounty to the Poor* (1671) remained a classic with readers of humanitarian sympathies for nearly a hundred years.[12] To Tillotson likewise the subject had a strong appeal: " How much better it is," he wrote in a typical passage, " to do good, to be really useful and beneficial to others, and how much more clearly and certainly our Duty, than to quarrel about doubtful and uncertain Opinions." [13] For Samuel Parker, as for his master Cumberland, the principle to which all the laws of nature could be reduced was " universal Justice or Humanity, or so much love and good-will to all Mankind, as obliges every man to seek the welfare and happiness of the whole Community and every Member of it, as well as his own private and particular Interest." [14] For William Clagett, writing in 1686 *Of the Humanity*

is a very cheap and easy, but withal a very worthless way of being religious ";
John Tillotson, *Works*, 4th ed., 1728, 2. 167: " When we come to die we can call nothing our own but the good works which by the grace of God we have been enabled to do in this life."

[12] See below, n. 56. The discourse is printed in *Theological Works*, 1830, 2. 169-258.

[13] *Works*, 1728, 1. 155. Cf. also *ibid*. 1. 160-1, 169-71; 2. 513, 595.

[14] *A Demonstration of the Divine Authority of the Law of Nature*, 1681, pp. 17-18; cf. *ibid.*, pp. 24-5.

and Charity of Christians, the obligation to do good to all men derives its force not merely from the fact that charity is enjoined upon us by Christ and his apostles; the obligation also has its basis in common humanity, since to "*Man* only of all Creatures under Heaven, God has given this quality, to be affected with the Grief and with the Joy of those of his own kind; and to feel the Evils which others feel, that we may be universally disposed to help and relieve one another." [15]

In the early eighteenth century the current of this humanitarian homiletic was flowing more strongly than ever. It was not necessary to read the works of the Earl of Shaftesbury to learn that " to love the public, to study universal good, and to promote the interest of the whole world, as far as lies within our power, is surely the height of goodness, and makes that temper which we call divine "; [16] the same lesson was being taught from hundreds of pulpits in London and the provinces by clergymen who had inherited the benevolistic spirit of their Latitudinarian predecessors of the generation before. Typical of these was Samuel Clarke, preaching in 1705 on *The Great Duty of Universal Love:*

> The true End and Design of Religion, is manifestly this; to make Men wiser and better; to improve, exalt, and perfect their Nature; to teach them to obey, and love, and imitate God; to cause them to extend their Love and Goodness and Charity to all their Fellow-Creatures, each in their several Stations, and according to the measure of their several Abilities; in like manner as the universal Goodness of God, extends it self over all his Works through the whole Creation. . . . [17]

Typical also was Francis Squire, rector of Exford in Somerset and author in 1714 of a sermon on *Universal Benevolence: or, Charity in its Full Extent,* " humbly dedicated to Richard Steele," the climax of which was this rhapsody on the peculiar merits of the benevolent man:

> Who can sufficiently express the *Dignity* of such a Person? What Trophies does he deserve? What endless Monuments of Praise and Glory belong unto him? He is in an implicit League of Philanthropy with the Guardian Angels, he carries on the great Cause of the Saviour of Mankind, he is the honourable Distributer of his

[15] Ed. 1687, p. 4. Cf. also pp. 8-9, 14.   [17] P. 2.
[16] *Characteristics,* ed. Robertson, 1. 27.

Creator's Blessings, he wears more emphatically the *Image* of his God, and shares with him in an universal Reverence, and (I was going to say) Adoration. For indeed, there are few that can withhold a Veneration from such a one; and for those impious Wretches who offer Violence to their Nature and their Consciences to detract from him, we have the Pleasure to observe they are forc'd to belye him before they can dishonour him; they must first maliciously hide the Vertue, before they can obscure those Beams of Glory that arise from it.[18]

Of the same school, finally, was George Stephens, author of *The Amiable Quality of Goodness as Compared with Righteousness, Considered* (1731):

Compare [he exclaims] the Characters of the Just and Good Man as already drawn before you: Set them in Contrast one against the other. *That* indeed strikes us with Awe and Reverence: *This* attracts our Love and Admiration.

It may, I conceive, be of Service to Religion, if we pursue this Reflexion a little farther. Moral Writers have well observed, that Justice is a Virtue of the greatest Consequence to Society, the very Cement, that binds it firmly together. And is it not equally true, that Goodness is the Ornament and Pleasure of it? Do not the Comforts and mutual Endearments of Life all flow from Goodness? Will not he, that is only guided by Justice, be led to many hard and cruel Things? And is not Extremity of Justice proverbially call'd the utmost Injury? Let us then learn indeed, and study to be just; but let us at the same time *love Mercy,* and hearken to the softer Dictates and Whispers of Humanity.[19]

[18] P. 25. Cf. pp. 6-7.

[19] Pp. 13-14. In addition to the texts quoted or referred to above, see the following: Samuel Parker, *A Free and Impartial Censvre of the Platonick Philosophie,* 1666, pp. 23-7; Thomas Hodges, *The Creatures Goodness,* 1675, p. 43, and *passim;* William Gould, *The Generosity of Christian Love,* 1676, pp. 12-13; Richard Kidder, *Charity Directed,* 1676, pp. 4-13, 22-5; Thomas Willis, *The Excellency of Wisdom,* 1676, pp. 27-30; Adam Littleton, *A Sermon . . . June 24, 1680,* 1680, p. 29; John Scott, *The Christian Life,* 1681, pp. 178, 186-7; Joseph Glanvill, *Some Discourses, Sermons and Remains,* 1681, pp. 101-02, 125-8; Robert South, "Sermon Preached May 3, 1685," in *Twelve Sermons,* 5th ed., 1722, pp. 436-8; Hezekiah Burton, "Of Doing Good to All Men," in *A Second Volume of Discourses,* 1685, pp. 491-4, 498-500, 518-26, 546-52, 604; Thomas Wagstaffe, *A Sermon Preached . . . Novemb. 24, 1687,* 1688, pp. 20, 26, 28; John Norris, *The Theory and Regulation of Love,* 1688, pp. 85-6; Henry Waring, *The Rule of Charity,* 1690, pp. 4, 21-2; Edward Pelling, *A Practical Discourse upon Charity,* 1693, pp. 3-5; Francis Atterbury, *The Power of Charity to Cover Sin . . . Preach'd . . . August 16, 1694,* 1708, p. 13; Robert Grove, *Profitable Charity,* 1695, pp. 12-14; William Sherlock, "The Nature and Measure of Charity" (1697), in *Sermons Preached upon Several Occasions,* 1719, pp. 211-12; Edward Synge, *A Gentleman's Religion,* Part 3 (1697), pp. 157-61; Benjamin Whichcote, *Select Sermons,* 1698, pp. 218-19, 272; John Smith, *An Essay*

2. *Benevolence as feeling.*—For most of the divines who were thus helping to set the tone of eighteenth-century humanitarian exhortation, the words " charity " and " benevolence " had a double sense, connoting not only the serviceable and philanthropic actions which the good man performs but still more the tender passions and affections which prompt to these actions and constitute their immediate reward. For this emphasis they had, it is true, an excellent warrant in various New Testament texts.[20] But there was more to their frequent statements of the idea than merely a development of I Corinthians 13, and an adequate explanation must also take into account the pronounced strain of anti-Stoicism which throughout the period characterized their ethical thought.

How consciously in revolt they were against the distrust of the passions and the exaggerated assumptions concerning man's rationality which they attributed to the Stoics can be seen in numerous places in their writings.[21] The passions, they insisted with Aristotle, are neither good nor evil in themselves; they may, however, be ordered to virtue, and when so ordered they have a positive value, since they and not our weak reason are the forces which make it possible for us to act at all; to wish to eradicate them from our nature is not only a futile but a

---

on *Universal Redemption*, 1701, p. 5; Thomas Lynford, *The Charitable Man Bears Much Fruit*, 1712, p. 12; William Lupton, *The Necessity . . . of . . . Charity*, 1713, p. 10; Gilbert Burnet, *Some Sermons Preach'd on Several Occasions*, 1713, pp. 224-7; Richard Bentley, "A Sermon Preached before King George I on February the Third, 1716-17," in *Works*, ed. A. Dyce, 3 (1838). 266-7; William Beveridge, "The Chain of Evangelical Graces " (1720), in *Theological Works*, 1845, 6. 114; John Leng, *A Sermon Preach'd . . . April 6, 1724*, 1724, pp. 6-8, 11; Alured Clarke, *A Sermon Preached . . . January the 25th, 1725*, 1726, pp. 6-7; Samuel Wright, *Charity in All Its Branches*, 1732, pp. v-ix.

[20] Cf. Richard Kidder, *Charity Directed*, 1676, p. 19; Anthony Horneck, *The Nature of True Christian Righteousness*, 1689, p. 20; Charles Hickman, *Fourteen Sermons*, 1700, Sermon 11; Richard Crossing, *Practical Discourse Concerning the Great Duty of Charity*, 1722, p. 7.

[21] See, in addition to the texts given above, Richard Baxter, *A Treatise of Self-Denyall*, 1660, p. 279; Henry More, *An Account of Virtue*, 1690, pp. 34-42 (originally published in Latin as *Enchiridion ethicum*, 1666) ; H. Lukin, *The Chief Interest of Man* (1670), 3d ed., 1718, pp. 55-69; Matthew Hale, *Contemplations Moral and Divine*, 1682, Part 1, pp. 104-06; Part 2, p. 71; John Hartcliffe, *A Treatise of Moral and Intellectual Virtues*, 1691, pp. 294-6; M. Burghope, *The Government of the Passions*, 1701, pp. 3-5; Francis Bragge, *A Practical Treatise on the Regulation of the Passions*, 1708, pp. 4-5, 6-7, 17-19; John Tottie, *A View of Reason and Passion*, 1736, pp. 6-8.

misguided desire. " The *Stoicks*," wrote James Lowde in 1694, "would make Man so wholly rational, that they will scarce allow him to be sensible, and would wholly exclude all natural affections and bodily passions out of humane Nature. . . . The Design . . . is, *First*, impossible; *Secondly*, it would be prejudicial thereunto, were it feisible; for these when duly regulated, become the subject matter of moral Vertue, and also add Vigour and Wings to the Soul in its pursuits of Vertue." [22] George Stanhope, in translating Epictetus in 1694, made the same point: " I think it cannot fairly be denied," he remarked, " that in their Way of Treating the Passions and Powers of the Soul, they [the Stoics] much overshot the Mark, and have quite mistaken the Case. . . . These are indeed the secret Springs that move and actuate us; and all the Care incumbent upon the Governing Part of the Mind, is to set them right. . . . So that in truth, the main, I might say the whole of our Duty and Happiness, consists, not in stifling these Affections, and condemning them to a State of utter Inactivity, but in moderating and regulating them." [23] And Charles Hickman, who became Bishop of Derry under Queen Anne, devoted some fifteen pages in one of his sermons (1700) to a formal refutation of the Stoic notion that because the passions lead us into dangers and betray us into sin, " 'tis fit they should be rooted out."

'Tis certain [he concluded] that when our passions are well regulated and reformed, they are great assistances and encouragements to Vertue. Our Reason is a cold and heavy principle, that moves us but slowly to our Work; but Passion puts an eagerness into our Desires, and a warmness into our Prosecutions, and makes the work go chearfully and vigorously on. . . .

Our Reason has but little to do in the forming of our minds, and bringing us to a Vertuous Religious Life; 'tis our Passions and Affections that must do the work, for till they begin to move, our Reason is but like a Chariot when the Wheels are off, that is never like to perform the Journey.[24]

So widely prevalent, indeed, were views like these in the later seventeenth and early eighteenth centuries that it is difficult to understand how it could ever have been supposed by modern

[22] *A Discourse Concerning the Nature of Man . . . with An Examination of Some of Mr. Hobbs's Opinions*, 1694, p. 24.

[23] *Epictetus His Morals*, 2d ed., 1700, Preface, sigs. [A 5]-[A 6].

[24] *Fourteen Sermons*, 1700, pp. 271-2.

students that the moral ideal of that age was one of " cold intellectuality." [25]

Such in any case was not the ideal preached by these Latitudinarian divines. And in nothing was their revolt against " the Stoic's pride " more evident than in their repudiation of the notion that though the good man must relieve the distresses of others he must not allow himself to be emotionally affected by the misfortunes he sees.

The doctrine against which they protested was familiar to the seventeenth century in the pages of Seneca [26] and of his various modern disciples.[27] It was stated with unusual explicitness by the Frenchman Antoine Le Grand, whose compendium of Stoic teaching was translated into English in 1675 under the revealing title of *Man without Passion: or, The Wise Stoick, According to the Sentiments of Seneca:*

For as these generous Philosophers [Le Grand wrote] strip their wise man of all the maladies of his Soul, they allow not that other mens misfortunes should be his miseries: they will have him as little concerned for his Neighbours afflictions as for his own disasters: They will have him to be fortune proof; and that that which discomposeth others, should teach him Constancy, and an even temper, What, say they, doth Vertue consist in infirmity? Must we be guilty of effeminacy, to perform Acts of Generosity? Can we not be charitable without being afflicted? And can we not relieve those that are in misery, unless we mingle our Sighs with their Sobs and Groans, and our Cries with their Tears? A wise man ought to consider the Poor for their Relief, and not himself to share in their Calamities; he ought to protect them from oppressions, and not to

[25] Many similar statements could of course be collected from the secular writers of the period. See, e. g., Meric Casaubon, *Marcus Aurelius . . . His Meditations,* 4th ed., 1673, Preface; Sir William Temple, " Of Gardening" (1685), in *Works,* 1814, 3. 208-10; Sir Thomas Pope Blount, *Essays on Several Subjects,* 3d ed., 1697, pp. 195-200; Tim. Nourse, *A Discourse upon the Nature and Faculties of Man,* 1697, pp. 104-09; Richard Steele, *The Christian Hero* (1701), ed. Blanchard, 1932, p. 74; Charles Gildon, *The Deist's Manual,* 1705, pp. 120-30; *Spectator,* No. 408, June 18, 1712; *Lover,* No. 32, May 8, 1714; Pope, *Essay on Man,* 1733, 2. 101-22.

[26] Cf., e. g., *The Workes of . . . Seneca,* trans. by Thomas Lodge, 1620, pp. 608, 609, in " Of Clemencie," Book 2, chap. 5, 6: " For it is nought else but a basenes of the heart which melteth in beholding another mans miseries. . . . He [the wise man] will assist his Neighbour that weepeth, without weeping himself. . . . He will not . . . be mooued, but will helpe, will profit, as being borne for the common good and the seruice of the Commonweale."

[27] E. g., Justus Lipsius. See *A Discourse of Constancy,* trans. by Nathaniel Wanley, 1670, 1. 12, pp. 67-70.

be inwardly disturbed for them; he ought to endeavour their comfort, and not to be a Partner in their misfortunes.[28]

To this creed of " stoical insensibility " our divines opposed what they insisted was the true Christian idea of a charity which derives both its force and value from the fact that the good man does permit himself to be " inwardly disturbed." There can be no effective benevolence, they declared again and again, that does not spring from the tender emotions of pity and compassion, and so far from suppressing these emotions we ought rather to look upon them as the marks which distinguish men of genuine goodness from those who are merely righteous or just. Not the Senecan wise man, relieving but not pitying, but the tenderhearted Christian, pitying before he relieves, was the ideal which they preached to their generation; and as time went on their emphasis tended more and more to dwell on those elements of " softness " and quick emotional response to the spectacle of human misery which were to constitute for the eighteenth century the peculiar traits of the " man of feeling." Of the many clergymen of the half century following the Restoration who helped to disseminate this kind of " sentimentalism "—a " sentimentalism " still distinctively Christian in its background and expression—it is possible to consider only a few. Let us begin with Robert South, commenting in a sermon of 1662 on the difference between the moral teaching of Christians and that of the Stoics:

Sorrow in their esteem was a sin scarce to be expiated by another; to pity, was a fault; to rejoice, an extravagance. . . . To us let this be sufficient, that our Saviour Christ, who took upon him all our natural infirmities, but none of our sinful, has been seen to weep, to be sorrowful, to pity, and to be angry: which shows that there might be gall in a dove, passion without sin, fire without smoke, and motion without disturbance.[29]

The essential doctrine is here, but the tone and emphasis are still those of the seventeenth century rather than the eighteenth. This can also be said of a development on the same theme in Richard Kidder's *Charity Directed* (1676):

[28] Pp. 277-8.
[29] " Of the Creation of Man in the Image of God," in *Sermons*, Philadelphia, 1844, 1. 28. Cf. also 1. 431.

The Doctrine of the *Stoicks* allowed the good man to *help,* but forbad him to *Pity* and *Compassionate* the *Needy.* [A note here refers to " Senec. de Clement. *l. 2. c. 5.*"] But we learn to do both from the Example and the Precepts of our Lord. Our Alms must be the Off-spring of our Charity and Kindness: and if we were allowed to be void of Pity and Compassion, 'tis to be feared our Relief would be but small. He is most likely to help his Neighbour that hath a great sense of his Misery. And Christianity hath provided better for the Poor than the Philosophy of the *Stoicks.* . . .[30]

From the middle of the next decade a change in tone becomes perceptible, manifesting itself, for example, in this passage on the duty of tenderheartedness in a sermon of Gregory Hascard (1685) :

[Tenderheartedness consists in] being extremely sensible of the common troubles and miseries of our Christian Brethren; this is the spring and original, the proper Source and cause of our Charity and Meekness, our Love and Relief of our fellow Beings. When our tempers are soft and sensible, and easily receive impressions from the Sufferings of others, we are pain'd within, and to ease our selves, we are ready to succour them, and then Nature discharging her Burthen and Oppression, creates both her own pleasure and satisfaction, and performs her Duty. The multitude of miserable Persons will not upon this account produce a continued trouble in your breast, for if the generality of mankind had this fellow-feeling, it would lessen the number; and as it is, the pleasure of doing good far surpasseth the pain in pittying. . . .[31]

The same note is sounded in a sermon preached in 1697 by William Sherlock, Dean of St. Paul's:

A Charitable Mind is very easy to receive the Impressions of Charity; and the more charitably it is disposed, still the more easy. Every pitiable Object moves and affects such Men; and they are no more able to resist the silent Oratory of meagre Looks, naked Backs, and hungry Bellies . . . than to deny themselves what is necessary to Life. . . . A soft and tender Mind, which feels the Sufferings of others, and suffers with them, is the true Temper and Spirit of Charity; and Nature prompts us to ease those Sufferings which we feel. . . . An inward Principle is more powerful than all external Arguments; and Sense and Feeling is this Principle, and Charity is this Sense.[32]

---

[30] P. 19.
[31] *A Sermon,* 1685, pp. 7-8.
[32] " The Nature and Measure of Charity " (April 6, 1697), in *Sermons,* 3d ed., 1719, 1. 214-15. Cf. also *ibid.,* pp. 206-08.

In much the same vein, again, were the reflections of Charles Hickman in his sermon, already quoted, against the Stoic distrust of the passions (1700) :

It is not a sign of *Goodness* in Man, to have no Passion in him, for such a Man is apparently Good for nothing at all. He does not hate his Brother, 'tis true: But then he does not love him neither. He does not oppress his Neighbour perhaps; but withal, he neither pities, nor relieves him. . . .
[In the character of the " good " man there is a certain] softening quality. 'Tis that which our Language very happily expresses by Good Nature. . . .
Indeed, goodness is the only excellence in Man, that deserves to be belov'd or priz'd. Good nature is all that a Man is good for in the World; without which, his riches only make him insolent, and his knowledge will but make him vain, and all his other admired qualities, render him the more dangerous, and suspected, and unfit for humane conversation. Nay, without this Goodness, and benignity of Mind, Righteousness is nothing else but Interest, and Vertue nothing but design, and Religion it self will dwindle either into frowardness, or formality.[33]

The word " sensibility," when these passages were written, had not yet come into fashion in the sense in which it was chiefly to be used by the writers and public of the mid-eighteenth century. It is clear, however, that the quality of mind later eulogized under the name of " sensibility " or " moral weeping " by the sentimentalists of the 1740's and 1750's was no other than the quality which was already being recommended so warmly as the distinguishing sign of the benevolent man by these anti-Stoic preachers of the later 1600's. " Humanity, in its first and general Acceptation," wrote an essayist of 1735 in what was certainly one of the earliest formal definitions of " sensibility " in its new sense, " is call'd by Holy Writers, *Good-will towards Men*; by Heathens, *Philanthropy*, or *Love*

[33] *Fourteen Sermons*, pp. 265, 321, 328-9. For other texts on the same theme see : Thomas Watson, *A Plea for Almes*, 1658, pp. 14-15; John Tillotson, *Works*, 1728, 1. 170 (preached December 3, 1678) ; John Scott, *The Christian Life*, 1681, pp. 184-5; Anthony Horneck, *The Nature of True Christian Righteousness*, 1689, p. 20; Edward Pelling, *A Practical Discourse upon Charity*, 1693, pp. 6-8; George Stanhope, *Epictetus His Morals* (1694), 2d ed., 1700, Preface, sig. [A 6ᵛ]; E. Young, *Sermons on Several Occasions*, 1703, 2. 365-6; Richard Crossing, *Practical Discourse Concerning the Great Duty of Charity*, 1722, p. 7; R. Skerret, *Alms-giving without Charity Unprofitable*, 1723; Alured Clarke, *A Sermon Preached . . . January the 25ᵗʰ, 1725*, 1726, p. 16.

of our *Fellow Creatures*. It sometimes takes the Name of *Good-nature*, and *delights* in *Actions* that have an *obliging* Tendency in them: When strongly *impress'd* on the *Mind*, it assumes a *higher* and nobler Character, and is not satisfy'd with *good-natured* Actions alone, but *feels* the *Misery* of others with *inward Pain*. It is then deservedly named *Sensibility*, and is considerably increased in its intrinsick Worth. . . ." [34] What was this but the doctrine of the " soft and tender mind " made widely familiar over a generation before by our divines ?

3. *Benevolent feelings as " natural " to man.*—When Shaftesbury in 1698 praised Benjamin Whichcote for his defence of " Natural Goodness " and bestowed on him the title of " Preacher of Good-nature," [35] he was using phrases which might have been applied, with little qualification, to most of the leading divines and many of their followers in the movement of which Whichcote had been an early pioneer. Without shutting their eyes to the great amount of actual selfishness and inhumanity in the world, they devoted much effort, nevertheless, to picturing the heart of man as " naturally " good in the sense that when left to its own native impulses it tends invariably to humane and sociable feelings—and this " without the Discipline of Reason, or the Precepts of Religion." [36]

There can be little question that this optimistic appraisal of human nature was in part a manifestation of the revolt against Puritanism which we have already observed in the early leaders of the Latitudinarian group. It would hardly have been possible had it not been for their vigorous insistence, against the one-sided Augustinianism of the Lutheran and Calvinistic traditions, that man was not completely depraved as a result of the Fall, that he has still some natural power of doing good, that " nature " can cooperate with " grace " to the end of his salva-

---

[34] *Prompter*, No. 63, June 17, 1735.

[35] Preface to *Select Sermons of Dr. Whichcot.*

[36] The phrase occurs in *A Sermon*, 1739, by Thomas Herring, Bishop of Bangor. See pp. 5-6 : " It is the Property of Mercy to pity the Infirmities of other Men ; . . . to cultivate a Tenderness and Humanity of Temper, a quick and ready Feeling of each others Wants and Pains. : . . And this is what indeed we are naturally carried to without the Discipline of Reason, or the Precepts of Religion.—There is something in the Human Constitution that naturally melts at Human Misfortunes. . . ."

tion.[37] But this is only part of the story; and what chiefly
provoked them to their frequent declarations of man's "natural
goodness" was undoubtedly not so much their enmity to the
Puritans as their zeal for combatting the dangerous political
and moral doctrines of Thomas Hobbes.

Of the many important issues raised for them by the publication of the *Leviathan* in 1651 we need concern ourselves with
only one: the issue involved in Hobbes' contention, which was
indeed central to his whole political theory, that without a
government possessed of complete power the natural passions
of man would lead to a state of constant social war. The
"Lawes of Nature," he had written, "(as *Justice, Equity, Modesty, Mercy,* and (in summe) *doing to others, as wee would be
done to,*) of themselves, without the terrour of some Power, to
cause them to be observed, are contrary to our naturall Passions, that carry us to Partiality, Pride, Revenge, and the
like." [38] And the reason is, as he said in another passage, that
"men have no pleasure, (but on the contrary a great deale of
griefe) in keeping company, where there is no power able to
overawe them all. For every man looketh that his companion
should value him, at the same rate he sets upon himselfe: And
upon all signes of contempt, or undervaluing, naturally endeavours, as far as he dares (which amongst them that have
no common power to keep them in quiet, is far enough to make
them destroy each other,) to extort a greater value from his
contemners, by dommage; and from others, by the example."
So that it is manifest, Hobbes concluded, "that during the time
men live without a common Power to keep them all in awe,
they are in that condition which is called Warre; and such a
warre, as is of every man, against every man." [39]

It is easy to understand why this doctrine should have
aroused the opposition of our divines. By reducing all human
motivation to egoistic passions of pride and self-esteem, Hobbes,

[37] Cf., e. g., Isaac Barrow, "Sermon XXVI," in *Theological Works,* 1830, 2. 36;
3. 533; Joseph Glanvill, *Some Discourses,* 1681, pp. 6-7, 29, 55-6; Sir Matthew
Hale, *A Discourse of the Knowledge of God, and of Our Selves,* 1688, pp. 54, 276;
Edward Synge, *A Gentleman's Religion,* Part 2 (1697), pp. 54-5, 62. See E. Gilson,
"Le Moyen Age et le naturalisme antique," *Archives d'histoire doctrinale et lit-
téraire du Moyen Age* 7 (1932). 5-37.
[38] Chap. 17.   [39] *Ibid.,* chap. 13. Cf. also chap. 11, beginning.

2

it seemed clear to them, had gone far toward making not only political justice but morality itself a purely arbitrary thing, dependent wholly upon the will of those in power. To offset so distasteful a conclusion it was obviously necessary to show the falsity of the conception of human nature upon which it rested. They devoted themselves, therefore, with much energy, to maintaining, against the *Leviathan*, that the nature of men is such that even without government they can be trusted to live together peacefully in sympathetic and helpful mutual relations. Our divines were not the first, of course, to uphold this thesis, and they made much of the fact that in Aristotle, in Cicero, in Juvenal, to say nothing of other classical and patristic authors, the capacity of human beings for amicable social living had been set in a much fairer light than in the writings of the cynical philosopher of Malmsbury.[40] But this did not prevent them from frequently giving to the old commonplaces a new turn and force or from developing them in some directions far beyond anything contained in the ancient texts.

From the point of view of the present study the most significant result of their efforts was the dissemination of the idea that man is essentially a gentle and sympathetic creature, naturally inclined to society not merely by his intellect, which tells him that kindness to others is the best means to the end of his own private happiness, but still more by " those passions and inclinations that are common to him with other Creatures " and which, like everything in his nature, have " a vehement tendency to acts of love and good-will." [41]

Among the anti-Hobbesist preachers of " natural goodness " in the years immediately following the Restoration, one of the most important was Isaac Barrow. In a number of sermons on the theme of charity delivered in the 1660's and early 1670's he protested vigorously against the " monstrous paradox, cross-

<hr>

[40] For Aristotle see, e. g., Barrow, *Theological Works* 2. 37, 80; Tillotson, *Works,* 1728, 1. 305; Samuel Parker, *A Demonstration of the Divine Authority of the Law of Nature,* 1681, p. viii; for Cicero, *ibid.*; for Juvenal, Barrow, *Theological Works,* 2. 141, 224. Many of the most important classical and patristic texts had been assembled by Grotius in his *De jure belli ac pacis,* 1625, Prolegomena, sects. 6-7, and Book 1, chap. 1.

[41] The phrase is Samuel Parker's in *A Demonstration of the Divine Authority of the Law of Nature,* p. 29.

ing the common sense of men, which in this loose and vain world hath lately got such vogue, that all men naturally are enemies one to another." [42] The truth is, he insisted, that if the practice of benevolent acts is our duty it is in part because such acts are in accord with, and not, as Hobbes had said, contrary to, our natural passions.

We are indispensably obliged to these duties, because the best of our natural inclinations prompt us to the performance of them, especially those of pity and benignity, which are manifestly discernible in all, but most powerful and vigorous in the best natures; and which, questionless, by the most wise and good Author of our beings were implanted therein both as monitors to direct, and as spurs to incite us to the performance of our duty. For the same bowels, that, in our want of necessary sustenance, do by a lively sense of pain inform us thereof, and instigate us to provide against it, do in like manner grievously resent the distresses of another, and thereby admonish us of our duty, and provoke us to relieve them. Even the stories of calamities, that in ages long since past have happened to persons nowise related to us, yea, the fabulous reports of tragical events, do (even against the bent of our wills, and all resistance of reason) melt our hearts with compassion, and draw tears from our eyes; and thereby evidently signify that general sympathy which naturally intercedes between all men, since we can neither see, nor hear of, nor imagine another's grief, without being afflicted ourselves. Antipathies may be natural to wild beasts [here he refers in a note to a well-known passage in Juvenal's fifteenth satire]; but to rational creatures they are wholly unnatural.[43]

Another expounder of the same doctrine was Samuel Parker, whose *Demonstration of the Divine Authority of the Law of Nature* (1681) was designed in the main as a reply to Hobbes. All our "natural desires," he wrote, "are not only just and reasonable in themselves, but they incline us to such designs and actions, as naturally tend to the good and welfare of mankind." [44] To this end in particular we have been endowed by the Creator with the passions of "Natural Pity and Compassion," the operation of which, when they have not been overlaid by contrary habits, is almost mechanical:

[42] *Theological Works*, 1830, 2. 79.
[43] *Ibid.* 2. 140-1. Cf. also *ibid.*, pp. 36-7, 78-80, 224-5. The theme is present in Barrow's "First Sermon" (preached at Cambridge, June 30, 1661) ; see *Sermons Preached upon Several Occasions*, 1678, pp. 24-5.
[44] P. 50.

... as for the generality of Men their hearts are so tender and their natural affections so humane, that they cannot but pity and commiserate the afflicted with a kind of fatal and mechanical Sympathy; their groans force tears and sighs from the unafflicted, and 'tis a pain to them not to be able to relieve their miseries. . . .[45]

Tillotson, likewise, among the divines of this generation, was given to frequent pronouncements of the same anti-Hobbesist sort. " So far is it," he wrote in one of his sermons, " from being true, which Mr. *Hobbes* asserts as the fundamental *Principle* of his *Politicks, That Men are naturally in a State of War and Enmity with one another*; that the contrary *Principle*, laid down by a much deeper and wiser Man, I mean *Aristotle*, is most certainly true, *That Men are naturally a-kin and Friends to each other*." [46] And the basis of this kinship, he explained elsewhere, is to be found in " the mere propensions and inclinations of their nature "—propensions comparable to " those instincts, which are in brute creatures, of natural affection and care toward their young ones." [47]

From the middle of the 1680's the number of such declarations would seem to have perceptibly increased; it had now become part of the recognized duty of the preacher of a charity sermon to picture human beings in an amiable light as creatures naturally disposed to impulses of pity and benevolence. The result was a long series of amplifications on the theme of man's essential " good nature," of which the following may serve as representative samples. From a sermon of 1686:

Tho *Nature* inclines us to Humanity, yet *Custom* and *bad Principles* may give us another *Bias*, and make us unconcern'd what others feel. But Nature, without Art and Force used upon it, seldom proves cruel; and we see that they which have the least of that we call *Breeding*, are prone to Pity and Commiseration. Men of a simple and rustick Education, and of mean Professions, easily fall into Compassion; and seldom fail of relieving one another, if the consideration of their own Interest does not prevail against it.[48]

[45] P. 55. Cf. pp. 21-2, 25-6, 29-30.
[46] *Works*, 1728, 1. 305. The date of the sermon was March 8, 1689.
[47] *Ibid*. 2. 298-9.
[48] William Clagett, *Of the Humanity and Charity of Christians, A Sermon Preached . . . Nov. 30, 1686*, 1687, p. 5. Cf. the same author's *A Paraphrase, with Notes . . . upon the Sixth Chapter of St. John . . .* , 1693, p. 76.

From one of 1700:

For our Incitement [to benevolence] ... there are natural Motions wrought within us, and moulded into our very Frame: For when we see a miserable Object, Nature it self moves our Bowels to Compassion, and our Hands to give; and those of the finest Temper are soonest affected with the Distresses of other Men.[49]

From one of 1701:

Nature has implanted in us a most tender and compassionate Sense and Fellow-feeling of one anothers Miseries, a most ready and prevailing propension and inclination to assist and relieve them; insomuch that pity and kindness towards our Brethren have a long time, passed under the name of Humanity, as properties essential to and not without Violence to be separated from humane Nature. . . .[50]

From another of 1708:

But if we are thus slenderly furnish'd for Speculative Knowledge, we are manifestly framed and fashion'd for Acts of divine *Worship,* and the Practise of *social* Vertues. Nature has endu'd us with the tenderest Passions: We are all Counterparts one of another: The Instruments *tun'd* Unison: the doleful Cry of one in extreme Distress, makes the Strings to tremble at our very Hearts. . . .

You have an Instance of this in the most Ancient History, *Gen.* 44 and 45. when Men follow'd closer the unsophisticated Dictates of Nature. [Then follows the story of Joseph and his brethren, after which the preacher concludes:] This is not alledg'd as an Instance of his Vertue, it was the Voice of Nature, *charity of the Machine,* and Formation. A Man must be disciplin'd into hardness of Heart, and neild into Cruelty. . . .[51]

From one, finally, preached some time before 1720:

God has implanted in our very Frame and Make, a compassionate Sense of the Sufferings and Misfortunes of other People, which disposes us to contribute to their Relief; so that when we see any of our Fellow-Creatures in Circumstances of Distress, we are naturally, I had almost said, mechanically inclined to be helpful to them . . . [And] as all the Actions of Nature are sweet and pleasant, so there is none which gives a good Man a greater, or more solid, or lasting Pleasure than this of *doing Good.* . . . Where Men follow Nature in those tender Motions of it, which incline them to

[49] Z. Isham, *A Sermon,* 1700, pp. 4-5.
[50] Sir William Dawes, *Self-love the Great Cause of Bad Times,* 1701, p. 9.
[51] Knightly Chetwood, *A Sermon Preach'd before the . . . Lord Mayor . . . , April 5, 1708,* 1708, pp. 8-9.

Acts of Kindness and Charity, they will not be easy, except they lay hold of the proper Occasions of exerting them. . . .

So strongly is this natural Tenderness, where Nature is not one Way or another corrupted, apt to operate in us; and which there- fore, from the *Greeks*, we very significantly render *Philanthropy*; from the *Latins*, *Humanity*; and which in the Language of our own Nation, and with a particular respect to the Genius of it, we express by *good Nature*. . . .[52]

It is no wonder that the deist Tindal in 1730, in referring to the doctrine that man is " a social creature, who naturally loves his own species, and is full of pity, tenderness & benevolence," should have prefaced his statement of it by the phrase " as our Divines maintain against *Hobbs*." [53]

The significance of their assiduous preaching of this doctrine for the problem with which we are here concerned scarcely needs to be pointed out. For clearly if a capacity for " pity, tenderness & benevolence " is what principally distinguishes man from other creatures, and if, as was generally assumed in

[52] Richard Fiddes, *Fifty-Two Practical Discourses on Several Subjects*, 1720, pp. 112-13.

I append here references to other texts of the period in which similar ideas are expressed: William Pike, *Observations, Censvres and Confutations of Divers Errors . . . of Mr. Hobs*, 1657, pp. 91-2; Thomas Tenison, *The Creed of Mr. Hobbes Examined*, 2d ed., 1671, pp. 140-1; Robert South, " Of the Origin, Nature, and Baseness of the Sin of Ingratitude " (1675), in *Sermons*, 1844, 1. 179; Richard Cumberland, *A Treatise of the Laws of Nature*, trans. 1727, p. 164 (the Latin original appeared in 1672) ; John Scott, *The Christian Life*, 1681, pp. 175-6; Thomas Mannyngham, *A Sermon Preached at the Hampshire Feast*, 1686, pp. 16 ff.; J. Lowde, *A Discourse Concerning the Nature of Man*, 1694, sigs. A4-A4ᵛ, pp. 164-6; Jeremy Collier, " Of General Kindness," in *Miscellanies*, 1694; H. Downes, *The Excellency of Publick Charity*, 1697, p. 3; Benjamin Whichcote, *Select Sermons*, 1698, pp. 92-3, 181-2, 217, 381-2, and *Works*, Aberdeen, 1751, 4. 257-8; Edmund Calamy, *A Sermon Preach'd before the Societies for Reformation of Manners*, 1699, pp. 12-13; W. Sherlock, " The Nature and Evils of a Vicious Self-love " (c. 1700), in *Sermons*, 3d ed., 1719, 1. 368-70, 379; Stephen Chapman, *A Sermon Preach'd before the Free-born Citizens of Bristol*, 1703, pp. 1-2; Samuel Clarke, *The Great Duty of Universal Love*, 1705, pp. 4-5; Andrew Snape, *A Sermon Preach'd before the Princess Sophia*, 1706, pp. 19-22; Benjamin Loveling, *The Best Use of Riches*, *A Sermon*, 1706, p. 14; William Colnett, *A Sermon Preach'd before the Societies for Reformation of Manners*, 1711, pp. 5-6; Gilbert Burnet, *Some Sermons*, 1713, pp. 232-3; Henry Grove, *Spectator*, Nos. 588, 601, Sept. 1, Oct. 1, 1714; Richard Bentley, *A Sermon Preach'd . . . Feb. 3, 1716-17* (1717), in *Works*, ed. Dyce, 3 (1838). 269; George Smalridge, *Twelve Sermons*, 1717, p. 199; Alured Clarke, *A Sermon Preached . . . January the 25ᵗʰ, 1725, 1726*, pp. 4-10; Samuel Wright, *Charity in All Its Branches*, 1732, pp. 2-3; T. Rundle, *A Sermon Preached . . . Feb. 17, 1733-34*, 1734, pp. 5-6.

[53] *Christianity as Old as the Creation*, 8vo ed., 1731, p. 49.

the seventeenth and eighteenth centuries, it is man's duty to live in conformity with his nature, then it follows that he does this most completely who not only practices an active benevolence toward all men but cultivates and makes manifest the " good Affections " of his heart. In a striking sentence by Isaac Barrow, written as early as the 1670's, this association between the psychology of " natural goodness " and the ethics of " sensibility " was already clearly expressed. " Since nature," wrote Barrow, ". . . hath made our neighbour's misery our pain, and his content our pleasure; since with indissoluble bands of mutual sympathy she hath concatenated our fortunes and affections together; since by the discipline of our sense she instructs us, and by the importunity thereof solicits us to the observance of our duty, let us follow her wise directions, and conspire with her kindly motions; let us not stifle or weaken by disuse, or contrary practice, but by conformable action cherish and confirm the good inclinations of nature." [54]

4. *The "Self-approving Joy."*—In still another way, finally, the preaching of the Latitudinarian clergy contributed to the formation of the state of mind which was later to be reflected in the popular conception of the " man of feeling." This was through their frequent exhortations to their hearers and readers to consider how enjoyable the benevolent emotions may be to the individual who allows himself to feel them. From the Restoration into the eighteenth century there came from Anglican pulpits a steady stream of such exhortations, varying in tone from simple developments on the Aristotelian topic of the inherent pleasantness of virtue to eloquent reminders of the " pleasing Anguish, that sweetly melts the Mind, and terminates in a Self-approving Joy " [55] which is the chief earthly reward of persons who indulge their naturally good inclinations.

The theme, as we might expect, was a favorite one with Barrow. " As nature," he wrote in 1671, in a passage which was long after to be quoted with approval by Fielding,[56] " as nature, to the acts requisite toward preservation of our life, hath annexed a sensible pleasure, forcibly enticing us to the

[54] *Theological Works* 2. 142.
[55] See above, p. 205.
[56] *Covent Garden Journal*, No. 29, April 11, 1752, ed. Jensen, 1. 308.

performance of them: so hath she made the communication of benefits to others to be accompanied with a very delicious relish upon the mind of him that practises it; nothing indeed carrying with it a more pure and savoury delight than beneficence. A man may be virtuously voluptuous, and a laudable epicure by doing much good; for to receive good, even in the judgment of Epicurus himself (the great patron of pleasure), is nowise so pleasant as to do it. . . ." [57]

Many others in the seventeenth century wrote in a similar strain. " There is no sensual Pleasure in the World," said Tillotson, " comparable to the Delight and Satisfaction that a good Man takes in doing good." [58] " He that shews Mercy to a Man in his misery," remarked Richard Kidder, " does a double kindness at once (and 'tis hard to say which is the greater) one to his Brother, and another to himself. There is a Delight and Joy that Accompanies doing good, there is a kind of sensuality in it." [59] " The first Reward of Vertue," Samuel Parker wrote, " is its own natural and intrinsick Pleasure," and he proceeded to bring out with remarkable frankness the strain of egoistic hedonism which the conception involved:

Acts of Love and Kindness are in themselves gratefull and agreeable to the temper of humane Nature; and all Men feel a natural Deliciousness consequent upon every Exercise of their good-natur'd Passions; And nothing affects the Mind with greater Complacency, than to reflect upon its own inward Joy and Contentment. So that the Delight of every vertuous Resolution doubles upon it self; in that first it strikes our Minds with a direct Pleasure by its suitableness to our Natures, and then our Minds entertain themselves with pleasant Reflections upon their own Worth and Tranquility. [60]

Here, in 1681, was the whole philosophy of the " man of feeling "! By the beginning of the eighteenth century the theme had become a commonplace of nearly every charity sermon, and preachers exhausted the resources of their rhetoric in depicting the exquisite pleasure which the good man feels in contemplating his own benevolent deeds. One example will suffice—a particularly illuminating one. The rewards of benev-

[57] *Theological Works* 2. 225. Cf. also 2. 141-2.
[58] *Works*, 1728, 1. 156. Cf. also 2. 599.
[59] *Charity Directed*, 1676, p. 12.
[60] *A Demonstration of the Divine Authority of the Law of Nature*, p. 64.

olence, Charles Brent told his congregation at Bristol in 1704, are not to be looked for merely in the life to come.

There is for certain, even now, a most Divine and Heavenly Pleasure in doing Good; a Pleasure that is suited to the truest Movings of Humanity, that gratifies the purest of all our natural Inclinations, that Delights and Comforts even to the cherishing of our own Flesh, that runs along with our Affections and our Bowels so very sympathetically, that some good Men have indulged and epicuriz'd in it, till they have been tempted to call it downright *Sensuality:* And yet a Pleasure without the least Abatement or Allay. A Pleasure too, that doth not lye lingering in the Futurities of a World to come, but commences with our very Act, nay before it; beginning even with our very Intensions: For we are no sooner entring upon a Design of serving Mankind, but we take up great Sums of Delight and Alacrity upon it, before-hand; and one Advantage here is, that the Pleasure does not leave us as soon as the Work is done, but lasts as long and lively upon our Minds, as our Memories will serve us to recollect it. . . .[61]

In these passages—and many more like them could be quoted from the sermon literature of the late seventeenth and early eighteenth centuries [62]—one can see a clear foreshadowing of that curious type of hedonism—the often frankly avowed pursuit of altruistic emotions for egoistic ends—which was to characterize most of the representative " men of feeling " of the next two generations. Sir Charles Grandison might have been a parishioner of Parker or Brent, and Parson Yorick their successor.

The hypothesis I have tried to suggest in this paper is not intended to be taken as an adequate or in any way exclusive explanation of the rise of the mid-eighteenth-century mode of sensibility in England. There is always the influence of Shaftes-

---

[61] *Persuasions to a Publick Spirit*, 1704, pp. 15-16.

[62] See, e. g., H. Lukin, *The Chief Interest of Man* (1670), 3d ed., 1718, pp. 46-50; Hezekiah Burton, *Several Discourses*, 1684, p. 80, and *A Second Volume of Discourses*, 1685, pp. 564-72; Gregory Hascard, *A Sermon*, 1685, p. 5; Edward Pelling, *A Practical Discourse upon Charity*, 1693, p. 25; Edmund Calamy, *A Sermon Preach'd before the Societies for Reformation of Manners*, 1699, p. 18; E. Young, *Sermons on Several Occasions*, 1702, 1. 391-2; Samuel Clarke, *The Great Duty of Universal Love*, 1705, p. 4; Daniel Waterland, " The Duty of Doing Good " (1712), in *Works*, 1823, 8. 372; Gilbert Burnet, *Some Sermons*, 1713, pp. 246-8; Francis Squire, *Universal Benevolence: or, Charity in its Full Extent*, 1714, pp. 12-13; Henry Grove, *Spectator*, No. 588, Sept. 1, 1714; Alured Clarke, *A Sermon Preached . . . January the 25th, 1725*, 1726, p. 5.

bury to be considered—a very real and important influence especially after 1725 when it was reinforced by that of his disciple Hutcheson. Even in the later seventeenth century, moreover, the ideas we have been discussing were not the exclusive property of writers of sermons. Mr. Ustick has recently called attention to their appearance in certain courtesy books of the 1680's,[63] and to the examples he gives others could doubtless be added. By 1714, as every one knows, they had begun to find their way into the popular literature of essays and plays.

My intention has not been to minimize these other factors in the preparation for sentimentalism, but merely to consider whether the whole movement does not become somewhat more intelligible historically than it has hitherto seemed when we bring into the picture, also, the propaganda of benevolence and tender feeling carried on with increasing intensity since the Restoration by the anti-Puritan, anti-Stoic, and anti-Hobbesian divines of the Latitudinarian school.

University of Chicago

---

[63] *Modern Philology* 30 (1932). 161-6.

J. H. HAGSTRUM

The Nature of Dr. Johnson's Rationalism

from

A JOURNAL OF ENGLISH LITERARY HISTORY

Volume XVII(1950), 191-205

THE NATURE OF DR. JOHNSON'S RATIONALISM

By J. H. Hagstrum

In *From Classic to Romantic* W. J. Bate has presented Samuel Johnson as " a Christian and a very English Socrates," classical rather than neo-classical in his dedication to humanistic and ethical rationalism and in his conception that art should be a revelation of general nature. Such an analysis, valuable though it is in emphasizing the dignity of Johnson's critical thought and sound though it is in perceiving the basic assumptions upon which the Johnsonian system rests, should not be allowed to stand without important qualification.[1] It is the purpose of this paper to describe briefly that which is traditionally rationalistic and humanistic in Johnson's conception of reason and then more fully to discuss the vitally significant empirical strains in his criticism, to clarify the hitherto unnoticed but, I think, perfectly clear relationship in him between the empirical and rational faculties, and finally to call attention to his perception that the reason was not only a restraining, normalizing force but was instinct with positive energy of its own. This acute awareness and the corollary one that literature is an expression of all the faculties of the mind energized and active enabled Johnson to transcend that dry and almost mathematical rationalism with which he has sometimes been accused of being tainted and to over-leap those boundaries which neo-classicism at its most rigid had fixed between the separate faculties of the mind.

1

Bate comments properly that Johnson's conception of the nature of rational insight " is not easy to define with precision." The basis of that difficulty (and what student of Johnson has not been vexed by it!) perhaps lies in the fact that his use of the word *reason*, although extensive and forcible, does not seem

---

[1] See Bate, pp. 59ff. Bate is aware of empirical and even anti-rationalist elements in Johnson's criticism, but he makes nothing of them. He says, in passing, that Johnson " certainly preferred an accurate presentation of empirical or particularized nature to a completely lifeless idealization " (p. 64). See also pp. 74 and 79.

to have rested upon a satisfactory abstract conception of the term. In *Idler* no. 24 (1758) he rejected a currently popular definition of the soul on the grounds that " it supposes what cannot be proved, that the nature of mind is properly defined," and eight years earlier, in *Rambler* no. 41, he averred that no accurate answer can be given to the question of how reason differs from instinct because " we do not know in what either reason or instinct consists." Nevertheless, the following conclusions (here stated in the briefest summary) can be drawn with confidence from a fairly thorough examination of all the important passages of both moral and literary criticism in which Johnson invokes reason and bases his argument upon it.

1. *Reason and universal truth.* When, in the *Life of Cowley,* Johnson says that " truth, indeed, is always truth, and reason is always reason; they have an intrinsick and unalterable value, and constitute that intellectual gold which defies destruction," he refers to the following universals which should always, in some way or other, be expressed by the poet and critic: (a) *moral and religious truth* and (b) *the immutable order of nature* and *the unalterable mind of man.*

(a) Since " he who thinks rationally thinks morally," reason, assisted by Christian revelation, will lead man to " those general and transcendental truths " which for Johnson were expressed in humanistic and Christian ethics. The writer, who must also be guided by this ethical insight, should " consider right and wrong in their abstracted and invariable state " and should not be a promiscuous recorder of things as they are. He ought rather to " distinguish those parts of nature, which are most proper for imitation " and exhibit " the most perfect idea of virtue, the highest and purest that humanity can reach." The highest literature thus becomes the result of a selective imitation, guided by ethical perceptions, of an ideal moral reality. In this important respect Johnson's position must be sharply distinguished from all literary naturalism and from all imitations of reality guided exclusively by aesthetic considerations.

(b) Johnson often uses fidelity to the *order of nature* and to the unalterable *mind of man* as a test of literary value: literature must conform to the " settled and unalterable nature of things," to " the order of nature and the operations of the intellect," to " the nature of things and the structure of the human mind "; it must be " adequate to our faculties and agreeable to nature." When followed, these principles have a two-fold effect upon literature: it attains permanent significance and avoids the temporary, the local, the superficial, and the accidental; it also represents reality and avoids the chimerical, the fantastic, the hypothetical, and that which is only the arbitrary prescription of authority and tradition.

To follow nature, in Johnson's view, is to represent in art observable reality. " What is commonly called *nature* by the critics," he says in the discussion of epitaphs which concludes the *Life of Pope*, is " a just representation of things really existing, and actions really performed." [2]

2. *The operations of reason considered as a faculty of the mind.* It is possible to distinguish five separate but closely related functions of reason, the human faculty, in Johnson's discussion of literature:

(a)   As that quality in man which understands and appropriates, to the practical purposes of life, general truth and reality, reason watches scrupulously the data of the senses and the combinations of the imagination (which creates fictions and adorns nature) to make certain that they resemble order of reality discussed under 1(a) and (b). It continually forces the mind back upon nature and life.

(b)   Reason, as a dividing, partitioning faculty, may be relied upon to " disentangle complications and investigate causes," to " divide the object into its parts, or mark the intermediate gradations from the first agent to the last consequence." Its function is directly antithetical to that of the imagination which unites disparate data into new combinations of imagery and which is accompanied by wonder, a " pause of reason, a sudden cessation of the mental progress."

(c)   But the reason is also a concatenating and synthesizing faculty, which establishes order, provides transitions, and properly arranges the disposition of materials—a mental architect which in philosophy constructs systems and in poetry creates plot, form, and structure.

(d)   Reason as a moderating force opposes excess and ecstasy, perceives the ethical and the aesthetic mean, and resists all tendencies to disproportion, lack of symmetry, inappropriateness of language and ornament.

---

[2] Citations from Johnson come from the nine-volume edition of his *Works* (Oxford, 1825) and appear in part 1(a) of the schematization in the following order: *Life of Cowley* (*Works*, 7.51), *Rasselas* (1.222), *Rambler* no. 4 (2.18, 19-20). Part 1(b): *Rambler* no. 140 (3.163), *Rambler* no. 156 (3.239-40), *Rambler* no. 92 (1.220-1), *Life of Pope* (8.348).

(e) Reason is an abstracting and generalizing power, of moral
importance in detaching the mind from the insistent claims
of sense and habit and of aesthetic importance in guiding
the writer to select general and therefore more permanent
reality. It operates not only as an intuitive and sudden
perception of general truth but also as the slower inductive
process of generalizing from specific data.[3]

Because the ideas that appear in the foregoing schematization
of the elements in Johnson's rationalism have their roots in the
entire intellectual legacy of Western Europe and had passed
current in the Republic of Letters for generations, any attempt
to determine their specific source would, of course, be futile.
They themselves, however, are the very bones and sinews of the
Johnsonian system of criticism. And yet, as the remaining
sections of this paper will attempt to show, they bear no more
resemblance to his total conception of the mind that creates
literature than does a skeleton to a man of living flesh.

2

All of the rational processes outlined in the preceding section
point to an antecedent operation of the mind—the appropriation of nature and life through the senses and the empirical
collection of materials upon which the reason can operate in
the functions mentioned above. The mind obviously cannot
watch, divide, combine, moderate, or generalize *in vacuo.*
" Judgment," said Johnson in the *Life of Pope,* " is forced upon
us by experience." The reason (no less than the picture-making
faculty of the mind, the imagination) depends upon raw
material from the world outside, and what Johnson once said
about the imagination is equally applicable to the reason. On
his tour with Boswell (19 September 1773) he expressed the
opinion that the poetry of St. Kilda must be very poor because
the locality was barren of images and therefore starved the
poet's fancy. To Boswell's objection that even what material

---

[3] For 2 (a) see the passages cited under " Truth " in Joseph E. Brown, *The
Critical Opinions of Samuel Johnson* (1926), pp. 250-3. For 2 (b) see *Rambler*
no. 137 (*Works*, 3. 147-8). For 2 (c) see *Rambler* no. 151 (3. 217), *Rambler*
no. 158 (3. 249-50), *Rambler* no. 139 (3. 157-62), *Life of Milton* (7. 139), and
Adventurer no. 95 (4. 81). For 2 (d) see *Rambler* no. 38 (2. 185-6), *Rambler*
no. 129 (3. 113), *Rambler* no. 122 (3. 28), and *The Fountains* (9. 181, 183, 190).
For 2 (e) see *Rambler* no. 208 (3. 462) and *Idler* no. 59 (4. 324).

there was could be combined into poetry by " a poetical genius,"
Johnson replied:

" But, sir, a man cannot make fire but in proportion as he has
wood. He cannot coin guineas but in proportion as he has gold."

Because Johnson is deeply concerned with the experience of
life and the empirical search antecedent to the operations of
reason, he cannot be denominated, without important qualification, a rationalist. In the Dictionary he defined a *rationalist*
as " one who proceeds in his disquisitions and practice wholly
upon reason," and the happy similes from Bacon which he used
to illustrate its meaning make it clear that Johnson, like Bacon,
was in no way satisfied with an exclusive reliance upon the
rational faculty.

He often used this comparison, the empirical philosophers are
like to pismires; they only lay up and use their store; the *rationalists*
are like to spiders; they spin all out of their bowels: but give me
the philosopher, who, like the bee, hath a middle faculty, gathering
from abroad, but digesting that which is gathered by his own
virtue.

Bacon's little fable of the bee leaves room for the rational
faculty, since the mind must, by its own power, digest at home
the materials presented to it. But before everything else it
must gather from abroad through empirical observation and
search.

Johnson not only accepted this Baconian conception of the
mind—empirical observation followed by rationalistic " digestion "—as an epistemological truth, but he made it fundamental
to his conception of the mental preparation of the poet for his
task. One of the most striking facts about Johnson's oft-
repeated " character " of the poet is the prominence he gives to
the empirical faculty. Although he often recommends, as he
does in *Rambler* no. 154, the humanistic labor of possessing
the " intellectual treasures which the diligence of former ages
has accumulated " and complains that " the mental disease of
the present generation is impatience of study, contempt of the
masters of ancient wisdom," the noteworthy fact about Johnson
is that he reveals impatience with an exclusive reliance upon
this somewhat academic and bookish knowledge of the great
traditions and insists repeatedly that the mind of the poet be

3

stocked with fresh, immediate observations of nature and men. Baconian philosophy and Lockean psychology provided him with a new touchstone for determining the excellence of literary imitation: has the poet, like the natural philosopher, collected accurate and extensive data? has he exercised the empirical faculty in gathering from abroad? have the senses stocked the mind with original impressions of nature and reality? As Imlac says, " no kind of knowledge was to be overlooked by the poet "; mountains, deserts, forests, flowers, crags, pinnacles, rivulets, summer clouds, plants, animals, minerals, meteors must all " concur to store his mind with inexhaustible variety." Milton apparently was content with less, for his

images and descriptions of the scenes, or operations of nature, do not seem always copied from original form, nor to have the freshness, raciness, and energy of immediate observation. He saw nature, as Dryden expresses it, ' through the spectacles of books; ' and, on most occasions, calls learning to his assistance.

But Shakespeare, on the other hand, " shows plainly that he has seen with his own eyes "; he is " an exact surveyor of the inanimate world; his descriptions have always some peculiarities, gathered by contemplating things as they really exist."

This important empirical strain in Johnson's criticism perhaps results from the fact that for him the principles of evoking literary pleasure did not possess the absoluteness and inflexibility of the moral and ethical principles mentioned earlier. In discussing the metrical harmony of Pope, for example, he denounced " the cant of those who judge by principle rather than by perception "—an almost complete reversal of his position in the realm of morals, where the cant lies in unprincipled reliance upon instinct. The simple but absolute principles of morality apply to art only to the extent that it instructs life. Since the belles lettres mix pleasure with instruction and thus introduce a somewhat more lawless element, Johnson approaches them from an entirely different point of view. In his Preface to Shakespeare he finds that works of literary pleasure like the drama are " gradual and comparative," " tentative and experimental," and are therefore to be distinguished from those " raised upon principles demonstrative and scientifick." Literature is thus neither morality nor science, and partakes only to a limited extent of the rational certitudes of these disciplines. But although the literature of pleasure is thus to be distinguished from demonstrative science, the empirical faculty becomes even more necessary than otherwise would be the case, and the appeal to experience takes on a deeper significance. Since works of pleasure appeal " wholly to observation and experience, no other test can be applied than length of duration and continuance of esteem "; their worth is discovered only in a " long succession of endeavours." Earlier, in *Rambler* no. 92, Johnson had said much the same thing about beauty, which he found to be a quality merely " relative and comparative," an epithet which we transfer from one object to another " as our knowledge increases " and as " higher excellence comes within our view."

It is not therefore remarkable that criticism, which attempts the evaluation of so protean a thing as beauty, " has not yet attained the certainty and stability of science." Johnson here (*Rambler* no. 92) holds out some hope that the critic may in time be able to " establish principles; to improve opinion into knowledge." But such principles could be determined on the basis not of universal notions of beauty nor of inner reason but only of continuing observation and experience. He thus praised, as " an example of true criticism," the treatise on the sublime by Edmund Burke, who certainly made it clear that he had sought a knowledge built upon a " more extensive and perfect induction " and had attempted, in his own words, to approach the method of the investigative sciences, a method which even in matters of aesthetics he considered " incomparably the best." [4]

This insistence in the criticism of literature upon the data of the senses and upon first-hand observations of life and nature reflect what is the natural bent of Johnson's mind, which always distrusted abstruse speculation and often demanded arduous and unrelenting search for factual verification. But this persistent empirical strain may also, I think, be properly related to what Johnson said about the nature of reason and the problem of intellectual certainty. It was observed at the outset of this paper that Johnson was impressed with the difficulty of arriving at an exact definition of reason and the mind. In the

[4] *The Writings and Speeches of Edmund Burke* (New York, 1901), 1.70, 81. For Johnson's praise of Burke's treatise, see Boswell's *Life of Johnson* (Hill-Powell ed.), 2.90.

preface to Dodsley's *Preceptor* (1748) he recommends first that the student consult books on logic by Crousaz, Watts, Wolfius, Le Clerc, and Locke, but that list is immediately followed by mention of works of " peripatetick logic, which has been, perhaps, condemned without a candid trial." This wavering between two leading schools of logic may have arisen from a fear that it would weaken morality and religion to rely, in all areas, upon induction. But when ethical considerations are not fully pertinent, Johnson reveals that it was with thinkers of the empirical school that he had the closest affinity.

He was a life-long and almost fervent admirer of the logical treatises of Isaac Watts, who says that " the old Aristotelian scheme of this science will teach us very little, that is worth knowing." [5] The fact that Locke (Watts' mentor and source), Bacon, Boerhaave, and Newton were all intellectual heroes to Johnson and that they all, up to a certain point at least, followed the methods of empirical logic is of some significance in determining Johnson's own concepts. But it is his own comments on the nature of certitude that are the most convincing. *Rambler* no. 41, in which Johnson despairs of determining exactly the meaning of reason and instinct, has already been cited. But after having admitted the semantic difficulty, he then forms a working conception of the terms:

... but surely he that contemplates a ship and a bird's nest, will not be long without finding out, that the idea of the one was impressed at once, and continued through all the progressive descents of the species, without variation or improvement; and that the other is the result of experiments, compared with experiments, has grown, by accumulated observation, from less to greater excellence, and exhibits the collective knowledge of different ages and various professions.

Memory is the purveyor of reason, the power which places those images before the mind upon which the judgment is to be exercised, and which treasures up the determinations that are once passed, as the rules of future actions, or grounds of subsequent conclusions.

It is indeed, the faculty of remembrance, which may be said to place us in the class of moral agents.

This passage is crucial to an understanding of Johnson on the mind. Doubtful of the abstract meaning of the term, he turns

---

[5] *Improvement of the Mind* (Boston, 1833), pp. 210-217. For Johnson's praise of Watts, see his *Life of Watts* (*Works*, 8. 385) and also Boswell's *Life*, 4. 311.

with almost obvious relief to nests and ships, to the certitudes of observation and experiment, of collecting data, and of storing the memory. He thus shifts the emphasis from the reason itself to the antecedent operations of the mind without which it would grope uncertainly in the dark. Memory, therefore, rather than the rational faculty itself, becomes here the distinguishing mark of human nature. Apparently Johnson, like Hamlet, finds " god-like reason " most meaningful when it exists with " large discourse looking before and after."

There is another most meaningful passage on intellectual certainty, written in the *Life of Boerhaave* when its author was thirty years of age. It deserves more attention than it has received, for it justifies placing Johnson " among th'asserters of free reason's claim," to use the language of Dryden, and shows comprehension of and admiration for the scientific method.

When he [Boerhaave] laid down his office of governour of the university, in 1715, he made an oration upon the subject of ' attaining to certainty in natural philosophy; ' in which he declares, in the strongest terms, in favour of experimental knowledge; and reflects, with just severity, upon those arrogant philosophers, who are too easily disgusted with the slow methods of obtaining true notions by frequent experiments; and who, possessed with too high an opinion of their own abilities, rather choose to consult their own imaginations, than inquire into nature, and are better pleased with the charming amusement of forming hypotheses, than the toilsome drudgery of making observations.

The emptiness and uncertainty of all those systems, whether venerable for their antiquity, or agreeable for their novelty, he has evidently shown; and not only declared, but proved, that we are entirely ignorant of the principle of things, and that all the knowledge we have, is of such qualities alone as are discoverable by experience, or such as may be deduced from them by mathematical demonstration.

In *Rambler* no. 137 (1751) Johnson expressed a principle of Locke which has been of crucial importance in all scientific advance and which Bertrand Russell in our own time has made basic to what he has called logical atomism—further evidence that Johnson understood the implications of the scientific revolution of the preceding century.

The chief art of learning, as Locke has observed, is to attempt but little at a time. The widest excursions of the mind are made by short flights frequently repeated; the most lofty fabricks of ' science are formed by the continued accumulation of single propositions.

The passages just cited refer primarily to the attainment of scientific truth. What is their relevance to literature? Literature, after the process of selective imitation, guided by ethical insight and devotion to general nature, and after the addition of imaginative elements designed to create pleasure, becomes, as an end-product, something different from a work purely scientific or informative. Nevertheless it was one of Johnson's most important critical emphases that before the process of rational and imaginative digestion takes place the poet must rigorously subject himself to a program of investigative and inductive exploration of reality. The result is that the quest of Johnson's poet (how unlike the Platonic quest of, say, Shelley's Alastor!) is a Baconian, Hobbesian, and Lockean quest for sense-data— for impressions of and information about nature and life. Johnson is always pre-occupied with the poet's mental stores and is under no illusion as to the way in which the shelves of the mind are stocked. Mental power, even when possessed by a poet, is the somewhat earth-bound ability to make use of what has already been supplied. Had Shakespeare (as he says in the *Preface*) waited upon the power of nature or the stirrings of inner genius, he had waited in vain, for

the power of nature is only the power of using to any certain purpose the material which diligence procures, or opportunity supplies. Nature gives no man knowledge, and, when images are collected by study and experience, can only assist in combining or applying them. Shakespeare, however favoured by nature, could impart only what he had learned . . .

3

In his best criticism Johnson was profoundly aware that a great work of literary art was an expression of all the powers of the writer—genius, invention, reason, imagination—working together and mutually energizing one another. This perception led him to transcend (without in any way destroying what he felt was the basic constitution of the mind) the rigidly defined categories of neo-classical psychology.

In Boswell's record of the journey to the Hebrides (15 August 1773) there is a passage in which Johnson expresses some important opinions about the mind. After the arrival of Dr. William Robertson the conversation, which then turned to the mental powers of Edmund Burke, became animated. Johnson said

he could not understand how a man could apply to one thing, and not to another. Robertson said one man had more judgment, another more imagination. JOHNSON. ' No, sir; it is only one man has more mind than another. He may direct it differently; he may by accident see the success of one kind of study and take a desire to excel in it. I am persuaded that had Sir Isaac Newton applied to poetry, he would have made a fine epic poem. I could as easily apply to law as to tragic poetry.' BOSWELL. ' Yet, sir, you *did* apply to tragic poetry, not o law, *JOHNSON*. ' Because, sir, I had not money to study law. Sir, the man who has vigour may walk to the east just as well as to the west, if he happens to turn his head that way.'

In this lively interchange of opinion Johnson denies any special place to literature, removing from it the mystification that has often surrounded it and relating it to the law, to mathematics, and to other co-ordinate disciplines. The assumption is that literature is, like the others, a rigorous mental pursuit. But the prevailing intellectuality is instinct with a kind of dynamism. Excellence depends upon *vigor* of mind—a quality that transcends the conventional distinctions, which Robertson introduced, between the imagination and the judgment. " No, sir; it is only one man has more mind than another."

Among the expected definitions of *vigour* in the Dictionary there occurs one that isolates a purely intellectual quality. Johnson describes it as " mental force, intellectual ability." Such metaphorical language about the mind that achieves excellence he persisted in using again and again. In *Rambler* no. 129 he urges everyone to " endeavour to *invigorate* himself by *reason* and reflection." In *Rambler* no. 145 he describes the impulse of genius as being " *invigorated* with stronger *comprehension*." Addison, who thinks justly but faintly, writes poetry that is the " product of a *mind* too judicious to commit faults, but not sufficiently *vigorous* to attain excellence." Pope's *judgment* often " makes the representation more *powerful* than the reality." Scientific projects are often the product of minds

" *heated* with intenseness of *thought*." For Johnson methodical deduction possesses " placid beauties "; transitions are lovely; a well-connected plan has " the power of attracting attention "; and generalization possesses grandeur and sublimity. All this points to a conception of reason somewhat different from the neo-classic and Lockean conception of the cold, restraining judgment and even from Rapin's conception of a " *Judgment* proportion'd to the *Wit* " in strength in order to " moderate the heat and govern the natural Fury " of the imagination.[6] For Johnson the purely intellectual faculty is impelled by heat and power of its own generation—a fact which it is important to notice as an important supplement to the functions of reason outlined in the first section.

Reason was also energized by its co-existence with other powers of the mind and by co-operation with them in literary creation. It had certainly been one tendency of neo-classic criticism to separate the mental faculties, partly in order to understand them more fully and partly in order to give emphasis to the qualities of judgment and good sense that would moderate the excesses to which other faculties were all too prone. But although, as was noted earlier, Johnson often makes these conventional separations, especially when writing with a moral view, his purely aesthetic pronouncements point often to a fusion of the rational and the imaginative. If, as he said in *Rambler* no. 122, " experience soon shows us the tortuosities of imaginary rectitude, the complications of simplicity, and the asperities of smoothness," an attempt to account for the complicated effects of literary pleasure would soon enough show him the impossibility of keeping the imagination and the reason in logic-tight compartments. Johnson might well have exclaimed with Pope: ''What thin partitions Sense from Thought divide! '' Johnson found it " ridiculous to oppose judgment to imagination; for it does not appear that men have necessarily less of one, as they have more of the other." [7] The co-existence

---

[6] *Reflections on Aristotle's Treatise of Poesie* tr. by Rymer (London, 1694), p. 23. For Locke on judgment, see *Essay concerning Human Understanding*, 1.xi.2. The phrases from Johnson in the two preceding sentences come from *Adventurer* no. 99 (4.87), *Rambler* no. 158 (3.249), *Life of Milton* (7.139), and *Life of Cowley* (7.38).

[7] *Life of Roscommon* (7.169). Irving Babbitt cites this passage in *On Being Creative* (London, 1932) as an " occasional remark of admirable perspicacity "

of these two powers, each of which has its own kind of anima-
tion, leads Johnson to forget, in some of his best critical comments, the antitheses between reason and fancy that are elsewhere sharply drawn. His very language is such that one cannot
always separate the rational from the imaginative strains. A
passage in the *Life of Milton* on the effect of the imagination in
that poet illustrates the point. I shall italicize those words and
phrases which normally concern the operation of reason but
which here comment upon the workings of the poet's imagination.

The *thoughts* which are occasionally called forth in the progress,
are such as could only be produced by an imagination in the highest
degree fervid and active, to which materials were supplied by
incessant *study* and unlimited *curiosity*. The heat of Milton's
mind may be said to sublimate his learning, to throw off into his
work the spirit of *science*, unmingled with its grosser parts.

The same type of fusion takes place between judgment and
invention, between judgment and genius. As we have seen,
there are passages in Johnson which do, in the more strictly
neo-classical manner, separate the concept of invention, wit,
natural genius, and imaginative power, on the one hand, from
judgment, restraint, and art, on the other hand. But such
passages do not represent his central conception of genius or
of original invention, which he calls " the highest praise of
genius." *Genius* is the inclusive term which refers, in the language of the Dictionary, to all " mental powers or faculties "
or to a man " endowed with superior faculties." And Johnson
refused to oppose the part to the whole. He ridicules, in *Idler*
no. 60, Dick Minim's cant that " a perfect writer is not to be
expected, because genius decays as judgment increases." In
commenting upon the " chief scene of enchantment " in *Mac-
beth* (Act IV, sc. 1) he observes the extraordinary use of
historical judgment in selecting the ingredients of the witches'
unholy brew: " These are the touches of judgment and genius."
But it is not only a matter of the necessary and plausible co-
existence of the two. As in the case of reason and imagination,

(p. 92), but he finds that usually Johnson tends, "like most neo-classic critics,
to set imignation and reason . . . in sharp opposition to one another " (p. 92).
In contrast, this paper argues that the fusion of the two is a central Johnsonian
insight, present in his best criticism.

there is a kind of mixing of essences. In quoting the conclusion of the *Life of Milton*, a passage on original genius, I shall again italicize those words and phrases that point to the presence of rational elements, which are here woven inseparably into the very fabric of the language itself.

> The highest praise of genius is original invention. Milton cannot be said to have *contrived* the *structure* of an epick poem, and, therefore, owes reverence to that *vigour* and amplitude of *mind* to which all generations must be indebted for the art of poetical narration, for the texture of the fable, the variations of incidents, the interposition of dialogue, and all the stratagems that surprise and enchain attention. But, of all the borrowers from Homer, Milton is, perhaps, the least indebted. He was naturally a *thinker* for himself, confident of his own abilities, and disdainful of help or hindrance . . .

Johnson early acquired the habit of introducing into his biographies (like those of Sarpi, Boerhaave, Barretier, Burman, and Sydenham) abstract and summary delineations of the moral and intellectual character of his subject. That habit he carried over into literary biography and criticism, and one finds a succession of " characters " of the poet from Imlac's to those that appear in virtually every one of the *Lives of the Poets*. Such delineations of literary persons and their mental qualities Johnson makes a functional part of his critical evaluations, since in his conception a work of art is a display, or proof, of those qualities. As early as the *Life of Savage* (1744) he found the poet's tragedy of Sir Thomas Overbury " an uncommon *proof* of strength of genius, and evenness of mind, of a serenity not to be ruffled, and an imagination not to be suppressed." He looked for " rays of genius " in all literary production. The point that has been made in this section is that literary excellence is the product of a reason that possesses vigor and power but not of reason, even thus considered, operating alone. The mind stimulated to literary activity is one in which all its powers are heightened and deeply and inextricably interfused.

I have not intended to deny what has always been perceived to be the central truth about Johnson as a critic, that he was a stout champion of the classical and humanistic ideal in letters. But I have found it necessary to point out what has often been ignored or perceived only dimly: that his devotion to general nature and ethical truth was freshened by a vigorous empiricism and by an imaginative *élan* which freed him from the springes of conventional categories of psychology and rhetoric. He probably never asked himself where fancy is bred, but he doubtless would have placed in the head what others have placed in heart, blood, bowels, and reins. He always cherished the *vivida vis animi*, for to him the mind of a great writer (like Pope, for example) was a mind energized and invigorated—

a mind active, ambitious, and adventurous, always investigating, always aspiring; in its widest searches still longing to go forward, in its highest flights still wishing to be higher; always imagining something greater than it knows, always endeavouring more than it can do.

Such powers of mind it is the aim of literature at its finest to display for the instruction and pleasure of man.

Northwestern University

RAYMOND D. HAVENS

Thomas Warton and the Eighteenth
Century Dilemma

from

STUDIES IN PHILOLOGY

Volume XXV(1928), 36-50

THOMAS WARTON AND THE EIGHTEENTH-CENTURY DILEMMA

By Raymond D. Havens

Thomas Warton is usually thought of as one who lifted high the banner of literary revolt " with gems and golden lustre rich imblazed." We picture him, both in critical theory and in poetic practice, a conscious rebel against the school of Pope. Such a misconception is natural enough, since we usually read both his prose and his poetry in anthologies that aim to give not his most typical, but his most significant writings, and his significance is thought to lie in revolt. Even if we turn to his complete works, we commonly read them with an eye for indications of romanticism; and, in any case, it is heterodoxy rather than conformity that makes the strongest first impression. As a result, we pass over the hundreds of satirical heroic couplets, the translations from Horace, the paraphrase of a chapter of Job, as well as the dozen humorous pieces and fasten upon " The Pleasures of Melancholy," " The Grave of King Arthur," and " The Crusade." In emphasizing these last two we do right, for they represent the real man, but " The Pleasures of Melancholy " does not. Though supposed to be typical of the Wartons and of their period, it is really typical of adolescence and tells us little about its sixteen-year-old author except that he was young, poetic, and a lover of Spenser and Milton. To be sure, it says a good deal about midnight, tombs, Gothic vaults, and solitude; but it is no more gloomy than is a ghost story. Its title describes it accurately, " The Pleasures of Melancholy." " Is there," the young bard asks, " a pleasure like the pensive mood,"

> To bend
> Th' uncertain step along the midnight mead,
> And pour your sorrows to the pitying moon? [1]

Far from being plunged in despair, he is having an excellent time and is very well satisfied with himself:

> Few know that elegance of soul refin'd,
> Whose soft sensation feels a quicker joy

---

[1] *Pleasures of Melancholy*, 168, 171-3.

36

> From Melancholy's scenes, than the dull pride
> Of tasteless splendor and magnificence
> Can e'er afford.[2]

And a hundred lines later he repeats, "These are delights . . . which alone the pensive soul can taste."[3] He piles up macabre and gloomy details, not because he really enjoys tombs and fogs, nor because he is discouraged and wishes his surroundings to accord with his mood; quite the contrary, out of the fullness of youth he seeks the thrill of a complete antithesis to the comfort, health, and high spirits that he enjoys. Partly it is bravado and partly roughing it from an easy chair. We do not judge Goethe by *Werther,* yet *Werther* describes a real phase of Goethe's development, whereas there is no reason to believe that Warton ever

> Genuine transport found, as on some tomb
> Reclin'd . . . [he] watch'd the tapers of the dead.[4]

Nor did he actually prefer a rainy, foggy, scowling morning to all the sweetness of a May dawn;[5] but in his ignorance of the emotions he attempted to describe he fell into exaggeration. Such pseudo-romanticism might well be significant if it were the affectation of one who had reached "years of discretion," but in the work of a boy not yet seventeen it has the same meaning as down on the lip and unpredictable breakings in the voice. At this particular time, indeed, it meant even less, for grave-yard poetry was just coming into vogue. Dyer's "Ruins of Rome" appeared in 1740, Young's *Night Thoughts* at intervals between 1742 and 1745 (the year in which "The Pleasures of Melancholy" was written), Blair's "Grave" in 1743, Hervey's *Meditations among the Tombs* in 1745-46, and in 1742 Gray began his "Elegy." The first three of these works, which (like his own effusion) were in blank verse, almost certainly influenced Warton, who also very naturally adopted the gloomy themes, congenial to an adolescent boy, that such productions were bringing into fashion.

Yet it is not because of his poetry alone that Thomas Warton has been pictured as one of the powers that led the enbattled seraphim to war against the neo-classic despotism. For in his *Observa-*

[2] *Ibid.,* 92-6.
[3] *Ibid.,* 194-5.
[4] *Ibid.,* 98-99.
[5] *Ibid.,* 130-52.

tions on the Fairy Queen (1754) he is said to have " produced a revolution in criticism." [6]   No doubt there is the possibility of a revolution in his remark, " It is absurd to think of judging either Ariosto or Spenser by precepts which they did not attend to," but unfortunately this utterance is not original and by no means represents his critical position.   I have said " position," but the plural should be used, since in the very section which contains this comment he twice shifts his ground and employs no fewer than three conflicting critical standards.   If the shifting were deliberately done in order to present contrasting points of view, it would indicate unusual keenness of discrimination and catholicity of taste; but it is unconscious and is due to the confusion in his mind, a confusion shared by many of his contemporaries.

Warton begins his book by presenting, in no uncertain terms, the neo-classic position: " When," he tells us, ". . . antient poetry and antient criticism . . . at last emerged from the depths of Gothic ignorance and barbarity; it might have been expected . . . that unnatural events, the machinations of imaginary beings, and adventures entertaining only as they were improbable, would have given place to justness of thought and design, and to that decorum which nature dictated, and which the example and the precept of antiquity had authorized."   But unfortunately " we find Ariosto . . . rejecting truth for magic, and preferring the ridiculous and incoherent excursions of Boyardo, to the propriety and uniformity of the Grecian and Roman models."   So, too, Spenser, who " copied the cast and construction of the antient Epic " and held to the " unity of the hero and of his design," was misled by Ariosto to disregard " that unity of action, by the means of which such a design should be properly accomplished." [7]

In consequence, though " not so confused and irregular as the Orlando Furioso "—in which " the reader's imagination is distracted, and his attention harrassed, amidst the multiplicity of tales,"—yet the *Faerie Queene* is in its plan and conduct " highly

[6] Clarissa Rinaker, " Thomas Warton," *University of Illinois Studies,* 1916, p. 43.

[7] *Observations,* I, 1-2, 6.   All references are to the second edition, of 1762, which differs considerably from the first.   Except where otherwise noted, all passages here quoted appear in the first edition and in substantially the same words.

exceptionable." [8]   These defects should have been remedied by
making Arthur the " leading adventurer " throughout, or, possibly,
by converting each book into a " detached poem . . . without any
reference to the rest." [9]   Warton alignes himself squarely with the
" regulars " by affirming: " Every classical, every reasonable critic
must acknowledge, that the poet's [Ariosto's] conception in celebrating the MADNESS . . . of a hero, implies extravagance and absurdity," and by gravely reminding us that Orlando, on his first appearance, " is placed in a situation not perfectly heroic. He is discovered to us in bed." [10]

By beginning his *Observations* with the consideration " Of the
plan and conduct of the *Fairy Queen* " Warton seems to lay great
stress upon the architectonic element, and by finding the poem
seriously deficient in this particular he seems to be condemning it
as a whole. In so doing he was merely accepting the neo-classic
assumptions and canons and repeating what Dryden, Hughes, and
others had said before him.[11] But he was not satisfied; he felt

---

[8] *Ibid.*, 12, 14.

[9] *Ibid.*, 6, 10. Warton failed to see that, although a certain formal unity
(about which neo-classic criticism was extremely solicitous) would have
been secured by making Arthur the leading character in all the books, this
change would not have affected the multiplicity of episodes, the lack of
real plot and of progress towards a goal which were presumably the
fundamental causes of his dissatisfaction.

[10] *Ibid.*, 12-13. Warton's limitations—his worship (in theory) of regularity and his willingness to accept the narrow standards of his day—are
distressingly apparent in his treatment of versification. The Spenserian
stanza, one of the chief glories of English prosody, he thinks " injudiciously
chosen," not adapted to " the genius of the english language," the source
of a " constraint " which " led our author into many absurdities " (*Ibid.*,
113-15). Inversion of accent (trochaic substitutions) are disapproved of—
except, apparently, at the beginning of a line—and it is " laid down as
a general rule, that an alexandrine cannot be harmonious without a full
pause after the third foot. . . . Consequently the sixth syllable must necessarily be a monosyllable, or the last syllable of a word." (*Ibid.*, II, 154).
Was even Bysshe more narrow and rigid? But Bysshe was not a poet; he
did not write alexandrines and use a variety of stanzas and other free
measures, as the future laureate did. It may be that Warton derived
more pleasure from Spenser's stanza than he realized and that he condemned it mainly because all his predecessors had done so.

[11] See H. E. Cory, " The Critics of Edmund Spenser " (*University of California Publications*, 1911), 114-15, 146-7, 165.

that something was wrong, though he did not know just what, and, accordingly, in the last two paragraphs of this first chapter, he attempts a defence of his beloved poem: " But it is absurd," he tells us, " to think of judging either Ariosto or Spenser by precepts which they did not attend to.   We who live in the days of writing by rule, are apt to try every composition by *those* laws which we have been taught to think the *sole* criterion of excellence.   Critical taste is universally diffused, and we require the *same* order and design which every modern performance is expected to have, in poems where they never were regarded or intended." [12]   It is here implied that a great poem must have order and design, must be tried by some laws, but that the neo-classic rules are not " the sole criterion of excellence."   We are led to infer that a study of poetry which was free from preconceptions and not limited to the ancient classics and to the French and English works patterned after them would give us other laws, other concepts of order and design, and that with these the *Faerie Queene* might be found to accord.

This is a most illuminating suggestion and might, had it been followed up, have led to great things.   But it is merely an after-thought which was added in the second edition.   Warton does nothing more with it and that, as is clear from his immediately

---

[12]*Observations*, I, 15; the italics are mine.   This passage was not in the first edition.   He had implied something like this a little earlier when he qualified his assertion that Spenser " does not . . . seem convinced of the necessity of that unity of action " by adidng, " At least, he has not followed the method practiced by Homer and Virgil, in conducting their respective heroes to the proposed end " (*Ibid.*, I, 6), which suggests that the *Faerie Queene* may observe this unity though not in the classic way.   Note also that Spenser is not explicitly accused of disregarding the unity; it is only said that he " does not . . . seem convinced of the necessity " of it.   Another instance of Warton's cautious statement of the neo-classic position without committing himself to it is his remark, two pages earlier, " It may be urged, that Spenser made an unfortunate choice, and discovered but little judgment, in adopting Ariosto for his example, rather than Tasso. . . . But our author naturally followed the poem which was most celebrated."   This seems to be a condemnation of Ariosto as a model, but Warton says only that Spenser's choice, which has been thought unfortunate, was due to Ariosto's popularity.   It is not unlikely either that he had arrived at no clear opinion about the matter or that he personally favored Ariosto.   The clauses " At least . . . end," " that Spenser . . . judgment " replace much more severe expressions in the first edition.

passing to another idea (which he treats as the same), because he has never thought it through but has merely appropriated it from John Hughes. In the preface to his edition of Spenser (1715), Hughes had said of the *Faerie Queene:* " The whole Frame of it wou'd appear monstrous, if it were to be examin'd by the Rules of Epick Poetry, as they have been drawn from the Practice of *Homer* and *Virgil.* But as it is plain the Author never design'd it by those Rules, I think it ought rather to be consider'd as a Poem of a particular kind, describing in a Series of Allegorical Adventures or Episodes the most noted Virtues and Vices: to compare it therefore with the Models of Antiquity, wou'd be like drawing a Parallel between the *Roman* and the *Gothick* Architecture." [13] It is to Hughes, therefore, a much more liberal, original, and penetrating critic than Warton, that all the credit for the often-quoted passage from the *Observations* is due.

Warton continues as follows:

> Spenser . . . did not live in an age of planning. His poetry is the careless exuberance of a warm imagination and a strong sensibility. It was his business to engage the fancy, and to interest the attention by bold and striking images, in the formation, and the disposition of which, little labor or art was applied. . . . Exactness in his poem, would have been like the cornice which a painter introduced in the grotto of Calypso. . . . we scarcely regret the loss of [" arrangement and oeconomy "] . . . while their place is so amply supplied, by something which more powerfully attracts us: something, which engages the affections the feelings of the heart, rather than the cold approbation of the head. If there be any poem, whose graces please, because they are situated beyond the reach of art, and where the force and faculties of creative imagination delight, because they are unassisted and unrestrained by those of deliberate judgment, it is this.[14]

Such criticism is sheer lawlessness. It belittles labor, judgment, selection, revision, and the entire architectonic, intellectual element to exalt spontaneity and emotional appeal as the only important things in poetry. According to it, the elaborate, monumental creation of " our sage and serious Spenser " is a piece of careless ex-

[13] Vol. I, p. lx; pointed out by Cory, p. 165, *cf.* p. 147. The greater part of Hughes's preface is reprinted in W. H. Durham's *Critical Essays of the Eighteenth Century*, New Haven, 1915.

[14] *Observations*, I, 15-16. The first part of the quotation, through " Calypso," is not in the first edition.

uberance possessing little plan or art and owing its greatness largely
to its faults, to the absence of " exactness " and " deliberate judgment." Furthermore, it seems to imply what Warton unconsciously
have believed that subject matter is the main thing in literature,
that Spenser's work is great not because of its beauty, its art,
but mainly because it furnishes the mind with a pleasant land in
which to wander.

It should be observed that all three appraisals of the *Faerie
Queene* stand: first, that it lacks plan; second, that it has plan but
not that of the classic epic; third, that it is without plan and is
better so. They are regarded not as optional but as supplementary
one to another; Warton believed them all. To be sure, he writes,
" It is absurd to think of judging either Ariosto or Spenser by
precepts which they did not attend to; " yet he does so judge them.
He lets his condemnation of Spenser's irregularity remain and even
places it at the beginning of his book. Furthermore, in his penulti-
mate paragraph he repeats the neo-classic condemnation though
with suggestion of the other two positions. " In analysing the
Plan and Conduct of this poem, I have so far tried it by epic rules,
as to demonstrate the inconveniencies and incongruities, which the
poet might have avoided, had he been more studious of design and
uniformity. It is true, that his romantic materials claim great
liberties; but no materials exclude order and perspicuity . . . I
have so far conformed to the reigning maxims of modern criticism,
as . . . to recommend classical propriety." [14a] In saying "his romantic materials claim great liberties," Warton seems to touch on
his own earlier suggestion that the *Faerie Queene* should be judged
by more liberal rules than those of neo-classicism; yet he concludes
that, after all allowances have been made, it cannot be brought
into conformity with any just standards. Does he, then, fall back
upon the romantic justification? By no means. " Nothing is more
absurd or useless," he asserted in the Postscript, " than the panegyrical comments of those, who criticise from the imagination
rather than from the judgment, who exert their admiration instead
of their reason, and discover more of enthusiasm than discernment." [15] Yet, useless and absurd as it was, he had done it, just
as he had vaguely held, and probably continued to hold, three

---

[14a] Not in the first edition.   [15] *Ibid.*, II, 263.

conflicting standards of esthetic judgment. In so doing, he showed himself to be much like the rest of us and thoroughly typical of the unsettled, transitional age to which he belonged.

He was an antiquary and a poet with little interest in the problems of literary criticism. The critical theories of his own and the immediately preceding age, he accepted, since they seemed to be in harmony with all the criticism he knew from Aristotle down, but probably gave them little real thought, just as he gave little space in his *Observations* to the subjects with which neo-classic criticism had been chiefly concerned. He seems not to have been analytical or to have cared much for the structural element in art— his own writings are notably lacking in it—but, since something had to be said about the plan and the unity of the *Faerie Queene,* he said it. So slight was his interest in such things that he merely repeated the condemnation of his predecessors, together with the suggestion of one of them that Spenser should not be judged by rules which he did not attend to. In his own words, "I have so far conformed to the reigning maxims of modern criticism, as . . . to recommend classical propriety." Yet his real taste and feelings are to be found in the earlier comment: "We scarcely regret the loss of these [proprieties] while their place is so amply supplied, by something which more powerfully attracts us; something, which engages the affections the feelings of the heart, rather than the cold approbation of the head."

This critical dualism, this sharp separation of judgment from enjoyment vitiates Warton's criticism. A writer who condemns what he really likes and approves of what he is actually indifferent to is a dubious guide in matters of taste. If Warton could have faced the issue squarely with a respect for his true likings and instincts, if he had asked himself, for example: "What are the things that I really like in Spenser? Are these things the bases of great poetry? Should the *Faerie Queene* be judged as a classic epic? How serious are the defects that have been pointed out in its plan? What effect did Spenser try to secure? Did he choose the best means to secure it? Are the effects and the means worthy of great poetry? if he had asked himself such questions and had possessed the ability to discuss them, he would have given us a really important book. But this is demanding too much. The hand of tradition lay heavy upon criticism and could not lightly be shaken off. None of the writers who felt the charm of medieval literature and architecture possessed at once the courage, the inclination, and the ability to furnish a reasoned justification for their novel taste. Certainly the easy-going Thomas Warton was unequal to so difficult a task; he had too much respect for tradition (natural enough in a lover of the past) and too little power of keen, analytical discrimination. Furthermore, it did not trouble him to condemn as a critic what he enjoyed as a reader; he showed no desire to prove that the beggar with whom he had fallen in love was really a princess in disguise.

But did he really think her a beggar, or are his adverse judgments mere lip-service to the authorities? We cannot be sure, but it looks as if the condemnation of Spenser's irregularities, though it did not disturb him, was genuine. As Percy " was long in doubt, whether . . . [the ballads] could be deemed worthy the attention of the public " and hoped " he need not be ashamed of having bestowed some of his idle hours " on them since they " only served as a relaxation from graver studies," [16] so Warton may have regarded Gothic architecture and medieval literature as his hobbies, possibly even as his weaknessess,[17] and not as important enough to be the life work of a serious man. It will be remembered that he had a number of tastes which he presumably did not defend— his fondness for public executions, for the music of a drum, and for the company of Oxford watermen. And the profound respect in which men of the eighteenth-century held high seriousness should never be forgotten; for them, enjoying a poem or a picture was one thing, taking it seriously was quite another. The real loves of Thomas Warton and of many of his contemporaries were degraded to the position of mistresses, to whom they gave most of their free time but for whom they asked toleration, not respect.

[16] Preface to the first edition of the *Reliques*. Percy's deprecatory tone, which reappears in his preface to the fourth edition, is not due solely to mock-humility and to deference to the opinions of others; for if he had respected the ballads as much as he liked them, he would not have garbled them as he did.

[17] Note Percy's words to Pinkerton, " I only considered these things as pardonable, at best, among the levities (I had almost said follies) of my youth " (Nichols's *Illustrations*, VIII, 94). It will be recalled that Johnson enjoyed medieval romances but disapproved of them.

Their homage, their names, their fortunes, their hope of posterity went, in the main, to their conventional wives who came of old families, ladies whom their judgments told them were suitable mates and whom they both admired and liked.

Sir Joshua Reynolds is a striking illustration of this inconsistency. In the *Discourses Delivered in the Royal Academy* he repeatedly warned young artists against the Venetian, Flemish, and Dutch painters; yet it was these painters who roused him to the greatest enthusiasm and who influenced him most profoundly. " Venice never conquered his reason, but she conquered his instincts and feelings and affections, and, for all that reason could do, for thirty years, from his return from Italy until his death, he poured forth work which owes all its power and charm to that very glow and suffusion of colour which year by year he denounced to the pupils of the Royal Academy as a delusion and a snare." [18]   Byron is another instance.   He preached,

> Thou shalt believe in Milton, Dryden, Pope; [19]

yet this very line occurs in a poem as unlike what Milton, Dryden, and Pope wrote as could well be. Byron knew this; he also recognized the greatness of *Don Juan*,[20] and he must have realized that as his poems grew in power they grew away from the works he held as models. He resembles Reynolds and Warton in that he preached and believed one thing but practiced and liked another.

In Warton's case, this inconsistency, this divided allegiance between wife and mistress, appears in the poetry as well as the criticism. " The Suicide," for example, pictures with notable understanding and sympathy the sufferings of an unfortunate, melancholy man who finally makes way with himself. But the poem does not end on the note of sympathy for the sinner. In the last four stanzas a " cherub-voice " speaks reproof and brings the poem into accord with orthodoxy and propriety:

> Forbear, fond bard, thy partial praise;
> Nor thus for guilt in specious lays
> The wreath of glory twine:

---

[18] Preface to the Everyman edition, pp. xiii-xiv.

[19] *Don Juan*, I, ccv; see also his letter to Murray, Sept. 15, 1817.

[20] See his letters to Murray, Aug. 31 and Sept. 4, 1821.

> In vain with hues of gorgeous glow
> Gay Fancy gives her vest to flow,
> Unless Truth's matron-hand the floating folds confine.

Here again Warton straddles. A little conventional morality patched on at the close will, he feels, do no harm and will prevent any possible misunderstanding. He has not thought the matter through and so does not see that his concluding stanzas seriously impair the unity and effectiveness of the poem which owes its original inception and all its vitality to that very sympathy for the sinner which its apparent purpose is to condemn.

A similar attempt to serve both God and Mammon disfigures the ode "Written at Vale-Royal Abbey." The first twenty stanzas of this poem are devoted to a pensive description of the ruins and to wistful imaginings of the days long since departed—harmless enough, it would seem, but the piece is not allowed to end so. Instead, "severer Reason" is brought in to remind us of the "more useful institutes . . . and new civilities" of modern life and of how

> Science, on ampler plume, a bolder flight
> Essays, escap'd from Superstition's shrine;
> While freed Religion, like primeval light
> Bursting from chaos, spreads her warmth divine.

It is safe to say that the poet-professor who rarely went to London but devoted his leisure to ancient manuscripts and medieval ruins had little real concern about "useful institutes" or "new civilities" and that he was more interested in Gothic superstitions than in the science which displaced them; yet, unlike later medievalists, he never asserted and probably would have denied the superiority of the middle ages to the modern. The enlightened eighteenth century was of course better—only he preferred to devote himself to a less civilized period.

Of all the vanished pomps of yesterday, that which seems to have appealed most strongly to Warton was Gothic architecture. Many of his vacations were given over to visiting old churches and castles and to making notes on them in preparation for an extensive work on medieval buildings. Like almost everything else he wrote, his poems give abundant evidence of this enthusiasm; yet they also leave no doubt that he regarded the Gothic as inferior to the classic. In the "Ode for Music," written in

1751, when he was only twenty-three, he says of the Oxford buildings:

> Nor wants there Graecia's better part,
> 'Mid the proud piles of ancient art,
> Whose fretted spires, with ruder hand,
> Wainflet and Wickham bravely plann'd.[21]

and thirty-one years later, in one of his last pieces, he not only condemns but ridicules the noble art which had been his study and his diversion in countless happy hours. So great an apostasy could not have sprung simply from seeing the pretty windows which Sir Joshua Reynolds painted for New College, Oxford. These were only the occasion which brought out once more the fundamental antagonism between what Warton liked and what his reason approved of, and again the palm was given to reason. " Ah, stay," he cries,

> Ah, stay thy treacherous hand, forbear to trace
> Those faultless forms of elegance and grace!

After a most sympathetic picture of the pleasure he has found in Gothic buildings, he again addresses the painter:

> Ah, spare the weakness of a lover's heart!
> Chase not the phantoms of my fairy dream,
> Phantoms that shrink at Reason's painful gleam!

Yet " of ravish'd pleasures why complain? " He acknowledges the " chaste design "

> The just proportion, and the genuine line;
> Those native portraitures of Attic art

of Reynolds's work and exclaims

> Thy powerful hand has broke the Gothic chain,
> And brought my bosom back to truth again;

---

[21] Compare the ode *On his Majesty's Birthday, 1785*, 21-36, especially the following:

> 'Tis his [the king's] to judgment's steady line
> Their [the arts'] flights fantastic to confine . . .
> And bind capricious Taste in Truth's eternal chain.
> Sculpture, licentious now no more,
> From Greece her great example takes . . .
> In native beauty simply plann'd,
> Corinth, thy tufted shafts ascend.

> To truth, by no peculiar taste confin'd,
> Whose universal pattern strikes mankind . . .
> To truth, whose charms deception's magic quell,
> And bind coy Fancy in a stronger spell.

He now finds humor in the "brawny prophets," the proud saints,
the fiercely-frowning virgins, and the mundane angels of Medieval
stained glass and bids them

> No more the sacred window's round disgrace,
> But yield to Grecian groupes the shining space.[22]

The point should be stressed; Warton ridiculed medieval stained
glass, its colors as well as its drawing, and wished it banished from
churches! Surely the force of reason could no further go! The
explanation is obvious: by no conceivable distortion of the canons
of classic art as they were then understood could highly-colored
windows filled with naïve, confusing, badly-drawn details be
justified. They could not be brought into the fold as Addison
had brought "Chevy Chase" and the "Children in the Wood;"
they must be justified in accordance with another aesthetic or
abandoned. Warton abandoned them. Their beauty, the pleasure
he had for years found in them, the importance of their contribu-

---

[22] It should be noted that Warton, who edited Greek texts and was one
of the most learned men of his day, speaks of "Attic" and "Grecian,"
not of classic or Roman art. Yet, while the lower tier of Sir Joshua's
windows may well be termed "classic" or "neo-classic," there is little in
any of them to recall the Greek. The largest was suggested by the
Nativity ("La Notte") of Correggio, surely one of the least Attic of
painters. Similarly the Radcliffe Camera, referred to as the contribution
of "Graecia's better part," is an eighteenth-century English adaptation
of Polladio's sixteenth-century Italian adaptation of the Roman, and in
spirit is scarcely more like the Parthenon than are the best cathedrals.
But of Greek architecture and sculpture little was known in Warton's day,
or, indeed, could have been known except by the rare traveller who went
to Greece itself. Not until 1815, when the Elgin marbles were first exhibited (the pediment from Aegina and the frieze from Phigaleia became
known about the same time), did Western Europe see any significant
number of important originals from the best period of Greek art. Those
we treasure most, aside from the Parthenon sculptures, were not yet ex-
cavated. As a result, the seventeenth and eighteenth centuries derived
their ideas of classic sculpture, buildings, and, to a considerable extent, of
poetry from the Romans, whose forte was not the arts.

tion to Gothic interiors—all these were as nothing in the face of their non-conformity.

Reynolds's " Grecian groups " did not seem to the laureate out of place in a Gothic church. On the contrary, their presence suggested that a happy union might be made of antique and medieval art. It was Reynolds's achievement

> Not of its pomp to strip this ancient shrine,
> But bid that pomp with purer radiance shine:
> With arts unknown before, to reconcile
> The willing Graces to the Gothic pile.

Warton does not stress the point, which may be little more than a graceful compliment; and there is no reason to believe that he had thought much about it or dreamed of a higher synthesis of the two styles.[23] He loved the Gothic but realized that it did not conform to the classic principles. Could it not be made to conform by the use of such expedients as " Greek " windows? What he had in mind was merely a superficial tinkering or patching up which should not interfere with the charm or the essential character of the medieval church but which should satisfy the rules. Such an attitude is typical of the man. To the last he remained true to the orthodox, neo-classic principles and at the same time a devoted admirer of medieval art which those principles condemned. The condemnation apparently troubled him little; it seems not to have interfered with his enjoyment and certainly did not drive him to any thorough-going examination of the bases of his taste. Criticism he seems to have regarded as a kind of intellectual golf, a game in excellent repute, played according to somewhat arbitrary rules of its own, but quite apart from the realities of life. If he had really grasped the principle underlying his oft-quoted assertion of the folly of " judging either Ariosto or Spenser by precepts which they did not attend to" he would not have condemned Gothic architecture as a " fond illusion " but would have come to see that it has its own laws, its own " reason," " truth," and " just proportion " quite as much as does the Greek.

" It may be," some one will perhaps reply, " but what of it? Do Warton's opinions matter much any way? " To which we may

---

[23] Miss Rinaker (*Thomas Warton*, 139), thinks otherwise.

4

answer with a paradox "which comforts while it mocks" that the truth of Warton's opinions does not matter but their inconsistences and other limitations do. We read the *Observations* and the "Verses on Reynolds's Window," not for light on the *Faerie Queene* or on Gothic architecture, but on a subject about which we know much less,—the mid eighteenth-century. If we are ever to understand this period, it will be through a careful study of such typical figures as Thomas Warton, a study, not only of their successes, but of their failures, a study which does not overlook their conventionality and conservatism in its search for originality and liberalism. Such a study will convince us of the impossibility of tagging the writers of the time as "romantic" or "classic." We have seen that the "Pleasures of Melancholy" is in the main pseudo-romantic, that its author's critical position is usually neo-classic, and had we discussed his best poems, we should have found that in them romantic strains predominate. Even true classicism might be discovered in his Latin poetry and his editions of the Greek anthology and of Theocritus. Yet in everything he wrote, characteristics may be discovered that are usually termed neo-classic, together with other characteristics commonly called romantic. Frequently the two are to be found on the same page, often in the same sentence. But, although evidence of both these qualities, is abundant, there is no warrant for attaching to Thomas Warton the epithet which is often associated with his name,—that of rebel.

The Johns Hopkins University.

EDWARD N. HOOKER

The Purpose of Dryden's 'Annus Mirabilis'

from

THE HUNTINGTON LIBRARY QUARTERLY

Volume X(1946), 49-67

The Purpose of Dryden's *Annus Mirabilis*

By Edward N. Hooker

I

D RYDEN's first long narrative poem appears so simple and lucid that nobody has seen fit to be puzzled concerning its intention. Yet its purpose has been generally misinterpreted, and our failure to catch its main intent has led to a false emphasis upon certain features of it and a mistaken evaluation of its proper intellectual and therefore esthetic effect.

Perhaps Dryden himself is partly responsible for the errors of critics concerning his poem, because he calls it "historical, not epic," in that it exhibits "but broken action, tied too severely to the laws of history"[1]—that is, it relates, without poetic fiction, things which actually happened, and in the order in which they happened. Furthermore, he says in his dedication to the city of London and its official representatives, "To you, therefore, this Year of Wonders is justly dedicated, because you have made it so; you, who are to stand a wonder to all years and ages; and who have built yourselves an immortal monument on your own ruins." *Annus Mirabilis*, then, is not merely an historical poem, but also a panegyric inspired by the vigor, courage, and resourcefulness of the metropolis.

So critics have understood it—where they have taken the trouble to discuss what seems almost too plain to invite discussion. Dr. Johnson took the work to be a simple historical poem, in which Dryden "had subjects equal to his abilities, a great naval war and the Fire of London." What can be expected of such an undertaking, thought Dr. Johnson, is a series of vivid pictures of scenes and events; and the great fault which he found with the poem as a whole is that the author "affords more sentiments than description, and does not so much impress scenes upon the fancy, as deduce

---

[1] "An Account of the Ensuing Poem," prefixed to *Annus Mirabilis*.

49

consequences and make comparisons."[2] To Mark Van Doren *Annus Mirabilis* "was almost the last echo of Lucan in English," a narrative poem that was "not a tale but a chronicle."[3] He also recognizes that it is a panegyrical poem, continuing the strain sounded previously in "To His Sacred Majesty" and "To My Lord Chancellor"; and that the panegyrical strain gives it a kind of unity, culminating nicely in the prophecy concerning London's future greatness. The poem is, says Van Doren in summary, "Dryden's most ambitious official compliment."[4] That, and nothing more? It is difficult to become excited over a poem with so simple a design, even if it is the work of a major poet.

But one may be sure that Dryden had something else in his mind when he wrote. In fact, he himself tells us as much, in words that meant far more to his contemporaries than they do to men of today. He dedicates his poem to the City, whose fame and glory have been dearly won in three terrible "trials": an expensive war, "a consuming pestilence," and "a more consuming fire." Now "trials" are the afflictions which God sends down upon the virtuous to test and *strengthen* them. Having introduced his explanation for the calamities of London, Dryden continues:

To submit yourselves with that humility to the judgments of heaven, and, at the same time, to raise yourselves with that vigour above all human enemies; to be combated at once from above, and from below; to be struck down, and to triumph,—I know not whether such trials have been ever paralleled in any nation: the resolution and successes of them never can be.

Here he repeats his theme with a slight variation; it is the City's rise through "trials" to strength and success.

But in the variation there is a significant word, which appears once and is quickly brushed away. The citizens had submitted themselves "to the *judgments* of heaven." *Judgments* suggest something quite different from *trials*, for a judgment, in the parlance of popular theology, is a punishment for grievous sins, as well as a warning of God's wrath to come if the sufferers continue in evil-

[2] Life of Dryden, in *Works of Johnson*, ed. Murphy (1824), VI, 376-77.

[3] *The Poetry of John Dryden* (Cambridge, Eng., 1931), p. 218.

[4] *Ibid.*, p. 118.

doing. Having barely suggested that idea, Dryden seems immediately to reject it, returning a few phrases later to interpreting London's calamities as *trials*. Later the City's troubles are referred to as "sufferings" and "afflictions." Lest anyone miss his intention Dryden puts it bluntly: the plague and the fire "are not more the effects of God's displeasure (frequent examples of them having been in the reign of the most excellent princes) than occasions for the manifesting of your christian and civil virtues."

By this time the careful reader has begun to suspect that there were men engaged in representing London's calamities as *judgments* inflicted upon a sinful people, and that Dryden was anxious to interpret the events in a different way. The latter part of the dedication presents three reasons why the disasters could not have been judgments. First, "heaven never made so much piety and virtue to leave it miserable." Second, virtuous individuals may end unhappily, but there is no example of virtuous nations coming to that fate. And third, the Providence which granted spectacular success to the country's naval forces could not intend utterly to ruin that nation at home. From these considerations Dryden arrives at the conclusion that the City's afflictions have been merely trials, which are now ended; and that it will speedily arise, like the phoenix, from its own ashes.

At this point we may state the problem. Why was Dryden anxious to show that what some men had construed as *judgments* consisted only of a series of *trials*? Who were the men thus bent upon seeing in London's woes the signs of God's wrath foretokening utter ruin? Why did these men insist upon this interpretation of the plague and fire? And finally, in view of the fact that Dryden intimates a clear connection, why were the misfortunes of the City taken to be an omen of the nation's doom?

The answers to these questions are to be found in history. After we have set them forth, we shall inquire how they affect our reading of Dryden's poem.

II

How did Dryden and his party view the course of events from the Restoration up to the Year of Wonders? Some light will be thrown upon their attitude by Bishop Parker, whose *De rebus sui temporis commentariorum libri quatuor* was published in 1726, and in the following year translated into English by Thomas Newlin. One would not go to Parker for an impartial summary of historical events in the Restoration, for he was a fierce royalist and a somewhat heated Churchman, who hated all Cromwellians, resented all dissenters, and opposed Comprehension and Toleration to the top of his bent. But he represents, in however inflated the form, many of the attitudes and beliefs which prevailed among the court party, with which Dryden had identified himself.

We learn at once from Parker that despite the apparently universal rejoicing that accompanied the return of Charles II, all was not peace and harmony. Various dissident groups still remained, and still cherished their hopes for a happy commonwealth, for a kingdom of God on earth, or at least for a place where one might worship without oppression or restraint. It is understandable that the harmony of the realm did not improve when it became evident that the spirit of the Declaration of Breda was not to be carried into effect, and the conduct of hundreds of ejected ministers, who braved poverty and ruin rather than to conform, shows that the courage to resist was not dead.

More specifically, however, Bishop Parker informs us that in the early years of the Restoration a good deal of agitation was stirring against the government. During these years, he says, innumerable libels of a seditious kind were published by republicans and dissenters, and of these the most flagrantly seditious were fantastic accounts of prodigies, omens, and portents from sky and sea, monstrous births and marvellous occurrences by land, all of them construed as dire warnings of the impending wrath of God, of divine judgments to be visited upon an erring nation.[5] And the title prefixed to these rebellious pamphlets recounting the aberrations of nature, was *Annus Mirabilis!*[6]

Was it a strange coincidence that Dryden in 1667 made use of a title which opponents of the Church and government had employed in their propaganda only a few years previously? Let us

[5] *Bishop Parker's History of His Own Time*, trans. Thomas Newlin (1727), pp. 23-25.
[6] *Ibid.*, p. 26.

look at the "seditious libels" which aroused such contempt, hatred, and fear in the doughty Bishop of Oxford.

Parker intimates that there were several, but only three such pamphlets seem to be extant, and only two of them are listed in Wing's Short-Title Catalogue.[7] The first was called *Mirabilis Annus, the Year of Prodigies*, and was published in 1661. The second, appearing in 1662, was entitled *Mirabilis Annus Secundus; or, The Second Year of Prodigies*. The third, printed late in 1662 and not long after the second, was called *Mirabilis Annus Secundus: or, the Second Part of the Second Years Prodigies*. All three of them omit the names of printer and publisher on the title pages—a caution undoubtedly well taken.

The first of these tracts included over a hundred accounts of strange apparitions and prodigious events, with frequent mention of the names of the persons concerned as well as of the places and dates of occurrences. There is no doubt whatever of the strong seditious tendency of the work; it was carefully calculated to arouse discontent against the Church and against the King and his ministers who supported the Church. To make it perfectly obvious that the omens should be regarded as a warning to the nation of judgments to come for their enduring an iniquitous monarch and an oppressive establishment, the tract included a collection of historical parallels pointing to national calamity, to the downfall of a monarch, and to civil war.

A general hue and cry followed the distribution of this pamphlet, and the cries of sedition were so loud that apparently some of the dissenters themselves were offended or alarmed by the work of their party. So much is indicated by the Preface to the second tract, the author or authors of which attempt (probably disingenuously) to disclaim any connection with or responsibility for the previous publication. After asserting that the stories related in the first *Mirabilis Annus* were largely true, the Preface goes on to dis-

---

[7]Edmond Malone first called attention to the fact that Dryden's title was not new and that a "prose tract thus entitled was published in 1662" (*Critical and Miscellaneous Prose Works of Dryden*, II, 249), but neither he nor any succeeding editor has commented on the tract or related it to Dryden's purpose in composing the poem.

cuss the charge of sedition which had been brought against the authors of that tract:

. . . we shall only say, That if any such thing were intended or designed by them, we cannot but openly testifie our Abhorrency of such Practices. The publishing of the Works of God ought not by any means to be made use of as a project to further and promote that which is so plainly repugnant to the Word of God. And we do ingenuously confess (though the Authors design might be never so innocent) yet that Collection of Parallels might well have been spared, in regard there was at least *an appearance* of ground for all those Imputations which were cast upon the *Book* and the *Author* also for their sakes.

As to the innocence of his own intentions the writer of the Preface wants nobody to be confused:

And truly, we can appeal to the *all-knowing God*, that our design is not to stir up any to *Sedition*, but seasonable *Repentance;* not to *Treason* against *man*, but *Loyalty* and *Subjection* to JESUS CHRIST. . . .

These are fair words, but the contents of the tract do not bear them out. The amazing tales are so slanted as to make it apparent that God's wrath is directed at the King and his Church. We are told, for example, of a special church-service in which an uncanny magpie by its inspired chattering confounded the prelatical parson in his attempts to deliver a sermon, and threw the bishop into confusion when he proposed to dismiss the congregation; the point of the story is made unmistakable by the information that the congregation and clergy had been summoned to the service to express their affections to the King.[8] Equally pointed is the account of the great storm that occurred on Tuesday, February 18, 1661. During the storm the Great Fane at Whitehall was blown down, the triumphal arches erected throughout London in honor of the King were shattered and torn, and from the arch in Leadenhall-street the King's Arms were wrenched loose and demolished.[9] Who could mistake such warnings?

The import of the third pamphlet is not less obvious. It was brought out under the same authorship, and it consisted of a batch of prodigies that had been left over from the previous publication.

[8]*Mirabilis Annus Secundus; or; the Second Year of Prodigies* (1662), p. 45.
[9]*Ibid.*, p. 59.

Three examples will illustrate the meaning which contemporaries found lurking in the work.

On April 13, 1662, we are told, the famous preacher Robert South of Christ Church, Oxford, delivered a sermon before the King at Whitehall. Just as he reached that moment when he would assert that the era of the late Rebellion was not a happier period than the present, he was stricken with a Qualm and forced to leave the pulpit.[10]

An even clearer manifestation of the anti-monarchical sentiments of the tract is found in the story of the two wastrels who made their way to Tyburn to witness the execution of three regicides, Berkstead, Okey, and Cobbet. After the execution, finding a portion of Colonel Berkstead's liver near the fire where his bowels were to be incinerated, one of the rascals seized the liver, wrapped it in a cloth, and along with his companion betook himself speedily to a tavern. Here the precious pair managed to get roaringly drunk, and in their riotous mirth they placed the Colonel's liver on the coals and, after it was sufficiently toasted, soon fell to consuming their unconventional feast. Then the bolt fell. Both were stricken at once; one died a few hours later, and the other seemed not like to continue long in this world. Thus God avenged a regicide![11]

Our third example is a direct, grim warning, though it has an overtone of humor for the modern reader. In October, 1662, great stores of mackerel were caught by the fishermen. So plentiful was the catch "that they have been sold in *Cheapside*-Market at reasonable rates; a thing which hath rarely happened heretofore, but upon some signal Changes and Revolutions."[12]

Such were the prodigies related of the years immediately following the return of Charles II. With Charles had come Maypoles and the spirit of Merry England, but the authors of the tracts were not primarily concerned with the frailties of the Old Adam in us; they were intent on bigger game. The prodigies were set forth as prophecies, giving fair warning of approaching judgments upon

[10]*Mirabilis Annus Secundus: or, the Second Part of the Second Years Prodigies* (1662), pp. 32-33.
[11]*Ibid.*, pp. 35-36.
[12]*Ibid.*, pp. 25-26.

a nation for tolerating an iniquitous monarch and oppressive clergy, or heralding "some signal Changes and Revolutions." In short, they led the people to expect disaster and civil war if they continued to submit to the Stuart regime.

These pamphlets, then, were alarming enough in themselves. But there was a special reason why they must have been feared: for years the minds of the people had been conditioned to expect disasters of extraordinary reach, which were to occur in the 1660's. The number of the year 1666 seemed to be fraught with supernatural significance, partly because 666 had the properties of a mystic symbol, and partly because 666 is mentioned in the very obscure "prophecy" of Revelations 13:18. A judicious and learned man like Selden could write upon this Scriptural passage without pretending to lay bare the future, but the temptation was too much for lesser minds. William Lilly, the famous astrologer, basing his foresight squarely upon both astrology and the Bible, predicted a series of broils and tumults to follow upon 1660 and to end, in 1666, in the pulverization of all false religions.[13] He could be even more specific. After examining a number of old prophecies, he arrived at the conviction that "in 1666. there will be no King here, or pretending to the Crowne of England."[14] Such predictions prepared the minds of Dryden's contemporaries to detect the republican odor in warnings concerning the horrible turmoil that lay in wait for England in the 1660's.

The ground, then, was made ready. But how effective were the *Mirabilis Annus* tracts themselves? Quite apart from Bishop Parker's rage, which indicates that they were considered dangerous, there is good reason for believing that friends of King and Church were perturbed.[15] In 1663, a year after the publication of the *Mirabilis Annus Secundus*, John Spencer, fellow of Corpus Christi in Cambridge, published *A Discourse concerning Prodigies*, a work of notable wit and learning, the success of which warranted a cor-

[13]*The Worlds Catastrophe* (1647), pp. 32-34.

[14]*Monarchy or No Monarchy* (1651), p. 57.

[15]The political unrest brought about by purposeful or irresponsible "vulgar prophecies" had been recognized in the sixteenth century, and laws were passed making them serious offenses. Cf. Thomas Tomkis, *Albumazar*, ed. Hugh Dick (Berkeley, 1944), Introduction, pp. 25-29.

rected and enlarged edition two years later. The author was no ordinary man. An eminent and erudite Hebraist, he was largely responsible for constructing the foundation on which the science of comparative religion was erected. Not only was he a follower of Bacon, and strongly sympathetic with the new movement in natural philosophy, but he was also a writer skilled in that style of urbane raillery which suited so well the cultivated Restoration taste. Two years after the second edition of his *Discourse* he was elected Master of Corpus Christi College by unanimous vote. Such a man would probably not have undertaken the book if the subject had not appeared important and the occasion serious.

That Spencer when he assumed his task had in mind the series of pamphlets called *Mirabilis Annus* is made manifest by his prefatory remark:

That which further engaged my thoughts upon the Argument, was a consideration of the *Seasonableness thereof.* We have been of late perswaded by three or four several impressions of Books (more then were ever vented in any Ethnick or Christian Common-wealth in a much larger period of time) that *England* is grown *Africa,* and presents us every year since the Return of His Majesty, with a new Scene of Monstrous and strange sights; and all held forth to the people, like black clouds before a storm, the harbingers of some strange and unusual plagues approaching in the State.[16]

Furthermore, he was convinced of the rebellious designs of the individuals who were circulating the tracts and eagerly devouring their contents. All such sullen murmuring, false reports, rumors, and libels hovering about the tales of prodigies and omens, he described briefly as "feminine sedition." They were the products of malcontents, lusting for revolution. Only when men are sick of the present times, he said, do they long for variety and look to prophecies and signs which seem to give them hopes and promises of a change.

As *Nature* hath seated in some bodies a kind of restless desire of change, and motion from their present state; so *humor,* or interest, hath placed in some minds a kind of perpetual motion, an eternal desire of change and alteration: And therefore *Prophecies, Omens, Stories of Prodigies,* shall be readily attended *to* and contended *for,* for these things feed

[16]*Discourse concerning Prodigies* (2d ed., 1665), sig. a5r.-v.

that humor; because encouraging in losers the hopes of a better game by some new shuffling and cutting, and in all persons not pleased with what pleaseth God, of a great change of Affairs in State.[17]

Reports of omens and prodigies are "symptomes of that common itch in men to tell strange stories," but these "camel-stories" are also dangerous. Therefore, by undermining their authority, Spencer proposed to secure the peace and tranquility of common life, to maintain the honor of religion (as against superstition, which he defines as religion scared out of its wits), and "to serve the just interest of State." In attacking superstitious prophecy he assumes the stand of scientist and philosopher. As scientist he affirmed his belief in the faithfulness of nature to its original laws of motion. What appears to be a "signal," or warning, prodigy is merely an event about the causes of which we are ignorant; a result of some unusual impediment in the course of nature, which yet does not destroy nature's general constancy and harmony. Why, he asks, would God interrupt nature in her regular motions in order to provide warning to those stiff-necked creatures who refuse to heed either the great examples of divine justice in the Bible, or the sermons of His clergy, or the lash of private afflictions? As a philosopher he adhered to the chain-of-being theory, which, interestingly enough, he employed to support his scientific assumptions; for the chain-of-being idea denies that any one event or phenomenon can be interpreted out of its context in the universal system. The diversity of men's minds, the "elegant variety of Beings in the world," and the "grateful disparity of occurrences which the history of every age of the world entertains us with," all warn us against the danger of drawing dogmatic conclusions from isolated or few or unrelated instances. Thus Spencer empties the "signal" prodigy of all significance.

There remained the "penal" prodigy, or judgment, and this was a subject far more gnarled and knotty, for the tradition of centuries had accustomed men to look upon certain dreadful and unusual events such as the defeat of armies, the devastations of the plague, and the coming of lean or unseasonable years, as punishments inflicted upon a nation for its iniquities. Moreover, Dryden

[17]*Ibid.*, p. 407.

and his contemporaries were all familiar with tales of God's judgments falling upon the sinful, upon the profane swearer and the Sabbath-breaker—illustrations of divine wrath such as one may find in *The Life and Death of Mr. Badman*. Against the overcredulous faith in judgments Spencer points out simply, "God often blasts the cause of truth and goodness by adverse Providences."[18] Because we know not His purposes, it is a dangerous kind of effrontery to set up our private interpretation of God's judgments as a criterion of right and wrong superior to His precepts and to the commands of His representatives on earth—especially as our interpretation will be based on self-interest or party bias. So Spencer pleads:

It were therefore heartily to be wish'd, that men had that *largeness of heart*, as not to think Heaven and Earth concerned in the standing or falling of their little Interests, Forms, and Opinions; that they would leave off (that worst kind of inclosure) the intailing Salvation soly upon their own party, and not go about to hedg in the Holy Dove, by appropriating the graces and influences thereof to themselves.[19]

In short, "The Ends of the Divine Judgments being thus various and unsearchable, they cannot be preferred Rules of trial in any sacred or civil differences. . . ."[20]

The restlessness and perturbation which Spencer had sensed when he published his *Discourse concerning Prodigies* in 1663 did not subside. In 1665 he wrote:

'Tis a time wherein (as 'tis usual) *Folly* is as busy as *Wisdom*. Never greater talk of terrible *Signs, Revelations, Prophecies and Visions* in our own and other Kingdoms then now.[21]

Up until the time of the great plague in 1665, we see, the air was full of rumors concerning strange prodigies and omens, which all pointed toward terrible judgments to be heaped upon the nation. Under the burden of this expectation it was obvious that if national disasters occurred many people would interpret them as God's punishment administered to a people who had turned from

[18]*Ibid.*, p. 357.
[19]*Ibid.*, p. 370.
[20]*Ibid.*, p. 367.
[21]*A Discourse concerning Vulgar Prophecies* (1665), p. 6. This work was issued with and bound up with the second edition of the *Discourse concerning Prodigies*.

Him toward pleasures and evil kings and an oppressive episcopacy. It seemed possible that in a crisis the King and Church might fall. What could be done to dissuade the people from resting their faith on judgments?

This problem was complicated by the fact that even the clergy of the Established Church were divided in their opinions of judgments. The distinguished Dr. Isaac Barrow in his "Sermon on the King's Happy Return" warned of the heinous provocations that lay in the dissoluteness of the times, and he urged that we have reason to be fearful of God's just displeasure.[22] Yet, like John Spencer, he condemned the assurance of bold men who professed to read God's intentions with certainty; and in his sermon called "The Unsearchableness of God's Judgments" he remarked that God may act upon rules too profound or subtle for our weak intellects. Such rules

we may not be able to perceive from the Meanness of our Nature, or our low Rank among Creatures; for beneath Omniscience there being innumerable Forms of Intelligence, in the lowest of these we sit, one Remove from Beasts. . . .[23]

We must therefore conclude nothing from judgments. (It is interesting to note that, again like Spencer, Barrow employs the chain-of-being theory to combat the popular inclination to prophesy from judgments.)

But on the other hand, that mighty preacher, ex-Presbyterian, and future Archbishop of Canterbury, John Tillotson, saw in the judgment an unmistakable sign of God's will and intention. In a sermon called "Of the End of Judgments, and the Reason of their Continuance," preached in 1667, he proclaimed that the plague of 1665 and the fire of 1666 had unquestionably been judgments of God upon England because the nation had turned away from Him; and because after those calamities the nation returned to its evil ways, a third judgment, the sally of the Dutch fleet up the Thames, had descended upon the people.[24]

It is hardly necessary to prove that the puritans of the day were quick to recognize the calamities of 1665-1667 as visitations of

[22]*Works*, ed. Tillotson (3 vols., 1700), I, 126.
[23]*Ibid.*, III, 229.
[24]Tillotson, *Works* (3 vols. 1752), I, 84-85.

God. Their own historian, Daniel Neal, proclaimed that the oppressions of the magistrates and the vices of the nation brought down the judgments of heaven upon England, and he listed the judgments: the Dutch war, the plague, and the fire.[25] The political excitement was intense, and the danger acute (or so it seemed). We know that, during the Dutch war, government circles were fearful lest the dissenters should rise in support of their co-religionists in Holland.[26] And we know that during this time there was a resurgence of strength and courage among the Presbyterians (partly because of their successful ministry during the plague) and that parliament viewed the trend with concern.[27] In this general state of tension and horrified anticipation Samuel Pepys entered in his Diary, on February 25, 1665/66, a record of a conversation which he had had with Lord Sandwich: "He dreads the issue of this year, and fears there will be some very great revolutions before his coming back again."

We are now better able to answer certain questions concerning Dryden's aims in the writing of *Annus Mirabilis*. As early as 1661 a group of sober citizens, clearly opposed to the Church, some of them anti-monarchical, thinking wistfully of the good old days and the good old cause, some of them restive and sullen under the oppressions of government and magistrates, some of them pious souls genuinely horrified at the wanton conduct of King and clergy and the effect of this upon the common people, published a series of anonymous pamphlets, issued without imprint, describing many "signal" prodigies that warned of approaching judgments or heralded "some signal Changes and Revolutions." They were understood by the court party to be seditious, and their effect upon the people was feared. One effect which they had was to lead the English people to expect some sort of national calamity, which would appear as heaven's condemnation of the government and Church; and with such an appearance of divine encouragement a rebellious people might rise again, as they had twenty-five years previously.

[25]*History of the Puritans* (2 vols., N.Y., 1871), II, 252-58.

[26]Von Ranke, *History of England, principally in the Seventeenth Century*, (6 vols., Oxford, 1875), III, 433.

[27]*Ibid.*, pp. 447-48.

The pamphlets were loaded with dynamite, because they strongly recalled and reinforced old prophecies, superstitions, and astrological predictions. Measures were taken, therefore, to counter their influence. Some friends of the court undertook to explain that the judgments of God were unsearchable and that He visited His wrath alike upon the wicked and the righteous; which is to say, that a calamity might be no judgment at all but only an accident of nature, or that it might be a trial to afflict the virtuous. Yet even some of the clergy of the Established Church feared judgments and expected them. The air was tense, and nerves were quivering. Then fell the first blow: the plague, in 1665. Out of it the Presbyterians emerged with heightened prestige and courage. In 1666 came the great fire of London. Besides, there was the costly and indecisive war with the Dutch. London, of course, was the seat of government and the source of England's power as well. If these calamities of the City betokened God's displeasure, then indeed the regime was doomed.

It was at this juncture that Dryden stepped forward and, taking over *the very title* of the seditious tracts, composed a poem to show that the disasters were merely trials (or, if they were allowed to be judgments, then they were judgments upon a people for persisting in their old spirit of rebellion against their rightful sovereign); to show that the disasters were but momentary interruptions in the path to wealth and glory, and that they had served to draw the King and his people together in the bonds of mutual suffering and affection. Such was Dryden's answer to the disaffected and seditious. Such was *Annus Mirabilis*. It stands as a political document as well as a poem, and it is remarkably adroit. Only a short while after it was published Dryden was nominated to the dignity of poet laureate.

III

How does this explanation of Dryden's intention affect our reading of the poem? Without attempting a detailed and exhaustive analysis, it may be profitable to note something of the poet's plan and maneuvering.

In the first place, it is obvious that Dryden is not writing an historical poem about a *Year* of Wonders, for the action begins with York's naval victory of June 3, 1665, and continues through the time of the great fire, which started on the night of September 1 and burned on until September 6, 1666. Nor is he writing of the *Wonders* of that period, for he religiously avoids the great plague, which reared up in June, 1665, and raged until January of the following year—a visitation more terrible and wonderful than the events described in the poem. Nor is the poet composing a panegyric to the city of London, because the praise of the City for its courage, enterprise, and loyalty occupies a relatively insignificant place in the poem.

Why he omitted an account of the plague is easy to understand. It was an unmitigated disaster, and he was much concerned to prevent emphasis upon this aspect of history. Moreover, he could not have welded it into his plan without ridiculously distorting the truth, for the King and his officials had been unheroic and many of the divines of the Church had shamefully deserted their posts. The plague was better left untreated.

Dryden's plan will be clearer if we outline the divisions of the poem.

I. (stanzas 1-12) An account of the importance of trade to England, together with an explanation of the necessity for the war against the Dutch.

II. (st. 13-18) A sketch of the preparations for the war, emphasizing the King's genius in naval affairs and the auspicious signs.

III. (st. 19-23) A relation of the first naval battle and York's great victory, a sign that heaven favors the cause of Charles II.

IV. (st. 24-31) The story of the attempt at Bergen, together with an illustration of the riches to be got by trade.

V. (st. 32-38) A digression on the vanity of human wishes—and the vanity of foreign alliances; leading up to

VI. (st. 39-45) A view of the sinister designs of France; and the harshness of the French king contrasted with the mercy and virtue of Charles II.

VII. (st. 46-53) An account of the preparations for battle, with praise of the English leaders, both favorites of fortune.

VIII. (st. 54-137) Story of the four-day naval battle, with praise for the generosity, courage, and virtue of the English leaders.

IX. (st. 138-154) An account of the return and repair of the ships, the skill of shipwrights and the genius of the King, and the inscrutable designs of heaven and kings, who must be obeyed without question.

X. (st. 155-166) A digression on the history of shipping, with praise for English enterprise and the practical contributions of the Royal Society to navigation.

XI. (st. 167-208) An account of the naval battle and victory, with an illustration of the riches to be found in commerce.

XII. (st. 209-282) Description of the fire, and the King's valiant efforts in behalf of his people.

XIII. (st. 283-291) Praise of the King's bounty, the loyalty and devotion of the people, and their determination to end the war in victory.

XIV. (st. 292-304) A vision of the future glory of London, greater than before: a symbol of the wealth and power of England—all this possible if the people obey their King and support the war to a victorious conclusion.

The seditious tracts which Dryden was answering agreed that the approaching disasters which would fall upon the nation were provoked by the iniquities of state and Church, of the King and his leaders. In reading *Annus Mirabilis* one cannot help noticing that the King and his chosen leaders are carefully represented as great and noble, and all splendid achievements are credited to them. The King himself is portrayed as a natural leader with a special genius in naval undertakings; he has extraordinary discrimination in selecting his admirals, he is generous and bountiful, vigilant in watching over his people, and wise in his provision for them; and, above all, his wisdom and virtue establish him (as if his divine right were not enough!) as the favorite of heaven.

Dryden's insistence that heaven and fortune are on the side of Charles could not be overlooked. The King's very birth was auspicious (st. 18); the fact that the Duke of York won the first notable victory of the war shows that heaven intended conquest to stem from the royal line (st. 19); the Dutch themselves in this battle had to acknowledge that heaven was present to favor the English fleet (st. 22); Charles's chosen leaders, Rupert and Albemarle, are favorites of nature and fortune (st. 49); the Duke reminds the sailors that heaven has chosen them to uphold the glory of Great

Britain (st. 75); fate has pledged the victory to the King (st. 81); the fates of Charles and his two admirals led the fleet irresistibly to victory (st. 191); the great fire is halted by a miracle, following upon the King's prayer (st. 271, 283); and the King supplies God's own place in his mercy and bounty to the distressed (st. 286). Thus Dryden opposes the superstitious acceptance of the vulgar prophecies.

So exalted a notion of the King and his chosen leaders stands in sharp contrast with Dryden's picture of the English people, who appear admirable only when they exhibit their loyalty and obedience to the King, and when they exert those talents for trade and shipping which can be given scope only by the fulfillment of the King's great design. By a dexterous twist the two comets which at the start give promise (apparently) of glorious success to Charles's arms (st. 18), later become dire influences accompanying God's wrath against the town (st. 291). In so far as the fire might be thought of as a manifestation of God's wrath, it was directed, not against the King or state, but against the people. It began, Dryden explains carefully, in the "mean buildings" of the town, and it was never allowed to touch the King's palace or his naval magazines, and only by the King's prayer was it finally checked. True, the flames were allowed to destroy St. Paul's, but Dryden intimates that the destruction came about only because the great church had been debased by rebellion and profaned by civil war. He does not tell us who started the fire, but in the exquisite stanza describing the ghosts of the regicides descending from the Bridge he lets us know what sort of people would rejoice in the fire. While the King in the midst of the conflagration was weeping with pity and exercising his fatherly care, what were the London crowds doing? Why, the wealthy were bribing the poor to assist them in saving their possessions, and the poor were haggling and bargaining for a higher price: "So void of pity is th' ignoble crowd. . . ." It was clearly on account of the sins of the people that punishment had fallen upon London.

But Dryden was not interested greatly in scolding the Londoners; it was rather his aim to enlist them in support of their King. He intimates quietly that the ignoble crowd had sinned grievously (that crowd which had driven the young Charles into exile, and which perhaps had circulated the very pamphlets from which the poet derived the title of his work). But the wrath which their errors had drawn upon them was not a wrath aimed to destroy. It was to purge them of their vices and tie them in tighter bonds of love and loyalty to their sovereign; it was a trial and not a judgment. It was to teach them that heaven's will and kings' designs are best effected when they "passive aptness in all subjects find."

If the poem is not a panegyric to the city of London, what motif can be found to unify the two main parts, the account of the naval battles and the account of the fire? For one may assume that there is some unity beyond mere chronological sequence. That unity, let us suggest, is to be sought in the passage following upon the description of the four-day naval battle. The battle had ended inconclusively, to the intense disappointment of Rupert and, presumably, the English nation. Rupert blamed his stars, but, says Dryden, he was wrong. Heaven's will is unsearchable, and kings' designs inscrutable. Great works come slowly to maturity, and what appears to be a check or a defeat may be the "rudiments of great success." Ours not to question why; our plain duty is loyalty and obedience to the King. In spite of disappointment the English, under the careful direction of Charles, undertake to fit out a new fleet. This finished, battle is joined with the Dutch navy, and a glorious English victory ensues. Thus the loyalty and obedience of the people are rewarded.

Then, in the moment of victory, as the English are swelled with pride and joy in their success, the great fire springs up to lay them low. Yet, however calamitous the fire, heaven stops it short of the royal palace and the naval magazines. It is not a judgment upon the state or Church, and the effect of it is to heighten the people's loyalty to their King. With this great end achieved, what at first seemed to be pure disaster has come to appear as preparation for the final effort; and now Charles's mighty designs can proceed. "Already we have conquer'd half the war, / And the less dang'rous part is left behind. . . ." And so the way is open to London's future greatness, and it is certain that Britannia shall rule the waves.

With high good judgment Dryden does not attempt to give a

direct answer to all of the threats in the *Mirabilis Annus* tracts. Instead, he appeals ingeniously to the self-interest of the citizens. The glory of their city and nation rests upon trade and the enormous riches that it can bring them. By great good fortune the genius of Charles II is perfectly suited to the command of ships and navies; his wisdom has revealed the aptitude of his people; and his care will develop their capacities for greatness. Since the plague and fire were visited upon the people, not their leaders, the people must purge themselves of sin and fractiousness, and support the designs of heaven and their sovereign in "passive aptness."

Dryden's poem was a piece of inspired journalism. It was published separately, and in the same size as most of the tracts which Restoration readers were familiar with. It seems to have been printed in fair numbers; there are, to my knowledge, at least four states represented in copies of the first edition still extant. The very title page shows a journalistic flair, displaying topics most likely to catch the eye of readers who were excited by current events and controversies. Altogether, the poem must be taken as part of a pamphlet-war. Dryden gave the official point of view dignity and prestige by setting it forth in skilful verse.

Conceived as a means to counter certain vague and superstitious terrors that filled the air, and in particular to oppose certain seditious tracts the effects of which, it was feared, would call the people forth to rebellion in times of disaster, *Annus Mirabilis* was developed as a plea that citizens should leave off their waywardness, pay their loyalty and obedience to their anointed leader, and vote him all the supplies which his purposes required. And the whole of it became an eloquent panegyric to trade, and a noble proclamation of Britain's manifest destiny.

RICHARD F. JONES

The Originality of 'Absalom and Achitophel'

from

MODERN LANGUAGE NOTES

Volume XLVI(1931), 211-18

THE ORIGINALITY OF *ABSALOM AND ACHITOPHEL*

Ever since Scott published his edition of Dryden's works, there has been little disposition to attribute any great degree of originality to *Absalom and Achitophel* in respect to the Biblical story selected to carry the satire. For Scott shows that not only had a Bible story been previously used in a poem, closely resembling Dryden's, for political purposes but that the very story of Absalom had been employed in 1680 to represent Monmouth's revolt against Charles.[1] Yet the extent to which the life of King David had been applied to political situations in the seventeenth century, and especially the degree to which "Achitophel" had become, prior to Dryden's poem, a conventional term for disloyal politicians have hardly been sufficiently recognized.

The work largely responsible for the popularity of this Biblical episode in political writings was Nathanael Carpenter's *Achitophel, or the Picture of a Wicked Politician,* the contents of which were first contained in three sermons preached before the University of Oxford. These, Wood says, were very much applauded by all the scholars that heard them, and were eagerly desired to be printed.[2] The first edition was published in Dublin in 1627, but was immediately withdrawn in order that certain passages suspected of attacking Arminianism might be deleted. The popularity of the work is evidenced by its enjoying five more editions, three published at London, 1629, 1633, 1638, and two at Oxford, 1640, 1641. In the dedication Carpenter defines his composition as " a sacred Tragedy, consisting of four chief Actors, viz. *David* an anointed King:

[1] *Works of John Dryden,* 1808, IX, 197-207.
[2] *Athenae Oxoniensis,* ed. P. Bliss, 1815, II, col. 421.

Absolon an ambitious prince: *Achitophel* a wicked politician, and *Hushai* a loyal subject: a passage of history for variety pleasant, for instruction useful, for event admirable." The author's purpose, however, is much the same as that of the "character" writers of the period, though his method is different. By thoroughly analyzing the story of Absalom and Achitophel as it is revealed in the Scriptures, he draws a "character" of a crafty politician, and applies it to local conditions, especially to the machinations of the Catholics.

It seems that Achitophel first became a popular term with the Puritans on the eve of the civil war to designate what they considered to be the evil influences surrounding the king. One speaker in supporting certain puritan policies characterized his time as an "Age (Mr. Speaker) that hath produced and brought forth Achitophells, Hammans, Woolsies, Empsons, and Dudlies. . . . And I doubt not, but when his Majesty shall be truly informed of such matters, as we are able to charge them withall, we shall have the same justice against them, which heretofore hath been against their Predecessours, in whose wicked steps they have trodden." [3] About the same time another puritan orator in speaking of the enemies of parliament proclaimed that all members of the latter had banded together "To defeat the Counsels of these Achitophels, which would involve us, Our Religion, our being, our Lawes, our liberties . . . in one universall and general desolation, to defeat I say, the Counsels of evil Achitophels." [4] Achitophel, as the representative of the whole tribe of wicked politicians, became so popular that he passed into ballad literature. After portraying with great gusto the imminent destruction of the bishops, the puritan poet concludes,

> Thus did the counsell of Achitophell
> Unto these Doctors prove a dismal Cell.[5]

Naturally the story proved popular in the pulpit, and due application was made of it to contemporary conditions, both from the puritan and the royalist points of view. In a sermon preached before the House of Commons, Sept. 24, 1645, and ordered printed

[3] *Mr. Grimston's Speech, In the High Court of Parliament,* 1641, p. 15.
[4] Densell Hollis, *Speech at the delivery of the Protestation to the Lords of the upper House of Parliament, 4 May,* 1641, p. 7.
[5] *The Prentises Prophicie,* 1642, p. 3.

by that body, Samuel Gibson first discussed the narrative and then applied it to the political crisis of his own day, with the fervent prayer that "all the enemies of the King and Parliament be as that young man *Absolom,* and that old Fox Ahitophel." [6] But the story could serve both parties equally well. The same year a Royalist thoroughly analyzed it, with a running application to the sad state to which the Puritans had reduced England, and concluded in this manner: "This is the true Story of this Rebellion, faithfully extracted out of the Holy Writ, where it is Recorded; Scarce to be parallel'd untill these unhappy Times, whence it seemes they have taken their President. *It needs no other Application."* [7]

Thus we see that in the unsettled conditions preceding and attending the civil war both Royalist and Puritan utilized the Bible story, or at least made use of the name of Achitophel to express their political condemnations. The restoration of Charles provided

---

[6] *The Ruine of the Authors and Fomentors of Civill Warres,* p. 27. This is one of the very few instances where the spelling of the name follows the authorized version. Richard Garnett (*Age of Dryden,* p. 21n.) thinks it "worth remarking that although not yet a Roman Catholic, Dryden in this name employs the orthography, not of the authorized version, but of the Vulgate." Needless to say, Dryden was merely following the usual spelling of the name in the seventeenth century.

[7] The italics are the author's; see *Absolom's Rebellion. As it is Recorded in the 2 Sam. Chap. 15, 16, 17, 18 & 19. With some Observations upon the Severall Passages thereof. Too fit a Patterne for the present Times, whereinto we are Fallen.* Oxford, 1645. Other examples of the conventional use of Achitophel are found in certain royalist effusions such as Francis Wortley's *Characters and Elegies,* 1646, p. 27, in which the author compares the treason of Britanicus [Marchmont Needham?] to that of Achitophel, and expresses the wish that all traitors may meet Achitophel's fate; and *Mercurius Britanicus His Welcome to Hell: With the Divills Blessing to Britanicus,* 1647, in which occur the lines

> Nay thou shalt set thy house in order too,
> And in thy death Achitophell out-do,
>
> *   *   *   *   *   *   *
>
> And therefore, in thy death thou shall excell
> That great grave Councellor Achitophell.

And another Royalist advises the puritan "Masters of Wit and Statecraft to have before their eyes the unsuccessful ends of Achitophel, the Oracle of the times he lived in." Peter Heylyn, *Cosmographie,* 1652, "To the Reader."

an even closer parallel with certain episodes in David's life, especially his exile and restoration,[8] which was seized upon with avidity by preachers and poets eager to stand in the good graces of their sovereign. One ecclesiastical congratulator says, with the air of a man making a new discovery, " If we compare the example of that king who is the present subject of our admiration with King David, as to those things we have spoken of him, we shall find them extreamly like one unto another," and the whole purpose of his sermon " is only to shew you the admirable conformity that is between those two Kings." [9]   In some sermons of the day the parallel was developed to the farthest possible limits, one preacher listing and discussing fifteen particulars in which the lives of the two kings were similar. He even compares the cave in En-gedi in which David took up his abode, with the hollow oak where Charles is said to have hidden.[10]

[8] Verrall says the " parallel was obvious enough, and it was indeed a common habit in political sermons to compare Charles with David." He also refers to such a comparison in Dryden's *Astraea Redux* and in Lee's verses prefixed to *The State of Innocence*, in which the latter urges Dryden to develop the parallel (*Lectures on Dryden*, pp. 56-58). A. W. Ward states that the parallel " was a commonplace of restoration poetry " (*Cam. Hist. Eng. Lit.*, VIII, 41). Scott refers (*op. cit.*, IX, 200n.) to John Rich's *Verses on the blessed and happy Coronation of Charles the II*, 1661, in which occur the lines,

> Preserve thy David, and he that rebells,
> Confound his Councells, like Achitophels.

Other poems that may be cited are John Quarles' *Rebellion's Downfall*, 1662, and an undated ballad, probably of this period, entitled *His Majesties miraculous Preservation By the Oak, Maid, and Ship*.

[9] Anthony Hulsius, *The Royal Joy. Or, A Sermon of Congratulation*, p. 11. This was preached at Breda, May 23, 1660, the day before Charles' departure for England. In a sermon preached June 28, 1660, William Creed claims that " The Author of this book of *Samuel*, or the *Kings*, seemes to have been a Register of our times, and to have foretold of these same changes, we in our days have lived to see," and he elaborates upon the comparison of the modern with the ancient king. *Judah's Return to their Allegiance, and David's Return to his Crown and Kingdom*, 1660, p. 1.

[10] R. Feltman in a sermon preached May 29, 1660, and entitled *Davids Recognition, with a Parallel betwixt his and our present Soveraigns Sufferings and Deliverances*. For another elaborate comparison consult Clement Barksdale's sermon delivered May 24, 1660, *The Kings Return*.

The sermons which have just been cited are sufficiently numerous to compel the conclusion that the association of the English sovereign with David must have accompanied the former until his death, though his life as king hardly conformed to scriptural teachings. Indeed, Charles himself seems to have courted the comparison. While his fate was still in the balance, the monarch addressed a letter to the peers of England in which he sought to make political capital of the parallel: "Again we call upon our Peers, who cannot be insensible that the Streams of your own Honour must necessarily fail, when the Fountain which should feed them is diverted; We advise you to learn of the Hebrews, who after that absence of their *King David* (more than seven times doubled by our sufferings) grew to contention for bringing home their persecuted Prince." [11] While it is quite possible that Charles gave the cue to his clerical adulators, the inference is unnecessary in view of the well established tradition regarding the use of the comparison. This letter, however, assumes some importance in the light of a widely accepted account, which has its origin in the 1716 edition of Tonson's *Miscellany Poems* (ii. 1), that Dryden undertook his poem at the instigation of Charles, for it strengthens this account, and indicates that the king may have been responsible for the form of the satire as well as its purpose.

Although the story of David's exile and restoration comprises the greater part of the parallels cited, Achitophel is by no means slighted, but is used generally to designate the enemies of the king.[12] As the poems mentioned in a previous note show, he still represented the false politician; in fact, he became so widely and frequently used as the prototype of traitors that a verb was coined from his name, the surest evidence of the identification of a type

See also James Buck's *St. Paul's Thanksgiving*, May 10, 1660; R. Mosson's *England's Gratulation For the King and his Subjects Happy Union*, May 10, 1660; George Willington's *The Thrise Welcome and happy Inauguration of our most Gracious Sovereign, King Charles*, 1660. The sermons and other references cited in this article, for the majority of which I am indebted to my wife, are only representative, and their number could easily be augmented by further investigation.

[11] *A Letter from His Maty. King Charles II^d. To his Peers the Lords in England*, 1660. Since Thomason gives March 20 as the date of publication, this letter preceded all the sermons that have been noticed.

[12] See especially W. Creed's *Judah's Return*.

with a name. In a poem of the period, the failure of the Puritans is ascribed to their plotting against each other:

> So all their Projects broke, not any held
> One by another out-Achitophel'd.[13]

And for a number of years Achitophel served a useful purpose in affording a term of reproach to be leveled at the discomfited Puritans. In speaking of the way in which the puritan leaders had misled the ignorant people, Samuel Parker remarks, " So easie a thing is it for your crafty Achitophels to arm Faction with Zeal, and to draw the Multitudes into Tumults and Seditions under Colour of Religion." [14] George Vernon applies the name more specifically in his attack on John Owen, when he says the latter " crept into his [Cromwell's] favour, was nourished in his bosome, and continued his Achitophel to his dying day." [15]

One might say that any political disturbance of any importance during this period was sure to inspire reference to the Biblical traitor. In a sermon preached on the anniversary of the gunpowder plot and largely inspired by the recent popish plot, Henry Dove introduces the deadly parallel, concluding with the words, " I shall leave it to your memories to run the parallel between David's Conspirators and these Traytors, in the secresie of their Counsels, designs laid deep as Hell, and black as utter darkness, in the maliciousness of their calumnies and imbitter'd slanders, in the insolence of their insurrection and bold-fac'd Rebellion." [16] But no political situation could possibly furnish so close a parallel as Monmouth's disaffection. Here was the story of a king's son egged on by politicians to revolt against his father and adopting practices

---

[13] H. Beeston Winton, *A Poem to His most Excellent Majesty Charles the Second*, 1660, p. 6. Two years later Wither, in *Verses intended to the King's Majesty*, expresses a desire for

> So much worth, at least, as did commend
> His loyalty, whom David call'd his friend;
> And wit enough to make a parallel
> Of evry traytor with Achitophel.

[14] *A Letter to a Friend Concerning some of Dr. Owen's Principles and Practices*, 1670, p. 27.

[15] *A Defence and Continuation of the Ecclesiastical Politie*, 1671, p. 684.

[16] *A Sermon Preached before the Honourable House of Commons . . . November 5, 1680.*

suggestive of the Scriptures. The application of the Biblical story to the affair was inevitable. We are not surprised, then, to find one who signs himself C. F. addressing a *Letter*[17] to Monmouth, which urges him to desist from his treasonable course, and makes the most out of the example of Absalom and his wicked politicians. In a very short tract published the same year an ever closer parallel is traced between the scriptural characters and Monmouth and Shaftesbury.[18] Certainly by the time Dryden's satire appeared, the comparison had been considerably overworked. It is not strange, then, to hear one of Shaftesbury's adherents say, evidently in scorn of Dryden's originality,

> Let them with their Poetick Malice swell.
> Falsely apply the Story, known so well,
> Of Absolom, and of Achitophel.[19]

It is not hard to understand why the vicissitudinous life of King David, and especially the episode of Absalom and Achitophel, should have figured prominently in the treatises, sermons, speeches, and poems of a period so troublesome for English kings as the seventeenth century. Even though it was not until the last years of the reign of Charles II that a clear parallel for Absalom was furnished, he could very well be used to represent rebellion in general. As for Achitophel, political strife was so intense and feeling ran so high that every faction needed some term into which could be packed all the hatred and contempt inspired by the supposedly wicked and deceitful practices of the other factions. Such

---

[17] *A Letter to his Grace the Duke of Monmouth, this 15th of July, 1680. By a true Lover of his Person and the Peace of this Kingdom.* This is to be found in the *Somers Tracts,* ed. Walter Scott, VIII, 216. See also Scott's edition of *Dryden's Works,* IX, 199-200.

[18] *Absolom's Conspiracy; or The Tragedy of Treason,* London, 1680. See the *Harleian Miscellany,* 1811, VII, 530. Malone pointed out that several months before the appearance of Dryden's poem, a satire entitled *The Badger in the Fox-Trap,* applied the name Achitophel to Shaftesbury:

> Some call me Tory, some Achitophel,
> Some Jack-a-Dandy, some old Machiavel.

See *Critical and Miscellaneous Prose Works of John Dryden,* ed. E. Malone, 1800, I, 141n. Malone, although he was familiar with Carpenter's book, thought Dryden was entirely original in his choice of the Biblical story.

[19] *A Loyal Congratulation To the Right Honorable, Anthony, Earl of Shaftesbury,* London, 1681.

a term as Achitophel was all the more useful when it was expedient to attack the counsellors of a ruler rather than the ruler himself, as in the case of Charles I, to castigate living Puritans for the deeds of Cromwell who was beyond punishment, and to show some tenderness to the son of a king.   Yet when everything is taken into consideration, the wide use of the story is still remarkable.   Dryden or possibly Charles, could not have shown less originality in the selection of the vehicle for the satire.   This fact, of course, does in no way detract from Dryden's originality in his treatment of the parallel, nor from his vigorous satire and energetic verse.

RICHARD F. JONES

Washington University,
St. Louis

F. B. KAYE

The Influence of Bernard Mandeville

from

STUDIES IN PHILOLOGY

Volume XIX(1922), 83-108

Reprinted by permission of the Editors

THE INFLUENCE OF BERNARD MANDEVILLE

By F. B. Kaye

Even to scholars Bernard Mandeville's *Fable of the Bees* is now little more than a name and the recollection of a long-dead scandal. Yet the book had an extraordinary effect on the history of thought, an effect international in scope and still felt. Indeed, so great was Mandeville's influence that he can, I believe, be shown to be a major dignitary of eighteenth century thought. To demonstrate this is the aim of the present paper.

After this introduction it may seem a humorous anti-climax to answer the question: What was *The Fable of the Bees?* but the way in which history has slighted the work renders such an answer necessary. The book opens with a twenty-page rhymed allegory called *The Grumbling Hive,* first published by itself in 1705. This hive is described as made up, like any human state, of the elements of selfishness, pride, ambition, viciousness, and dishonesty. Yet all this evil is the stuff out of which is made the complicated mechanism of a great and prosperous state with

> Millions endeavouring to supply
> Each other's Lust and Vanity (*Fable*, I, 3).[1]

Indeed, it is precisely this lust and vanity, as it shows itself in the desire for power, the love of splendor, the round of fashions, and the give-and-take of prodigality and avarice, that is the motive force of the whole commonwealth.

> Thus Vice nurs'd Ingenuity,
> Which join'd with Time and Industry,
> Had carry'd Life's Conveniences,
> Its real Pleasures, Comforts, Ease,
> To such a Height, the very Poor
> Liv'd better than the Rich before (*Fable*, I, 11).

The bees, however, are not satisfied to have their viciousness mixed with their prosperity. All the cheats and hypocrites disclaim

---

[1] My page references apply equally to a number of editions—to those of 1724, 1725, 1728, and 1732 of the first part, and to the editions of 1729 and 1733 of Part II of the *Fable.*

83

about the state of their country's morals, and pray the gods for honesty. This raises the indignation of Jove, who unexpectedly grants them their wish.

> But, Oh ye Gods! What Consternation,
> How vast and sudden was th' Alteration! (*Fable*, I, 13)
>
> As Pride and Luxury decrease,
> So by degrees they leave the Seas . . . .
> All Arts and Crafts neglected lie;
> Content, the Bane of Industry,
> Makes 'em admire their homely Store,
> And neither seek nor covet more (*Fable*, I, 21).

In this way, through the loss of its vices, the hive at the same time loses all its greatness.

Now comes the moral:

> *Then leave Complaints: Fools only strive*
> *To make a Great an Honest Hive.*
> *T' enjoy the World's Conveniences,*
> *Be fam'd in War, yet live in Ease,*
> *Without great Vices, is a vain*
> EUTOPIA *seated in the Brain.*
> *Fraud, Luxury and Pride must live,*
> *While we the Benefits receive . . . .*
> *So Vice is beneficial found,*
> *When it's by Justice lopt and bound;*
> *Nay, where the people would be great,*
> *As necessary to the State,*
> *As Hunger is to make 'em eat (Fable, I, 23-4).*

In 1714 Mandeville republished *The Grumbling Hive* with a prose commentary of about two hundred pages appended. This commentary was in the form of some twenty essays—or "Remarks," as he called them—each Remark serving as note to some line or lines of the little rhymed allegory. This time he named his book *The Fable of the Bees: or, Private Vices Publick Benefits.* In 1723 he added several new passages, among them two long prose essays (one of them an attack on charity schools); in 1724, he included a "Vindication" of his book from the attacks already accumulating; and in 1728 (by title-page, 1729) he published a Part II, of size equal to the first volume.

Obviously, such a framework gave Mandeville the opportunity of incorporating any thought he liked on any topic he liked; and he took advantage of the fact. An extraordinarily fertile speculator, he throws out original or suggestive opinions—some of much interest—on education, evolution, feminism, criminology, medicine, duelling, vegetarianism, public stews, psychology, economics, French literature, and theology. Among his educational conceptions, for example, is a foreshadowing of the Montessori system (*Fable,* II, 183-5 and 211). Then, too, Mandeville's theories in Part II of the *Fable* concerning the evolution of society were quite extraordinary.[2] He seems unique at the time in appreciation of the great slowness of the thing, the small part in it played by the individual, the unsteadiness of its progression, and its control by physical law. A similar anticipatory modernity will be found in Mandeville's embryonic feminism.[3] These, however, are side issues for this paper, and are noted merely in passing.

We shall be occupied here with Mandeville's influence in three fields only: literature, ethics, and economics.

I

Mandeville's purely literary influence was not considerable. The *Fable* had no direct imitators. Its influence was limited to the offering of tid-bits for amalgamation or paraphrase by other writers. Such an influence, however, it did have, and on some big figures—chiefly, Pope, Johnson, Adam Smith, and Voltaire. Pope paraphrased the *Fable* both in the *Moral Essays* and in the *Essay on Man.*[4] The manuscript of the latter, it should also be noted, had,

[2] There are, before Mandeville, only embryonic and fragmentary considerations of the growth of society from an evolutionary point of view. Of the ancients (Horace, *Satires,* I, iii, Lucretius, *De Rerum Natura,* book 5, and Aeschylus, *Prometheus Bound,* lines 442-506) Lucretius is the most elaborate. The moderns until Mandeville added nothing. There is either no or slight anticipation of Mandeville in Matthew Hale (*Primitive Origination of Man*), Bossuet (*Discours sur l'Histoire Universelle,* ed. 1845, pp. 9-10), or Temple (*Essay upon the Original and Nature of Government*); nor is he anticipated in such works as those of Giordano Bruno, Bodin, Thomas Burnet, Whiston, John Woodward, John Keill, or Vico.

[3] See *Fable,* II, 187-9, and also the passage in Mandeville's *Virgin Unmask'd,* ed. 1724, pp. 115-7, beginning: "They have enslaved our Sex."

[4] Elwin considers the following passages derived from Mandeville: *Moral Essays,* III, 13-14 and 25-26; *Essay on Man,* II, 129-30, 157-8, and 193-4. That the *Essay on Man,* II, 129-30 and 157-8, owes anything to Mandeville, however, is doubtful, although the other lines are probably Mandevillian.

instead of the present line II, 240, this direct paraphrase of the sub-title of the *Fable of the Bees:*

And public good extracts from private vice.

It is just possible also that Pope derived the famous "To err is human, to forgive, divine" from a passage in another well-known book by Mandeville—the *Free Thoughts*.[5]—Dr. Johnson, who said that Mandeville opened his views into real life very much,[6] and whose economic theories were borrowed from Mandeville,[7] limited his literary indebtedness to a passage in one of his *Idlers* (No. 34), which is a paraphrase of a witty portion of the *Fable* (I, 106), and to some able discussions with Boswell about the book.—Adam Smith's literary obligation extends to at least one famous passage, but this matter will be considered later as incidental to Smith's debt to Mandeville in the field of economics.—The literary borrowings of Voltaire, whose great general indebtedness will also be touched on later, consisted in the paraphrasing in French verse of some seven pages of the *Fable* (I, 190-6), Voltaire's poem being called *Le Marseillois et le Lion* (*Œuvres*, ed. Garnier, 1877-85, X, 140-8) ; and of passages in *Le Mondain* and the *Défense du Mondain,* and in the *Observations sur MM. Jean Lass, Melon et Dutot; sur le Commerce,* which have parallels in the *Fable*.[8]

All this, however, constitutes an unimportant phase of Mandeville's influence. His great effect was on ethics and economics, and a very practical effect it was; no mere interchange of theories, but one bound up with the destinies of England and of France.

Before undertaking an analysis of this effect, however, I wish to give some impression of the enormous vogue of the *Fable,* and the eighteenth century's interest in it, for in the light of this vogue points of relationship between the *Fable* and subsequent developments take on fuller significance.

The *Fable* first attracted attention in 1723, when Mandeville added to it his "Essay on Charity and Charity-Schools." There-

---

[5] *Free Thoughts* (1729), p. 61: "If to err belongs to human fraility, let us bear with their errors."

[6] Boswell, *Life,* ed. Hill, New York, 1889, III, 292.

[7] See below, note 66.

[8] Derivations from Mandeville in these three works are noted in André Morize's interesting dissertation, *L'Apologie du Luxe au XVIIIe Siècle et "Le Mondain" de Voltaire* (Paris, 1909).

upon, the newspapers focussed on it at once, and within a year whole books began to be aimed at it. At the same time the public commenced to exhaust an edition a year.[9] Then it went into foreign editions.[10] Meanwhile, other books by Mandeville were being frequently printed in England and, translated, on the Continent.[11] Moreover, his works must have been made familiar to thousands who never saw the books by the many reviews of them (often of considerable length) in periodicals such as the *Bibliothèque Britannique* and the *Histoire des Ouvrages des Savans*,[12] in theological bibliographies like those of Masch, Lilienthal, and Trinius, and in encyclopedias like Chaufepié's and the *General Dictionary*. The many attacks, also, on the *Fable* not only illustrated the fame of the book, but diffused this fame still further—a celebrity often commented on by contemporaries.[13] The following is a partial list

[9] New editions were published in 1724, 1725, 1728, 1729 and 1732 (all by Tonson), and of Part II in 1729, 1730, and 1733 (all by Roberts). Further editions appeared in 1734, 1755, 1772, 1795, and 1806.

[10] French versions in 1740 and 1750; German versions in 1761 and 1818 and, possibly, 1817.

[11] The *Treatise of the Hypochondriack and Hysterick Diseases* had three or four printings; the *Virgin Unmask'd*, at least five; the *Modest Defence of Publick Stews* at least six English editions and some nine French ones; the *Free Thoughts*, five English editions, one German edition, an edition in Dutch, and four in French.

[12] For instance, the *Bibliothèque Angloise* for 1725 gave the *Fable* 29 pages and Bluet's reply to the *Fable* the same amount of space; the *Bibliothèque Raisonée* for 1729 reviewed the *Fable* in 44 pages; the *Bibliothèque Britannique* in 1733 gave 52 pages to Mandeville's *Origin of Honour;* *Maendelyke Uittreksels* for 1723 devoted 71 pages to the *Free Thoughts;* and the *Mémoires de Trévoux* (1740) allotted the *Fable* over a hundred pages.

[13] For instance: "La Pièce . . . fait grand bruit en Angleterre" (*Bibliothèque Angloise* for 1725, XIII, 99) ; "Avide lectum est in Anglia et non sine plausu receptum" (Reimarus, *Programma quo Fabulam de Apibus examinat*, 1726) ; "The *Fable* . . . a Book that has made so much Noise" (*Present State of the Republick of Letters* for 1728, II, 462) ; "La Fables des Abeilles *a fait tant de bruit en* Angleterre" (preface to French version of *Fable*, ed. 1740, I, i) ; "Nicht nur die Feinde der christlichen Religion, sondern auch viele Christen zählen ihn unter die recht grossen Geister" (J. F. Jacobi, *Betrachtungen über die weisen Absichten Gottes*, 1749); "Such is the system of Dr. Mandeville, which once made so much noise in the world" (Adam Smith, *Theory of Moral Sentiments*, ed. 1759, p. 486); "La fameuse fable des abeilles . . . fit un grand bruit en Angleterre" (Voltaire, *Œuvres Complètes*, ed. Garnier, 1877-85, XVII, 29).

of some of the better known men who at some time gave him specific and often sustained attention: John Dennis,[14] William Law,[15] Reimarus,[16] Hume,[17] Berkeley,[18] Hutcheson,[19] Godwin,[20] John Brown,[21] Fielding,[22] Gibbon,,[3] Diderot,[24] Holbach,[25] Rousseau,[26] Malthus,[27] James Mill,[28] Mackintosh,[29] Adam Smith,[30] Warburton,[31] John Wesley,[32] Herder,[33] Montesquieu,[34] Hazlitt,[35] and Bentham.[36]

---

[14] *Vice and Luxury Publick Mischiefs: or, Remarks on . . . the Fable of the Bees* (1724).

[15] *Remarks upon . . . the Fable of the Bees* (1724).

[16] *Programma quo Fabulam de Apibus examinat . . .* (1726).

[17] *Essays,* ed. Green and Grose, 1889, I, 308-9.

[18] *Alciphron: or, the Minute Philospher* (first and second dialogues); *Discourse Addressed to Magistrates,* 1736 (*Works,* ed. Fraser, Oxford, 1871, III, 424).

[19] Letter in *London Journal* for Nov. 14 and 21, 1724; *Inquiry into the Original . . . of . . . Virtue . . . . In which the Principles of . . . Shaftesbury are . . . defended against . . . the Fable of the Bees* (1725); three letters in the *Dublin Journal,* Feb. 5, 12, and 19, 1726—reprinted as the latter half of *Reflections upon Laughter, and Remarks upon the Fable of the Bees* (Glasgow, 1750).

[20] *Political Justice*—ed. 1793, II, 815; ed. 1796, II, 484-5, note.

[21] *Estimate* (1758), II, 86; *On Honour* (1743), lines 176-9; *Essays on the Characteristics* (1751), in the second essay.

[22] *Tom Jones,* book 6, chap. I; *Amelia,* book 3, chap 5; *Covent-Garden Journal,* ed. Jensen, New Haven, I, 258-263.

[23] *Memoirs,* ed. Hill, 1900, p. 23.

[24] *Œuvres,* ed. Assézat, Paris, X, 299 and IV, 102-3 (the latter sometimes attributed to Rousseau).

[25] *La Morale Universelle* (1820), I, xxi-xxiii.

[26] *Narcisse,* preface (*Œuvres,* ed. Petitain, 1859, V, 142). See also Masson's edition of the *Profession de Foi du Vicaire Savoyard.*

[27] *Essay on . . . Population,* ed. Bettany, 1890, p. 553, note.

[28] *Fragment on Mackintosh* (1835), pp. 55-63.

[29] "Disertation Second," in *Encyclopœdia Britannica,* ed. 1842, I, 323.

[30] Letter in *Edinburgh Review* (1755), No. 1, pp. 63-79; *Theory of Moral Sentiments* (1759), pp. 474-87 and 492.

[31] *Divine Legation of Moses* (1846), I, 156ff.

[32] Diary, entry for Apr. 14, 1756, and letter cited in Abbey's *English Church and its Bishops* (1887), I, 32.

[33] *Adrastea,* IV (2), 234-252.

[34] *De l'Esprit des Lois,* book 7, chap. 1.

[35] See index of Waller and Glover edition for some twenty-three references.

[36] *Works,* ed. Bowring, 1843, I, 49, note, and X, 73.

Some of these, such as Fielding, referred to him repeatedly, and some wrote whole books on him. William Law devoted a volume to him; so did John Dennis; and Francis Hutcheson, no mean figure in the history of philosophy, wrote two books against him; while Adam Smith allotted him half of a special article, and Berkeley, a dialogue.

Nor was this vogue merely academic. The *Fable of the Bees* made a public scandal, and reached through the resultant notoriety not only the public eye but the public emotion. Mandeville, with his teaching of the usefulness of vice, inherited the office of Lord High Bogey-man, which Hobbes had held in the preceding century. The *Fable* was twice presented by the Grand Jury as a public nuisance; minister and bishop alike denounced it from the pulpit.[37] The book, indeed, aroused positive consternation, ranging from the reprehension of Bishop Berkeley [38] to the horror of John Wesley,[39] who protests that not even Voltaire could have said so much for wickedness. In France, the *Fable* was actually ordered burned by the common hangman.[40]

It would, in fact, be difficult to overrate the degree and extent of Mandeville's eighteenth-century fame. A letter of Wesley's,[41] in 1750, indicates that the *Fable* was current in Ireland. In France, in 1765, we find Diderot complaining that the tenets of the book had become so familiar as to be a conversational nuisance.[42] In 1768, the friend of Laurence Sterne, John Hall-Stevenson, thought a good title for one of his pieces would be "The New Fable of the Bees." As late, indeed, as 1787, and in America at that, the

[37] Some of the sermons against it that got into print were *The True Christian Method of Educating the Children both of the Poor and Rich*, preached in 1724 by Thomas Wilson, Bishop of Sodor and Man; Chandler's *Doing Good . . . . an Answer to . . . the Fable of the Bees* (1728); a sermon delivered in 1727 by Isaac Watts (printed as *An Essay towards the Encouragement of Charity-Schools*, 1728); and Barnes's *Charity and Charity Schools Defended* (delivered 1724, printed 1727).

[38] *Works*, ed. Fraser, 1871, III, 424.

[39] *Journal*, ed. Curnock, IV, 157.

[40] G. Peignot, *Dictionnaire . . . des Principaux Livres Condamnés au Feu* (Paris, 1806), I, 282.

[41] Cited in Abbey's *English Church and its Bishops* (1887), I, 32.

[42] *Œuvres*, ed. Assézat, x, 299.

author of our first American comedy—a play meant for popular consumption [43]—refers to Mandeville as if the latter's theories were as well known to the audience as the latest proclamation of General Washington.

This outline of Mandeville's vogue will serve as a prelude to the search into his specific influence, and may also give some initial intimations of the justification for the claims I made at the outset concerning his importance.

II

Now, to understand the effect which Mandeville exercised on ethical theory, it will be necessary to sketch briefly his general philosophical position. A good part of Mandeville will escape in the process: the wit, humor, and worldly-wise cynicism which gave his thought its edge must be omitted; but that cannot be helped.— Mandeville called his book " Private Vices, Publick Benefits." Now, by that he did not mean that all evil has a good side to it, and that this good outweighs the ill. His paradox turned, instead, on a matter of definition. He adopted certain current ethical conceptions as to the prerequisites of morality. But when he came rigorously to apply the definition of virtue which he had thus derived he found that the world did not furnish any examples of people who lived up to the definition, and thus it became an obvious deduction that, since all is vicious, even matters beneficial to us arise from vicious causes, and private vices are public benefits.

The conception of virtue propounded by Mandeville proclaimed, first, that no action was really virtuous if inspired by selfish emotion; and this assumption, since Mandeville considered all natural emotion fundamentally selfish, implied the ascetic position that no action was virtuous if done from natural impulse. Secondly, Mandeville's definition of virtue declared that no action was meritorious unless the motive that inspired it was a " rational " one. As Mandeville interpreted " rational " to imply an antithesis to emotion and self-regard, both aspects of his ethical code — the ascetic and the rationalistic—alike condemned as vicious all action

---

[43] Royall Tyler, *The Contrast*, III, ii.

whose dominant motive was natural impulse and self-regarding bias—or, to put it from a different angle, his code condemned all such acts as were caused by the traits man shared with the animals.

This conception of morality was no invention of Mandeville's. He merely adopted the creed of two great popular groups of the period. The first group comprised the theologians who, from the orthodox belief in the depravity of human nature, concluded naturally that virtue could not be found except in such action as unselfishly denied or transcended the working of the nature they condemned.[44] To all logical inferences from Mandeville's position as to the moral necessity of unselfishness and the conquest of natural impulse these ascetics were also fairly committed. The other group comprised the rationalistic or "intellectualistic" ethical thinkers, who identified morality with such action as proceeded from rational motives. This group was committed to conclusions logically deducible from Mandeville's position only in so far as, like him, they made an antithesis between reason and emotion; but, since this antithesis was very commonly made, at least implicitly,[45] these thinkers too were largely implicated in Mande-

[44] This was the respectable orthodox position. Thus Luther wrote, "All things in thyself are unrighteous, sinful, and damnable" (*Select Works*, trans. Cole, 1826, I, 13 and passim). And Calvin argued (*Institutes*, III, ix, 2), "For there is no medium between the two things: the earth must either be worthless in our estimation, or keep us enslaved by an intemperate love of it. Therefore, if we have any regard to eternity, we must carefully strive to disencumber ourselves of these fetters"; and he speaks (*Institutes*, III, ix, 3) of the "contempt which believers should train themselves to feel for the present life." This belief in the corruption of human nature the Synod of Dort authenticated as the official Protestant doctrine. It is found in representative moral works of all sorts. For example, in his *Rule and Exercises of Holy Dying* (Temple Classics, p. 68), Jeremy Taylor wrote, "He that would die holily and happily, must in this world love tears, humility, solitude, and repentance." In 1722, in his *Conscious Lovers* (III, i), Steele satirized this attitude as if it were of general currency: "To love is a passion, 'tis a desire, and we must have no desires."

[45] Rationalism, of one aspect or another, in seventeenth and eighteenth century ethics was, it is almost unnecessary to note, very marked, whether in a writer such as the Cambridge Platonist Culverwel, who states (*Of the Light of Nature*, ed. Brown, 1857, p. 66) that "the law of nature is built upon reason," or in a more systematic thinker like the "intellectualist" Samuel Clarke, who argues (*Works*, ed. 1738, II, 50-1): "From this first,

ville's conclusions. The implications, then, which Mandeville was to deduce from the rigorous application of his definition of virtue were such as could genuinely involve and provoke the thought of his day.

The conclusion reached by Mandeville that all human action is at bottom vicious was attained by a psychological analysis of human

original, and literal signification of the words, *Flesh* and *Spirit;* the same Terms have, by a very easy and natural figure of Speech, been extended to signify *All Vice* and *All Virtue* in *general;* as having their Root and Foundation, one in the prevailing of different *Passions and Desires* over the Dictates of *Reason*, and the other in the Dominion of *Reason and Religion* over all the irregularities of *Desires and Passions*. Every *Vice*, and every instance of *Wickedness*, of *whatever* kind it be; has its Foundation in *some unreasonable Appetite* or *ungoverned Passion, warring against the Law of the Mind.*" And again—" All Religion or Virtue, consists in the Love of Truth, and in the Free Choice and Practice of Right, and in being influenced regularly by rational and moral Motives " (*Sermons*, ed. 1742, I, 457). Even so empirical a thinker as Locke holds, in contradiction to his main philosophy, that a complete morality can be derived by the exercise of pure ratiocination from general *a priori* principles, without reference to concrete circumstances; and Spinoza also, who had placed so great a stress on the dependence of thought upon feeling, nevertheless attempts to demonstrate his ethics " ordine geometrico."

However, although the general thought identified virtue with conduct in accord with " reason," " reason " was usually an ill-defined and contradictorily employed term. The ethical rationalism of the period implied, first, that the organization of the universe was a geometrically rational one, and that, therefore, moral laws were the " immutable and eternal " affairs whose disconnection with the facts of human nature Fielding was later to ridicule in *Tom Jones*. To such a conception the tastes and emotions in which men differed from one another were either irritating or negligible; and its stress was naturally laid upon the abstract, rational relationships which were true alike of all men. To this conception, therefore, " reason " tended to imply an antithesis to taste and individual impulse.

Secondly, the ethical rationalism of the day insisted that acts were virtuous only if their motivation was from " reason." It is at this point— the phase of rationalistic ethics of chief importance in relation to Mandeville—that current philosophy was most inchoate. No real attempt was usually made to define motivation by " reason." " Reason " sometimes implied any practical action, sometimes a proper blend of deliberation and impulse, and very often, indeed, it was used, as Mandeville used it, in connection with acts the decision to perform which was not determined by emotional or personal bias (which might, however, provided it did not determine the will to act, legitimately accompany the action). Again and

(159)

emotions and their relation to opinion never before equalled, except possibly by Spinoza, for scientific penetration and completeness. I shall not here attempt to detail the examination through which Mandeville reached the conclusions that reason is not a determinant factor in men's actions, our most elaborate and apparently detached ratiocination being basically only a rationalizing and excusing of the demands of dominant emotions; that all our acts—even those apparently most altruistic and unselfish—are, traced to their source,

again it is manifest upon analysis that action according to reason is thought of (even by thinkers who sometimes take a different position) as action done despite the insistence of natural impulse and self-regarding bias, in spite of one's animal nature. Sometimes the writer makes this antithesis comparatively obvious, as when Culverwel reasons: "Yet grant that the several multitudes, all the species of these irrational creatures [animals] were all without spot or blemish in . . . their sensitive conversation, can any therefore fancy that they dress themselves by the glass of a [moral] law? Is it not rather a faithfulness to their own natural inclinations? . . . A law is founded in intellectuals, in the reason, not in the sensitive principle " (*Of the Light of Nature*, ed. Brown, 1857, p. 62). The tendency of the rationalistic school to make reason a quite abstract function is illustrated in the work of Mandeville's contemporary Wollaston, whose rationalistic *Natural Religion Delineated* considered virtue simply as truth, and vice as untruth. The antithesis between reason and natural impulse is very sharp and explicit in Richard Price, who summed up the principles of the " intellectualist " school of which he was a belated member in the statement that "*instinctive benevolence* is no principle of virtue, nor are any actions flowing merely from it virtuous. As far as this influences, so far something else than reason and goodness influence, and so much I think is to be subtracted from the moral worth of any action or character " (*Review of the Principle Questions in Morals*, ed. 1787, pp. 323-4).

There were certain characteristics of the ethical rationalism of the day which explain and illustrate the tendency to disassociate reason and feeling. In the first place, rationalism was from one aspect transcendental. With its stress on " immutable and eternal laws " of right and wrong and its love of the formulable, it was largely an attempt to transcend the merely relative, and hence personal and individual emotions. Like the theological asceticism of its day (see above, note 44), it was a method of transcending concrete human nature. Secondly, it could hardly help being affected by this current theological asceticism and its condemnation of natural impulse, especially since so many rationalists were also theologians. The tendency to identify the theological and the rationalistic attitudes is evidenced in the prayer with which Thomas Burnet closed the second book of his *Theory of the Earth:* "*MAY we, in the mean time, by a true Love of God above all things, and a contempt of this Vain World which passeth* due to some variety or interplay of selfish emotion; that man, after all, is only " the most perfect of animals " (*Fable,* I, 31) and, no matter how much trained and preached at, can never transcend or contradict this fact. It is enough to note that he found his ethical code impossible of achievement, and, therefore, advised all pretenders to statesmanship not to worry about unselfishness and " rationality," but to content themselves with so ordering things that there should be such proper mixture of various self-counteracting selfish passions as would produce harmonious results. For practical purposes, then, Mandeville offered, not rigorism, but utilitarianism [46] as a guiding principle to the actual worldly world.

away; By a careful use of the Gifts of God and Nature, the Light of Reason and Revelation, prepare our selves . . . for the great Coming of our Saviour." Note the paralleling of *" a contempt for this Vain World "* with *" the Light of Reason."* In the third place, because of the problem of the soul a sharp distinction was drawn between man and the animals. The belief that animals have no soul (rational principle) combined with the conviction that the soul is the ultimately important thing tended naturally to cause contempt for the animal functions and a belief that they could form no ingredient in virtue. Berkeley illustrates this tendency when, in his reply to Mandeville (*Alciphron*), he says, " Considered in that light [as he is an animal], he [man] hath no sense of duty, no notion of virtue " (*Works*, ed. Fraser, 1871, II, 81). Finally, to cause too sharp an antithesis between the conceptions of reason and feeling there was the all important fact of mental and literary inexactness, of failure to make and maintain proper distinctions. Since Mandeville's day philosophical speculation, to an appreciable extent on his account (see below, note 53), has become more precise as regards the distinction between reason and feeling, but in his time it so generally fell into assertions or implications of an antithesis between reason and impulse, even in the face of speculations in the same work maintaining an opposite position, that so great a thinker as Spinoza was not entirely exempt from the contagion, as is apparent in his *Ethica*, part 4, props. 53 and 56.

From the above it may be seen that, even though the position taken by Mandeville that no conduct can be virtuous unless the will to perform it was undetermined by natural impulse and selfishness may have been somewhat more extreme than the average, yet it is evident that his position was none the less in accord with a great body of contemporary theory. And, indeed, this close relation to his age is demonstrated by the violence of the popular reaction to his book.

[46] I use the term " utilitarian " in a looser sense than that in which specialists in philosophy ordinarily employ it. I use it as a blanket term for such teleological forms of ethics as eudaemonism and universal hedon-

And he felt it a pretty good world, too, in which, although abstract virtue might be absent, yet human self-seeking, properly controlled, could be made to produce a prosperous and happy state of affairs.

But then came the paradox. All this actual scheme of things, although it produces or can be made to produce such pleasant results, is, he announced, wrong, because not in accord with the demands of rigoristic morality. The passions are indispensable to proper conduct, but they are wicked. Prosperity is a pleasant thing, but it is evil. The utilitarian viewpoint is highly practical, but it will send you to Hell. Indeed, all the things which Mandeville has shown so necessary and desirable he then rejects as vicious. His philosophy, accordingly, has two aspects. First, he presents the actual world and how to get along in it, and after he has expounded the means of making it exceedingly pleasant, he places a candle snuffer on his previous thought by declaring that all these good things of the world are vicious because not based and impossible of being based on the rigoristic demand for unselfishness and rationally motivated action. *The Fable of the Bees,* then, holds in solution two opposite points of view—the utilitarian and the rigoristic or formalistic.

By juxtaposing these two in this manner, Mandeville has achieved a latent *reductio ad absurdum* of the rigoristic point of view. But he never educed this *reductio ad absurdum.* Although he spent most of his book in the demonstration that a life regulated by the principles of rigoristic virtue is not only impossible but highly undesirable, he continued to announce the sanctity of the formalistic creed. This paradoxical ethical duet which Mandeville carried on with himself is the point to note here, for it is this fact which gives the clue to the influence on ethics which he exerted.

The attacks on Mandeville focus on this paradox, but the type of attack varies according to the intellectual leanings of the par-

ism; and intend by it always an opposition to the insistence of rigoristic or formalistic ethics—rationalistic or ascetic—that not results but motivation by right principle determines virtuousness. To have used the technical vocabulary of the philosophical specialist would have needlessly hampered the reader trained in other fields; and, besides, my non-technical use of the term parallels the condition of ethical theory in Mandeville's day, when utilitarian theory had not yet taken to itself the specific connotation it now has, but was thought of simply as an ethics whose moral touchstone was results and not abstract principle.

ticular polemicist.   First there were the critics who, like William
Law and John Dennis, adhered to the rigoristic school of ethics.
On these the effect of the *Fable* was that of the insane root which
takes the reason prisoner.   William Law was almost alone in keeping his head, although not his temper.   It was not merely the
theories of Mandeville that caused this riot of reason, but the tone
of the doctor's writing.   Mandeville employed a humorously cynical
downrightness of statement that made him so provocative that even
now, after two hundred years, he has kept almost unimpaired his
ability to irritate those who disagree with him.   But, apart from
their expression, there was enough in Mandeville's tenets to upset
those who believed virtue necessarily unselfish and rational.   Mandeville accepted their own position to argue them into unbearable
predicaments.   He agreed that only such behaviour is virtuous as
is motivated not by selfish emotion but through the conquest of
one's natural impulses or through sheer respect for a moral code;
and then he demonstrated that there can be no such conduct in
this world.   He admitted that a state based on selfishness is corrupt and that luxury is contrary to the Christian religion, and
then he proceeded to show that all society must be based on selfishness and that no state can be great without luxury.   He agreed
that men must transcend their animal nature, and then he proved
that it could not be done.   In other words, he took advantage of
his opponents' own standards to show them that according to these
ideals they had never done a virtuous action in their lives, and
that, even if these standards could be lived up to, they would inevitably cause the total collapse of society.   Meanwhile Mandeville
stood in the middle of this spectacle roaring with laughter; which
did not help to soothe his critics.

The thing was like an argument between Bernard Shaw and a
synod of revivalists.   They lost their heads.   If only Mandeville
had accepted the *reductio ad absurdum* latent in his book and
rejected the rigoristic system of ethics, things would have been
simple for the William Laws.   They would merely have rushed to
the defense of their code, and been quite comfortable.   But Mandeville didn't reject it; the force of his demonstration of the value of
vice and impossibility of virtue rested on his accepting their position.

There were, therefore, only two rational [47] courses open to the rigorists. They could argue, first, that Mandeville's vivisection of human nature was faulty and that men really can act in a manner fundamentally unselfish and rational. This they tried.[48] But Mandeville's analysis had been so keen and thorough that few of his opponents dared claim that they had demonstrated more than that in some few cases a man might conceivably be virtuous in their sense of the word. This was hardly very comforting, for it left them still drowning in a sea of *almost* undiluted iniquity.

The other method was to abandon the ascetic point of view and deny that only such actions were virtuous as were done from unselfish devotion to principle, and to call for another criterion of virtue. Now, the strange fact is that almost every rigorist who undertook to answer Mandeville did at some time or other in this fashion repudiate his own basal position.[49] William Law was

[47] I say "rational" advisedly. Many of Mandeville's attackers simply misunderstood him. They took his terms quite literally, interpreting "vice" as something contrary to the welfare of the individual practising it. From this they proved "by rule demonstrative" that vice must therefore be injurious to society, the sum of individuals. But, of course, Mandeville meant by vice not something harmful to its devotees, but something contrary to the dictates of a strictly rigoristic morality. John Dennis is a good example of the literal-minded whose attack on the *Fable* was largely an excited attempt to prove that if a thing has a bad effect it has an effect which is bad.

And then, besides the logomachy arising from a too literal reading of the *Fable*, much of the controversy was mere vituperation, as in Hendley's *Defence of the Charity-Schools. Wherein the Many False, Scandalous and Malicious Objections of those Advocates for Ignorance and Irreligion, the Author of the Fable of the Bees . . . are . . . answer'd* (1725).

[48] Notably Hutcheson (*Inquiry into . . . Beauty and Virtue*). But Hutcheson's attempt to prove the fundamental benevolence of humanity is not entirely an attack on Mandeville's psychological analysis; it is largely a giving of different names to the same emotions. Hutcheson, like Mandeville, denied the possibility of entirely dispassionate action; and Mandeville, like Hutcheson, admitted the reality of the compassionate impulses. Mandeville, however, insisted on terming all natural emotions selfish, whereas Hutcheson defined some of them as altruistic.

As to the effects of distinguishing between selfish and unselfish natural impulse, see below, note 53.

[49] That is, if he did not indulge merely in vituperation or in the misunderstanding considered above, note 47.

perhaps as staunch and unmitigated an ascetic as ever urged his
dogmas on other people; to Law an act done simply because a
person wanted to do it was *ipso facto* a bad act.[50] Yet Law, in his
answer to the *Fable,* at times approaches the utilitarian position,
and approves natural impulse.[51]

Law was typical. Of the rigorists who attack the *Fable* with any
insight, almost all [52] are driven at some point or other to turn upon
their own rigorism and to set up instead some form of utilitarianism; that is, to maintain that moral laws are justly to be shaped
and qualified according to the human ends to be served, and to
measure the service of these ends in terms of human happiness.[53]

[50] See his *Serious Call to a Devout and Holy Life* (1727), *passim.*
[51] *Remarks upon . . . the Fable of the Bees* (1724), pp. 33-37.
[52] Examples of rigoristic critics thus forced to repudiate their position
include Law, Dennis, Fiddes (*General Treatise of Morality,* 1724), and Bluet
(*Enquiry whether . . . Virtue tends to . . . Benefit . . . of a People,*
1725).
[53] Of course there were ways for the rigorists to evade Mandeville's attack
without quite giving up their position. Their very inconsistencies were a
means of defense; and Mandeville, too, really had taken a rigoristic position
more accentuated and bald than the average. But the devices by which the
rigorists sought to defend themselves without shifting ground were a very
incomplete defense. Thus, they argued that there was such a thing as
morally neutral activity, and that, therefore, self-regarding action and
natural impulse, while not sufficient by themselves for virtue, were not
necessarily vicious. This destroyed Mandeville's demonstration that the
rigoristic position implied everything to be necessarily vicious, but it left
him able still to claim that nothing could be virtuous, moral neutrality
being then the utter limit of moral achievement. This, of course, was hardly
satisfactory to the rigorists. Similarly, the ascetics could and did argue
that they did not deny the moral value of man's nature nor quite condemn
selfishness—indeed, that, properly understood, man's real nature and greatest happiness is found only in obeying the *a priori* dictates of Heaven, and
that, therefore, enlightened selfishness demands adherence to the rigoristic
code. Not to notice the important shift of sense in the word "nature,"
it is enough to point out here that the "theological utilitarianism" here
adopted is definitely an approach to more empirical utilitarianism, and,
therefore, that here again Mandeville's pressure towards utilitarianism is
only partially evaded. Again, the rigorists might deny, like non-rigorists
such as Adam Smith, that all natural feeling was selfish, maintaining that
some compassionate emotions were genuinely altruistic. But since they could
not say this of all compassionate feeling (some of this being obviously a
self-indulgence) they had to find a criterion to distinguish between selfish

On the other hand, there was another class of critics of the *Fable*, comprising those men by intellectual bias anti-rigoristic, like Hume and Adam Smith. These men took the *Fable* more calmly. Not holding the formalistic premise, they were not upset by Mandeville's deductions therefrom. They agreed with his analysis; but when he came to his rigoristic candle-snuffer and said, "All these good things are due to vice," they answered with Hume: If it be vice which produces all the good in the world, then there is something the matter with our terminology; such vice is not vice but good.[54] These critics then, simply accepted the *reductio ad absurdum* which Mandeville refused to educe, and, rejecting the formalism which gave rise to Mandeville's paradox, adopted instead a utilitarian scheme of ethics.

This may seem the simple and obvious thing to do. And it *is* simple and obvious now—after two hundred years. But in that simple and obvious step is the germ of the whole modern utilitarian movement; in that rejection of absolute *a priori* codes and that refusal to dissever man from the animals is the core of the modern scientific, empirical attitude. With the solving of Mandeville's paradox, indeed, is bound up our whole present-day intellectual atmosphere, the development of which the utilitarian movement has done so much to foster.

and non-selfish compassionate emotion; and, a strictly rigoristic test being here not possible, a utilitarian criterion naturally forced itself upon them. And, waiving the efficacy of their replies to Mandeville, the very fact that they had to frame replies on profoundly significant ethical questions was itself a service to the progress of speculation. One may look long in pre-Mandevillian literature for such careful distinctions between reason and emotion and their respective virtuousness as Law, for example, is forced to make in his effort to show that Mandeville misunderstood the rigoristic position. Whether he misunderstood it or not, he forced its adherents to attempt a liberation of their creed from the contradictions and indefiniteness which by themselves had given enough ground for his satire.

And apart from the sheerly logical side of the matter, there was a psychological reason why the attempt to cope with Mandeville so weakened the power of the formalists. Formalism affirms its transcendence; it professes absoluteness. When, therefore, imperfection in a formalistic creed is sufficiently felt to induce a desire for modification, the impulsion to formalism —a craving for the absoluteness and perfection which the creed promised— is weakened at its source, for the creed is now seen to be somewhat a thing of uncertainty.

[54] See Hume, *Essays*, ed. Green and Grose, 1889, II, 178.

Now, recognition of the inexpediency of rigoristic codes, which recognition eventually led to the utilitarian movement, was to be found elsewhere than in Mandeville, and the Mandevillian paradox was to be found latent in every-day points of view; but it was in dealing with Mandeville's especially forceful statement of this paradox that the utilitarian leaders were first caused to solve it. It was Mandeville who furnished them the specific stimulus. Their first statements of the utilitarian theory will be found in those books of theirs which deal with Mandeville, and were largely evolved through the controversy. This is true of three who wrote of him at considerable length—Francis Hutcheson, John Brown, and Adam Smith, while, of the other major leaders of the utilitarian movement, Hume was acquainted with Mandeville, Bentham and Godwin praised him, and James Mill strongly defended him.[55] And, turning from the leaders to the intellectual soil upon which they had to work, it should be recalled that contemporary anti- or non-utilitarian opinion had been qualified, and thus prepared for change, by the insistent paradox of the *Fable,* the outstanding ethical irritant of its generation. The case might be put more formally: Mandeville's critics are forced in their consideration of him to adopt in common the utilitarian attitude. Yet these critics were very dissimilar thinkers. Their agreement, therefore, must in considerable measure have been due to the nature of the subject—the *Fable of the Bees.*

The paradox of the *Fable,* indeed, supplied a spur which, on contact, almost necessarily forced all groups toward utilitarianism; and the enormous vogue of the book, together with the facts that its paradox was based on dominant types of ethical theory and thus involved and affected their many adherents, and that the book was so studied and reacted to by the utilitarian leaders, is proof of how generally and efficaciously the spur was applied.

As a matter of fact Mandeville has an even fuller claim than this to be considered a prime mover in the development of modern utilitarianism: it was not only through forcing a solution of the paradox that private vices are public benefits that the *Fable* fathered the utilitarian philosophy; another salient feature of Mandeville's ethical scheme had effect of a similar sort. This feature can be

---

[55] For references see above, notes 19, 21, 30, 17, 36, 20, and 28.

equally well described as moral nihilism, philosophical anarchism, or pyrrhonism. In morals, declared Mandeville, there are no universally valid rules of conduct. No person believes one thing but someone professes the opposite; no nation approves one form of conduct but another nation as strongly condemns it. ". . . hunting after this *Pulchrum & Honestum* is not much better than a Wild-Goose-Chace" (*Fable*, I, 380). "What Mortal can decide which is the handsomest, abstract from the Mode in being, to wear great Buttons or small ones? . . . In Morals there is no greater Certainty" (*Fable*, I, 377-9).

How Mandeville reconciled this pyrrhonism with the rigoristic ethics which he accepted superficially and the utilitarianism which was basic in his thought need not concern us here. The point is that he put his denial of general moral standards with his usual pungency, and that it produced noticeable reactions in a number of his critics.[56] It affected them in much the same way that his famous paradox had. It presented what was to them an intolerable scheme of things, which, for their peace of mind and soul, they had to remodel. And this remodeling—the furnishing of those valid ethical standards whose existence Mandeville denied—led them either to assert some *a priori* code and to maintain a rigoristic scheme of ethics (in which case the other edge of Mandeville's blade — his paradox — drove them toward utilitarianism); or it caused them to appeal to the utility of actions to supply, for judging those actions, the moral criteria Mandeville denied.

Thus with a double lash Mandeville drove his critics toward utilitarianism. By making the rigoristic position intolerable and the anarchistic position plausible, he forced his readers to formulate a way out. He furnished the necessity which is the mother of invention.

Nor is this all; for not only did Mandeville have the effect of a horrible example by driving people away from the position he ostensibly supported; he must also have exercised the influence of a model to be copied. As I indicated earlier, he himself had adopted

---

[56] For instance, in Law (*Remarks*, section 3), Berkeley (*Works*, ed. Fraser, 1871, II, 76 and 82), Brown (*Essays*, second essay, section 4), Adam Smith (*Theory of Moral Sentiments*, ed. 1759, p. 474), and Fiddes (*General Treatise of Morality*, preface).

the utilitarian point of view, and his whole viewpoint and method is strongly empirical.   Indeed, he gave the utilitarian principle one of its earliest statements in its modern form.[57]   " If a Publick Act," he said, " taking in all its Consequences, really produces a greater Quantity of Good, it must, and ought to be term'd a good Act." And again, " No sinful Laws can be beneficial, and *vice versa, . . .* no beneficial Laws can be sinful." [58]   Now, while I find no certain evidence of anyone's having copied directly after Mandeville's statements of the utilitarian philosophy, yet it is only rational to suppose that some of his myriad readers and students must have adopted such beliefs from the *Fable.*

Furthermore, considering the effect of the book on those who wrote about it, and its enormous vogue, it is only fair to assume that its influence was considerable on those who did not write about it.   Such an influence would have been exerted not only through the *Fable* itself, but through the works of disciples and opponents. This last matter is not entirely conjectural.   Bentham, for instance, said that one of the books which most affected him was the *De L'Esprit* of Helvétius.[59]   Now, this book is in many ways simply a French paraphrase of the *Fable.*[60]

This unspecific influence might be much further enlarged upon, but it is hardly worth the while thus to elaborate conjecture when

[57] Hutcheson's dictum that " *that Action* is *best,* which accomplishes the *greatest Happiness* for the *greatest Numbers* " (*Inquiry into . . . Beauty and Virtue,* ed. 1725, p. 164), was not pronounced till 1725.

[58] *Modest Defence of Publick Stews* (1724), pp. 68 and 69. Similar statements of the utilitarian position are found in the *Fable,* I, 274, II, 196, II, 333, and II, 335.

[59] See Leslie Stephen, *English Utilitarians* (1900), I, 177.

[60] Helvétius' derivation from Mandeville has been noted by Jodl, *Geschichte der Ethik* (Stuttgart, 1882), I, 189; Tabaraud, *Histoire Critique du Philosophisme Anglois* (1806), II, 186; Malesherbes (see Erdmann, *Grundriss der Geschichte der Philosophie,* ed. Berlin, 1870, II, 121) ; Morize, *L'Apologie du Luxe* (1909), p. 69; Sakmann, *Bernard de Mandeville* (Freiburg, 1897), p. 212; Schlosser, *History of the Eighteenth Century* (1843-52), I, 50; Guyot, *La Science Économique* (1907), p. 8; Hasbach, "Les Fondements Philosophique de l'Économie Politique" (in *Revue d'Économie Politique* for 1893, VII, 785) ; Buckle, *History of Civilization in England* (1872), II, 218; Robertson, *Short History of Freethought* (N. Y., 1906), II, 238. The Sorbonne blamed Helvétius' theories partly on Mandeville's teachings (see Sakmann, *Bernard de Mandeville,* p. 212).

the positive facts already noted suffice to prove the *Fable of the Bees* one of the most fundamental and persistent influences underlying the whole modern utilitarian movement.

III

Let us consider now Mandeville's effect on the course of economic theory, where his dominance was perhaps at its greatest.

One aspect of Mandeville's effect on the history of economic thought was his association with the famous division of labor theory. It is generally known that Adam Smith made this principle into one of the foundation stones of modern economic thought, but it is not so well known that Adam Smith took this theory largely from Mandeville. Mandeville, in the *Fable of the Bees,* as early as the first edition in 1714, definitely developed this conception not only once but several times.[61] Now, of course, the mere fact that Mandeville anticipated Smith would not mean that Smith derived his tenets from Mandeville, for Smith had been anticipated by others besides Mandeville. But Mandeville has special claims to influence. We know that Smith was intimately acquainted with the *Fable of the Bees.* He gave a most able analysis of it in his *Theory of Moral Sentiments,* and devoted half an essay to the influence of Mandeville on Rousseau.[62] Moreover, Mandeville not only sets forth the division of labor principle, but does so in the words that Smith was to make famous, speaking several times of " dividing " and " subdividing" "labour." Furthermore, one of the most famous passages in the *Wealth of Nations*—that about the laborer's coat—is only a padded paraphrase of a similar passage in the *Fable of the Bees.*[63] Finally, Dugald Stewart, who knew Smith personally, credits Mandeville [64] with having been Smith's inspiration. It does not seem that more need be said to indicate that considerable credit for putting the division of labor theory on its feet belongs to Mandeville.

---

[61] See *Fable,* I, 182-3, I, 411-4, II, 149, II, 335-6, II, 386, II, 391, and index to Part II under, " *Labour.* The usefulness of dividing and subdividing it."

[62] See above, note 30.

[63] Compare *Fable,* I, 182-3 and 411-4 with *Wealth of Nations,* ed. Cannan, I, 13-14. Cannan notes the parallel.

[64] Stewart, *Collected Works,* ed. Hamilton, VIII, 323. Cf. also VIII, 311.

But, though important, his influence on the establishment of this doctrine is a minor aspect of Mandeville's effect on economic tendencies. A more important phase was his place in the international discussion concerning the usefulness of luxury, one of the most widely agitated questions in the eighteenth century. The *Fable of the Bees* contains many passages—perhaps the best known passages in the book—in which Mandeville shows not only the inseparability of luxury from a flourishing state, but holds that the production and consumption of luxuries is necessary to make it flourishing. This opinion was in opposition not only to all the more ascetic codes of morality, but in contradiction to what might be called the classic economic attitude, which set forth the ideal of a Spartan state, exalted the simpler agricultural pursuits, and denounced luxury as the degenerator of peoples and impoverisher of nations. The question of the value of luxury was to be one of the great battle-grounds of Voltaire and the Encyclopedists.

Now, the *Fable of the Bees* was the practical starting place of the defense of luxury, and exerted an international effect, greatest, perhaps, in France. From Mandeville descend the chief exponents of this defense: Melon, Montesquieu,[65] Voltaire, and the Encyclopedists, and even defenders who were no economists, like Dr. Johnson.[66] Voltaire, perhaps the most influential of all the defenders, is especially indebted to Mandeville. The famous *Mondain* of Vol-

[65] The indebtedness of Melon and Montesquieu is treated in Morize's *L'Apologie du Luxe*. Melon's debt is noted also by Espinas, "La Troisième Phase et la Dissolution du Mercantilisme" (in *Revue Internationale de Sociologie* for Mar. 1902, p. 166).

[66] Johnson's economic tenets were apparently drawn from the *Fable*. Mandevillian passages abound; see *Works* (1825), XI, 349; Boswell, *Life*, ed. Hill, New York, 1889, II, 170-1, II, 217-9 (cf. *Fable*, I, 118 ff.), III, 56, III, 265 (cf. *Fable*, I, 108-10 and ff.), III, 282 (cf. *Fable*, I, 198-9), III, 291-2, and IV, 173; *Lives of the English Poets*, ed. Hill, I, 157 (Hill notes the origin of this in Mandeville). Johnson himself practically admits his debt (*Life*, III, 291): "He as usual defended luxury; 'You cannot spend money in luxury without doing good to the poor . . .' Miss Seward asked, if this was not Mandeville's doctrine of 'private vices publick benefits.'" And Johnson responds with a brilliant criticism of the *Fable*, the statement that he read the book forty or fifty years ago, and the acknowledgement that it "opened my views into real life very much."

taire, one of the chief works which drove the defense of luxury into the public mind, is in large part simply a versification of some of the theories set forth in the *Fable of the Bees*.[67]

Nor was the *Fable* merely a potent influence in the works of other writers. It not only spurred on the others, but was itself in the van of the attack. In 1785, the learned Professor Pluquet, in a work approved by the *Collège Royal,* called Mandeville the first to defend luxury from the standpoint of economic theory; [68] and so thoroughly in the public mind was Mandeville conceived as spokesman for the defense of luxury that a popular American play [69] as late as 1787 apostrophized not Voltaire, not any of the well-known encyclopedists, but Mandeville as the arch-advocate for this defense.

We now come to perhaps the most important aspect of Mandeville's economic influence. In the *Fable of the Bees* Mandeville maintains, and maintains elaborately, the theory at present known as the *laissez-faire* theory, which dominated modern economic thought for a hundred years and is still a potent force. This is the theory that commercial affairs are happiest when least regulated by the government; that things tend by themselves to find their own proper level; and that unregulated self-seeking on the part of individuals will in society so interact with and check itself, that the result will be for the benefit of the community. But unnecessary interference on the part of the state will tend to pervert that delicate adjustment. Mandeville develops this hypothesis in regard both to national and international matters. In national affairs, he says—and elaborates the thesis—" Proportion as to Numbers in every Trade finds it self, and is never better kept than when no body meddles or interferes with it " (*Fable,* I, 342). This advocacy of the *laissez-faire* theory he put into the most discussed part of the *Fable*—the notorious " Essay on Charity and Charity-Schools "; and the effect of his defense is evidenced by the number of replies directed specifically at this part of the *Fable*.

---

[67] This is demonstrated in Morize's *L'Apologie du Luxe au XVIIIe Siècle*.

[68] For the college's approval see Pluquet, *Traité Philosophique et Politique sur le Luxe* (Paris, 1786), II, 501. Pluquet's statement concerning Mandeville's priority (*Traité,* I, 16) is not quite accurate. Bayle had preceded Mandeville in defending luxury. However, the very error shows how closely Mandeville had become indentified popularly with the defense of luxury.

[69] Tyler, *The Contrast,* III, ii.

His application of the *laissez-faire* attitude to international concerns took the form of an attack on the then prevailing mercantile
theory—the belief that a nation's wealth could be gauged by the
amount of money in the country, and that, consequently, to keep
bullion in the country, imports should be either limited or pro-
hibited. In opposition to this, Mandeville, in keen analysis, demonstrated that a community's imports cannot be restricted without
affecting the ability of other nations to buy that community's ex-
ports; and he developed, also, some of the disadvantages of a nation's
possessing a disproportionate amount of the world's bullion.[70] This,
of course, is a predominant phase of the philosophy underlying
English free trade, and of the philosophy of free trade in general.

Some historians of economics have considered the *Fable of the
Bees* [71] an effectual source of the doctrine; but here the case must
be developed by other means than such definite citations as those
which demonstrate Mandeville's relation to the division of labor
theory and the defense of luxury. To begin with, considering the
effect of Mandeville's other economic tenets, and the extraordinary
popularity of the *Fable;* and in view also of the fact that the great
apostle of the *laissez-faire* theory (both in its national and international applications), Adam Smith, had such a knowledge of and
such a debt to the *Fable of the Bees,* it becomes more than possible
that as regards the *laissez-faire* theory also Mandeville's influence
must have been considerable. And to these considerations must
be added another more weighty. In the thought of the great leaders
of the *laissez-faire* movement—Hume and Smith—economic theory
is, as has been noted, the outgrowth of their ethical systems. They
saw man as a mechanism of interacting passions which he cannot
help indulging as they come uppermost. Fortunately, however,
according to their belief, these passions, although 'at first sight

[70] For Mandeville's defense of free trade see especially *Fable,* I, 110-4 and
284, and, for his theories concerning money, I, 213-5 and 345.

[71] Thus Hasback, " Les Fondements Philosophique de l'Économie Politique
de Quesnay et de Smith " (in *Revue d'Économie Politique* for 1893, VII,
782); Lange, *Geschichte des Materialismus* (1887), p. 743; Laviosa, *La
Filosofia Scientifica del Diritto in Inghilterra* (Turin, 1897), p. 683. Schatz
calls it (*L'Individualisme Économique et Social,* ed. Paris, 1907, p. 62)
" l'ouvrage capital ou se trouve tous les germes essentiels de la philosophie
économique et sociale de l'individualisme."

their dominion might seem to threaten anarchy, are so composed and arranged that under the influence of society their apparent discords harmonize to the public good. This immensely complicated adjustment is not the effect of premeditated effort, but is the automatic reaction of man in society; premeditated effort could only bungle and interfere with the complex social harmony which the facts of man's nature have of themselves created and will maintain. Thus, from this conception of human nature, the *laissez-faire,* or individualistic, theory of economics naturally followed— a descendant of ethical speculation.

Now, as has been indicated above, the relations between Mandeville and the ethical philosophers of his age were very close, especially as to the conception of human nature which underlies the economic theory of Smith and of Hume. Indeed, this conception of human nature, without which there would have been no philosophy of *laissez-faire,* and with which there could hardly help but be, is specifically Mandeville's. It is Mandeville who describes man as a mechanism of personal interests, which, however, functions in society for the public benefit. Mandeville is the creator of the "economic man" about whom Smith and Hume built their system. The *laissez-faire* theorists who followed Mandeville, whatever they may have said about his terminology of "vice" and "virtue," accepted his analysis of human nature, and used it, without adding essentially to its completeness, as the foundation of their systems.[72]

This sketch of Mandeville's influence on economic thought through the division of labor theory, the defense of luxury, and the *laissez-faire* philosophy does not exhaust his consequence in the field of economics; nor is our view of his general importance complete when we have added to his total effect on economics his commanding position in the development of the utilitarian movement. To complete our picture we should have to study the significance of that mass

[72] Schatz has developed this matter in his "Bernard de Mandeville" (in *Vierteljahrschrift für Social- und Wirtschaftsgeschichte* for 1903, I, 434-80).

Hume, it is true, came finally to assert the reality of benevolence, and Smith had always maintained this. However, their analysis of human nature really paralleled Mandeville's; they differed only in giving the same compassionate emotions contrary names, as Hutcheson did (see above, note 48). And, apart from that, in their economic writings they concentrated on man as a selfish mechanism, leaving his benevolence to be considered in more ethical works.

of fertile theory, embracing everything from anthropology to criminology, with which his work is crammed; we should have to analyze the possible effect of his other books, such as his once popular *Treatise on the Hypochondriack and Hysterick Diseases* and his *Enquiry into the Causes of the Frequent Executions at Tyburn,* which, according to J. M. Robertson, anticipated Howard's prison reforms; [73] we should need to consider the effect he exerted on outstanding figures like Hazlitt and Rousseau, and to add to our estimate a fact with which this paper has not been concerned— that the *Fable of the Bees* is the work of a literary genius. Only then should we have a full portrayal of the significance of a man who was perhaps among the half dozen English writers of the eighteenth century who most profoundly influenced the course of civilization.

Northwestern University.

---

[73] *Essays towards a Critical Method* (1889), p. 219.

LOUIS A. LANDA

Jonathan Swift

from

ENGLISH INSTITUTE ESSAYS, 1946

(1947), 20-40

Reprinted by permission of the Columbia

University Press

Jonathan Swift

鈴

By LOUIS A. LANDA

IT IS RARE INDEED that a commentator appraises any work of Jonathan Swift without reference to biographical fact. If one of Swift's minor efforts is under discussion, as the poem "The Lady's Dressing Room," we may expect the critical judgment to rest upon some such basis as that presented by Sir Walter Scott, who wished the poem to be interpreted in the light of the author's peculiar habits and state of mind. If Part III of *Gulliver's Travels,* where Swift attacks the corruptions of learning, is the object of consideration, the commentator is certain to make an excursion back to Swift's student days at Trinity College, Dublin, to explain that here began his life-long hatred of science and philosophy. And so with the other works, to the point that the criticism of Swift is a sustained endeavor to interpret the writings in the light of the man, although anyone who reads the critics of Swift will be aware too of a simultaneous and converse process—attempts to interpret the man in the light of the works.

With respect to Swift we are often confronted not

(177)

only with the critical significance of biographical evidence but as well with the biographical significance of critical evidence. It is easy to find commentators who will have it both ways, commentators, for example, who assume a morbid state of mind in Swift as an explanation of his scatalogical verse, then use the scatalogical verse to prove that the author undoubtedly was morbid. Traditionally the criticism of Swift's works is so inextricably mingled with biography that one looks almost in vain for critical judgments based upon merely aesthetic assumptions.

The persistent tendency of the commentators has been to assume a direct and fairly simple reflection in the works of the nature and personality of Swift; and such a work as *Gulliver's Travels* has as often as not been viewed as both a strange and puzzling psychological case history and a representation of its author's objective experiences. No one can doubt for a moment the validity and the fruitfulness of the biographical approach to *Gulliver's Travels* in particular or to Swift's works in general. Considering the character of his writings—their personal, intimate, and topical nature—this approach is the natural one. Yet I think that the interpretation of Swift has at times suffered somewhat from this tendency, this unwillingness of the commentator to detach the work from the man. But the overemphasis upon this approach is rather less disturbing than its misapplication or its loose and incautious use. Commentators who would doubtless feel some hesitation in equating Fielding with Tom Jones or Sterne with Tristram Shandy can accept with ap-

(178)

parent ease as a premise of their criticism that Swift is
Gulliver. In what follows I wish, first of all, to comment on certain recurring biographical considerations
which have played a part—a not very happy part—in
the criticism of Swift's works for a period of two centuries, and, secondly, to present some instances in
which other biographical considerations of value for
criticism have not been explored sufficiently.

The problem which has most preoccupied Swift's
critics has been the pessimism and misanthropy of
Gulliver's Travels and the endeavor to explain these
qualities in the work by searching for exactly corresponding qualities in Swift himself. Part IV of *Gulliver's Travels,* with its contrasting picture of Yahoo
and Houyhnhnm, has been the focal point of the discussions, and ordinarily the commentators have acted
on the assumption, though not always consciously,
that here in Part IV is the real key to Swift. It is maintained or implied that in Part IV are the possibilities of
a final comprehension and the basis of a final judgment. The image of Swift—the rather horrendous
image—which has been transmitted from generation
to generation is chiefly the image deduced from Part
IV, enforced by a careful selection of biographical
fact or myth appropriately chosen to stress the severe
lineaments of his character. Only occasionally is the
image, a monochrome, softened by reference to the
playful Swift, to Swift the author of delightful light
verse, the punster, the genial companion of Queen
Anne's Lord Treasurer and her Secretary of State, or to
the Swift who was a charming guest at great houses and

(179)

who had a genius for friendship among both sexes.

Perhaps for purposes of discussion we may ignore the volume and range of Swift's works and grant the unwarranted assumption that the masterpiece is somehow the man, and that a particular portion of the masterpiece—Part IV of *Gulliver*—is of such fundamental significance as to outweigh various other considerations. If we trace the progress of the criticism of *Gulliver's Travels* from Swift's earliest biographer, the Earl of Orrery, to the twentieth century, we find preponderantly and repetitiously a set of severe judgments passed on Part IV, judgments referable back to Swift the man. In his *Remarks on the Life and Writings of Dr. Jonathan Swift* (1752), Orrery climaxes his comment with the statement that "no man [was] better acquainted [than Swift] with human nature, both in the highest, and in the lowest scenes of life" (p. 338). Yet, contradictorily, in discussing Part IV of *Gulliver* he observes that Swift's misanthropy is "intolerable," adding that "the representation which he has given us of human nature, must terrify, and even debase the mind of the reader who views it" (p. 184). Orrery then proceeds to a lengthy vindication of mankind mingled with violent charges against Swift, among them that in painting the Yahoos Swift became one himself and that the "voyage to the Houyhnhnms is a real insult upon mankind" (p. 190). Orrery is significant because with few exceptions his is the tone and pretty much the method of criticism of the Fourth Voyage for a century and a half. The fundamental points raised are concerned with the motives or the personality of the author who would present this particular conception of human nature; and Orrery's explanation of Part IV in terms of injured pride, personal disappointments, and a soured temper becomes as time goes on the traditional one.

Even an occasional defender of Swift, as his good friend Patrick Delany, who answers Orrery point by point, is unwilling to undertake the defense of the last book of *Gulliver;* and he too lets fall such phrases as "moral deformity" and "defiled imagination." The eighteenth-century commentators, taking a high moral line, maintained that Swift's misanthropy had led him to write, as James Beattie phrased it, "a monstrous fiction." It was variously and characteristically stated: the gloomy and perverse Dean had talents that tended toward the wicked rather than the sublime; he was motivated by a malignant wish to degrade and brutalize the human race; he had written a libel on human nature. Though generally these commentators prefer to denounce the moral aspects of the Voyage to Houyhnhnmland and the degraded nature of the author, they leave no doubt that they think Part IV an artistic failure as well. In their eyes moral culpability and artistic failure have a necessary connection. The premise seems to be that a person of unsound views concerning human nature or of false moral views cannot write an artistically sound work. It is as though a Buddhist should deny literary value to Dante's *Divine Comedy* or Milton's *Paradise Lost* because these works are ethically and religiously unsound.

Yet it ought to be said to the honor of the eighteenth-

(181)

century commentators that they generally paid the author of *Gulliver* the compliment of believing him a sane man. It remained for certain nineteenth-century critics to take a new tack and to elaborate a less defensible charge. Though they accepted the view that the Fourth Voyage could be explained in terms of a depraved author, they *added* that it might well be explained in terms of a mad author. The charge of madness was usually presented with a certain caution. Two commentators in the middle of the century may be taken as examples of the willingness to accuse Swift of insanity and the unwillingness, at the same time, to come out unreservedly. In the *North British Review* of 1849 a reviewer writes of Swift's work that it is *"more or less* symptomatic of mental disease" (italics mine); and in the following year, in the London *Times,* a writer says that Swift was "more or less mad." It is possible that Sir Walter Scott is responsible for this wavering between outright and qualified assertion. In his edition of Swift's *Works* (1814) he writes that we cannot justify, by saying that it has a moral purpose, "the nakedness with which Swift has sketched this horrible outline of mankind degraded to a bestial state" (1883 ed., I, 315). He prefers to explain the misanthropy of *Gulliver* as the result of "the *first* impressions of . . . *incipient* mental disease" (italics mine). There are nineteenth-century commentators who felt that the Fourth Voyage should not be read. Thackeray gave such advice to the audience who listened to his lectures on the English humorists of the eighteenth century in 1851; and, later, Edmund Gosse—using such phrases as

(182)

"the horrible satisfaction of disease" and a brain "not wholly under control"—declared that the "horrible foulness of this satire on the Yahoo . . . banishes from decent households a fourth part of one of the most brilliant and delightful of English books." It is somewhat more surprising to find W. E. H. Lecky, who usually showed a well-balanced and sympathetic understanding of Swift, falling into the jargon. He can see Swift's misanthropy as a constitutional melancholy "mainly due to a physical malady which had long acted upon his brain." [1] It is not surprising, however, that in the twentieth century the psychoanalysts have seized on so attractive a subject as Swift; and now we find *Gulliver* explained in terms of neuroses and complexes. The following quotation is taken from the *Psychoanalytic Review* of 1942: *Gulliver's Travels* "may be viewed as a neurotic phantasy with coprophilia as its main content." It furnishes

abundant evidence of the neurotic makeup of the author and discloses in him a number of perverse trends indicative of fixation at the anal sadistic stage of libidinal development. Most conspicuous among those perverse trends is that of coprophilia, although the work furnishes evidence of numerous other related neurotic characteristics accompanying the general picture of psychosexual infantilism and emotional immaturity.

By a diligent search this psychoanalyst was able to discover in *Gulliver's Travels* strains of misogyny, misanthropy, mysophilia, mysophobia, voyeurism, exhibitionism, and compensatory potency reactions. If

[1] Introduction to the *Prose Works of Jonathan Swift,* ed. T. Scott, 1897, I, lxxxviii.

this psychoanalytic approach seems to have in it an element of absurdity, we should recognize that it is only a logical development of the disordered-intellect theory of the nineteenth-century critics, the chief difference being that the terminology has changed and that the psychoanalyst frankly sees *Gulliver's Travels* as case history, whereas the critics were presumably making a literary appraisal. Perhaps these crude and amateur attempts deserve little attention, yet they are a phenomenon that the serious student of Swift can hardly ignore in the light of their recurrence and their effectiveness in perpetuating myths. And they sometimes come with great persuasiveness and literary flavor, as witness Mr. Aldous Huxley's essay in which, by virtue of ignoring nine tenths of Swift's works, he can arrive at an amazingly oversimplified explanation of Swift's greatness: "Swift's greatness," Mr. Huxley writes, "lies in the intensity, the almost insane violence, of that 'hatred of bowels' which is the essence of his misanthropy and which underlies the whole of his work" (*Do What You Will*, 1930, p. 105).

I suggest that the commentators who have relied on a theory of insanity or disordered intellect to explain Swift's works have weakened their case, if they have not vitiated it entirely, by resorting to ex post facto reasoning. The failure of Swift's mental faculties toward the end of his life—some fifteen or sixteen years after the publication of *Gulliver's Travels*—was seized upon to explain something the critics did not like and frequently did not understand. It seemed to them valid to push his insanity back in time, to look retrospectively at the intolerable fourth book of *Gulliver's Travels,* and to infer that Swift's insanity must have been at least incipient when he wrote it. One recent commentator, rather more zealous than others, hints that the madness can be traced as far back as *A Tale of a Tub.* Commentators who observe manifestations of a disordered intellect in the Fourth Voyage have not thought to question the intellect behind the Third Voyage, yet we know now that the third was composed in point of time after the fourth. And these commentators have nothing but praise for the vigor, the keenness, the sanity, and the humanity of the mind that produced the *Drapier's Letters,* yet we have reasonable assurance that Swift completed the draft of Part IV of *Gulliver* in January of 1724 and was at work on the first of the *Drapier's Letters* in February.

Another procedure of which the critics of Swift are fond deserves to be scanned: the habit of taking an isolated statement or an isolated incident and giving it undue significance to support their prepossessions. In a recent study of Swift, in many respects of more than ordinary perceptiveness, the author considers Part IV of *Gulliver* as an embodiment of the tragic view of life. In so doing he passes from the work to the facts or presumed facts of Swift's life to enforce his interpretation, adducing as evidence the report of Swift's manner, in his later years, of bidding friends good-by: "Good night, I hope I shall never see you again." If Swift really used this remark, if he used it seriously, some weight may be attached to it; but I should want to know to whom he used it and in what tone or spirit.

It sounds very much like his usual banter, his manner of friendly insult and quite genial vituperation which so often distinguishes his letters to friends who understood his ironic turn and his liking for the inverted compliment. How can we rely on such casual remarks or possibly know what weight to give them? But such a remark is related to Swift's habit of reading certain parts of the Book of Job to prove that he hated life, and is made to seem of a piece with the Fourth Voyage of *Gulliver's Travels*. This is typical of the commentators who have culled from Swift's letters, from the biographies, and from other documents all the presumed evidence of gloom and misanthropy in order to uncover what they have a strong prepossession to uncover, the essential misery of his existence. This is the way to prove, in support of the interpretation of the Fourth Voyage, that "Swift's life was a long disease, with its disappointments, its self-torture, its morbid recriminations."

But a matter of statistical balance is involved here: the facts listed and weighted heavily have been too much of one complexion. Too much has been made of the last years of Swift's life, when he bothered less to conceal his moods and his irritations—and when he seemed to get a certain satisfaction in talking about his ailments. I should like to see some biographer counter the gloomy approach by emphasizing Swift's zest for life, his vitality, and the playfulness of his mind. There is ample evidence in his letters—and in what we know of his activities—of high spirits, good humor, and daily satisfactions. Such a study might very well, without distortion, evidence an unexpected mathematical balance between happiness and unhappiness.

I should not want to be put into the position of denying Swift a considerable pessimism and a fair share of misanthropy. These qualities, however, were not so raw or so unassimilated or so crudely operative in his daily existence as has been often represented. The manner in which these personal qualities have been used to explain *Gulliver* deserves to be questioned. It has been an overly simple process of equating biographical fact and artistic statement, of viewing the work as a transcription of the author's experiences or as a precise and complete representation of his personal philosophy—or as a final explanation of his personality. There is an obvious danger in seeing an artistic or imaginative construction as mere duplication. *Gulliver's Travels* is a work of mingled fantasy and satire; it is Utopian literature, highly allusive and symbolic, charged with hidden meanings and projected to a level several removes from the real world of its author.

To leaven the biographical approach other questions deserve attention. What are the artistic necessities of a work of this type? What are the aesthetic principles, quite apart from other considerations, that shape the work? To what extent is there a compromise between these principles and the conscious or the undeliberate tendency of the author to reflect his experiences and his personality?

If the biographical approach to Swift has been crudely used or overemphasized in certain respects,

(187)

there are other respects in which biographical considerations of critical value have been left almost
wholly unexplored. The most significant of these
seems to me to be Swift's profession as a Christian
divine. Is there in this some clue to an explanation of
Part IV of *Gulliver*? If a reading of the sermons can
be trusted, the eighteenth-century divine relished his
duty to expatiate on the evils and corruptions of this
world and the inadequacies of this life. He seemed to
enjoy measuring the imperfections before him against
a higher set of values. Swift, I think, would have held
an optimistic divine to be a contradiction in terms;
and his own pessimism is quite consonant with the pessimism at the heart of Christianity. One of Swift's sermons begins as follows:

The holy Scripture is full of expressions to set forth the
miserable condition of man during the whole progress of
his life; his weakness, pride, and vanity, his unmeasurable
desires, and perpetual disappointments; the prevalency of
his passions, and the corruptions of his reason, his delud-
ing hopes, and his real, as well as imaginary, fears . . .
his cares and anxieties, the diseases of his body, and the
diseases of his mind. . . . And the wise men of all ages
have made the same reflections.[2]

If Swift had written his own comment on *Gulliver's
Travels*, he might very well have used the words of
this sermon. *Gulliver's Travels* certainly is full of expressions to set forth the miserable condition of man—
his weakness, pride, and vanity, his unmeasurable desires, the prevalency of his passions and the corrup-

[2] *On The Poor Man's Contentment.*

tions of his reason—and so on through the catalogue. Indeed, Swift's few sermons and those of other eighteenth-century divines could easily be used to annotate *Gulliver's Travels*. It is difficult for me to believe that a contemporary could fail to see the affinity between the Fourth Voyage—or the whole of *Gulliver*—and many of the conventional sermons on human nature and the evils of this life. Swift's emphasis on depraved human nature and his evaluation of man's behavior are certainly *not* at odds with Christian tradition. There is no need to ascribe such views solely to personal bitterness or frustrations or melancholia. His thinking and status as a divine had an effect much more profound than is generally recognized. A good case can be made for Part IV of *Gulliver* as being in its implications Christian apologetics, though of course in nontheological terms; in a sense it is an allegory which veils human nature and society as a Christian divine views them. It is by indirection a defense of the doctrine of redemption and man's need of grace.

Only an occasional commentator has recognized and stressed the essentially Christian philosophy of the Fourth Voyage. The first was Swift's relative, Deane Swift, who declared that the Christian conception of the evil nature of man is the "groundwork of the whole satyre contained in the voyage to the Houyhnhnms." Then this cousin of Jonathan Swift, this lesser Swift, delivers himself of a catalogue of vices worthy of his great cousin:

(189)

Ought a preacher of righteousness [he asks], ought a watch-man of the Christian faith . . . to hold his peace . . . when avarice, fraud, cheating, violence, rapine, extortion, cruelty, oppression, tyranny, rancour, envy, malice, detraction, hatred, revenge, murder, whoredom, adultery, lasciviousness, bribery, corruption, pimping, lying, perjury, subornation, treachery, ingratitude, gaming, flattery, drunkenness, gluttony, luxury, vanity, effeminacy, cowardice, pride, impudence, hypocrisy, infidelity, blasphemy, idolatry, sodomy, and innumerable other vices are as epidemical as the pox, and many of them the notorious characteristicks of the bulk of mankind? [3]

"Dr. Swift," he adds, "was not the first preacher, whose writings import this kind of philosophy." Surely those clergymen who week after week exposed the deceitfulness of the human heart would have agreed with Deane Swift.

It seems to be true, as T. O. Wedel has pointed out,[4] that Swift's view of human nature was opposed to certain contemporary attitudes in which the passions of men were looked on kindly and in which the dignity of human nature was defended in such a way that the doctrine of original sin lost its efficacy. In his *Reasonableness of Christianity* (1695) John Locke could deny, without raising much serious protest, that the fall of Adam implies the corruption of human nature in Adam's posterity. It is this same current of thought

[3] *Essay upon the Life, Writings, and Character of Dr. Swift* (1755), pp. 219–20.
[4] For the relationship between Swift and Wesley stated in this paragraph see an article to which I am much indebted, T. O. Wedel, "On the Philosophical Background of *Gulliver's Travels*," *Studies in Philology*, XXIII (1926), 434–50.

that later in the century disturbed John Wesley who complains in one of his sermons (No. XXXVIII, "Original Sin") that "not a few persons of strong understanding, as well as extensive learning, have employed their utmost abilities to show, what they termed, 'the fair side of human nature in Adam's posterity.' " "So that," Wesley continues, "it is now quite unfashionable to say anything to the disparagement of human nature; which is generally allowed, notwithstanding a few infirmities, to be very innocent, and wise, and virtuous." Is it not significant, when Wesley comes to write his treatise on *The Doctrine of Original Sin* (1756), that he should turn to Swift, to Part IV of *Gulliver* for quotations? In this treatise Wesley refers scornfully to those "who gravely talk of the dignity of our nature," and then quotes several times from what he calls "a late eminent hand." The "late eminent hand" is Swift's, whose words from Part IV of *Gulliver* describing man as "a lump of deformity and disease, both in body and mind, smitten with pride" Wesley has seized on. Wesley refers again and again to the "many laboured panegyrics . . . we now read and hear on the dignity of human nature"; and he raises a question which is, I think, a clue to Swift. If men are generally virtuous, what is the need of the doctrine of Redemption? This is pretty much the point of two sermons by Swift, where he is obviously in reaction to the panegyrics on human nature which came from Shaftesbury and the benevolists, from the defenders of the Stoic wise man, and from proponents of the concept of a man of honor. Swift sensed the

(191)

danger to orthodox Christianity from an ethical system or any view of human nature stressing man's goodness or strongly asserting man's capacity for virtue. He had no faith in the existence of the benevolent man of Shaftesbury and the anti-Hobbists, the proud, magnanimous man of the Stoics, or the rational man of the deists; his man is a creature of the passions, of pride and self-love, a frail and sinful being in need of redemption. The very simple and wholly unoriginal strain of apologetics in Swift's sermons is based upon an attitude common in traditional Christian thought; and to my way of thinking Swift the clergyman repeats himself in *Gulliver's Travels*.

It might be of value to carry the consideration of Swift the clergyman beyond application to *Gulliver,* to discover whether his activities in his profession may not throw some light on his other works—the Irish tracts, for example. Those who make a case for Swift's misanthropy, his pessimism and gloom, his tragic view of life, can point to these tracts to enforce their views. Can we accept the Irish tracts as "monuments to despair, pessimism, bitterness, hopelessness and hate; and like his other works . . . distillations of the man"? It is certainly true that the tracts reflect disillusionment, and are filled with statements that reflect hopelessness. Undoubtedly they are charged with bitterness; yet it is not necessarily the bitterness of a man who hates his fellow men or thinks them not worth saving. The real note is perhaps despair, despair at corruption and weakness; but it is obvious that Swift's *words* of despair were tempered by hope that something might be achieved to relieve the Irish people. Until the end of his active life he persisted in writing and working to achieve reforms. His continued zest for reform is significant, even though he assures us frequently that he is without hope. He did not withdraw to nurse his bitterness or his misanthropy. Is it not conceivable that the tone, the emotional coloring, the violent rhetoric of the Irish tracts are susceptible to an explanation in terms other than personal bitterness or pessimism? Are not the rhetorical qualities, the strong expressions, appropriate to the purpose in hand and proper from a clergyman and reformer bent on seeing maladjustments corrected? Swift's occupation, his position as dean and dignitary, gave him the opportunity and imposed on him the obligation to take cognizance of private and public distresses. He dispensed the Cathedral funds for private and public benefactions; he sat on numerous charity commissions; he was requested and expected to make his views known on public ills. As a dignitary in a hapless country, it was—to say the least—mathematically probable that he should encounter conditions to call forth gloomy expressions. If a sensitive, public-spirited, socially conscious Irishman of Swift's day were anything but gloomy, then indeed we would need an explanation. Irish conditions being what they were, Swift's lamentations, the fierce and desperate rhetoric, are a natural product of a man doing his duty in an appropriately chosen diction. It was Swift's job to spy out the worst and to call attention to it in the strongest language he could command. By his calling he was a

(193)

specialist in disorders; and here we have possibly a sufficient explanation of the tone of the Irish tracts without recourse to any theory of personality or misanthropy.

The Irish tracts, including the *Drapier's Letters,* offer another instance of the way in which interpretation and biographical considerations enforce each other—and at the same time a further instance of how easily divergent views may be arrived at. If a person without any knowledge of Swift came to the tracts without prepossessions, he would carry away with him, despite certain qualifications, the general impression of an Irish patriot moved by a genuine desire for the national welfare. Swift would obviously appear to be concerned to protect Ireland from exploitation at the hands of a powerful England. There is, certainly, a note of scorn for the slothful and dirty native Irish; but there is also a note of strong compassion and a tendency to absolve them from blame in the light of intolerable conditions which they could hardly be expected to transcend. In a letter of 1732 he writes that the English ought to be "ashamed of the reproaches they cast on the ignorance, the dulness, and the want of courage, in the Irish natives; those defects . . . arising only from the poverty and slavery they suffer from their inhuman neighbors . . . the millions of oppressions they lie under . . . have been enough to damp the best spirits under the sun." [5] It is not accidental that the English authorities viewed Swift as dangerous, and certain of his tracts as openly inciting

[5] *Correspondence,* ed. E. Ball (1910–14), IV, 328.

the Irish to make themselves independent of England. Indeed his sense of Ireland's rights as a nation to develop its own economy and to control its own destiny is at times so vigorously expressed—his words probably go beyond his intention—that he can easily be taken as a confirmed nationalist.

And thus the Irish claim Swift as the Hibernian Patriot. In 1782, when Grattan secured the adoption of the declaration of Irish independence in the Irish House of Commons, he took the floor to apostrophize Swift (and Molyneux) in these words: "Spirit of Swift! Your genius has prevailed. Ireland is now a nation!" This view of Swift as the "first and greatest of Irish nationalists" found stronger and stronger proponents as time went on. In the last part of the nineteenth century we find this not uncharacteristic utterance: "No one can now talk of Irish liberty, the Irish nation, Irish manufactures, Irish grievances, and Irish rights without speaking the language and echoing the thoughts of Swift. When [he] denounced Wood's Halfpence he was not thinking at all of finance and currency. He was after quite other game. He meant to build up an Irish nation." In the twentieth century such enthusiasm eventuates in the view, recently propounded, that Swift's sympathies were with the silent and hidden Ireland rather than with the Protestant Ascendancy and that the native Irish "made him a God of their Gaelic Olympus, and even imagined that he was secretly of their faith." A year does not pass without discussion in some Irish journal of the exact nature of Swift's Irishism.

(195)

Yet there is the other side, equally well supported by biographical materials. Certain fierce defenders of Irish nationalism will have none of Swift. Admitting that some of his efforts had good results, they still insist that the facts of Swift's biography leave no interpretation possible but that Swift was an Englishman of the hated Protestant Ascendancy. The Irish nation was for him the English Pale. Catholic and Celtic Ireland hardly existed for him. It has been pointed out that in Swift's day the Gaels had hundreds of poets to express their feelings and that these poets were often politically self-conscious; yet in their works are no references to the Dean or the Drapier.

The case is strengthened by a careful selection of biographical fact: Swift's insistence that his birth in Ireland was mere accident; his pride in his Yorkshire ancestry; his desire for residence and a career in England; and his reference to his being exiled in Ireland; his resistance to any attempt to spread the use of the Irish language. But what weighs most heavily with the proponents of this view is that Swift had, they insist, no real concern for Catholic Ireland, that he favored the harsh penal laws against the Catholics, and that his concern was only for the Anglo-Irish Anglicans. As usual, Swift's words and actions are interpreted with considerable asperity, and he is seen as defending Ireland less out of humanity than out of a desire to revenge himself on his enemy, Robert Walpole and the Whig administration in England. This is the familiar Swift—and the familiar application of his biography to interpretation—Swift, the man of violent personal prejudices, moved by envy and disappointed ambition, whose every act, known or surmised, whose every utterance, public or private, and whose personality in every facet, real or imagined, are brought to bear in the interpretation of his works.

ALAN D. McKILLOP

Epistolary Technique in Richardson's Novels

from

THE RICE INSTITUTE PAMPHLET

Volume XXXVIII, No. 1(April, 1951), 36-54

Reprinted by permission of the Rice Institute
Committee on Publications

EPISTOLARY TECHNIQUE IN RICHARDSON'S
NOVELS

IN PASSING from Samuel Richardson's little volume of
familiar letters to *Pamela* we find, in place of a collection of brief letters touching on various situations, a massive
collection of long letters developing a single situation.
Richardson calls his new method "writing to the moment";
he uses a letter-writer who records the passing thought,
gesture, and incident in great detail while moving toward
the novelist's foreordained end.[1] But the story told in this
way is not merely a series of direct communications from
the correspondent. Richardson, as an experienced printer,
knew every step in the making of a book, and saw the completed and published novel as the result of a long and
intricate process; he extended "writing to the moment" to include every step in the history of a published correspondence. The writing of the letters is only the beginning; they
are copied, sent, received, shown about, discussed, answered,
even perhaps hidden, intercepted, stolen, altered, or forged.
The relation of the earlier letters in an epistolary novel to
the later may thus be quite different from the relation of the
earlier chapters of a novel to the later. It may seem obvious
to say that the writing of the letters is an important part of
the action of an epistolary novel, but this is not always so;
the letters may be just sections of a narrative told in the
first person, or may otherwise be submerged in the story. In
a scholarly and well documented study of the subject, Professor Frank Gees Black makes the significant comment:
"Though skill in particular cases qualifies the statement, it
would seem that in letter fiction the epistle should be kept
as a means of presenting the story and not be unduly ob-

truded as an agent in the narrative."[2] But in Richardson's
work the emphasis on the letter is almost incessant and
highly characteristic. And his putting the writing of the
novel into the novel itself is far from artless. One would have
to go no farther than Cervantes to find an author who puts
the discovery of documents conveying the story into the
story, and who represents the characters thinking of themselves as in a book. But the device of writing, editing, and
even reading the novel within the novel is, I think, essentially
new in Richardson—it has even been taken to be new and
ingenious as recently as Gide's *Les Faux-Monnayeurs* (1925).
A brief survey of the ways in which letter-writing, or, as we
may say more pompously and accurately, the provision and
transmission of documents, figures in Richardson's novels,
may help to dispel the idea that Richardson simply cut up
his moralizing narrative into long lengths which he called
letters.

It is appropriate that Mr. B. should find Pamela in the first
letter writing a letter, and that he should soon order her not
to spend so much time in correspondence.[3] The first complication appears when the servant John regularly shows what
she writes to Mr. B. before he carries her messages to her
parents, as he later confesses in a surreptitious note. Then
Pamela's pen gains momentum, and she begins to keep a
continuous record which is relatively independent of the receipt and delivery of letters: "I will write as I have Time,
and as Matters happen, and send the Scribble to you as I
have Opportunity."[4] She even writes a letter when she expects to see her parents within twenty-four hours: "I will
continue my Writing still, because, may-be, I shall like to
read it, when I am with you, to see what Dangers I have
been enabled to escape; and tho' I bring it along with me."[5]

There is an underlying compulsion to explain that Richardson's major correspondents love writing in the epistolary way for its own sake.

When Pamela is removed to Lincolnshire and kept a prisoner there, the novelist himself has to intervene for several pages to tell the incidents leading to the visit of her father to Mr. B., since he has no one on hand to make the record—something that would never happen in Richardson's fully developed work. Pamela is now forbidden to carry on correspondence, and Richardson extends the principle of continuous record and has her keep a journal. Since she is expected to show all that she has written to her keeper Mrs. Jewkes, she has to conceal writing materials and smuggle out letters, as to the friendly Parson Williams. These letters are included in the journal; the process includes not only the writing but the copying of letters—one's own and those lent one to read. It is sobering to reflect that unless we remember this duplication of copies, we underestimate the paperwork done by Richardson's characters. Richardson, at least after 1740, kept copies of letters sent and sometimes of letters received, and his characters follow the same plan after they have hit their epistolary stride. This begins in Pamela's journal, and develops enormously. She becomes to a large extent her own compiler and editor. Much of this may seem mere *paperasserie*, such as the formal set of proposals for keeping her as his mistress which Mr. B. submits in writing: "I took a Copy of this for your Perusal, my dear Parents."[6] Richardson also begins in a small way the device of the fabricated or falsified letter when he has Mr. B. prescribe a short letter to be sent to her parents.[7] There is occasional dramatic use of letters, such as the misdelivery and interchange of letters from Mr. B. to Pamela and Mrs.

Jewkes, so that Pamela discovers his plot against Parson Williams, and later the anonymous note warning her that Mr. B. intends to use the device of a mock-marriage—both important in raising and prolonging Pamela's suspicions.[8] Even more important is the impact of the journal on the later action. Pamela had managed to send the early part of the record to her parents by way of Williams; the second part she hid under a rosebush in the garden, and Mrs. Jewkes seized it. Thereafter the prudent girl kept the rest of the journal "sew'd in my Under-coat, about my Hips."[9] The part seized by Jewkes is turned over to Mr. B. Just as Pamela is represented as the author and editor of her own story, so Mr. B. is represented as the first reader.

> You have so beautiful a Manner, that it is partly that, and partly my Love for you, that has made me desirous of reading all you write; tho' a great deal of it is against myself: for which you must expect to suffer a little. And as I have furnish'd you with a Subject, I have a Title to see the Fruits of your Pen.—Besides, said he, there is such a pretty Air of Romance, as you relate them, in *your* Plots, and *my* Plots, that I shall be better directed in what manner to wind up the Catastrophe of the pretty Novel.[10]

At his demand Pamela gives him the later part, including the account of her attempted escape. His comments and reactions are at this point a delayed response to the journal, though not of course an epistolary response; assuming that the reader has been interested in the original narrative, Mr. B.'s responses reënforce this original appeal and at the same time advance the action. Even if we do not agree that Richardson is completely successful in putting over this device, we should recognize the novelist's ingenuity.

Mr. B. is now in melting mood, and finds Pamela's insistence on returning to her parents perverse. The action moves quickly here; Richardson is not always tedious, and

letters may precipitate as well as suspend the action. After
the parting, as Pamela stops for the night, she sees in advance a letter which was to have been delivered to her at
noon the next day, a letter which tells her that Mr. B. had
been about to make honorable addresses to her when she
expressed the preference for a return to her parents.[11] A
record of Mr. B.'s underlying intentions is thus put before
Pamela in time to dispose her to accept another letter the
next day imploring her to return, the result of Mr. B.'s reading the rest of the journal. Perhaps, as the moralists tell us,
she should not have gone back, but at least the premature
opening of the first letter, with its touch of feminine curiosity,
is ingeniously timed, and the climactic action produced by
the reading of the journal is skillfully presented.

This climax is the most effective use of documentation in
Pamela. The rest of the two-volume novel published in November 1740, which we may call *Pamela I*, is of less interest
for epistolary technique, though Mr. B.'s sister Lady Davers,
the strongest opponent of the marriage, is well presented in
some vigorous quarrel scenes. The epistolary methods used
in the two-volume sequel *Pamela II* of December 1741 do
not show successful experimentation. The device of repeating and commenting on the earlier action is ineffectively extended, as when Mr. B. tardily supplements Pamela's original
report of the early situation.[12] One of the most effective
episodes in *Pamela II*, the showdown with Mr. B. about his
incipient affair with a beautiful countess, is told by Pamela
to Lady Davers in letters which are then read and supplemented by Mr. B., but without heightening the dramatic
effect.[13] The new social perspectives of *Pamela II* make the
early story seem crude and awkward in retrospect: Pamela
comments on the elevation of her own style, is ashamed to

have strangers read her account of Mr. B.'s clumsy attempts at seduction, and remarks regretfully that she knew no "polite Courtship."[14] Some comparatively light social notation on the new level is developed in the letters of Polly Darnford, Pamela herself, and Lady Davers, and points forward to the later novels. The novelist at times tries to keep up an evenly balanced two-way correspondence. But the decline of dramatic interest invites digression and interpolation, always a threatening possibility in the epistolary novel.[15]

In line with the social setting, the action, and the psychology, *Clarissa* shows a more elaborate epistolary structure. Pamela is the only major correspondent in her story; whereas all readers of *Clarissa* are likely to remember the enormous narrative in terms of parallel series of two-way communications between Clarissa Harlowe and Anna Howe on the one hand, Robert Lovelace and John Belford on the other. Yet this is not the scheme as actually worked out; for a considerable span we are likely to find that one correspondent dominates, often writing long letters journal-wise, in which other letters or documents may be included or absorbed. The early action centers with morbid intensity on Harlowe Place, and Clarissa reports the crisis in the family circle in practically continuous narrative. The correspondence is carried on under difficulties; Clarissa is imprisoned by her family, and has to smuggle out letters to Anna Howe with the aid of trusted servants. There is also a carefully motivated secret correspondence with Lovelace: she wishes to pacify him so that he will not take violent action; she seeks a line of retreat in case her family forces the repulsive Solmes upon her; and, more vaguely, it is intimated that Lovelace appears as a possible lover and husband. But Lovelace's letters are not immediately pushed to the fore; as summarized and reported by Clarissa to Anna, they at first fall into the predominant line. We are told that Clarissa keeps complete files—"I have promised to lay before you all his Letters and my Answers."[16] Her task of copying is even more laborious than Pamela's. The arrangement seems clumsy, but the total effect is impressive: the elaborate documents connect Clarissa with the world and at the same time emphasize her tragic isolation. She carries on written negotiations with her family, even though they are under the same roof; Lovelace's world of pride and passion threatens in this sequence, but is kept at a distance; Anna Howe's world of normal social relationships, in which girls can innocently indulge their whims and quarrel harmlessly with parents and suitors, comes tantalizingly close, but Clarissa can never reach it. Anna's is sometimes a light epistolary comedy with Richardson's characteristic devices; thus in the long communication containing her sketch of Solmes, the earlier part of the letter is the theme of a discussion with her mother reported in the later part.[17]

Richardson does not go about his work simply by having everybody in the story write letters. No protracted correspondence ever takes place between Lovelace and Clarissa; their ambiguous relationship is described, always imperfectly, in letters to and by others, and does not allow the sharp commitments of direct written communication between principals. The novelist uses his secondary correspondents with great skill. Anna, like Belford later in the other series, gains for a time in importance; the crescendo of her letters presents the happy normal world denied to Clarissa and the shrewd yet inadequate judgments of that world; she sides against the Harlowes more sharply than the heroine herself, and points out that Clarissa is in love with Lovelace, and that if she takes flight with him, marriage is her only choice. After the actual flight, we come closer to parallel series, Clarissa to Anna and Lovelace to Belford, but the scheme does not become mechanical. Where there would be excessive duplication, Richardson continues to abridge and summarize Lovelace's letters, and sometimes to omit letters which the formal scheme of the novel would require. The originals of such letters may have existed, in some part, in the novelist's writing desk. He "restored" letters and passages to *Clarissa* in the third edition, and later made additions on a smaller scale to *Grandison;* no doubt other letters produced in the working out of the plans for the novels remained unpublished.

With the advance of Lovelace to the foreground of the correspondence, about the time of the removal of Clarissa from Hertfordshire to London, he enters on an elaborate series of forged and garbled letters, beginning with the faked letter from "Doleman" which tricks Clarissa into thinking that the lodging with the infamous widow Sinclair is eligible and respectable. Clarissa is plied with forged letters purporting to come from Lovelace's relatives, and is cruelly duped by an agent of Lovelace's, "Tomlinson," who pretends to be negotiating on behalf of her uncle. Lovelace also gets access to the Anna-Clarissa letters, and of course sends copious extracts to Belford. Thus one of the two main lines of letters is presented as impacted in the other. As the crisis approaches, Lovelace intercepts a letter in which Anna tells Clarissa the truth about the plots against her; since he knows Clarissa would expect a letter, he imitates Anna's hand and garbles the text. His *libido dominandi* does not adequately motivate these cumbersome devices, yet Clarissa's tragic isolation can still evoke an imaginative response. While, with

mingled credulity and pride, she thinks that marriage negotiations are under way and that the situation is still largely
within her control, a veil of deceptive documentation cuts
her off from normal and rational humanity. Outrage follows
deception. Clarissa escapes to Hampstead, is traced thither
and confronted by Lovelace, lured back to London, and
there drugged and violated. Lovelace's reports still enlarge
upon his tricks and stratagems, but the curtain drops temporarily at the curt sentence, "The affair is over. Clarissa
lives."[18] After Clarissa's later escape to Covent Garden she
again becomes principal correspondent for a time and re-
sumes connections with the outer world. She unravels the
web of Lovelace's deceptions, and in unimpeded letters to
Anna tells for the first time the details of the tragic return
from Hampstead.[19] This is a masterly piece of narrative, sur-
charged with almost intolerable apprehension and agony; its
power is partly due to the skill with which Richardson has
held it back until Clarissa could tell the story with the tre-
mendous weight of deliberate recollection. It is after all the
complex letter mechanism that produces this powerful delayed effect, this merciless iteration of doom.

With the false arrest of Clarissa at the suit of the bawd
Sinclair, her temporary imprisonment at Rowland's, and her
final asylum at Smith's in Covent Garden, Belford intervenes
and becomes for the first time the reporter of important matters; indeed for a considerable time he gains what we may
call epistolary dominance not only in the Lovelace-Belford
series but in the whole system of the book. His is the pen of
a ready writer; both he and Lovelace use shorthand for their
confidential correspondence with each other and for other
records.[20] He begins his new role as an intermediary between
Lovelace and Clarissa. Clarissa would be ready to tell her

story herself, if she could; but after seeing specimens of
Lovelace's letters and finding that Belford is worthy to be
"the protector of her memory," she makes him her executor
and the editor of the letters that tell her story.[21] As a reformed rake, he offers too much edifying comment to suit
our taste; he divagates, for example, into the warning tale of
the sad end of his fellow-rake Belton, and into a comparison
between Rowe's *Fair Penitent* and Clarissa's story, yet he is
by no means superfluous. In the reprisals and regrets of the
latter part of the story the correspondence is more widely
scattered; various members of the family have their say, including Colonel Morden, Clarissa's one true friend among
her kinsfolk, and it is Belford's part to keep the story from
running into excessive fragmentation. Though Anna Howe
is directed to collaborate with him, he remains in control.
Anna's wit and spirit become irrelevant, and she naturally
drops into the background, though Richardson goes too far
when he sends her on a trip to the Isle of Wight during the
last days of Clarissa's life.[22] Yet Belford is never dramatically
central, like Clarissa and Lovelace, and Richardson slackens
his grip at the end when he says that the Conclusion is "supposed to be written by Mr. Belford."[23]

The story runs its course to a foreseen conclusion, yet the
shock of surprise can still be felt. The inept letters of the
pedant Brand almost at the hour of Clarissa's death may remind us that Richardson had sought comic relief even in
this tragedy; and now that Anna Howe and Lovelace can
no longer write with gusto, he offers this heavy and heartless
humor, with its remarkable burlesque of formal and didactic
letter-writing. Finally, in contrast to the protracted reports
and discussions connected with Clarissa's death, we have the
swift denouement in which Lovelace goes to the Continent

and falls in a duel with Morden—a short span in which Lovelace uses epistolary dominance only for a few curt words.

In summing up the use of letters in *Clarissa*, we may say that the correspondents report conflict and offer commentary. The conflict is not typically a head-on collision between one correspondent and another, assertion and reply; rather it is presented largely within the letters of a dominant correspondent, who may report dialogue in great detail, sometimes with dramatic notation, interpreting all signs and considerations in their bearing upon motives, intentions, and future action. A report of conflict thus becomes an elaborate assertion of personality, and here Richardson often dramatizes "the divided mind." This is preëminently true of the principal characters, Clarissa and Lovelace. For Miss Howe and Belford, the provision of comment outweighs the report of conflict, but when Richardson is at his best there is an organic connection. Secondary characters may be given over to one aspect or another; thus the Harlowe family represent conflict in its most brutal and sullen form, and are not enlightened enough to provide a significant commentary. Other secondary characters show a considerable variety of function.

In *Pamela* and *Clarissa* Richardson experiments with and extends epistolary technique. There is less innovation in *Grandison*, though some new effects and values appear. Instead of the isolated and distressed heroine writing her own history almost single-handed, as in *Pamela*, or with the aid of other correspondents who are primarily concerned with her affair, as in *Clarissa*, we now have an enormous expansion of social correspondence carried on without serious obstruction or threat, and usually intended to be shown about to a circle of friends. It has been noted that such work had already been done in *Pamela II* and in Anna Howe's

part of *Clarissa*. The story and the letters go by groups—the
Selby group in Northamptonshire, the Grandisons, and later
the della Porrettas in Italy. The lending and forwarding of
long files of letters, so that one group may be informed about
the other, is part of the pattern of the book. The groups
ramify into the casual contacts of actual society. Letter-
writing thus loses dramatic intensity and sometimes becomes
a pastime for young ladies, while the protestations about
long letters become conventional: "What a length have I
run! How does this narrative Letter-writing, if one is to
enter into minute and characteristic descriptions and conversations, draw one on!"[24] Thus Richardson moves in the
direction taken later by Fanny Burney and Jane Austen. The
danger is that such a record will be too trivial and discur-
sive. The age was ready to call almost any batch of sketches
or essays "letters." Richardson had already fallen into this
trap in *Pamela II*, however, and is generally aware of the
danger. Though at the beginning of *Grandison* he is capable
of reporting a long argument about ancient and modern
learning, he tries to make it part of the social record; we
may well feel that there is too much set discussion here, but
the dialogue is well dramatized.[25]

In general, Richardson keeps to the relatively simple plan
already described: one major correspondent is likely to
dominate a considerable section of the book, and other documents are taken into this sequence. The correspondent may
send installments numbered as letters ("Harriet in continuation") which are really chapters or long entries in a record
kept journal-wise. The attempt of Sir Hargrave Pollexfen to
abduct Harriet and her rescue by Sir Charles Grandison
introduce new characters and potential correspondents, but
Harriet continues to transmit the mail. In presenting the
ideal gentleman Sir Charles, Richardson has a new problem;

the hero cannot report *in propria persona* all his noble deeds and thoughts. Others must chant his praise, as in Voltaire's *Zadig:*

> Que son mérite est extrême!
> Que de grâces! que de grandeur!
> Ah! combien monseigneur
> Doit être content de lui-même!

Harriet at times becomes a collector and transcriber of records about Sir Charles and the history of the Grandison family. The novelist is at some pains to provide her with documents. Thus, when Sir Charles answers Sir Hargrave's challenge to a duel, Sir Charles's own copy of the letter is shown to Mr. Reeves, who shows it to Harriet, who in turn sends it to Lucy Selby. Reeves also gives Harriet a copy of the record of the dialogue between Sir Charles and Sir Hargrave's friend Bagenhall, made by the young clerk whom Bagenhall had brought with him. When Sir Charles comes to breakfast with Sir Hargrave, he likewise brings along a precautionary stenographer.[26] The natural inclination of Richardson's busybodies in our own enlightened times would be to tap telephones and plant dictaphones.

But these are extreme cases; Richardson usually falls back on the assumption of a ready journal-keeper and letter-writer, perhaps seconded by an industrious assembler and editor of memoranda. When the Grandison sisters tell Harriet the story of their father's tyranny, Charlotte seems to be using notes—"But what say my minutes?"[27] Characters regularly provide one another with files of letters; thus Harriet furnishes the Grandison group with the record down to the time of her abduction, letters already given in the text.[28] When letters not already given are thus provided, the effect is that of a cut-back in the narrative. After Sir Charles has told Harriet directly the earlier part of the Italian story (she re-

members it word for word, of course), Dr. Bartlett, Sir
Charles's tutor and revered friend, sends Harriet successive
"pacquets" of letters recounting the story of the della Porretta
family and the early stages of the long negotiations and
parleys about a possible marriage of Clementina and Sir
Charles. His nephew and amanuensis extracts the story from
his papers.[29] But when Sir Charles makes his second journey
to Italy, and the match with Clementina seems imminent
until her religious scruples come to be decisive against it,
the hero himself, for the only time in any long sequence,
relays the account to Dr. Bartlett in a one-way correspondence. Clementina herself is never a Richardsonian heroine in
the full sense, for she never becomes a major correspondent.
Her story was intended to provide dramatic suspense and a
note of tragedy, but Richardson never allows her to write
letters "to the moment" on a large scale. Thus the one character in *Grandison* who shares in some degree the tragic
isolation of Clarissa is denied epistolary dominance. Somewhat similarly, though Richardson presents the jealous Olivia
as a rival both to Clementina and Harriet, she does not develop as a character or a correspondent, and we may conjecture that the novelist at first intended to give her a larger
place in the story and then prudently dropped her. It is almost startling to find the indefatigable Dr. Bartlett telling
Harriet that it will not be necessary to give Olivia's story
at length.[30]

While Dr. Bartlett is sending his consignments and later
while Sir Charles is reporting at length from Italy, Harriet
and the English story might seem to be outweighed. There
is a mechanical set-up by which Harriet sends the Bartlett
installments to Lucy Selby; later Sir Charles's sister Charlotte
likewise forwards his advices from Italy to Harriet in

Northamptonshire. But the Italian story does not keep the social comedy from developing in England, and this gives a new importance to Charlotte Grandison, now Lady G. She is obviously an extension of the character of Anna Howe, and her letters also elaborate the suggestions for a comedy of manners contained in Harriet's London-to-Northampton-shire letters at the beginning of the story. With the Italian plot kept at arm's length, and Harriet's affairs at a stand, Charlotte is given more freedom to develop her wit and her temperament than Anna Howe ever had. Her husband Lord G., she feels, leaves much to be desired, and she becomes perverse, whimsical, and "arch" to a degree, and is duly rebuked by the more sedate Harriet. Her letters are of major importance in keeping us in the well-bred English world, and for the first time in the story we have a genuine two-way correspondence, Harriet and Charlotte both carrying weight.

After Clementina's renunciation and Sir Charles's return to England, this social tone still dominates. Richardson's problem is to maintain interest now that the way is clear for the union of Harriet and Sir Charles. He still strives for dramatic range, and to this end Clementina and the della Porretta family invade England. When this irruption falls short, as it does, one would expect padding and digressions, along with tedious eulogies and congratulations such as we find in *Pamela II*. Some of our fears may be realized, but not our worst fears; Richardson does not, for example, give us extended travel letters when Harriet and her party take a tour in Northamptonshire, and even the glories of Grandison Hall are largely reported, we are told, in letters by Lucy Selby which "do not appear."[31] There are some rather set general conversations, one on the possibility of the intellectual life for women and another on young girls' romantic no-

tions and the folly of a first love,[32] but Richardson does not
sink his story by interpolation. The more serious difficulty
is that he does not succeed in blending the Italian story and
the English social comedy as they converge. Clementina and
Charlotte are "scarce cater-cousins."

The vein of social notation does, however, produce ingenious variations of the device of making dramatic play
with letters, and this sometimes stands in contrast to the
plodding and mechanical provision of documents. At the
very beginning, one of Harriet's Northamptonshire suitors,
Greville, reads the company passages from a letter from
Lady Frampton about Harriet, and "passages from the copy
of his answer." He then lends a copy for Harriet to read,
scratching out some sentences, but, it is added, only faintly.[33]
There is a good deal of by-play of this kind. Letters that are
being written may be shared with friends at the elbow of
the ready writer; Harriet may begin a letter and Lucy finish
it. Charlotte can tantalize Harriet with the possibility of
reading a letter from Sir Charles to Dr. Bartlett, though
Charlotte of course had no right to pick the letter up in the
first place.[34] The surface of the story is rippled with feminine
curiosity about the contents of letters. Sir Charles has great
reserve; he does not tell all his affairs to his sisters (a piece
of masculine psychology ingeniously used by Richardson),
and inquisitiveness adds point to the insistent questions as
to what has been written, what should be written, what
should be sent, read, shown, and to whom. The opening and
extension of social relationships, the growth of friendship
and love, are figured in this endless process of divulging
letters and deciding just how much may be conveyed in
confidence at a given time. Negotiations about letters admit
of very fine shading. Thus, when the Grandison sisters ask to

see Harriet's letters with the proviso that Harriet may omit certain passages, she resents even their assumption that some things she has written should be kept from them.[35] Again, Sir Charles picks up a stray sheet of a letter in which Harriet says that his young ward Emily Jervois secretly loves him; he is of course too much of a gentleman to read it, but the fact that Harriet doesn't want him to read something she has written about Emily carries appreciable weight.[36]

Thus the characteristic contribution of *Grandison* is not the elaboration of epistolary mechanism, but the refining of the letter-form and the letter-situation as a device for the notation of social and psychological detail. An interesting by-product is the ingénue type of letter written, not at great length, by Emily Jervois, but destined to be developed in various ways by Fanny Burney and Jane Austen. There are even hints that the lighter letters in *Grandison* could be made a delicate instrument for high comedy, that is, for criticism of the basic assumptions of the book. Charlotte's picture of the eternal friendship struck up between Harriet and Clementina, heroines both, "each admiring herself *in* the other," raises large issues and opens an important page in Meredith's Book of Egoism.[37] The persistent interest which Meredith showed in Sir Charles Grandison is highly significant. Both Charlotte and Harriet are capable of speaking of Sir Charles with salutary irreverence. There is a minor strain of uneasiness or dissatisfaction after his return from Italy, a hint of impatience at his very proprieties and virtues. Should he come unannounced to Selby House to claim, as all expect, the hand of Harriet? Should he send word in advance? "Or does he think," asks Harriet, "we should not be able to out-live our joyful surprize, if he gave us not notice of his arrival in these parts before he saw us?"[38] Richardson doesn't quite make it, but he comes close to taxing his letter-form beyond the limits of Harriet's scrupulousness and propriety, and it may be added, beyond the limits of his own rationality as well. Once he goes so far as to record at length a troubled dream of Harriet's, recapitulating with broken imagery the principal events of the story.[39] "Incoherences of incoherence!" she cries, and her "resveries" are not extended or made the staple theme of other letters; but even here Richardson can be seen experimenting with his forms and testing their possibilities to the last.

Perhaps the most common criticism of Richardson is that he had an imperfect knowledge of his own principles and themes, that he was in part duped by convention, entrapped by his underlying interest in sex, and constantly in danger of being swamped by his own verbosity. But if he falls short of classic control of his themes, the reason may be, not that he was inept or incompetent, but on the contrary that his use of the letter form led him in one direction toward a specific analysis of the enmeshing complexities of life, and in another direction toward a heightened awareness of the discontinuities and blockages, the frustrations and loose ends, that seem to make up the plight of man.

ALAN D. McKILLOP

NOTES

References to Richardson's novels are to the Shakespeare Head Edition, 18 vols., Oxford: Blackwell, 1929-31. The three novels, *Pamela, Clarissa,* and *Grandison,* are designated by the abbreviations *P., Cl.,* and *Gr.* Small Roman numerals refer to the numbering of the letters in the Shakespeare Head Edition; Arabic numerals refer to pages.

1. For an excellent brief statement of what "writing to the moment" means in keeping a journal or writing a novel, see Frederick A. Pottle's Introduction to *Boswell's London Journal 1762-1763* (New York, 1950), pp. 12-13.

2. Frank Gees Black, *The Epistolary Novel in the Late Eighteenth Century* (Eugene, Ore., 1940), p. 58. (University of Oregon Monographs: Studies in Literature and Philology, No. 2.) See also, for good comments on the dramatic function of letters in Richardson's novels, with special reference to *Pamela*, Ernest A. Baker, *The History of the English Novel* (10 vols.; London, 1924-39), IV, 22-24.

3. *P.*, I, 3, 23-24.
4. *P.*, I, 49.
5. *P.*, I. 111.
6. *P.*, I, 263.
7. *P.*, I, 127, 154-55.
8. *P.*, I, 218-21, 307.
9. *P.*, I, 311.
10. *P.*, I, 317.
11. *P.*, II, 6-7.
12. *P.*, III, xxx.
13. *P.*, IV, xxxi-xxxvi.
14. *P.*, III, 14, 35-36, 159-60.
15. For further comment on Richardson's methods in *Pamela II*, see Alan D. McKillop, *Samuel Richardson, Printer and Novelist* (Chapel Hill, N.C., 1936), pp. 57-61.

16. *Cl.*, I, 180.
17. *Cl.*, I, xxvii.
18. *Cl.*, V, xxxii.
19. *Cl.*, VI, xliv-xlvi.
20. *Cl.*, VI, 113, 315.
21. *Cl.*, VII, xix, xx.
22. *Cl.*, VII, 109, 247.
23. *Cl.*, VIII, 278.
24. *Gr.*, I, 86.
25. *Gr.*, I, x-xiv.
26. *Gr.*, I, 319-20, 337-43, 378.
27. *Gr.*, II, 79.
28. *Gr.*, II, 385.
29. *Gr.*, III, 42.
30. *Gr.*, III, 406.
31. *Gr.*, VI, 32, 75, etc.
32. *Gr.*, V, lviii; VI, lxii.
33. *Gr.*, I, i, ii.
34. *Gr.*, II, xxxiii.
35. *Gr.*, II, xix.
36. *Gr.*, V, 255-56.
37. *Gr.*, VI, 255-56.
38. *Gr.*, V, 88.
39. *Gr.*, V, xxxv.

MAYNARD MACK

The Muse of Satire

from

THE YALE REVIEW

Volume XLI, Number 1(1951), 80-92

THE MUSE OF SATIRE
By MAYNARD MACK

I T grows plainer every year that literary study in our part
of the twentieth century has been very considerably stimulated by one important event. This event is the gradual
reëmergence of rhetoric—by which I mean the reëmergence of a number of interpretive skills and assumptions about
literature that under the name of rhetoric once formed part of
the medieval trivium and together with grammar made up a
study somewhat resembling what we now call literary expli-
cation. As we begin the second half of the century, the signs of
this rhetorical quickening seem to me to be multiplying very
fast.

To begin with a whimsical example, I notice that my reprint of Puttenham's "Arte of English Poesie" (1589), frequently on loan to students, is well thumbed chiefly at the
twelve chapters where the rhetorical figures are named and
illustrated. Forty-five years ago, when Gregory Smith reprinted Puttenham in his collection of "Elizabethan Critical
Essays," these were precisely the chapters, and the only chapters, he chose to leave out. This is a straw in the wind from
readers.

There is ampler evidence from writers. One might cite,
at the level of research, the speedy proliferation of studies
dealing with aspects of rhetorical history: investigations like
J. W. H. Atkins' of classical, medieval, and Renaissance
criticism, or T. W. Baldwin's of Shakespeare's grammar
school training, or Miss Tuve's of sixteenth-century rhetorical manuals. At the level of practical criticism, one could point
to the reappearance of rhetorical concepts in literary discourse.
One hears the word *decorum* used nowadays without a sneer;
one comes across mentions, though as yet no illuminating
discussions, of the "three styles"—high, middle, and low; one

even hears the admission that there may be something in genre: "Paradise Lost," Mr. C. S. Lewis has been trying to persuade us, is what it is at least as much because it is a *heroic* poem as because it was written by John Milton.

But doubtless the climactic evidence at the critical level is the so-called—the so ineptly called—"new" criticism. The enormous influence of this body of writing can only be properly understood, I think, if we realize that it has been the pioneering phase—that is to say, the most applied and "practical" phase—in a general revival of rhetorical interests and disciplines. Evoked by the absence of a continuing tradition of rhetorical analysis (for the classical tradition was unfortunately discredited by the time the new critics began to write), this criticism has been an effort, often fumbling, often brilliant, to recapture some of the older exegetical skills, or at any rate to formulate their equivalents, for modern use.

Now rhetoric being a body of learning that insists on the recognition of artifice, one of the effects of its renascence is bound to be the reinvigoration of our sense of distinctions between art and life. If we compare ourselves with the nineteenth century in this respect, we realize that we no longer write, or care to read, books like Mrs. Cowden Clarke's on "The Girlhood of Shakespeare's Heroines" (1850–2); nor do we care to inquire, even with so great a critic as A. C. Bradley, where Hamlet was when his father was being murdered, or with Ellen Terry, how the Boy in Henry V learned French: "Did he learn to speak the lingo from Prince Hal, or from Falstaff in London, or did he pick it up during his few weeks in France with the army?" We realize, too, that unlike the nineteenth century we can no longer speak of Shakespeare's "Dark Period" or his "Joyous Comedies," except by enclosing the words in quotation marks. We acknowledge, to be sure, that a playwright and his plays are involved with each other in important ways, but we are much too conscious of artifice to be willing to risk a direct reading from comedy or tragedy to the author's states of mind.

In our dealings with the drama, in fact, most of us are now

willing to add to the study of how a work grows or what it does the study of what it is. Inquiries into biographical and historical origins, or into effects on audiences and readers, can and should be supplemented, we are beginning to insist, by a third kind of inquiry treating the work with some strictness as a rhetorical construction: as a "thing made," which, though it reaches backward to an author and forward to an audience, has its artistic identity in between—in the realm of artifice and artifact. With respect to drama, there has lately been building a valuable even if by no means uniformly sound criticism of this kind. But outside the drama, and a few other areas recently invaded, we cannot point to very much. On the subject of poetry in general, Mr. Ricardo Quintana has complained, most of our commentary still "turns out to be either description of our impressions" (i.e., effects), "or reconstruction—largely imaginary—of a precise moment in the poet's emotional history with which we have chosen to equate the poem" (i.e., origins).

One need not share Mr. Quintana's doubt as to the effectiveness of other approaches to feel that in the case of satire, at any rate, what is desperately needed today is inquiry that deals neither with origins nor effects, but with artifice. Criticism of satiric literature has barely begun to budge from the position of Macaulay, Elwin, Leslie Stephen—all of whom seem, at one time or another, to have regarded it as a kind of dark night of the soul (dank with poisonous dews) across which squibs of envy, malice, hate, and spite luridly explode. Here is a sample from 1880, referring to Pope's "Sporus": "that infusion of personal venom"; "the poet is writing under some bitter mortification"; he is "trying with concentrated malice to sting his adversary"; he is "a tortured victim screaming out the shrillest taunts at his tormentor" (Sir Leslie Stephen). Here is a sample from 1925, referring to Pope's epistles and satires in general: at the time of their creation, "they resembled nothing so much as spoonsful of boiling oil, ladled out by a fiendish monkey at an upstairs window upon such of the passers-by whom the wretch had a grudge against"

(Lytton Strachey). And here is a sample from 1941, referring to the "Dunciad"—if anything the tone is shriller: "impossible to admire it without an unenviable pleasure in sheer spite"; "the tone of furious indiscriminate hatred"; "the half-crazed misanthropy of the whole poem"; "a general indictment of the human race"; "this universal shriek of loathing and despair" (Gilbert Highet).

In this essay, I should like to ventilate this fetid atmosphere a little by opening a window on one or two rhetorical observations. These observations will be commonplaces, but the record suggests that they can bear repetition. My illustrations will be drawn from Pope, especially from his formal satires, such as the "Epistle to Dr. Arbuthnot"; and my thesis will be that even in these apparently very personal poems, we overlook what is most essential if we overlook the distinction between the historical Alexander Pope and the dramatic Alexander Pope who speaks them.

It is to underscore this distinction that I have ventured in my title to name the Muse. For the Muse ought always to be our reminder that it is not the author as man who casts these shadows on our printed page, but the author as poet: an instrument possessed by and possessing—Plato would have said a god, we must at any rate say an art. And, moreover, the Muse ought to remind us that in any given instance the shadow may not delineate even the whole poet, but perhaps only that angle of his sensibility which best refracts the light from epic, elegy, pastoral, lyric, satire. The fact is not without significance, it seems to me, that though Pope, following the great victories of naturalism in the seventeenth century, had to make do with a minimum of mythology and myth, he never discarded the Muse, either the conception or the term. She appears with remarkable regularity even in his satires, and there, for my present purposes, I am choosing to regard her as a not entirely playful symbol of the impersonality of the satiric genre—of its rhetorical and dramatic character.

Rhetorically considered, satire belongs to the category of *laus et vituperatio*, praise and blame. It aims, like all poetry,

in Sidney's phrase, through the "fayning notable images of
vertues [and] vices," to achieve "that delightful teaching
which must be the right describing note to know a Poet by."
And it has, of course, its own distinctive means to this. Prominent among them to a casual eye is the *exemplum* in the
form of portrait, like Dryden's Zimri or Pope's Atticus; and
the middle style, which stresses conversational speech (more
than passion or grandiloquence) along with aphoristic phras-
ings, witty turns, and ironical indirections. Less prominent
but more important than either of these is (the satiric fiction)
into which such materials must be built.

All good satire, I believe it is fair to say, exhibits an appreciable degree of fictionality. Where the fiction inheres in familiar elements like plot, as in "Absalom and Achitophel" or
"The Rape of the Lock" or "The Dunciad" or "The Beggar's
Opera," its presence is, of course, unmistakable; and it is unmistakable, too, in such satires as Swift's "Argument against
Abolishing Christianity" or his "Modest Proposal," where the
relation of the speaker to the author is extremely oblique, not
to say antithetical. But when the relation is only slightly oblique, as in Pope's formal satires, the fictionality takes subtler
forms and resides in places where, under the influence of romantic theories of poetry as the spontaneous overflow of
powerful emotions, we have become unaccustomed to attend
to it. (How far unaccustomed is seen if we reflect that the
extraordinary views of Gulliver in Houyhnhnmland have
been repeatedly cited as identical with Swift's. And this despite
the fact that the incidents of the book show the author to be
studiedly undercutting his hero-gull and to be using the
metaphor of the rational *animal*, the Houyhnhnm, to make
it plain that pure rationality is neither available nor appropriate to the human species—just as in the "Essay on Man"
Pope's fully rational angels show "a Newton as we show an
Ape.")

One aspect of the fictionality in Pope's case resides in the
general plan of the formal satiric poem. This, as Miss Ran-
dolph has observed in the work of Horace, Persius, and Juvenal, contains always two layers. There is a thesis layer attack-

ing vice and folly, elaborated with every kind of rhetorical device, and, much briefer, an antithesis layer illustrating or implying a philosophy of rational control, usually embodied in some more or less ideal norm like the Stoic *vir bonus*, the good plain man. The contours of a formal verse satire, in other words, are not established entirely or even principally by a poet's rancorous sensibility; they are part of a fiction.

We encounter a further aspect of this fiction when we pause to consider that the bipartite structure just mentioned apparently exists to reflect a more general fictive situation. This situation is the warfare of good and evil—differentiated in satire from the forms it might take in, say, lyric, by being viewed from the angle of social solidarity rather than private introspection; and from the forms it might take in, say, tragedy, by being carried on in a context that asserts the primacy of moral decision, as tragedy asserts the primacy of moral understanding.

Tragedy and satire, I suspect, are two ends of a literary spectrum. Tragedy tends to exhibit the inadequacy of norms, to dissolve systematized values, to precipitate a meaning containing—but not necessarily contained by—recognizable ethical codes. Satire, on the contrary, asserts the validity and necessity of norms, systematic values, and meanings that *are* contained by recognizable codes. Where tragedy fortifies the sense of irrationality and complexity in experience because it presents us a world in which man is more victim than agent, in which our commodities prove to be our defects (and vice versa), and in which blindness and madness are likely to be symbols of insight, satire tends to fortify our feeling that life makes more immediate moral sense. In the world it offers us, madness and blindness are usually the emblems of vice and folly, evil and good are clearly distinguishable, criminals and fools are invariably responsible (therefore censurable), and standards of judgment are indubitable. All this, too, results from a slant of the glass, a fictional perspective on the real world—which, as we know, does not wholly correspond either with the tragic outlook or the satiric one.

Finally, we must note, among these general and pervasive

aspects of fictionality in satire, the *ethos* of the satirist. Classical rhetoric, it is well to recall, divides the persuasive elements in any communication from one man to another into three sorts: the force of the arguments employed, the appeal to the interest and emotions of the hearer, and the weight of authority that comes from the hearer's estimate of the speaker's character, his *ethos*. For the satirist especially, the establishment of an authoritative *ethos* is imperative. If he is to be effective in "that delightful teaching," he must be accepted by his audience as a fundamentally virtuous and tolerant man, who challenges the doings of other men not whenever he happens to feel vindictive, but whenever they deserve it. On this account, the satirist's *apologia* for his satire is one of the stock subjects of both the classical writers and Pope: the audience must be assured that its censor is a man of good will, who has been, as it were, *forced* into action. *Difficile est saturam non scribere:* "It is difficult *not* to write satire."

Moreover, the satirist's *ethos* is the *rhetorical* occasion (even though vanity may be among the *motives*) of his frequent citations of himself. As a candid fellow, for instance, and no pretender to be holier than thou:

> I love to pour out all myself, as plain
> As downright Shippen, or as old Montaigne. . . .
> In me what Spots, (for Spots I have) appear,
> Will prove at least the Medium must be clear.

A man, too, of simple tastes, persistent loyalties:

> Content with little, I can piddle here
> On Broccoli and mutton, round the Year;
> But ancient friends, (tho' poor, or out of play)
> That touch my Bell, I cannot turn away.

A man whose character was formed in the good old-fashioned way by home instruction and edifying books:

> Bred up at home, full early I begun
> To read in Greek, the Wrath of Peleus' Son.
> Besides, My Father taught me from a Lad,
> The better Art, to know the good from bad.

Consequently, a man who honors the natural pieties:

> Me, let the tender Office long engage
> To rock the Cradle of reposing Age:

who is sensible of life's true ends:

> Farewell then Verse, and Love, and ev'ry Toy,
> The rhymes and rattles of the Man or Boy,
> What right, what true, what fit, we justly call,
> Let this be all my Care—for this is All:

and who is valued by distinguished friends. If the friends happen to be out of power, or drawn in part from a vanished Golden Age, so much the better for *ethos:* our satirist is guaranteed to be no time-server.

> But does the Court a worthy Man remove?
> That instant, I declare, he has my love.
> I shun his Zenith, court his mild Decline;
> Thus Sommers once, and Halifax were mine.
> Oft in the clear, still Mirrour of Retreat
> I study'd Shrewsbury, the wise and great. . . .
> How pleasing Atterbury's softer hour!
> How shin'd the Soul, unconquer'd in the Tow'r!
> How can I Pult'ney, Chesterfield forget
> While Roman Spirit charms, and Attic Wit? . . .
> Names which I long have lov'd, nor lov'd in vain,
> Rank'd with their Friends, not number'd with their Train.

By passages of this kind in Pope's satires, the rhetorically innocent are habitually distressed. They remark with surprise that Pope insists on portraying himself in these poems as "lofty, good-humored, calm, disinterested." Or they grow indignant that an epistle like "Arbuthnot" reveals "not what Pope really was, but what he wished others to think him." They fail to notice that he speaks this way only in a certain kind of poem, and so enlarge irrelevantly—though to be sure with biographical truth enough—upon the subject of his vanity. Meantime, on a rhetorical view, the real point remains, which is simply that in passages of this sort, as also in his notes to the "Dunciad," and probably, to some extent, in the publication of his letters (both these enterprises, significantly, accompanied his turning satirist), Pope felt the necessity of supporting the *ethos* a satirical poet must have.

Obviously, the two agents to be considered in the fictive situation are the person speaking and the person addressed. We may, however, dismiss the second, for though he is often a true *adversarius*—a friend calculated like Job's friends to be egregiously mistaken in his views and values—no one, I think, has ever seriously misinterpreted a satire because he failed to see that the *adversarius* was a fiction. It is with the satiric speaker that the difficulty has come. We may call this speaker Pope, if we wish, but only if we remember that he always reveals himself as a character in a drama, not as a man confiding in us. The distinction is apparent if we think of Wordsworth's use of the word *young* in a famous passage from "The Prelude" about the early days of the French Revolution: "Bliss was it in that dawn to be alive, And to be young was very heaven"—and then compare it with Pope's remark to the friend with whom he professes to be conversing in the first dialogue of the "Epilogue to the Satires": "Dear Sir, forgive the Prejudice of Youth." Wordsworth's *young* is determined by something outside the poem, something true (in the years to which the poet refers) of himself in real life. But in real life, when Pope wrote his dialogue, he was already fifty; his *youth* is true only of the satiric speaker of the poem, who is an assumed identity, a *persona*.

This *persona* or speaker has almost always in Pope's formal satires three distinguishable voices. One is the voice of the man I have partly described in connection with *ethos:* the man of plain living, high thinking, lasting friendships; who hates lies, slanders, lampoons; who laughs at flatteries of himself; who is "soft by Nature, more a Dupe than Wit"; who loves of all things best "the Language of the Heart"; and who views his own poetry with amused affection qualified with Virgilian tenderness for the tears of things in general:

> Years foll'wing Years, steal something ev'ry day,
> At last they steal us from ourselves away;

In one our Frolicks, one Amusements end,
In one a Mistress drops, in one a Friend:
This subtle Thief of Life, this paltry Time,
What will it leave me, if it snatch my Rhime?

Then, secondly, there is the voice of the *naïf*, the *ingénu*, the simple heart: "the Prejudice of Youth." The owner of this voice is usually the vehicle of ironies about matters he professes not to understand, and is amazed by his own involvement in the literary arts. "I lisp'd in Numbers, for the Numbers came"—says this voice, speaking of one of the most carefully meditated poetries in literature. Or else: "Why did I write? What sin to me unknown Dipt me in Ink . . . ?" To the owner of this voice, his proficiency in satire is particularly puzzling. Should it be explained as the by-product of insomnia? .

I nod in Company, I wake at Night,
Fools rush into my Head, and so I write;

a scheme of personal defense like jiujitsu?

Satire's my weapon . . .
Its proper pow'r to hurt each Creature feels,
Bulls aim their Horns, and Asses lift their Heels;

or is it a species of harmless madness, a kind of psychosomatic twitch that nothing short of death will stop?

Whether the darken'd Room to Muse invite,
Or whiten'd Wall provoke the Skew'r to write,
In Durance, Exile, Bedlam, or the Mint,
Like Lee and Budgell, I will Rhyme and Print.

Pope's third voice is that of the public defender. If the first voice gives us the satirist as *vir bonus*, the plain good private citizen, and the second, the satirist as *ingénu*, this one brings us the satirist as hero. A peculiar tightening in the verse takes place whenever this *persona* begins to speak, whether he speaks of the mysterious purposes of

That God of Nature, who, within us still,
Inclines our Action, not constrains our Will;

or of the time when

> Inexorable Death shall level all,
> And Trees, and Stones, and Farms, and Farmer fall;

or of his own calling:

> Yes, I am proud; I must be proud to see
> Men not afraid of God, afraid of me.

The satirist as *vir bonus* was content to laugh at flatteries, but the satirist as hero feels differently:

> Fr. This filthy Simile, this beastly Line,
> Quite turns my Stomach—P. So does Flatt'ry mine;
> And all your Courtly Civet Cats can vent,
> Perfume to you, to me is Excrement.

Similarly, the satirist as *ingénu* chose to find the motives of satire in a nervous reflex; the satirist as hero has other views:

> O sacred Weapon! left for Truth's defence,
> Sole dread of Folly, Vice, and Insolence!
> To all but Heav'n-directed hands deny'd,
> The Muse may give thee, but the Gods must guide.

Without pretending that these are the only voices Pope uses, or that they are always perfectly distinguishable, we may observe that the total dramatic development of any one of his formal satires is to a large extent determined by the way they succeed one another, modulate and qualify one another, and occasionally fuse with one another. In a poem like Pope's imitation of the first satire of Horace's second book, the structure is in a very real sense no more than a function of the modulations in tone that it takes to get from the opening verses, where the *naïf* shows up with his little slingshot and his five smooth pebbles from the brook:

> Tim'rous by Nature, of the Rich in awe,
> I come to Council learned in the Law;

through the point, about a hundred lines later, at which we realize that this fellow has somehow got Goliath's head in his hand (and also, the hero's accents in his voice):

Hear this, and tremble! you, who 'scape the Laws.
Yes, while I live, no rich or noble knave
Shall walk the World, in credit, to his grave;

then back down past a window opening on the unimpeachable integrity of the *vir bonus*, instanced in his ties with men whom it is no longer fashionable to know: "Chiefs, out of War, and Statesmen, out of Place"; and so, finally, to a reassumption of the voice of the *ingénu*, surprised and pained that he should be thought to have any but the noblest aims. "Libels and Satires!" he exclaims, on learning the category into which his poems are thrust—"lawless things indeed!"

But grave Epistles, bringing Vice to light,
Such as a King might read, a Bishop write,
Such as Sir Robert would approve ————?

Indeed? says the friend; well, to be sure, *that's* different: "you may then proceed."

Though the construction in Pope's satires is by no means always so schematic as in this example, it seems almost invariably to invoke the three voices of the *naïf*, the *vir bonus*, and the hero. And their presence need not perhaps surprise us, if we pause to consider that they sum up, between them, most of what is essential in the satirist's position. As *naïf*, the satirist educates us. He makes us see the ulcer where we were accustomed to see the rouge. He is the child in the fairy story forever crying, "But mamma, the king *is* naked." As *vir bonus*, on the other hand, he wins our confidence in his personal moral insight. He shows us that he is stable, independent, urbane, wise—a man who knows there is a time to laugh, a time to weep: "Who would not weep, if Atticus were he?" And finally, as hero, he opens to us a world where the discernment of evil is always accompanied, as it is not always in the real world, by the courage to strike at it. He invites us, in an excellent phrase of Mr. Bredvold's, to join "the invisible church of good men" everywhere, "few though they may be—for whom things matter." And he never lets us forget that we *are* at war; there *is* an enemy.

We should never have made, I think, so many mistakes about a portrait like "Sporus" if we had grasped the fact that it is primarily a portrait of the enemy (one of the finest Pope ever drew), evoked in a particular context at a particular point. We know, of course, that the lines were based on Pope's contemporary, Lord Hervey, whom he passionately disliked; and therefore we may justly infer that personal animus entered powerfully into their motivation.

But to read with this animus as our center of interest is to overlook the fact that, though the lines may be historically about Hervey, they are rhetorically about the enemy. It is to fail to see that they sum up in an *exemplum* (of which the implications become very pointed in the references to Satan) the fundamental attributes of the invader in every garden: his specious attractiveness—as a butterfly, a painted child, a dimpling stream; his nastiness—as a bug, a creature generated in dirt, a thing that stinks and stings, a toad spitting froth and venom; his essential impotence—as a mumbling spaniel, a shallow stream, a puppet, a hermaphrodite; and yet his perpetual menace as the tempter, powerless himself but always lurking "at the ear of Eve," as Pope puts it, to usurp the powers of good and pervert them. Because the lines associate Sporus with Evil in this larger sense, his portrait can be the ladder by which Pope mounts, in the evolution of the epistle as a whole, from the studiedly personal impatience of the pestered private citizen in the opening lines: " 'Shut, shut the door, good John!' fatigu'd I said," to the impersonal trumpet tones of the public defender on the walls of *Civitas Dei*—"Welcome for thee, fair Virtue, all the past." Without Sporus prostrate on the field behind him, the satiric speaker could never have supported this heroic tone. Something pretty close to the intensity exhibited by this portrait was called for, at just this point, not by the poet's actual feelings about a contemporary, but by the drama of feelings that has been building inside the poem—the fictive war—"the strong Antipathy of Good to Bad," here projected in its climactic symbol.

JAMES M. OSBORN

The Search for English Literary Documents

from

THE ENGLISH INSTITUTE ANNUAL, 1939

(1940), 31-55

Reprinted by permission of the Columbia

University Press

The Search for English Literary Documents

By JAMES M. OSBORN

Yale University

IT IS GENERALLY AGREED that among the various activities which pass under the name "literary scholarship" the finding of documents is not the most important. And yet I imagine it will also be agreed that finding documents (using the word in the widest sense) is the primary task of the literary researcher.[1] Documents are the basic evidence to be gathered and sorted before attempts are made to explain what an author wrote or why he wrote it. Finding literary documents is thus the foundation of literary research, upon which interpretative criticism must rest.[2]

In the following remarks I shall take the term

1 Since this lecture was delivered before the outbreak of the war between England and Germany, many of the statements now need to be qualified.

2 It is scarcely necessary to emphasize the importance of knowing your subject or author thoroughly before you set out to find new manuscripts. By having a greater mastery of detail than your predecessors, you will find significance in documents they passed over. But in the absence of such knowledge, information will be overlooked and the next man to cover the ground may make a monkey out of you.

"literary documents" to include every piece of evidence which throws light on the text of a literary work or on the life of the author. These documents fall into three categories, which may be briefly distinguished as official, personal, and textual documents. Official documents are those which have passed through the hands of an office holder in the performance of his duties. Personal documents are the letters, diaries, notebooks, and other personal papers of the author. And textual documents include manuscript copies of literary work, whether or not in the author's holograph, as well as proof sheets or other versions of the text before it reached final revised form.

Of these three groups, official documents are frequently given the position of stepchildren and barely allowed a place on the fringe of literary research. We have much to learn on this subject from our cousins the historians. Except for the Chaucerians and Shakespeareans, whose research techniques have led literary scholarship for two hundred years, our profession has made little use of official archives. It is true that each year more and more students of literature are seen in the Public Record Office, but even so, the caverns of that institution will not be exhausted for many generations to come. Moreover, literary researchers are too often satisfied with public records at second hand, going no further than the printed calendars and indexes instead of scrutinizing the documents themselves. Yet the calendars are often most untrustworthy, and Percy Simpson has reported some instances in which the meaning in the calendar is quite the opposite of that in the actual document. Another trouble is that pilgrimages to Chancery Lane are frequently made without remembering that the Public Record Office may contain only a small portion of the documents that are involved in an investigation. Municipal, manorial, and ecclesiastical records are as much neglected today as those of the Public Record Office were yesterday.

The situation is understandable, however. To the beginner the ocean of documents appears as wide and trackless as the Pacific did to stout Cortez. American life is organized very differently from that of the mother country, and our scholars are often baffled when confronted by the ancient legal, ecclesiastical, and governmental structures of England. To be specific, how many persons can distinguish a "Coram Rege Roll" from a "Pipe Roll," or the Pells office from the Petty Bag office? And how many graduate students of pre-Georgian literary history are encouraged to make a study of diplomatic? Indeed, the majority of our graduate students are turned out as finished products without receiving any specific training in research among manuscripts. In the matter of official documents even their seniors are handicapped, for no proper guidebook has been written to help literary scholars find their way among the bulging archives of Great Britain. Perhaps the best practical procedure is to observe the methods of those who have gone over the field with care. For the Elizabethan period Sir Edmund Chambers's treatment of the records in his *William Shakespeare* is a model. Much can be learned also from the Marlowe researches of Hotson, Brooke, Bakeless, and Eccles. Specialists in the later centuries may well examine Dixon Wecter's brilliant monograph on *Edmund Burke and His Kinsmen*. The digger after biographical facts who will honestly compare Wecter's documentary researches with his own will profit much. He will either be immensely stimulated or be content to relapse into the tranquillity of administrative work. Chambers, Wecter, Hotson, and others show by example the type of documentary evidence that you may hope to discover in your own researches.

The other two categories, personal documents and textual documents, present enough common problems to be discussed jointly, with occasional digressions. In pursuing them it is necessary to use a variety of methods, devices, and techniques, the choice depending on the nature of the documents sought. I shall begin by making a fundamental distinction between documents that have been exposed to public view and those that are in the hands of the original owners or their descendants. In effect, the distinction is between documents that have passed through the auction rooms or the hands of dealers and those that have not.

Seeking the latter class of documents, those that have never been on the market, is like prospecting for oil. The rewards are those of oil prospecting too, for one good strike may compensate for many disappointments. There are four places where such hidden documents are likely to be found. The most natural is in the possession of the heirs of the author in question, and in their garrets you may discover a cache to rival the Malahide papers. The finding of heirs involves a little genealogical work, usually not a difficult task. If the ordinary genealogical tools are inadequate, good use can sometimes be made of obituary articles in newspapers. This applies especially to the nineteenth century and after. In other cases effective use can be made of wills, for as most of you know, the law requires that the wills of all British subjects must be recorded at the Probate Registry, located in Somerset House. After paying a fee of one shilling one may there inspect registered copies of wills, but much time will be saved if you will send the fee by mail and ask that a photostatic copy be sent to you. Those who have wasted an afternoon in the dark chambers of Somerset House will agree with me that the latter procedure should be adopted whenever possible and that actual visits should be made only as a last resort. Some wills are not lodged there, but with respect to most modern wills the authorities will tell the inquirer where they can be found.

The second likely place to look for hidden documents is in the possession of the heirs of an author's friends, correspondents, and patrons. Perhaps the outstanding discovery of this sort was the Boswell bonanza at Fettercairn House, in the possession of the descendants of Sir William Forbes, Boswell's literary executor. The first scholar to make a systematic census of heirs was Edmond Malone, who did so while searching for Dryden papers. He drew up a list of "Persons in whose cabinets letters written by Dryden may probably be found," [3] which is still consulted by Dryden scholars. Malone's example may be profitably followed by those who wish to be systematic in their research.

An appropriate word may here be inserted about the need for tact in approaching the present representatives of English worthies. Most Englishmen of position resent being molested, especially by Americans. To the great families it is generally necessary to present an introduction, and one is not always easily found. Introductions can often be obtained through Mr. Willard Connely of the American Universities Union,[4] to whose intermediary offices many of the most successful manuscript searchers are indebted.

When writing to titled personages, be sure to study the correct form of address. This can be found in *Whitaker's Almanack*. If possible, try in a subtle manner to appeal to family pride. A method that may be successfully employed is to put the family in the position of recipient. Send them one of your books or articles in which their illustrious forebear plays a role, for though the article may not be read by them, it will have a psychological effect. Moreover, it will

[3] *The Prose Works of John Dryden*, 1800, I, 567–69.

[4] Address, 1 Gordon Square, London W.C. If that institution should close its doors as rumor prophesies, the paths of American students in England will be even more thorny.

show that you have more than curiosity to recommend
your petition. In a few cases I have sent a typewritten
account of information, preferably new, about their
ancestor with the request that it be added to the family archives, a gesture that has usually been well received. I will also describe a device that a member of
this institute found useful in gaining admission to the
papers in one of the great ducal houses. By digging
around a bit he learned the shelf mark of one manuscript in the library, and although it was of no interest to him, he wrote and asked to be allowed to come
and consult it. Permission was granted. After sitting
with the decoy manuscript open before him for a
while, our friend returned it to the librarian, and
asked to see the set of papers in which he was really
interested. The librarian was obliging, and the sought-
for documents were produced for examination. Obviously this device should not be tried by every neo-
phyte.

The attitudes of humbler families may be far different. They are often pleased with attention and willing
to assist in every way possible the glorification of
their literary ancestor. An exceptional incident occurred this summer. One of our countrymen applied
to the heirs of an eighteenth-century poet for the use
of papers in their possession and was told that he could
use them only upon payment of twenty pounds. After
having recovered from the blow, he agreed to pay
provided they would sign an agreement prepared by
a lawyer granting him exclusive publishing rights to

the collection. Thus he ended by getting more than his money's worth.

The author's publishing house should also be investigated, for among its papers highly interesting documents may be discovered, such as proof sheets, financial agreements, and letters in which the author discusses his own writings. Once again the Dryden researches of Edmond Malone provide an example of a new technique. From the heirs of Jacob Tonson he obtained a treasure trove. Reputedly the house of Murray still owns manuscripts written by Byron and his contemporaries. In the case of modern authors the publisher's files are invaluable. An illustration is found in the recently dispersed papers of John Lane, the publisher of the *Yellow Book* and friend to two generations of literary men. If the Lane papers could have been preserved intact, they would have constituted an unrivaled reservoir of information on the poets and the literature of his time. American publishers have shown more responsibility to posterity, and many of them make a practice of sending most of their papers to the Library of Congress or to the New York Public Library.

The literary remains of earlier scholars often repay attention, since in addition to valuable hints they may contain copies of important documents. For example, when Francis Child was preparing his great edition of *English and Scottish Popular Ballads,* he derived substantial help from the collections of David Herd. Herd was an Edinburgh accountant who had published only a small selection of ballads, but had made extensive collections. Another interesting example is Walter Graham's experience in tracking down Addison letters. He learned that a long series known to be among the State Papers in Dublin had been burned in the Irish Rebellion of 1916. But by a happy stroke Graham found that his predecessor in Addison research, A. C. Guthkelch, had made transcripts of them. The letters can now be printed from these copies.

A somewhat special category must be made for the documents described in the reports of the Historical Manuscript Commission. Like those we have been discussing, most of them are in the possession of the original owners, but with the significant difference that in trailing these manuscripts there is some specific information to go by. The first step is to discover whether the manuscripts are still in the possession of the same family or if they have been sold in the years since the report was printed. This is not always easy. Last year the Institute of Historical Research published in their *Bulletin* for February, 1938, an article by Miss Eleanor Upton, of the Yale Library staff, which lists a number of collections that have been dispersed or deposited in new locations. For collections not mentioned in Miss Upton's list it is prudent to write to the secretary of the commission, C. T. Atkinson, whose quarters are above the gate at the Public Record Office. If he can supply no further information, then application may be made directly to the present representative of the former owner. Due to the fact that only seventy years have elapsed since the earliest reports were issued, the present generation of owners is easily traceable. In making overtures to them one should take the same types of precaution that I mentioned earlier—introductions whenever possible, and tact always. And do not neglect the new reports that appear from time to time; at present nine new volumes are in the press, and the third part of the *Guide* to all the reports is in active preparation.[5]

A great change in technique is required when we pass from the pursuit of documents that are still in the original place of deposit and begin to search for those that have been placed on the market and have been scattered to the four winds. The method in the former case was to get permission to fish in private waters and then to rely on skill with the rod and hook. But to catch fish that have found their way into the sea, it is necessary to use a net. And the net must be spread wide so that good luck may supplement piscatory prowess.

[5] The volumes in the press are known by the following short titles, which refer to the names of the collections: Lindsey, Polwarth volume IV, Sackville volume I, De L'Isle and Dudley volume I, Hastings volume IV, Salisbury (Cecil) volume XVIII, Downshire volume IV, Graham of Fintry, Bath volume IV. Material has accumulated for additional volumes in the Salisbury (Cecil), Polwarth, Downshire, De L'Isle and Dudley, and Sackville series, as well as a volume in the "Various Collections" series. While using these valuable reports, their limitations should not be forgotten. The failure of a report to list certain manuscripts is no reason to suppose that they are not in fact to be found in the collection. And many important collections of papers are in existence that, for one reason or another, have never been reported on.

When you set out to use your net, it is advisable to let the rest of the world know what kind of quarry you seek, since help may come from unsuspected quarters. Letters to the *Times Literary Supplement* and its American counterparts will cost no more than a few stamps and an hour at the typewriter, and although such announcements often fail to bring a response, many searchers have had lucky results. The officials of many American libraries, notably the Folger, take their responsibility seriously, and usually reply with a list of their holdings on your subject. In some cases it is wise to insert paid advertisements in the British newspapers. If you try this, remember that the *Times* is not the only important paper in England. Choose the *Telegraph* or other papers that the propertied class who own manuscripts might read, and do not forget the local newspapers. The scholar writing on Sir Thomas Browne, for example, should try the Norwich papers, and for Walter Savage Landor, the newspapers in Florence. When searching for local materials it is well to correspond with a local antiquary. In case you cannot discover one easily, write to the vicar of the local church, for in many cases he will be the very man you seek. His name can usually be found in *Crockford's Clerical Directory*.

Another way of making your research known, if you will allow me to drum up trade, is to see that it is announced in *Work in Progress*. But passive use of *Work in Progress* is not enough. Look up the projects that border on your own and write to the scholars involved, offering to exchange information. Since generosity begets generosity, enclose several items with your initial letter. Even if you receive only a third as much in return, that amount will be all gain. Once cordial relations have been established with fellow laborers, the fruits of time will be yours. And don't be backward about talking to other scholars about your subject, for many significant clues can be picked up in conversation.

In the case of documents that have appeared on the market, the chances are ten to one that they are still preserved somewhere. The tenth instance allows for accidents, especially fires and other calamities. The reason they have been preserved is that once a man has paid cash for anything, he and his heirs will thenceforth consider it a potential source of cash. There are three places where you can look for such documents: in the hands of dealers, on the shelves of collectors, or in the vaults of institutions. Most of such items pass through the hands of dealers more than once, and some of them a dozen times, as collectors die or become financially embarrassed or bored with their collections. But sooner or later, through gift or purchase, nearly all documents of any value reach a permanent home in some institution. This trend, and the fact that salable documents are usually preserved somewhere, should be considered corollaries of documentary research.

The relations between you, as a manuscript seeker, and the dealer, as manuscript merchant, must receive your attention. Most dealers are well versed in literary lore, a type of information which may be invaluable on certain occasions. In transactions with them, however, do not lose sight of the facts that the dealer is a merchant and that he is not in business because he loves to read *Gondibert* or *Paracelsus*. Most dealers are kindly disposed toward scholars, and at your request many of them will allow you to make copies of low- or medium-priced documents; but they rightly feel that the existence of a duplicate lowers the marketability of their merchandise, and so they may demur if you ask for copies of expensive manuscripts. It is highly desirable to establish personal relations with at least one dealer, preferably the one who is most active and learned in your field. For medievalists and Elizabethans, Goldschmidt and Quaritch might be most satisfactory; for the Restoration and the eighteenth century, Percy Dobell is preëminent; for the Victorian period John Carter, of Scribners, is second to none. Of course there are also specialists on particular subjects; for example, Francis Edwards on travel literature. Of American dealers, Gabriel Wells is the most active in literary documents, although Rosenbach's name is seen in the newspaper headlines more frequently. As an all-around expert I recommend Percy Dobell, whose learning and generosity are attested in the prefaces of numerous scholarly books.

The best way to build up personal relations with a dealer is, naturally, to give him an occasional order.

If it happens that you are not in a position to buy even five or ten dollars worth of merchandise per year from your chosen dealer, you may be able to arrange with your college library to route a few of their orders or inquiries through his firm. If the dealer knows you have his interests at heart, he will not forget your interests, and when he sees a letter or diary that is essential for, let us say, your definitive biography of Eustace Budgell, he may pass along a hint of its whereabouts. Even more important, the dealer may offer you or your library a chance to acquire important documents that he has purchased privately. For example, Gabriel Wells recently obtained from the heirs of John G. Lockhart the heavily annotated proof sheets of Lockhart's *Life of Scott*. He promptly offered them to a scholar who, he knew, would be interested in them. Without the existence of this personal relationship the documents might have been sold privately and have remained inaccessible, if not unknown, for decades to come. The scholar who is alert will find frequent opportunities to purchase, at very modest prices, documents that are of definite literary importance. Except for the "high spots," literary manuscripts are really very cheap, and there are at least a dozen opportunities a year to pick up for ten dollars or less manuscripts that can be used as the basis of an article or as part of a longer study.

But regardless of your success in establishing personal relations with someone in the trade, it is necessary to keep an eagle eye on the catalogues of the principal dealers in order that knowledge of available manuscripts may not escape you. In addition to the dealers already mentioned, the most interesting catalogues of manuscripts are issued by Maggs, Robinson, Pickering and Chatto, Myers, Colbeck Radford, and Bernard Halliday. Most dealers will send you their catalogues if encouraged to do so, and in any case you must see that your university library does not lack them. Catalogue reading can become a time-consuming habit if one does not keep in mind the law of diminishing returns, yet I have heard no less a scholar than Nichol Smith admit that booksellers' catalogues had made a definite contribution to his education. In the case of work that is intended to be definitive in scope it is necessary to make a systematic perusal of the back numbers of catalogues issued by the principal manuscript dealers since the beginning of the nineteenth century. The task may take a fortnight or more, but it will yield information about documents whose existence might not otherwise be known to you.

Analogous to the catalogues of dealers are those of the leading auction houses, Sotheby's and Hodgson's, in England, and the Parke-Bernet (which has succeeded the Anderson-American Art Gallery) in New York. Their catalogues can be obtained for a small subscription, five shillings for Sotheby's and four dollars for the Parke-Bernet's. They should be in every college library, and in my opinion every serious literary historian should subscribe to them himself, at least to the Sotheby catalogues. Each year many highly important manuscripts are placed on the market for the first time. Even the shelf-worn stock sold by the trade, usually catalogued as "Other Properties," may be important for your purpose. It is even more important to examine the auction catalogues of former years than the catalogues of dealers, although actually the two complement each other. These catalogues often reproduce passages from interesting documents, which may be useful to you even if the original cannot be found. Some day there may be an index to the most important contents of these sale catalogues, but at present each man must traverse the ground for himself. In such a search there is another tool, of limited utility—the compilation known as *Autograph Prices Current,* an index to manuscripts sold at auction between the years 1914 and 1922.

To keep yourselves well informed about newly available manuscripts, several other steps may be taken. Most of the important libraries include in their annual reports a summary of their principal acquisitions. These publications can be inspected in your library or, better yet, can be subscribed for directly. The *Annual Report* of the Curators of the Bodleian, for example, can be obtained for a shilling. Interim reports are found in the bulletins of the Yale University Library, the New York Public Library, and the Bodleian Library, to mention only a few examples.[6] The single most useful publication for this purpose is the *Bulletin* of the Institute of Historical Research. It should already be known to you, because it prints in each issue corrections to the *Dictionary of National Biography* and the *Oxford English Dictionary*. Each issue also devotes ten pages or more to news about historical manuscripts that have recently changed ownership. One section lists those acquired by British libraries and permanent repositories; the other part is called "Migrations" and lists manuscripts sold at auction, offered by dealers, or otherwise changing hands among private parties. Fortunately the editor's definition of "historical manuscripts" is broad enough to include many documents of interest to literary researchers. Perhaps some day one of our periodicals will publish a similar list called "The Migrations of Literary Manuscripts." It is urgently needed.

When you begin to seek manuscripts that have already passed from dealers to collectors, a different set of problems must be faced. Probably the most difficult situation is that in which the manuscript and its location are known, but the collector wishes to keep his prize to himself. Generally, there is little that can be done in such a case. The best approach is through some intermediary who has the collector's confidence, for example, someone with whom he sits on a board

[6] Every American scholar should subscribe to the *Bulletin* of the New York Public Library. The dollar so expended will bring twelve issues of various and valuable information, not the least of which is news of acquisitions.

of directors or one of his cronies at the Grolier Club. But even the best ambassador will fail if the collector is a real hoarder, or if, as has occurred in several notorious cases, his collections are in pawn. But such collectors are the exception; most of them are generous almost to the point of cordiality in allowing *bona fide* students to use their treasures. Many collectors consider themselves patrons of learning and the arts. A psychological factor is also involved—one of the motives behind collecting is the hope of obtaining erudition vicariously. So, too, attention from a scholar implies that the manuscript in question was worth the price the collector paid for it. Once access to the inner sanctum has been granted, most collectors will display their rarities as long as you show a polite interest, for you may be the first intelligent audience in months. It is unnecessary to warn you against the greatest insult you can make to any collector: never imply that he has paid too much for anything. And don't expect him to know much about literary or bibliographical matters outside his own collection.

In attempting to locate manuscripts in collections unknown to you, about all that can be done is to trust to luck and keep on trying.[7] Here is where personal relations with a dealer bear fruit. Sometimes his knowledge will be confidential, but at other times the

[7] A number of collectors have published accounts of the manuscripts that they have brought together. It is worth while to look over the following, in particular: *Catalogue of the Collection of Autograph Letters Formed by Alfred Morrison,* 1885; *Meditations of an Autograph Collector,* by A. H. Joline, New York, 1902; *An Autograph Collection,* by Lady Charnwood, London, 1930.

information can be passed along openly. Whatever
the topic of your research may be, it is advisable to
assume that someone somewhere has made a collection on the subject. Inquiries should be made before
the work has advanced very far, but even then you
may discover a collection of your special material
after plans for publication have been made. Arthur
Case had this experience with his valuable bibliography of *Poetical Miscellanies*. The book was already
in proof when he learned that unknown to specialists
the world's best collection of miscellanies was in Chicago, not ten miles from his own door.

In attempting to find such collections only a few
blind steps can be taken. First, consult the directory
Private Book Collectors and Their Hobbies, compiled
by John A. Holden. For obvious reasons this directory
is very incomplete, but when used intelligently, it
will yield valuable clues. Secondly, the dealer with
whom you have contact may know of a collection on
the subject you seek, or he may be persuaded to keep
his ear to the ground. Any collector with whom you
may be acquainted should also be questioned. And if
a choice manuscript appears at an auction, tracing it
may lead to a whole collection of material useful to
you. Similar clues may be derived from tracing the
ownership of manuscripts loaned for exhibitions. De
Ricci's *Census* is also useful within the limits of time
and geography that governed its compilation.[8]

[8] Seymour De Ricci, *A Census of Medieval and Renaissance Manuscripts in the United States and Canada,* 2 vols., New York, 1935-37.

The greatest private collections in the world are, however, mere molehills compared to those amassed by the great national and institutional libraries. As I suggested a moment ago, nearly all documents sooner or later come to rest in permanent repositories. This process is nowhere better revealed than at the Bodleian, which, as everyone knows, was the national repository for one hundred and fifty years before the British Museum came into existence. And the great component collections still kept under the names of their donors—Laud, Selden, Junius, Tanner, Rawlinson, Malone, Douce, and others—show that Bodley's manuscript treasures essentially consist of great collections arranged next to one another. The British Museum, of course, was founded on the great Cottonian and Harleian collections, to which many other notable ones have been added. The same is true to a limited degree of even the modern libraries like the John Rylands and the Huntington.

For most seekers of English literary documents the British Museum is the first port of call. But that is no reason to rush there blindly before investigating how many of its treasures would be available without the expense of a steamship ticket. Most Americans wait until they have entered the portals at Great Russell Street before making a systematic search of the catalogues of the Museum's manuscripts; indeed, the average graduate student does not know that these catalogues are available in his university library. By going through them carefully one can determine how much preliminary material is available, and microfilms or photostats can be ordered without waiting for a traveling fellowship or a sabbatical year. It is my observation that most traveling fellows who come to England spend at least half their working time hovering over materials that could have been photostated and sent to them in America. A shelf load of microfilms or photostats can be bought for the price of a steamship ticket. Of course, other values are derived from a literary pilgrimage to England, but in few cases does the amount of completed research justify the financial sacrifices involved. Expensive journeys for research should be made only after adequate preparation, and the printed catalogues to the great British libraries should be exhausted before placing a foot on the gangplank. The catalogues of manuscripts in the Bodleian and the British Museum, not to mention others, are the most neglected tools for research in English literature. For browsing purposes their pages are a scholar's delight.[9]

In addition to the printed catalogues there is in the Student's Manuscript Room at the Museum a series of class catalogues, of which only one copy exists. If your subject is a fairly specific one—a biography of Eustace Budgell, to use our former example—a letter can be sent directly to the superintendent of the Manuscript Room asking him to send a list of entries

[9] Interesting documents are sometimes found in "grangerized" volumes, of which the British Museum copy of Moore's *Life of Byron* is perhaps the best known.

which may appear in the class catalogues under the name Budgell. This will be done without charge, but further work, such as transcribing and photographing, involves a small fee. There is in process of compilation a new combined catalogue, which will include all the entries in the class catalogues, as well as those in printed catalogues to "Additional Manuscripts." Three volumes have been completed, extending through the letter C, and the whole series will be ready in about ten years.

If your research concerns a poet or a type of poetry, full use should be made of the Museum's First Line Index to manuscript poems. There are more than 17,000 poems listed in this index. A transcript of it is now in course of preparation and when completed should be available in the Yale University Library.[10] In general, first-line indexes have not been sufficiently employed by literary students. When properly used they may add a number of poems to the canon of your chosen author, Budgell. A first-line index has also been begun at the Bodleian; all the poems in the Malone manuscripts have been entered, and progress is now being made with those in the Rawlinson collection. At the Folger Shakespeare Library there is a first-line index to poems in manuscript before 1650, compiled by Giles E. Dawson. It contains more than three thousand entries.

The same type of written inquiry may be sent to

[10] The outbreak of the war has interrupted the copying of this catalogue.

the Bodleian as to the British Museum, but their slip
index to the manuscripts is based on the printed catalogues, and so it will add little to what you have
already found in them. The University Library, at
Cambridge, does not contain manuscripts comparable
to the Bodleian or the British Museum, but its catalogues should not be neglected. Some of the colleges,
especially Trinity and St. Johns, have very valuable
collections, particularly of medieval and Elizabethan
literature. Their catalogues, like those of the Oxford
colleges, the Ryland's Library, the Bretherton Library, the Hunterian Library, and the National Library of Scotland, should be systematically examined
before written inquiries are made. You may be surprised at the richness of their contents. Indeed, our
pride in the Pierpont Morgan and other great manuscript collections in the United States is rudely de-
flated when the contents of some of the smaller English libraries, for example, Corpus Christi College,
Cambridge, are compared with them. Students whose
researches center on Anglo-Saxon documents or Chaucer manuscripts do not need to have this truth em-
phasized. Only one original Anglo-Saxon document is
on this side of the Atlantic, the "Blickling Homilies,"
and it is a recent immigrant. While stressing the riches
of these smaller British libraries, I do not wish to
imply that the holdings of American libraries are
inconsiderable. But the value and extent of their
manuscript treasures are so well known to you that
a delineation of the subject would be superfluous.

And the intelligent assistance rendered by the authorities at the Folger, the Huntington, the Pierpont Morgan, the Boston Public, the Historical Society of Pennsylvania, and a score of other libraries should be a source of national pride.

The most systematic method of determining whether these institutions in Europe and in America have any manuscripts of use to you is to conduct a so-called "census" by mail. If your query is brief and specific, then a reply postcard may be used. For longer inquiries a form letter is preferable, prepared so that information may be supplied in blank spaces on the letter before it is returned to you.

Once you have made full use of the printed catalogues and have supplemented them with postal inquiries, the time will have come to go to the places where you suspect manuscripts will be found. Many important discoveries have resulted from this simple procedure of going to the places concerned. Perhaps the most spectacular example is that of James Clifford, of Lehigh, who set out on a bicycle to visit all the haunts of Mrs. Thrale-Piozzi. At a remote farmhouse in a Welsh valley he was finally rewarded by discovering several bushels of manuscripts, including some of Dr. Johnson and Fanny Burney. Back in London, he visited the brewery that had once belonged to Thrale, and there he uncovered a hundred more letters. Just being on the spot and active in the pursuit may result in unexpected good fortune. The luck of Anna Kitchel, of Vassar, is also an example to be remembered. While riding on a London bus she was discussing her pursuit of materials about George Henry Lewes. The woman sitting in front of her turned suddenly and asked, "Would you be interested in Lewes's diaries?"

Less dramatic discoveries are also to be made in the libraries among uncatalogued and miscatalogued documents. Arthur Case's recent discovery of the anecdotes about Pope which Spence had sent Warburton is a clear instance of an important document being miscatalogued. If you will "go to the places" and make a thorough examination of the evidence, you cannot fail to discover new documents and find new significance in some of the old ones.[11] In the phrase of Wilmarth Lewis, "expose yourself to luck."

Thus the finding of literary documents, like the finding of anything else, depends less on the devices, tricks, and techniques than on the amount of diligence, common sense, and imagination put into the task. It is after you have found the documents that the real work will begin.

[11] Students should consult the catalogues of manuscripts listed under the heading "Manuscripts" in C. S. Northup's *Register of Bibliography* (New Haven, 1925, or the revised issue which is expected in 1940). Another excellent list is found under the same heading in the *Aslib Directory*, London, 1928. The various catalogues of the manuscripts in the British Museum and the Bodleian deserve special attention, as does that of the National Library of Scotland.

RICARDO QUINTANA

Situational Satire: a Commentary on
the Method of Swift

from

THE UNIVERSITY OF TORONTO QUARTERLY

Volume XVII(1948), 130-6

SITUATIONAL SATIRE:
A COMMENTARY ON THE METHOD OF SWIFT

Ricardo Quintana

MUCH depends on the readiness with which we acknowledge the element of impersonality in literary art. The impersonality of drama we perceive and accept instinctively, since our normal responses to a play are grounded in this very acceptance. We do not confuse the dramatist with his characters; unless we are Romantic critics writing on Shakespeare, we do not take the play as direct expression of the writer's personality. The play stands forth as an artifice; we are willing to think of it and discuss it in terms of structural form. How different in this respect our reactions are to most non-dramatic forms of literary art can be measured by the degree to which we confound the writer and the written work. When we see the work and its author as interchangeable, when we take the work to be an act at the level of every-day behaviour, we have pretty well lost sight of the impersonal element and the presence of anything in the nature of deliberate method and form. For such reasons we often find it hard to come to terms with the lyric poem as a poem, as a construct, with the result that much of our commentary on poetry turns out to be either description of our impressions or reconstruction—largely imaginary—of a precise moment in the poet's emotional history with which we have chosen to equate the poem. Perhaps we find it hardest of all to admit of any distinction between a satirist and his satiric composition—and this despite the fact that satire is much more obviously a form of rhetoric than is lyric poetry. It is scarcely surprising, therefore, that Swift's satiric method, which everywhere stares us in the face, is only dimly recognized to be a method. We praise Swift's style; we speak of his use of allegory and his mastery of disgust; but we do not follow through with conviction. Sooner or later we allow the personality of Swift to take over and in consequence to obscure the artist, the craftsman, who after all is only Jonathan Swift's distant relative.

It is perfectly apparent—and here is a key that will unlock the first door—that in every one of Swift's more notable prose satires we have a fictional character or group of characters: Lemuel Gulliver; Isaac Bickerstaff; M. B., Drapier; the humanitarian projector who writes *A Modest Proposal*; the three brothers in the *Tale of a Tub*. What we refuse to see is that Swift himself is *not* present, that it is the characters who are in complete charge. Swift's method is uniformly by way of dramatic satire. He creates a fully realized character and a fully realized world for him to move in. Sometimes, as in *Gulliver's Travels*, the satiric action is developed in terms of the character's reactions to this world; but frequently the action is of essentially another sort, deriving from the crazy assurance with which the character makes himself at home in his cloud-cuckoo-land, tidies the place up, and proceeds to enlarge the bounds of his estate. The difference referred to is a real one, a genuine difference of method, something much more ponderable than the words which must be used to describe it. It is the difference between Gulliver and Bickerstaff, between the *Travels* and the Partridge-Bickerstaff Papers. Gulliver is a reluctant explorer, cast by storms and tides upon strange countries where he is compelled to live at the mercy of the inhabitants. Isaac Bickerstaff, by contrast, is at the mercy of nothing: he assumes such complete control over the laws of logic and astrology that he does not hesitate to condemn a man to death and carry out the sentence.

The latter method is more characteristic of Swift than the method employed in *Gulliver's Travels*. Both are dramatic in the sense suggested, consisting of the depiction of characters and worlds, the character being sometimes projected into a world prepared for him in advance, but more often being allowed to create one for himself. It is in regard to the character's creation of his own world that we begin to suspect that something more than what we ordinarily think of as a dramatic method has perhaps entered into the compositions of Swift. In the *Tale of a Tub* we hear of "many famous discoveries, projects, and machines," of noteworthy devices, of arts highly useful to the commonwealth. In point of fact, the entire *Tale* and its accompanying *Discourse concerning the Mechanical Operation of the Spirit* are one long series of projects, devices, and machines, spun out with amazing bravura. What was there about projectors and projects that so fascinated this particular satiric artist?

II

Before pressing on in further search of Swift's satiric method, we ought perhaps to establish our larger view. The misinterpretation of Swift is proverbial, but with fewer exceptions than is sometimes realized those who have written about him have fought energetically against the deep-lying prejudices of the sort voiced so deplorably and so brilliantly by Thackeray. It happens that we know a good deal of both the private life of Swift and his public career, and much about his motives, interests, prejudices, and theoretical convictions. Criticism, as distinct from biography, is concerned to find the relationship between the man and the artist, but this it can do with some degree of effectiveness only through a sense of the general problem. How do the writer as man and the writer as artist stand to one another? Where does personality end and impersonality begin?

Satire, as much as and no less than drama and lyric poetry, is a construct. It is precisely devised literary composition, a form of rhetoric. It may proceed, as we have seen, by way of characters whose actions are recorded objectively or who speak as in a play; but even in the absence of such ikons there is still the assumed character of the satirist, which despite a convincingly deceptive egotism is quite as much an imaginative creation as any ikon.   Nor, in another and more vital respect, is there any substantial difference between satire on the one hand and drama and lyric poetry on the other.   Each of these fashions its own world, not as Swift creates the land of the Houyhnhnms or Shakespeare the island of Prospero, but rather in the sense that *Gulliver's Travels*—all of it—is a world, that *The Tempest*—the play as a totality—is its own, complete universe.   This special world is a most complex structure, having a logic of its own which governs feeling and speech.   It is at once a way of looking at things, a way of feeling, and a way of speaking.

The writer himself, the man with a human character and practical motives, is present of course, but he stands several levels away from this manner of feeling and speech.   The avowed intention of the satirist is to expose folly and evil and to castigate them, and there is no satire worthy of the name which does not in fact establish a moral dichotomy: right over against wrong, rectified vision or virtue against twisted vision, human dignity and freedom against stupidity, blindness, perversity.   If the moral sense of some satirists—of Byron, for instance—seems elementary, the moral sense of Swift we recognize as that inherited from the humanist tradition, in which man's freedom was defined in terms of ethical responsibility and in accord with the Christian awareness of human incapacity and failure.   The drift of Swift's satiric statements, their intellectual-ethical significance, the practical effects they were designed to achieve are made clear by the history of the age and our knowledge of Swift's character.   The impact of his satires is another problem, for their meaning as satiric constructs embraces something which is more than their practical meaning and qualitatively different from it.   What this other thing is, is the question, or rather, how to find the terms which will enable us to talk about it without evasion. It is a way of thought and feeling, but only as it is a method—a tone, a style, a manner of execution—can it be described in the language which criticism must come to when it seeks to put close observation in the place of impressionism.

III

It is essential to sense the fact that the method of Swift is a good deal more than what we often think of as a method.   Fundamentally, it is an imaginative point of view, making possible and controlling a kind of translation into terms peculiar to a certain angle of perception.   This means that it cannot be exclusively identified with any single procedure or device however characteristic of Swift.   Though dramatic construction marks all of his best-known satiric works, it would be a mistake to regard such construction as the gist of the matter.   Similarly, we have to resist any temptation to single out Swift's use of allegory or of parody in an effort to isolate his method.   All of these devices operate together; they are modes of expression within a single language; they are functions of something larger. What name we find for this enclosing method is not particularly important, since there is no precise term that can do all the necessary work. *Situational satire* will serve.

A satire of Swift's is, we may say, an exhibited situation or series of such situations. Once the situation has been suggested, once its tone, its flavour have been given, it promptly takes command of itself and proceeds to grow and organize by virtue of its own inherent principles. It is a state of affairs within which, as we mistakenly put it, "anything can happen"—mistakenly because everything that does happen is instantly recognized as a part of *this*, a unique situation. Nevertheless, the room for self-improvisation seems limitless, and the comic scale ranges from the hilarious to the grim. It is to be observed that the satirist is himself not involved: he is as much an observer, as much outside all the fuss and nonsense, as we are. (Is it this that we mean when, in speaking of the satires, we comment on the "coldness of Swift"? We know that he was not cold, else we should not be quoting his epitaph as we do.) For the incidents which come to pass no one can be held responsible, any more than for the ideas and emotions which appear. What we have is, literally, an exhibition: everything is shown; everything is at least one degree removed from reality. In short, the situation may be thought of as a kind of chamber within which ideas and emotions are made to move and collide at accelerated speed.

With a recognition of the situation as such comes a perception of the functional character of Swift's favourite devices, which serve both in the creation of the situation and in the generation of the kinetic energy by which it is sustained. There are at least five of these devices that strike us forcibly: drama by way of created characters; parody, or at any rate the imitation of a specific literary *genre*; allegory; the "myth"; and "discoveries, projects, and machines." Of the first of these enough has already been said. Nor is it necessary to dwell at length on Swift's use of parody; we find epic parody in the closing passages of the *Battle*, parody of modern scribblers throughout the *Tale*, parody of the projector's pamphlet in the *Modest Proposal*, and the faithful reproduction, in *Gulliver's Travels*, of the style, tone, and matter-of-fact reporting found in the genuine travel-books of the time. Parody is in itself so close to the dramatic method that the two are sometimes difficult to distinguish; in Swift, parody is only another means of creating and exploiting a situation having its own unmistakable thickness. The world which the *Modest Proposal* invites us to live in is our own familiar world twice refracted, our world as remade in the enthusiastic imagination of a typical projector, and that remade world further distorted through parody.

Allegory in Swift's satires is really of two sorts. When it sets up a recognizable parallelism between two systems of events or ideas it derives quite directly from the kind of allegory which was constantly being used by post-Restoration writers in commenting on contemporary events. The

olitical allegory running through *Gulliver's Travels* is of this nature. Much
he same are the short fable (the spider-bee episode in the *Battle*) and the
xtended fable (the story of the animated books in the *Battle* and the story
f the three brothers in the *Tale*). The whole point of allegory thus em-
loyed lies in clear correspondence, one set of details suggesting and in-
erpreting another set. But if we agree that the *Mechanical Operation of
he Spirit* is "by way of allegory," we find ourselves confronted by something
hat does not fully answer to this kind of running parallelism. In this
atter satiric fragment, attached to the *Tale* and the *Battle*, we are re-
ninded that Mahomet refused fiery chariots, winged horses, and celestial
edans, and "would be borne to Heaven upon nothing but his ass"; and to go
n "by way of allegory," we are asked to use, for the term *ass*, that of *gifted* or
nlightened teacher and for *rider, fanatic auditory*. In this case, it seems,
almost any parallelism no matter how fantastic will serve, since what is
equired is only an initial correspondence. The "allegory" does not throw
ight; rather, it is a challenge in response to which there arises a crazy
world where religious fervour is created by mechanical means. And even
where Swift is using allegory for sustained correspondence, one sometimes
observes that the emerging situation tends to assert its independence. In
the *Tale of a Tub*, for instance, the allegorical base on which the story of
the three brothers rests never drops from sight, but with Peter and again
with Jack we have an exuberant and perverted sense of power, of capacity
to improvise and invent, which though in accord with the religious allegory
is altogether in excess of it.

What have been called Swift's "myths" are familiar to every reader of
the satires. Thus, it is the animal myth which informs both the *Modest
Proposal* and the fourth book of *Gulliver's Travels*. Others appear in the
Tale of a Tub, giving us that sect who worship tailors because of a belief
that the universe is a large suit of clothes, the Aeolists who affirm "the gift
of belching to be the noblest act of a rational creature," and the philosophical system which holds that all notable achievements are the result of
madness. The Hobbian myth is of frequent occurrence: a set of principles,
a practical programme, worked out from the assumption that man is a
physical mechanism, his acts a phase not of intelligence but solely of matter.
It is this kind of systematized make-believe, a nonsensical "as is," that
gives life to the latter part of Gulliver's description of the Grand Academy
of Lagado (Book III, chapter VI), where we are told of that school of
political projectors whose admirable practices result from a clear understanding of the strict universal resemblance between the natural and the
political body.

In what sense are these expanded metaphors to be taken as myths?
The distinctive character of Swift's intuition, of his imaginative grasp of
the human dilemma, is a moral realism which renounces with superb pride
any mythological vision of human destiny. Only the fool believes he can
see better through coloured glasses. The burden of civilization can be

borne solely by such as have learned that human dignity is achieved not through hope but through wilful disillusion, acceptance, resolution. If one sought to be paradoxical, one could say that the only myth genuinely embraced by Swift is the myth that there are no myths, the myth for which he found many statements, all of them variants of the single theme of the outside vs. the inside. "Last week I saw a woman flayed, and you will hardly believe how much it altered her person for the worse." This moral realism, emphasizing so mordantly and so insistently the deceptive fairness of the surface in contrast with what lies inside, was with Swift a passionate belief. Its metaphorical expressions, however, are less in the nature of myths than anti-myths, being in fact a kind of parody with a grim and earnest purpose. As statements they are designed to narrow to shrink, not to enlarge.

The myths previously referred to (the Hobbian myth, etc.) are clearly of the fantastic order, and often blend into those "discoveries, projects and machines" of which so much is said in the satires. Indeed, what for the projector himself is a cherished myth is for us an anti-myth, a machine art, or device concocted in that madhouse which is the enthusiast's brain. The myth and the project, no less than dramatic form, parody, and allegory are means whereby situations are brought about.

IV

That the method we have been speaking of appears for the first time in the great satire published in 1704, comprising the *Tale*, the *Battle*, and the *Mechanical Operation*, and not at all in the earlier Pindaric odes, written during the first years at Moor Park, is perhaps a sufficient reminder that Swift attained artistic maturity when he discovered and put on a hitherto unknown personality, a non-self who spoke and therefore thought a new idiom. The assurance which marks every passage of the 1704 satire is of one who has found creative freedom by learning how to avoid direct partici pation. The comedy of ideas, the self-developing irony of the situation require no intervention. Yet somehow, in this comedy that enacts itself and improvises its own language, Swift's passionate intuition has found it proper form.

Though each of the satires included in the 1704 volume is in itself an unmistakable comedy, we must not miss the larger comedy presented by the book as a whole, which by bringing the *Tale*, the *Battle of the Books*, and the *Mechanical Operation* into forced relationship establishes a context within which the three pieces are to be construed. Everything about them the forms they are cast in, the deplorable gaps in the text, the marginal notes, the impertinence with which they ask to be taken as a trilogy, is part of this inclusive situation.

From this time on the method so brilliantly sustained in *A Tale of a Tub* becomes a part of Swift. It is his *alter ego*, his personality as prose satirist Seen from the outside (how else can analysis view it?) it is method at the lower level of stratagem, and Swift knew he had fashioned something in the way of comic technique. "There is one thing," he wrote in the "Apology" (1710) for the *Tale*, "which the judicious reader cannot but have observed, that some of those passages in this discourse . . . are what they call parodies, where the author personates the style and manner of other writers, whom he has a mind to expose." That it is far more than technique, that it is imagination and intuition, we acknowledge consciously or otherwise through our response to the satiric work of Swift taken as a whole—consciously when we recognize the presence of the artist, instinctively when we think we see a soul writhing in indignation.

Because the method of Swift is more than anything else a creative perception it cannot be summarized. Its essence is its history, its occurrence under different modes in the satires which came to be written. It operates in one fashion in *Gulliver's Travels*, notably in Books I, II, and IV (the comparative ineffectiveness of the third book being attributable to a relaxation of the method save in those passages concerning the virtuosi and the Struldbrugs). We can find it in the Drapier Letters: "They say 'Squire C—y has *Sixteen Thousand Pounds a Year*, now if he sends for the *Rent* to Town, as it is likely he does, he must have *Two Hundred and Forty Horses* to bring up his *Half Years Rent*. . . .'" There is nothing to stop such ready calculation, and we shortly find ourselves with £40,000 and 1,200 horses on our hands. Leslie Stephen, speaking with the gravity of a cabinet minister, took exception to the economic heresies which gave rise to such arithmetic. But the Drapier was right, after all. Walpole and Wood were forcing on Ireland a monetary situation that was preposterous. The Drapier's inspired vision of a team of 1,200 horses drawing £40,000—all in copper halfpennies—about the streets of Dublin was no mere Irish myth.

Two final instances of the method. *An Argument against Abolishing Christianity* can perhaps be adequately described as ironic disputation. However, it is disputation that is more than a colloquy between A (who views abolition with concern) and B (all who, for various reasons, would abolish). A is likewise a multiplicity of voices, each point of view that is pressed into service carrying with it a somewhat different personality. It is a dialogue between the speaker's various selves, each of whom has a myth wherewith to confound his adversary; the full pattern of the "argument" emerges solely from eccentric points of reference.

If the *Argument* is Erasmian (and Platonic), *A Modest Proposal* is pure Swift. Nowhere else is the method clearer, nowhere else is the fusion of moral insight and imaginative translation so complete. It is a character in action, a parody, a project, and an animal myth all at once, a situation within which any distinction between art and propaganda seems meaningless.

GEORGE SHERBURN

Fielding's 'Amelia': an Interpretation

from

A JOURNAL OF ENGLISH LITERARY HISTORY

Volume III(1936), 1-14

ELH

A Journal of English Literary History

| VOLUME THREE | MARCH, 1936 | NUMBER ONE |

FIELDING'S *AMELIA:* AN INTERPRETATION

By GEORGE SHERBURN

Fielding is a novelist of many intentions. On the original titlepage of his *Amelia* he placed two lines from Horace and two from Simonides of Amorgos [1] that perhaps sufficiently indicated (to those who could translate) that the novel was by its author intended to present a picture of durable matrimony and of the beauty of virtue in woman. But if his readers thought *Amelia* a police-court tract, he could hardly deny that he had shown concern over the failure of the courts to dispense true justice. Other readers have liked to regard the story as one of an exposed and neglected wife. The book, again, is plausibly regarded as a sort of monument to the author's lasting love for his first wife, Charlotte. It is not my present purpose to deny any of these interpretations, but it does seem possible that to re-study the novel may serve to emphasize certain important shaping ideas in the domestic drama that Fielding wished to unfold.

If an author of established reputation changes his tone or technique, his public is apt to be surprised and even disappointed. Hence, in general, the unfavorable reception of *Amelia* in 1751. There are so many reasons for the relative failure of this novel that critics have tended to attack or defend its repu-

---

[1]
Felices ter et amplius
Quas irrupta tenet Copula. Horace, *Carm.* 1. 13. 18.
γυναικὸς οὐδὲν χρῆμ' ἀνὴρ ληΐζεται
ἐσθλῆς ἄμεινον, 'οὐδὲ ῥίγιον κακῆς. Simonides, *Iamb.* 6.

1

tation rather than to search out just what Fielding was trying
to do in it.

Amelia is not necessarily duller than his earlier stories, but
obviously it is more serious and less high-spirited. This seriousness is not accidental; it is intentional. It is not that ill health
has robbed Fielding of his facetious humours. Parts of *Amelia*
—the History of Captain Trent (Bk. 11, ch. 3), for example—
abound in brilliant and caustic facetiousness, and so does much
of the later *Covent-Garden Journal.* Fielding had not lost that
tone: he had simply changed it for another. A bit of superficial
evidence will show the consciously serious and " high-class "
intention here dominant, and that evidence is his quotation of
the classics. Fielding knew his classics far better than did most
of his contemporaries, and he quotes them in all his works; but
the quotation in *Amelia* is much more frequent, comes from a
wider range of reading, and at least a score of passages of Latin
and Greek are given without translation. Some of these
(notably one from Claudian) are essential to the motivation
of his characters or situations, and the failure to translate them
obviously limited appreciation of the story to readers who were
not, to use Fielding's word, " illiterate." Amelia herself knew
neither Latin nor Greek, and most of Fielding's readers were
probably in the same state.

Similar evidence of Fielding's " high-brow " seriousness is
seen in the imitation of the classical epic that marks the structure of the novel. *Joseph Andrews* and *Tom Jones* had been
described by Fielding as comic prose epics. The phrase in
variant forms caught on, and has since obsessed critics of the
novels. In spite of the comic-epic label placed on these works
by Fielding, there is less of epic tradition in them than in the
more serious *Amelia.* But in *Amelia* he follows, not the tradition of the comic epic—really that of Cervantes and Scarron,
among others,—but rather a newer tradition of the epic in
prose. The epic in prose, in its turn, is not so much the tradition of *Telemachus* as it is a tradition of private history done
with fidelity to the facts of every-day life. Fielding has left us
various accounts of this tradition, the best of which perhaps is
the last—found in the *Journal of a Voyage to Lisbon.* Here a
passage contrasts Fielding's own plodding, prosaic Voyage with
the marvels to be found in the *Odyssey* and in *Telemachus;*

thus pointing the favorite antithesis between " romance and true history, the former being the confounder and corrupter of the latter."

I am far [he says] from supposing, that Homer, Hesiod, and the other antient poets and mythologists, had any settled design to pervert and confuse the records of antiquity; but it is certain they have effected it; and, for my part, I must confess I should have honoured and loved Homer more had he written a true history of his own times in humble prose, than those noble poems that have so justly collected the praise of all ages; for though I read these with more admiration and astonishment, I still read Herodotus, Thucydides, and Xenophon, with more amusement and more satisfaction.[2]

In this spirit Fielding undertook in *Amelia* to write a sober, faithful history of his own times in humble prose—a history that yet should, in its structure, its organizing themes, and in its pictures of domesticity, recall at least remotely the masterpiece of Vergil. Soon after the book was published, its author had to defend it, and in so doing he asserts its epic pattern unmistakably in the *Covent-Garden Journal* for 28 January, 1752:

I . . . avow, that of all my Offspring she is my favourite Child. I can truly say that I bestowed a more than ordinary Pains in her Education; in which I will venture to affirm, I followed the Rules of all those who are acknowledged to have writ best on the Subject; and if her Conduct be fairly examined, she will be found to deviate very little from the strictest Observation of all those Rules; neither Homer nor Virgil pursued them with greater Care than myself, and the candid and learned Reader will see that the latter was the noble model, which I made use of on this Occasion.

It would be possible to take this statement too seriously, but *Amelia* does have serious and semi-serious relations to the Vergilian epic. These certainly include the epic " cut-back " in which Booth narrates his past fortunes to Miss Matthews, as Æneas does his to Dido. A touch worthy of James Joyce is the using of Newgate Prison to parallel the palace of the Carthaginian queen and the cave where was consummated the fateful *furtivum amorem*. More serious[3] is the preoccupation

---

[2] *The Journal of a Voyage to Lisbon*, Oxford World's Classics, 1907, p. 8.

[3] One respect should be noted in which the seriousness of *Amelia* is no innovation. Fielding had always been grimly severe when portraying London high society. His early comedies—*The Temple Beau, The Modern Husband, The Universal Gallant*—

of Fielding with an organizing theme—held in his day to be a prime essential in epics. This epic proposition, the *arma virumque* of the novel, is stated in the first sentence in a style consciously suited to the idea of an epic in prose. It reads:

The various accidents which befel a very worthy couple after their uniting in the state of matrimony will be the subject of the following history.

The utmost malice of Fortune, he continues, might seem to have been working against this couple, except that (as he avows) it is doubtless a mistake to blame Fortune when we involve ourselves in misfortune " by quitting the directions of Prudence, and following the blind guidance of a predominant passion." " To retrieve the ill consequences of a foolish conduct, and by struggling manfully with distress to subdue it, is one of the noblest efforts of wisdom and virtue."

This then is the theme that the novel attempts to dramatize. There is nothing new in it. The idea of a predominant or ruling passion doubtless developed out of the physiology and psychology of the four humours. It was well established long before Pope popularized it for the eighteenth century in his *Essay on Man.* Fielding seems to agree that only the passions stimulate to action; and he asserts, as do most of his contemporaries, a dualism of passion: the good passions headed by benevolence or love of man; the bad by self-love (in the selfish sense) or pride. Booth's error is variously stated: sometimes we are told that men's actions are ruled by a single predominant passion; at others, that men act from whichever passion happens to be uppermost.[4]

It is necessary to consider the relation of these ideas to the characters of Fielding's " worthy couple " — and first of all necessary to insist that they are a worthy couple. Amelia

---

are as censorious of the upper classes, are as completely lacking in comic playfulness, as anything he ever wrote, though their picture is not, like that in *Amelia*, pointed by the presence of definitely rationalized social themes. Fielding drops his high spirits whenever he writes about London. Even in *Tom Jones* the London episodes are all sombre, and Lady Bellaston and Lord Fellamar belong as much to the atmosphere of *Amelia* as they do to that of *Tom Jones.*

[4] Bk. 3, ch. 4, 5; Bk. 4, ch. 6; Bk. 10, ch. 9. Booth is nowhere depicted as the victim of one ruling passion; he is rather the victim of a belief that men act from their passions, whether permanently predominant or only temporarily so. As a result of this belief he lacks moral courage to struggle against misfortune.

doubtless is far the worthier of the two; for she is a devout Christian with no doubts or beliefs in a ruling passion. Born of a gentle family and reared as a considerable heiress, she nevertheless more than once suggests eagerly that she be allowed to work with her own hands to help support the family. Such "low-mindedness" on her part was disgusting to lady novel-readers of the period, but it seemed heroic to the man who had been Charlotte Fielding's husband. Amelia is not merely the idealization of the *ewig-weibliche*; she is an embodiment of moral courage—precisely what her husband lacks.

Booth's sins live after him more vigorously than his virtues; but Fielding tries always to insist on his essential nobility of character. Booth acts almost always from benevolent instincts —not like most of his friends from self-interest only; he is, all told, a devoted husband; and all his faults (which are not so many) are those of the eighteenth-century gentleman. No man of his station (except Sir Charles Grandison) could have refused the overtures of Miss Matthews in Newgate. The lady, furthermore, plies him with rack-punch before he yields; and once out of Newgate he forsakes her as promptly as Æneas does Dido. He is arrested three times; but once it is through the malice of his Wiltshire neighbours who have lied about him to Dr. Harrison; another time illegally through the trickery of Captain Trent (for debts of honour were not actionable in law) ; and the first time he is arrested, he is sent to Newgate through the grossest miscarriage of justice when actually he deserved the thanks of the court. He sets up a coach before he can afford one, and that snobbishness on his part brings distress: he once gambles at cards (again through the machination of Captain Trent) ; and when his wife pawns all her trinkets to pay the debt, Booth unwisely gives the money to a great man in the war office, who (he has reason to believe) thus will be led to get Booth back his commission at once. We naturally blame Booth for bribery; but Fielding's comment indicates that such presents were probably quite the normal thing in 1750. He says:

The great man received the money, not as a gudgeon doth a bait, but as a pike receives a poor gudgeon into his maw. To say the truth, such fellows as these may well be likened to that voracious fish, who fattens himself by devouring all the little inhabitants of the river.[5]

This sort of thing, however, is not the worst of Booth: the worst is that his moral courage is weak because he believes men act from their natural and not from their rational appetites— to use the jargon of his day. His " chief doubt " in matters moral or religious was, he said, " that, as men appeared . . . to act entirely from their passions, their actions could have neither merit nor demerit." [6] Booth, to be sure, despises Mandeville's perverse account of the passions, and believes heartily in benevolence; but he says of his friend Colonel James:

The behaviour of this man alone is a sufficient proof of the truth of my doctrine, that all men act entirely from their passions; for Bob James can never be supposed to act from any motive of virtue or religion, since he constantly laughs at both; and yet his conduct towards me alone demonstrates a degree of goodness which, perhaps few of the votaries of either virtue or religion can equal.[7]

Doubtless this idea (that goodness asks no sanction from religion) is what at times led the pious Amelia to fear that her husband " was little better than an atheist." Of this last error, however, he was not guilty. At the beginning of the story Fielding tells us:

. . . as to Mr. Booth, though he was in his heart an extreme well-wisher to religion (for he was an honest man), yet his notions of it were very slight and uncertain. To say truth, he was in the wavering condition so finely described by Claudian:

> labefacta cadebat
> Religio, causaeque viam *non sponte* sequebar
> Alterius; vacuo quae currere semina motu
> Affirmat; magnumque novas per inane figuras
> Fortuna, non arte, regi; quae numina sensu
> Ambiguo, vel nulla putat, vel nescia nostri.[8]

---

[5] Bk. 11, ch. 5.　　　　　[6] Bk. 12, ch. 5.　　　　　[7] Bk. 3, ch. 5.

[8] *In Rufinum*, 1.14-19. Fielding does not translate this passage for his readers. For the Loeb Classical Library Platnauer has translated it as follows: " then in turn my belief in God was weakened and failed, and even against mine own will I embraced the tenets of that other philosophy [Epicureanism] which teaches that atoms drift in purposeless motion and that new forms throughout the vast void are shaped by chance and not design—that philosophy which believes in God in an ambiguous sense, or holds that there be no gods, or that they are careless of our doings."

This way of thinking, or rather of doubting, he had contracted from the same reasons which Claudian assigns, and which had induced Brutus in his latter days to doubt the existence of that virtue which he had all his life cultivated. In short, poor Booth imagined that a larger share of misfortunes had fallen to his lot than he had merited . . . (Bk. 1, ch. 3).

It was the psychological and moral task of the novel to rescue Booth from this mental state. Obviously a change of character is necessary, but neither Fielding nor his contemporaries had any modern technique for such portrayal. In *Tom Jones* there is some improvement in Tom's prudence alleged at the end of the novel as due to the ripening effects of experience and age. Booth, however, is no boy, and supernatural intervention seems almost essential. And so, during Booth's last incarceration he reads Dr. Barrow's sermons in proof of the Christian religion, and is quite suddenly convinced of his errors. Little is done by way of direct preparation for this conversion, which, however, seems requisite to the plot from the very beginning—from the moment, in fact, when the parallel to Claudian's state is given.

Any possible milestones on the road to this conversion are more apparent to the reader than they were to Booth: after all, for moral effectiveness, it was more essential that readers should be convinced than that Booth should be; and so Fielding's views, expressed for the reader rather than to Booth frequently concern Booth's problems and the problems involved in reconciling pagan ethics (that is, Stoicism) with Christian principles. Dr. Harrison is the usual mouthpiece; his thinking is scarcely novel, but Fielding clothes it with tactful eloquence, and at times it is effectively dramatized. One exposition of the superiority of the Christian system is as follows:

If the poor wretch, who is trudging on to his miserable cottage, can laugh at the storms and tempests, the rain and whirlwinds, which surround him, while his richest hope is only that of rest; how much more cheerfully must a man pass through such transient evils, whose spirits are buoyed up with the certain expectation of finding a noble palace and the most sumptuous entertainment ready to receive him! [9]

The best discussion of these matters is that between Harrison and a young cleric, destined obviously to become a second

[9] Bk. 3, ch. 10.

Thwackum. Here, to the discouraged, Harrison says: "A true Christian can never be disappointed, if he doth not receive his reward in this world; the labourer might as well complain that he is not paid his hire in the middle of the day." [10] The discussion then turns to philanthropy, charity, and universal benevolence—which Harrison holds to be essentially Christian. The uncharitable young cleric protests:

'Pardon me . . . that is rather a heathenish than a Christian doctrine. Homer, I remember, introduces in his Iliad one Axylus, of whom he says,—

$$—\phi\text{í}\lambda os \; \delta'\tilde{\eta}\nu \; \alpha\nu\theta\rho\acute{\omega}\pi o\iota\sigma\iota$$
$$\pi\acute{\alpha}\nu\tau as \; \gamma\grave{\alpha}\rho \; \phi\iota\lambda\acute{\epsilon}\epsilon\sigma\kappa\epsilon\nu$$

But Plato, who, of all the heathens, came nearest to the Christian philosophy, condemned this as impious doctrine; so Eustathius tells us, folio 474.'

'I know he doth,' cries the doctor, 'and so Barnes tells us, in his note upon the place.'

And the doctor proceeds to heap up counter authorities on the point (not to be found in Barnes) and concludes triumphantly, "Whom is it, therefore, we imitate by such extensive benevolence?" The impressed but unsympathetic response from the father of the young man is: "What a prodigious memory you have!"

Then the argument turns to the forgiveness of enemies—one of Fielding's favorite topics—on which we get expressions of opinion from many persons in *Amelia*—even from Billy Booth, jr., aged six. Harrison throughout the story embodies the recognition, held by Fielding, of the superiority of Christian thinking over ancient philosophy. His last pronouncement to Booth on the passions is central in his thinking and in the thought of Fielding's day:

. . . if men act, as I believe they do, from their passions, it would be fair to conclude that religion to be true which applies immediately to the strongest of these passions, hope and fear; choosing rather to rely on its rewards and punishments than on the native beauty of virtue which some of the ancient philosophers thought proper to recommend to their disciples.[11]

In converting Booth, Fielding does not stress process, but it

[10] Bk. 9, ch. 8.
[11] Bk. 12, ch. 5.

is nevertheless curious that he should not have used Booth's selfish and false friend, Colonel James, to bring about disillusionment with free-thinking and to arouse an impulse towards religion. James seems a good friend, though he laughs at virtue and religion. Either through selfish policy or through casual impulse he is often generous in an undiscriminating fashion; [12] but he is quite without emotions of benevolence. His mind, Fielding tells us,

was formed of those firm materials, of which nature formerly hammered out the Stoic, and upon which the sorrows of no man living could make an impression. A man of this temper, who doth not much value danger, will fight for the person he calls his friend, and the man that hath but little value for his money will give it him; but such friendship is never to be absolutely depended on; for, whenever the favourite passion interposes with it, it is sure to subside and to vanish into air. Whereas the man whose tender disposition really feels the miseries of another, will endeavor to relieve them for his own sake; and, in such a mind, friendship will often get the superiority over every other passion.

But, from whatever motive it sprung, the colonel's behaviour to Booth seemed truly amiable. . . . [13]

Later on when it is perfectly evident to the reader that James is trying to win Amelia as a mistress, Booth might well have been made aware of his friend's true character, and the disillusionment might have been used to strengthen religious inclinations in Booth. Fielding, however, strangely enough never makes Booth really conscious of James's designs, and the day after Booth is finally released from the bailiff's house the worthy couple, at the instance of Dr. Harrison, dine with the Jameses. Whether this is by implication forgiveness of one's enemies, or whether Fielding is ironically indicating that life goes on as usual even after conversion, or whether it is simply the outburst of exuberant good-nature that frequently affects English authors (even Shakespeare) at a joyful conclusion, it is hard to say. Certainly Colonel James is typical of the callous sort of aristocrat that causes most of Booth's troubles.

It will be remembered that Booth's religious and moral doubts were ascribed vaguely to the same causes as those of Claudian and Brutus—that is, to the prosperity of the wicked in high places. *Diu floruere nocentes*, complains Claudian,

[12] Bk. 8, ch. 6.   [13] Bk. 8, ch. 5.

whose Rufinus is remotely paralleled by Fielding's colonels and noble lords.

The nature of man [Dr. Harrison tells Amelia] is far from being in itself evil; it abounds with benevolence, charity, and pity, coveting praise and honour, and shunning shame and disgrace. Bad education, bad habits, and bad customs, debauch our nature, and drive it headlong as it were into vice. The governors of the world, and I am afraid the priesthood, are answerable for the badness of it. Instead of discouraging wickedness to the utmost of their power, both are too apt to connive at it.[14]

Booth's personal problem is a private concern—like the wrath of Achilles; but the corruption of the aristocracy and their failure to distinguish and reward merit is as public a theme as the fall of Troy. It is clear from many passages in Fielding's works that he had an interesting philosophical class-consciousness. Its basis is a belief in the necessity of " allegiance to the whole " on the part of the individual. In the *Essay on Man* this idea received perhaps its most popular statement in Fielding's day. There the universe, socially considered, is a " vast chain of being," an ordered *continuum,* kept cohesive by the mutual dependence of all the parts.

> Nothing is foreign: Parts relate to whole;
> One all-extending, all-preserving Soul
> Connects each being, greatest with the least;
> Made Beast in aid of Man, and Man of Beast;
> All served, all serving: nothing stands alone;
> The chain holds on, and where it ends, unknown.

In a pamphlet published less than two years after *Amelia* Fielding (addressing the governing classes in behalf of the unemployed) makes the following observations on the duties of the extremes in the social scale:

Those duties . . . which fall to the higher Ranks of Men, even in this Commonwealth, are by no Means of the lightest or easiest Kind. . . . It is true, indeed, that in every Society where Property is established and secured by Law, there will be some among the Rich whose Indolence is superior to the Love of Wealth and Honour, and who will therefore avoid these Public Duties, for which Avarice and Ambition will always furnish out a sufficient Number of Candidates; yet however idle the Lives of such may be, it must be observed, First, That they are by no Means burthensome to the Public, but do support themselves on what the Law calls their

[14] Bk. 9, ch. 5.

own; a Property acquired by the Labour of their Ancestors, and often the Rewards, or Fruits at least of Public Services. 2dly, That while they dispose what is their own for the Purposes of Idleness, (and more especially, perhaps, if for the Purposes of Luxury,) they may be well called useful Members of trading Commonwealths, and truly said to contribute to the Good of the Public.

But with the Poor (and such must be in any Nation where Property is, that is to say, where there are any Rich) this is not the Case: For having but their Labour to bestow on the Society, if they withhold this from it, they become useless Members; and having nothing but their Labour to procure a Support for themselves, they must of Necessity become burthensome.[15]

This is Fielding's typical view, but in *Amelia* he is less tolerant of the idle rich, or the governing classes. In the earlier parts of the story he illustrates most vividly the miscarriages of justice in the established courts of law, and in the later books he repeatedly exclaims over the callousness of the upper classes, over their selfishness and lack of benevolence. Hearing the story of honest Bob Bound, a half-pay officer of the same regiment as Booth, Amelia cries:

' Good Heavens! . . . what are our great men made of? are they in reality a distinct species from the rest of mankind? are they born without hearts?'

' One would, indeed, sometimes,' cries Booth, ' be inclined to think so. In truth, they have no perfect idea of those common distresses of mankind which are far removed from their own sphere. Compassion, if thoroughly examined, will, I believe, appear to be the fellow-feeling only of men of the same rank and degree of life for one another, on account of the evils to which they themselves are liable. Our sensations are, I am afraid, very cold towards those who are at a great distance from us, and whose calamities can consequently never reach us.' [16]

Their fault seems to be that they act either carelessly or only from motives of self-interest. Repeatedly this idea is dramatized by Fielding. The colonel at Gibraltar is willing to lend money to Booth while he thinks Booth has married a fortune; but when he is really in need, the colonel will not help.[17] Tom Bennet's noble friend of college days has forgotten him, and does not wish to renew an acquaintance with a needy clergyman (8, 5). Mrs. James implies that her class grants preferments according to policy, not merit, when, coyly starting a

[15] *A Proposal for making an Effectual Provision for the Poor*, 1753, pp. 5-6.
[16] Bk. 10, ch. 9.   [17] Bk. 3, ch. 7.

movement for bigger and better guardsmen, she insists that
her husband (acting out of interest only) shall *not* get Booth
a commission in an American regiment but shall place him
nearer home: " Are we resolved [she exclaims] never to encourage merit, but throw away all our preferments on those who do
not deserve them? What a set of contemptible wretches do we
see strutting about the town in scarlet?" The central plot
problem of getting Booth back into the commission he so richly
deserves is the most glaring case of this callousness. Colonel
James could get him back in a moment, but, as he says, he has
just secured " two places of a hundred a year each for two of "
his " footmen, within this fortnight " (Bk. 11, ch. 1), and feels
unable to ask further favours at the moment. The noble lord
(of amorous propensities) could, if he liked, get the coveted
commission within twenty-four hours—he did it for Atkinson,
and he had lavishly provided for such a creature as Captain
Trent. But this peer is perhaps not quite an average sort, and
so Fielding introduces (Bk. 11, ch. 2) another peer, made ex-
pressly to enforce the point of this phase of the plot. This is the
lord whom Dr. Harrison approaches in behalf of Booth. His
lordship is perfectly willing to be of service, not as he frankly
avows, because of Booth's obvious merits, but purely out of
regard for the worthy Doctor—though it immediately appears
that his regard for the Doctor depends entirely on whether that
clergyman will use his influence in favour of an inferior candidate who wants to be mayor. Dr. Harrison will not. Whatever the office at stake, this peer does not scrutinize the qualifications of his candidate. " With regard to the personal merit
of these inferior officers, I believe I need not tell you that it is
very little regarded." Later Doctor Harrison comes doggedly
back to this point:

' Is his own merit, then, my lord, no recommendation ? ' cries the
doctor.

' My dear, dear sir,' cries the other, ' what is the merit of a subaltern officer ? '

' Surely, my lord,' cries the doctor, ' it is the merit which should
recommend him to the post of a subaltern officer. And it is a
merit which will hereafter qualify him to serve his country in a
higher capacity. And I do assure you of this young man, that he
hath not only a good heart but a good head too. And I have been
told by those who are judges that he is, for his age, an excellent
officer.'

'Very probably!' cries my lord. 'And there are abundance with the same merit and the same qualifications who want a morsel of bread for themselves and their families.'

'It is an infamous scandal on the nation,' cries the doctor; 'and I am heartily sorry it can be said even with a colour of truth.'

'How can it be otherwise?' says the peer. 'Do you think it is possible to provide for all men of merit?'

'Yes, surely do I,' said the doctor; 'and very easily too.'

'How, pray?' cries the lord. 'Upon my word, I shall be glad to know.'

'Only by not providing for those who have none. The men of merit in any capacity are not, I am afraid, so extremely numerous that we need starve any of them, unless we wickedly suffer a set of worthless fellows to eat their bread.'

'This is all mere Utopia,' cries his lordship; 'the chimerical system of Plato's commonwealth, with which we amused ourselves at the university; politics which are inconsistent with the state of human affairs.'. . . 'Do you not know, doctor, that this is as corrupt a nation as ever existed under the sun? And would you think of governing such a people by the strict principles of honesty and morality?'

Harrison is quite conscious of the dangers of political degeneracy, and hotly urges:

'Wherever true merit is liable to be superseded by favour and partiality, and men are intrusted with offices without any regard to capacity or integrity, the affairs of that state will always be in a deplorable situation. . . . But, my lord, there is another mischief which attends this kind of injustice, and that is, it hath a manifest tendency to destroy all virtue and all ability among the people, by taking away all that encouragement and incentive which should promote emulation and raise men to aim at excelling in any art, science, or professsion.'

At this point the two themes [17] that Fielding uses in depicting Booth's lot most nearly meet: his belief in a dominant passion has sapped his zest for life as a moral struggle, and the lack of recognition of his undisputed merit has destroyed incentive that might lead him to excellence as a servant of his country.

Many critics have thought that the happy ending of *Amelia* to a certain extent contradicts the narrative premises of the story. Such an idea is partly based on a lower conception of the character of Booth than Fielding intended; and Booth's

---

[17] For analysis of epic structure into a remotely similar dual motivation see Bossu's *Treatise of the Epick Poem* (2d. English ed., 1719), Bk. 1, ch. 8 (the *Iliad*), ch. 10 (the *Odyssey*), ch. 11 (the *Æneid*).

conversion, whether through argument with Harrison or through Barrow's sermons, is more than once foreshadowed in the book—though hardly more than foreshadowed. The recovery of Amelia's fortune through the confession of Robinson is certainly an artificial, though time-honoured device. It saves Booth from the army, and Henry Fielding was enough of a pacifist to be pleased with that result. But could Henry Fielding the political and social reformer—or as the consistent artist, for that matter—regard this result as a proper "happy ending"? Obviously, if the fears of political and social degeneracy were not to be justified, what was really needed was the conversion, not of Booth, but of some noble lord, who acting from pure desire to secure an able officer for the guards would get the long-coveted commission for Booth. No such person appeared; no Rufinus fell: *diu floruere nocentes.* Fielding simply turns his back on his larger theme, and content to make his worthy couple happy, lets them retire to Wiltshire and an untroubled country life.

Amelia was published in December, 1751. Its attack on the aristocracy for callousness and lack of recognition of merit was, of course, nothing new. About two months before the death of Alexander Pope, much of whose writing decries the bad taste and corruption of the aristocracy, Dr. Johnson had published his *Life of Richard Savage,* which told a story motivated much as Booth's was to be. In 1748 in *Roderick Random* Smollett had displayed the acidity of his heart in the story of the difficulties of Melopoyn in securing a patron for his tragedy—transparently the story of Smollett's own difficulties over his *Regicide.* Four years after *Amelia,* Dr. Johnson penned his famous letter to the Earl of Chesterfield about patronage, and in 1759 Goldsmith's *Enquiry* reiterated this tale of the lack of recognition of merit. In brief, this sort of thing, always evident in literary circles, was in the eighteenth century by way of becoming an agent to dissipate respect and regard for noble lords. It consequently is wise to realize that none of these authors was an intentional or conscious revolutionary: they were practically all of them thorough conservatives of the best sort, who wrote with a desire to reform the aristocracy and thus to make the world safe for what we now call the *ancien regime.*

University of Chicago

H. T. SWEDENBERG, JR.

Rules and English Critics of the Epic, 1650-1800

from

STUDIES IN PHILOLOGY

Volume XXXV(1938), 566-87

RULES AND ENGLISH CRITICS OF THE EPIC,
1650-1800

By H. T. Swedenberg, Jr.

For a hundred and fifty years after Davenant and Hobbes published their treatises occasioned by *Gondibert,* English critics looked
upon the epic as one of the most important genres of literature.
Many moribund epics were produced and scores of treatises were
written about the form. Several forces contributed to this activity.
Homer and Virgil were universally accepted as two of the greatest,
if not the greatest, writers of antiquity, and Milton, during the
eighteenth century, came to be considered worthy of a place beside
them. As a matter of course, the epics of these three, admittedly
their noblest works, received marked attention. Furthermore Aristotle and Horace had given critical pronouncements on the form,
and their works had been embellished and interpreted by critic
after critic on the Continent, especially the French of the seventeenth century. Therefore with the *Iliad, Odyssey,* and *Aeneid* as
classic examples, with *Paradise Lost* as a native one, with Aristotle, Horace, and the French classical critics as preceptors, English writers almost inevitably turned their attention to the theory
of the epic. In fact practically every great critic of the 1650-1800
period, and a vast number of the less great, wrote about the epic
poem.

Knowing and using constantly the critical theory of the past,
these English writers naturally quite often took notice of such
popular subjects as the theory of the rules and the power of critical
authority. Since the critics of the epic numbered among their
ranks the great and the small, their opinions are fairly representative of their time. In other words, a study of their opinions will
indicate not only what they as critics of a certain type of literature
thought, but also what they as typical writers of their period believed. A survey of their remarks will, therefore, throw further
light on the general theory of the period in regard to rules and
critical authority.

The material which is presented below is divided into three sections, each division containing the theory of a fifty-year period.
No attempt is made to suggest that any remarkable change took

place in English criticism in 1700 or in 1750. It is true that a fairly distinct belief is apparent in each of the fifty-year periods, but the exact dates have been chosen primarily for convenience.

I

In writing *Gondibert* Davenant had consciously departed from certain established methods of epic structure, and therefore he might well be expected to attack certain rules and critics. But he is singularly silent on the subject. His preface to *Gondibert* (1650), it is true, contains material which indicates clearly that he was quite aware of his departure from Homeric and Virgilian modes. Thus he declares:

> If I be accus'd of Innovation, or to have transgressed against the method of the Ancients, I shall think my self secure in beleeving that a Poet, who hath wrought with his own instruments at a new design, is no more answerable for disobedience to Predecessors, then *Law-makers* are liable to those old Laws which themselves have repealed.[1]

Again he writes in the same essay that, contrary to his method most writers " are apter to be beholding to Bookes then to Men." [2] These statements, however, obviously have reference to ancient practice rather than theory. But, at the same time, they indicate that Davenant was skeptical of authority *per se*.

It is not at all surprising to find Hobbes even more opposed to literary authority than was Davenant. Hobbes exalted the power of reason and concluded that the man of judgment must avoid dependence upon mere authority: " he that takes up conclusions on the trust of authors, and doth not fetch them from the first items in every reckoning, which are the significations of names by definitions, loses his labour; and does not know anything, but only believeth." [3] This general philosophic truth applies, in Hobbes' opinion, to art also. Rather scornfully he writes in his " Answer " (1650) to Davenant's preface about those who " take not the laws of art, from any reason of their own, but from the fashion of

---

[1] *Critical Essays of the Seventeenth Century*, ed. J. E. Spingarn (Oxford, 1908-1909), II, 20. All subsequent references to this work will be designated by the use of the name Spingarn.

[2] *Ibid.*, p. 26.

[3] " Leviathan " (1651), *English Works*, ed. Sir William Molesworth (London, 1839-1845), III, 32.

precedent times." [4]   Therefore he cannot see why a Christian poet should preface his epic with an invocation, except that it is "a reasonless imitation of custom; of a foolish custom." [5]

Hobbes and Davenant, then, are not concerned with customs and authority in practice or theory. Cowley, a friend of both, is likewise doubtful of mere authority. In the Pindaric "To Mr. Hobs" he shows clearly his opinion by writing:

> The *Fields* which answer'd well the *Ancients Plow*,
> Spent and out-worn return no *Harvest* now,
> In barren *Age* wild and unglorious lie,
>   And boast of *past Fertilitie*,
> The *poor relief* of *Present Povertie*.[6]

His poem "*Reason. The Use of it in* Divine *Matters*" indicates that his praise of Hobbes is not idle courtesy; he was a follower of Hobbes in elevating reason. It is not surprising, therefore, to find him approving Davenant's departure from the epic norm. Some, says Cowley, seem to think everything ill save that which comes from Rome. But Davenant is to be praised for deserting the beaten way.[7] In a note on an ode which he inserted in his *Davideis* he shows the same tendency toward revolt, saying he had no authority, but declaring that "We must sometimes be bold to innovate." [8] In these remarks Cowley is definitely of a stamp with Hobbes and Davenant in defending reason as opposed to authority. But he does not follow this theory in all his statements about the epic. He declares that he followed the ancients in prefacing his *Davideis* with an invocation;[9] he explains that he divided the poem into twelve parts after the manner of Virgil;[10] and he notes that he did not carry the poem on to David's anointing because the method of the ancients was to conclude the poem without the final details.[11] Quite obviously, then, Cowley was not a complete convert to the cause of Davenant and Hobbes. His criticism is, in fact, an early example of what was to appear later in epic theory: a blending of authority and reason.

---

[4] *English Works*, ed. cit., IV, 447.

[5] *Ibid.*, p. 448.

[6] *Works* (London, 1668), p. 26, 3d pag.

[7] "*To Sir* William Davenant. *Upon his two first Books of* Gundibert, *finished before his voyage to* America," *Works*, p. 25, 1st pag.

[8] *Works*, p. 37, 4th pag.   [10] *Ibid.*, sig. C₃

[9] *Ibid.*, p. 24, 4th pag.   [11] *Ibid.*

Thomas Rymer took essentially the same stand. As Spingarn has pointed out,[12] Rymer had respect for the theory of Hobbes. Thus in *The Tragedies of the Last Age* (1678) he writes of the importance of reason in making great poetry. But in his preface to the translation of Rapin's *Reflections* (1674), just before he begins a survey of English epic poetry, he shows his respect for authority. Furthermore, he blends reason with authority and accepts both:

The truth is, what *Aristotle* writes on this Subject are not the dictates of his own magisterial will or dry deductions of his Metaphysicks: But the Poets were his Masters, and what was their practice he reduced to principles. Nor would the *modern Poets* blindly resign to this practice of the *Ancients*, were not the Reasons convincing and clear as any demonstration in *Mathematicks*.[13]

This is, of course, a statement of the very popular neo-classic doctrine that rules are based on nature and reason and are therefore to be accepted.

Another follower of reason was Edward Phillips, who contended that a poet might know all the laws of epic and tragedy, and still, lacking " Poetic *Energie*," fail. A critic, in his opinion, must use his reason and common sense as well as his knowledge of the ancients. At the conclusion of his preface to *Theatrum Poetarum* (1675) he declares that he has judged by what truth has " suggested to my reason, perswading my self, that no right judgement can be given or distinction made in the Writings of This or That Author, in whatever Art or Science, but, without taking ought upon trust, by an unbiass'd and, from the knowledge of ancient Authors, judicious examination of each." [14]

The Earl of Mulgrave had a wholesome respect for reason, " that substantial, useful part " [15] which governs with fancy, and he was even more enthusiastic about the laws of epic structure, in particular those set forth by Le Bossu, who showed the world the " sacred Mysteries " of the epic. In these and other statements Mulgrave blends reason and authority, until authority, leaving reason a little behind, becomes important for itself. Le Bossu,

[12] *Critical Essays of the Seventeenth Century*, I, lxiv.
[13] *Ibid.*, II, 165.
[14] *Ibid.*, II, 272.
[15] " An Essay upon Poetry " (1682), Spingarn, II, 287.

says Mulgrave, has clearly shown the way in epic poetry, but there is no one to follow it.[16]

In the mind of "W. J.," who translated Le Bossu's treatise on the epic, there was no doubt about the efficacy of the rules. In enumerating various reasons for the low state of epic poetry in his time, he gives as one of the most important the disregard for the rules:

> The third and last Reason I shall mention for the declining State of *Epick* Poetry among the *Moderns* is, *their notorius neglect of following the Rules which* Aristotle *and* Horace *have prescrib'd*: This, and not want of *Genius*, has been the true Cause why several of our *English Epick Poets* have succeeded so ill in their Designs.[17]

But "W. J." does not desert the cause of reason. In defending the method of Le Bossu he points out that Le Bossu has indeed followed the theory of Aristotle and Horace, but he has always employed his judgment in using any of their ideas. Many will disagree with some of Le Bossu's theories, but, says "W. J.," it is to be hoped that no serious reader will condemn him until

> he has seriously weigh'd his Reasons, and consider'd the Arguments he uses to maintain his Cause: and then if our *Critick* can be convinc'd of any Error, he is too modest not to submit to the Suffrage of better Judgments. But if, on the other hand, he has Reason on his side, it may with Justice be expected, that he will be a means of opening the Eyes of a great many unprejudic'd Persons.[18]

"W. J." is obviously much more concerned about the efficacy of the rules than the sanctity of reason, but he nevertheless remembers that reason and judgment are still important in criticism.

Equally respectful of the rules is Sir Richard Blackmore, who observes that for seventeen hundred years no one has succeeded in the epic, and then notes: ".That the modern Poets have been so unsuccessful, has not, I imagin, proceeded so much from want of *Genius*, as from their Ignorance of the Rules of writing such a Poem; or at least, from their want of attending to them." [19] Although, as we shall see, he later made a pretense of revolting

---

[16] *Ibid.*, p. 296.

[17] *Monsieur Bossu's Treatise of the Epick Poem* (London, 1695), sig. b₂v.

[18] *Ibid.*, sig. b₅.

[19] "The Preface" to *Prince Arthur* (London, 1695), sig. a₂

against authority, in 1695 Blackmore is awed by it. He does not seek to justify the rules of epic construction by reason; he is satisfied that they are correct, because they have been propounded by great critics. It is useless, he declares, for him to censure modern epics, for

whoever will be at the Pains to read the Commentators on *Aristotle*, and *Horace's* Rules of Poetry; or that will but carefully consider *Rapin, Dacier,* and *Bossu,* those great Masters among the *French*, and the Judicious Remarks of our own *excellent Critick Mr. Rymer,* who seems to have better consider'd these matters, and to have seen farther into them, than any of the *English Nation*; will be soon able to see wherein the Heroick Poems that have been publish'd since *Virgil* by the *Italian, French,* and *English Wits* have been defective, by comparing them with the *Rules* of Writing set down by those *great Masters.*[20]

At variance with Blackmore and others on a number of subjects, John Dennis was nevertheless at one with his age on the subject of rules and reason. He elevated reason, but at the same time managed to show that nature, the rules, and common sense are all the same. In *The Impartial Critick* (1693) he makes one of the characters say: "The Rules of *Aristotle* are nothing but Nature and Good Sence reduc'd to a Method." [21] And he reiterates even more forcefully in his work on Blackmore's *Prince Arthur*:

For the Rules of *Aristotle* . . . are but Directions for the Observation of Nature, as the best of the written Laws, are but the pure Dictates of Reason and Repetitions of the Laws of Nature. For either this must be granted, or *Aristotle* must be confess'd to have contradicted the Design which he had in prescribing those Rules: Which Design was to teach Men to please, more than they could do without these Rules. . . . For Poetry is nothing but an Imitation of Nature, which *Aristotle*, who knew her well, has very well taught us to imitate. And he who keeps up strictly to his Rules, is as certain to succeed, as he who lives up exactly to Reason is certain of being happy. But it is as impossible for any Man who has not a great Genius, strictly to observe the Rules; as it is for any one who has not super-natural Assistance to live up to the Dictates of Reason.[22]

Rules, reason, nature, common sense—all are intertwined, all are closely related in the opinion of Dennis.

Finally there was Dryden, who, as might be expected, took a

[20] *Ibid.,* sigs. c_1-c_1v.
[21] Spingarn, III, 194.
[22] *Remarks on a Book Entituled, Prince Arthur, an Heroick Poem* (London, 1696), pp. 106-107.

middle-of-the-road approach. He recognized the value of rules and of reason, but he was skeptical of that reason which would shackle the flights of great poetry. In " A Parallel of Poetry and Painting " (1695) he defends rules as being rational, because they are founded on nature:

the way to please being to imitate nature, both the poets and the painters in ancient times, and in the best ages, have studied her; and from the practice of both these arts the rules have been drawn, by which we are instructed how to please, and to compass that end which they obtained, by following their example; for nature is still the same in all ages, and can never be contrary to herself.[23]

It is not necessarily true, he goes on, that that which pleases the greatest number is greatest. What " ought to please " is important. Our judgments have become warped, and we sometimes mistake for an imitation of nature that which has no nature in it. Therefore " rules were invented, that by them we might discern— when nature was imitated, and how nearly." [24]

Reason, in Dryden's opinion, is all very good, but if it is used to condemn imaginative work it must be the result of a majority opinion, not merely the judgment of one man. Many condemn the flights of heroic poetry as bombast. Such critics had better doubt their own judgment than that of Homer, or Virgil, or Milton. It is true, says Dryden, there are limits to which the poetic spirit may range, " but he must understand those limits who pretends to judge as well as he who undertakes to write." [25] Mere individual reason is not enough to cast aside the hyperboles of the great masters:

And if you would appeal from thence to right reason, you will gain no more by it in effect, than, first, to set up your reason against those authors; and, secondly, against all those who have admired them. You must prove, why that ought not to have pleased, which has pleased the most learned, and the most judicious; and, to be thought knowing, you must first put the fool upon all mankind.[26]

Thus also is Dryden a member of the rational-rule group. He will not use reason to carp at the excellencies of imagination, but

[23] *Works*, ed. Sir Walter Scott and George Saintsbury (London, 1882-1893), XVII, 310.

[24] *Ibid.*, p. 313.

[25] " Apology for Heroic Poetry and Poetic Licence " (1677), *Works*, V, 116.

[26] *Ibid.*, pp. 116-117.

neither will he allow imagination to run riot. Established judgment, then, is to be the norm for criticism, not the mere whim of each succeeding critic. The judgment established by the great minds is the basis of rules, which are to be considered not because they are rules, but because they are founded on nature, a nature that is always constant.

From the foregoing remarks of various critics of the epic, the fact is obvious that a gradual development toward authority took place in the last half of the seventeenth century. Neo-classic theory of the epic started with Davenant and Hobbes and grew until it reached a fairly mature state in the work of Blackmore, Dennis, and Dryden. During this development opinion on rules and authority changed. Hobbes and Davenant, basing their belief on the importance of reason, scouted the value of authority in epic construction. This respect for reason continued throughout the century, but it soon changed from a thoroughgoing love of reason as opposed to authority to a love of reason and authority as harmonious guides. Even Cowley, an intimate and admirer of Hobbes and Davenant, could not go all the way with them in rejecting Homer and Virgil as models. As the century progressed and the study of the epic became more popular, established method and rules were looked upon with ever increasing respect. But reason and common sense likewise became more and more a part of every critic's lexicon. It followed, therefore, that rules and reason became companions. By the time of Dryden's death the familiar neo-classic theory that rules are founded on nature and that men of judgment accept them because they are reasonable was established.

II

The first fifty years of the eighteenth century is a period particularly fruitful for an investigation of the theory of rules, for it is universally accepted as the age in which English neo-classicism was at its flood tide. In this period John Dennis continues in the attitude he had expressed prior to 1700. In the "Epistle Dedicatory" to *The Advancement and Reformation of Modern Poetry* he explains his belief in regularity. There are, says Dennis, some things in great poetry, like some phenomena in nature, which seem at first sight to be "against Reason," but upon close examination those things in nature and poetry prove to be necessary to a " just Design." Thus Homer and Virgil certainly followed the rules of composition, for they had " too much Discernment, not to see the Necessity of knowing and practising the Rules, which Reason and Philosophy have prescrib'd to Poets." [27] Dennis is willing to admit that Milton broke the laws of Aristotle and that he was justified in this course.[28] But apparently this praise of Milton's latitude does not apply to the work of lesser folk who might eschew rules. Dennis goes on to say that poetry has lately fallen to a low level because its devotees are ignorant of the essential laws of the art:

In short, Poetry is either an Art, or Whimsie and Fanaticism. If it is an Art, it follows that it must propose an end to it self, and afterwards lay down proper Means for the attaining that end: For this is undeniable, that there are proper Means for the attaining of every end, and those proper Means in Poetry, we call the Rules. Again, if the end of Poetry be to instruct and reform the World, that is, to bring Mankind from Irregularity, Extravagance and Confusion, to Rule and Order, how this should be done by a thing that is in it self irregular and extravagant, is difficult to be conceived. Besides, the work of every reasonable Creature must derive its Beauty from Regularity, for Reason is Rule and Order, and nothing can be irregular either in our Conceptions or our Actions, any further than it swerves from Rule, that is, from Reason.[29]

Here is, of course, a restatement, in the most explicit terms, of the theory that rules and reason are the same.

Addison felt that rules were not always to be honored, and he was particularly irritated with those who judged only by them: " A few general rules extracted out of the French authors, with a certain cant of words, has sometimes set up an illiterate heavy writer for a most judicious and formidable critic." [30] He declares that in writing the critique of *Paradise Lost* he has not bound himself by the rules of any critic. He has taken something from one and something from another, and at times he has differed from all. That, says Addison, was " when I have thought that the reason of the thing was on my side." [31]

[27] *The Advancement and Reformation of Modern Poetry* (London, 1701), sig. a₂.
[28] *The Grounds of Criticism in Poetry* (London, 1704), sigs. a₆-a₆v.
[29] *Ibid.*, pp. 5-6.
[30] *The Spectator*, ed. George A. Aitken (London, 1898), No. 291.
[31] *Ibid.*, No. 321.

Pope was the first English writer to ridicule the rules of Le Bossu,[32] who was looked upon with great respect by most English critics. In the "Receipt to make an Epic Poem," first published in number 78 of the *Guardian*, he burlesques Le Bossu's method of criticizing an epic, prefacing his work with a statement about criticism in general. As criticism is known, he says, "it consists only in a knowledge of mechanic rules which contribute to the structure of different sorts of poetry; as the receipts of good housewives do to the making puddings of flour, oranges, plumbs, or any other ingredients."[33] Also, in the "Postscript to the *Odyssey*" he declares that he is "sawcy enough to think that one may sometimes differ from *Aristotle* without blundering, and . . . I am sure one may sometimes fall into an error by following him servilely."[34] Pope, then, was also skeptical of the rules *per se*.

Well in the ranks of those who venerated the methods of the classics is Thomas Parnell, who is firm in the belief that the modern can imitate only the ancients. He admits that the modern is not forced to follow the fables of the ancients, but he is certain that he will do well "to observe their Manner."[35] He knows that Milton and Spenser have given evidence that "Invention is not bounded" but he is certain that these two are exceptions and not to be followed by the ordinary man.

On the other side is John Hughes. He finds difficulty in harmonizing strict classic rules with the structure of the *Faerie Queene*. Thus, while admitting that one of the major defects of the *Faerie Queene* is its want of unity, he goes on to say that the poem must not be judged by rules "drawn from the Practice of *Homer* and *Virgil*."[36] And having made this statement, he proceeds to draw a parallel in a manner dear to Augustan critics:

to compare it therefore with the Models of Antiquity, wou'd be like drawing a Parallel between the *Roman* and the *Gothick* Architecture. In the first there is doubtless a more natural Grandeur and Simplicity: in the latter, we find great Mixtures of Beauty and Barbarism, yet assisted by the

[32] See A. F. B. Clark, *Boileau and the French Classical Critics in England (1660-1830)* (Paris, 1925), p. 247.
[33] *The British Essayists*, ed. A. Chalmers (London, 1817), XVII, 127.
[34] *The Odyssey of Homer* (London, 1725-1726), V, 314.
[35] *An Essay on the Different Stiles of Poetry* (London, 1713), sig. A₄.
[36] *The Works of Mr. Edmund Spenser* (London, 1715), I, lx.

Invention of a Variety of inferior Ornaments; and tho the former is more majestick in the whole, the latter may be very surprizing and agreeable in its Parts.[37]

Henry Felton also had a questioning attitude toward the authority of rules. He is certain that many of the greatest works were written before the rules were evolved: " For those who first prescribed the Rules of Writing, did not take Nature stripped and naked for their Copy; but they looked upon her, as she was dressed and adorned by her Adorers." [38] Rules, then, were simply founded on the models of the greatest writers; and those who have written after these early writers have, in following nature, followed the rules. " And perhaps," concludes Felton rather daringly, "(for I love to doubt in Matters of so hazardous Conjecture) if the Rules had not been given, we had been troubled with many fewer Writers; for then those who had not Nature for their Rule, could have had no Rule at all." [39] As it is, there are many scribblers who think only of the rule and care not at all for the meaning.

We have already noted Sir Richard Blackmore as a staunch defender of authority in 1695. But by 1716 he had reversed his position and was taking a definite stand against the conventional rules. In his " An Essay on the Nature and Constitution of Epick Poetry " he admits Aristotle " as a great Genius, and a Person of more than common Erudition," [40] but he refuses to accept his dictates as the final decree in poetry. Poets and critics, says Blackmore, should trust their reason and judgment and not rely solely upon authority. If this attitude were taken, men would no longer be slaves to commentators and grammarians. Also modern poetry would not be tried by the laws of the ancients alone. Critics would " produce clear Evidence from the Nature and Constitution of that kind of Poetry, to make good their Opinions; and not rely on the single Authority of ancient Writers, tho of the greatest Name, to support them." [41]

Seven years later Blackmore said essentially the same thing. In the preface to *Alfred* he again calls for freedom from ancient

[37] *Ibid.*, I, lx-lxi.
[38] *A Dissertation on Reading the Classics, and Forming a Just Style* (2d ed., London, 1715), pp. vii-viii.
[39] *Ibid.*, p. ix.
[40] *Essays upon Several Subjects* (London, 1716-1717), I, 12.
[41] *Ibid.*, p. 13.

authority. If Homer and Virgil are judged with an exercise of reason, says Blackmore, it is apparent that they are not free from faults; and therefore modern writers are under no particular obligation to follow their patterns. A slavish imitation of them " manifestly sets up Authority and Example, above Judgment and Reason." [42] It is, after all, only " the half Critick " who will admit nothing in the epic which is not also in Homer and Virgil.[43]

Joseph Trapp, first professor of poetry at Oxford and translator of Virgil, also objected to a complete subjection to authority, though he did not believe that poetry can be free of all rules. In speaking of his own criticism he declares that he has examined various authorities, and goes on to say, " I don't slavishly adhere to their Decrees. For Books are to be consider'd as Helps to Learning, not Fetters to it; and it is just, in these sort of Studies especially, that every Man, after he has weigh'd the Opinion of others should be at Liberty to follow his own." [44] But he goes on to point out that the art of poetry is as susceptible to laws as other arts, and that these laws are " founded upon Truth and right Reason." [45] In another place, however he shows that rules may be submitted to reason, for he argues that Aristotle's rules cannot be used to limit all subsequent epic poetry, since Aristotle based his statements primarily on the work of Homer.[46]

Of all those who honored the rules, none more completely revered them than Charles Gildon. He is certain that no man ever achieved a lasting fame without " coming up " to the rules of

[42] *Alfred: An Epick Poem in Twelve Books* (London, 1723), p. xxxv.

[43] It should be noted here that, despite Blackmore's pretended rebellion against rules, he slavishly followed the established scheme of criticizing an epic. His various essays on the epic had practically nothing in them that had not already been said by other critics of the neo-classic school. Blackmore was not alone in this inconsistency. Many of the eighteenth-century critics continued to follow established theory, even though they denounced authority and rules. The limits of this study preclude a consideration of the theory of the epic in neo-classic England, but the writer plans to publish an extended discussion of the subject at some time in the future.

[44] " Author's Preface," *Lectures on Poetry Read in the Schools of Natural Philosophy at Oxford. Translated from the Latin, with additional Notes* (London, 1742), p. iii.

[45] *Ibid.*, p. 3.

[46] *The Æneis of Virgil, translated into Blank Verse* (London, 1718-1720), I, xx.

poetry,[47] and he can see no sense in the argument concerning art and nature in a poet, for art is *" Nature reduc'd to Form."* It is all very well for the man of genius to exercise his natural abilities, but he must at the same time use his judgment, which is based on the rules of art. When the question of Homer's knowledge of rules is proposed, Gildon can only answer that his belief is that the poet proposed rules to himself.[48]

Three years after making these statements Gildon is still worried about the " low state of Poetry " and the lack of taste of the people in general.[49] He feels that the rules would alleviate this condition, if only the public were acquainted with them. And he is particularly wroth with those " messieurs of *Port-Royal* " who question whether Virgil was concerned with the rules. Gildon is convinced that Virgil knew the rules of composition as well as those of grammar.[50]

Though he is concerned only incidentally with epic, Leonard Welsted writes with so much force and directness on the subject of regulation by rule in poetry that he may very profitably be noted here. His essay " A Dissertation concerning the Perfection of the *English* Language, the State of Poetry, &c." contains some extremely sensible and logical material on the subject. Though Welsted was inclined to the school of taste, he also saw the value of reason and restraint in poetry. But his conception of reason differs somewhat from that held by others of his period, and therefore his pronouncements are particularly interesting.

According to Welsted all that the ancients and moderns together have written on the subject is only what a man of sense would know anyway. The rules have done little except produce a group of very inferior writers.[51] He goes on to say—in striking contrast to Gildon's conception of Virgil's method of composition—that

Those Observations or Rules were primarily form'd upon and design'd to serve only as Comments to the Works of certain great Authors, who compos'd those Works without any such help; the mighty Originals, from

---

[47] *The Complete Art of Poetry* (London, 1718), I, 94.
[48] *Ibid.*, I, 97.
[49] *The Laws of Poetry* (London, 1721), p. 39.
[50] *Ibid.*, pp. 58-59.
[51] *Epistles, Odes, &c written on Several Subjects. With a Translation of Longinus's Treatise on the Sublime* (London, 1724), pp. xvi-xvii.

whence they were drawn, were produc'd without them; and unluckily for all Rules, it has commonly happen'd since, that those Writers have succeeded the worst, who have pretended to have been most assisted by them.[52]

The " arts " of poetry, says Welsted, can touch only the mechanical side of poetry, ignoring the more important internal fire. Rules cannot teach a writer true poetry:

What Instruction shall convey to him that Flame, which can alone animate a Work, and give it the Glow of Poetry? And how, or by what Industry shall be learn'd, among a Thousand other Charms, that delicate Contexture in Writing, by which the Colours, as in the Rainbow, grow out of one another, and every Beauty owes its Lustre to a former, and gives Being to a succeeding one?[53]

Welsted declares that he does not wish to throw poetry into a mysterious vagueness. He understands the necessity for reason. The important point, however, is that reason of poetry should be differentiated from that of mathematics:

Poetry depends much more on Imagination, than other Arts, but is not on that Account less reasonable than they; for Imagination is as much a Part of Reason, as is Memory or Judgment, or rather a more bright Emanation from it, as to paint and throw Light upon Ideas, is a finer Act of the Understanding, than simply to separate or compare them: The Plays, indeed, and the Flights of Fancy, do not submit to that sort of Discussion, which moral or physical Propositions are capable of, but must nevertheless, to please, have Justness and natural Truth: The Care to be had, in judging of Things of this Nature, is to try them by those Tests that are proper to themselves, and not by such as are proper only to other Knowledges. Thus Poetry is not an irrational Art, but as closely link'd with Reason, exerted in a right Way, as any other Knowledge; what it differs in, as a Science of Reason, from other Sciences, is, that it does not, equally with them, lie level to all Capacities, that a Man, rightly to perceive the Reason and the Truth of it, must be born with *Taste* or a Faculty of Judging, and that it cannot be reduc'd to a formal Science, or taught by any set Precepts.[54]

The reason which governs poetry, then, is not to be acquired by rules; it is rather born in a person. Welsted's opinion seems to be rather Hobbesian, since his reason is the reason which is individual, a reason based on the natural endowment of a man, not that arrived at by the use of set principles. His attitude is therefore particularly interesting, because of his attempt to harmonize reason and taste, and his rejection of set rules.

[52] *Ibid.*, p. xvii.   [53] *Ibid.*, p. xix.   [54] *Ibid.*, pp. xxii-xxiii.

Joseph Spence also realized that art may be above rules, when he wrote " Eloquence has its *Je ne scai quoi's,* as well as Beauty." [55] But he was, nevertheless, thoroughly convinced that certain rules are to be followed in judging a poem. He was particularly irritated with the critics who simply carp at an author's work. The great critics of antiquity were aware that a poet may make some minor errors and still be praised, if only he have a " generous Spirit." " Agreeable to this was the behaviour of these great Men in laying down rules, or making observations: their intention was to distinguish the beauties of Language or Sentiments, from the defects and vices of either." [56]

Jonathan Richardson likewise felt that rules may at times be transcended. In regard to Milton's treatment of the rules of epic structure in *Paradise Lost* he writes:

> if the Sublimity and Peculiarity of the Matter of this Poem, if its Superiority in That Respect has rais'd it above Some of the Rules given by *Aristotle*, or Whatever Other Criticks, and Gather'd From, or Founded on the *Iliad, Odyssey,* or *Æneid,* it has Distinguish'd it to its greater Glory; 'tis not only an Heroic Poem, but the Most So that Ever was Wrote. *Milton* did not despise Rules, Such as were Built upon Reason, So far as those Establish'd Reach'd; but as his Free and Exalted Genius Aspir'd Beyond what had Yet been Attempted in the Choice of his Subject, Himself was his Own Rule when in Heights where None had gone before, and Higher than Which None Can Ever go.[57]

Henry Pemberton expressed a similar doubt in the beginning of his *Observations on Poetry*:

> WERE the precepts of critics always consistent with one another, and with truth, nothing more would be necessary towards deciding upon any poetic performance, than to compare it with their dictates. But as the most approved are on some points divided, and, where they are more unanimous, not always in my apprehension free from error; I intend to examine into the genuine principles, whereby our opinion . . . ought to be regulated, independent on any authority whatever.[58]

---

[55] *An Essay on Pope's Odyssey: In Which Some particular Beauties and Blemishes of that Work are consider'd* (London and Oxford, 1726-1727), Part I, p. 144.

[56] *Ibid.,* p. 145.

[57] *Explanatory Notes and Remarks on Milton's Paradise Lost* (London, 1734), p. cxlvii.

[58] *Observations on Poetry, Especially the Epic: Occasioned by the Late Poem upon Leonidas* (London, 1738), pp. 1-2.

Many, says Pemberton, are still enslaved by "the pedantry of submitting implicitly to ancient authority," but the world is at length largely freed from that bondage. He, therefore, is not afraid to disagree with Aristotle's precepts on the epic.

In this manner the critics of the epic talked about rules in the first half of the eighteenth century. Any attempt to evaluate their position leads inevitably, in the first place, to the conclusion that there was a division of opinion. Some strongly favored the rules, others were equivocal, and others deprecated them. The time-honored explanation that rules were founded on nature appeared often. Those critics who were concerned with defending modern epics naturally could not accept ancient rules as the only correct interpretation of nature. Spenser and Milton, for instance, were so careless of some of the established theories that their works would probably suffer if judged solely by them. And therefore critics like Hughes and Richardson were forced to side-step some of the old laws. Occasionally outright questioning of the value of rules made itself apparent.

It is particularly noticeable that reason was a constant guide, no matter what the critic thought of the rules themselves. He might identify rules with reason or he might put reason against rules, but he was always calling reason to justify his position. Never were rules defended on the basis that they were promulgated by Aristotle or Horace and therefore must be right. As a matter of fact, during this period in which the classics were honored above all, there is a notable tendency among critics of the epic to question the established rules of composition. Not many were ready to declare boldly that these laws should be disregarded, but a goodly number showed plainly that they were restive under the dominion of a system too inflexible. This tendency looks forward to the change in belief that was to come in the last half of the century.

III

In his essay on Pope, Joseph Warton comments on Pope's line "nature methodiz'd," saying that the rules of poetry were all "posterior to practice."[59] Furthermore he adds that "A petulant rejection, and an implicit veneration, of the rules of the ancient

[59] *An Essay on the Genius and Writings of Pope* (3d ed., Dublin, 1764), p. 97.

critics, are equally destructive of true taste." [60] Warton takes the middle of the way. Critical bigotry is not, he affirms, to be confused with true critical endeavor. Such rules as those that the epic action should begin as late as possible, that the action be great and complete, that the episodes rise from the " main fable," and that the hero be distinguished are " indispensable rules, which nature and necessity dictate, and demand to be observed." [61] He is, however, perfectly willing to damn such absurd theories as those that an epic should have only twelve books, and should end happily.

Thomas Warton was thoroughly convinced that classical rules cannot be applied to the romantic epic:

> But it is absurd to think of judging either Ariosto or Spenser by precepts which they did not attend to. We who live in the days of writing by rule, are apt to try every composition by those laws which we have been taught to think the sole criterion of excellence. Critical taste is universally diffused, and we require the same order and design which every modern performance is expected to have, in poems where they never were regarded or intended. Spenser, and the same may be said of Ariosto, did not live in an age of planning. His poetry is the careless exuberance of a warm imagination and a strong sensibility. . . .
>
> If the FAIRY QUEEN be destitute of that arrangement and œconomy which epic severity requires, yet we scarcely regret the loss of these, while their place is so amply supplied, by something which more powerfully attracts us: something, which engages the affections the feelings of the heart, rather than the cold approbation of the head.[62]

Arthur Murphy was even more thorough in rejecting the rules of epic structure. In number 92 of the *Gray's-Inn Journal* for July 20, 1754, he reviews rules for the epic which " *Bossu* and other Critics " have given the world, such as those of the unity of time, of *in medias res,* and machinery. These he concludes " do not any Way conduce to the Refinement of Taste, or the Improvement of true Genius." [63]

Goldsmith sees the ruin of literature in the popularity of rules and critics. He declares that common sense " might suggest, that those rules were collected, not from nature, but a copy of nature, and would consequently give us still fainter resemblances of

---

[60] *Ibid.*   [61] *Ibid.*, pp. 99-100.

[62] *Observations on the Fairy Queen of Spenser* (2d ed. London, 1762), I, 15-16.

[63] *Gray's-Inn Journal* (London, 1756), II, 251.

original beauty." [64] In a review of Roger Kedington's *Critical Dissertations on the Iliad of Homer* (1759), Goldsmith [65] expresses a like opinion. Kedington had worshipped Homer abjectly. Goldsmith points out in his review that one of the main reasons for the poor quality of epic writing is that too many people have followed Homer and forgotten nature. As a result all epics

seem to be cast in the same mould: the muse is invoked, she tells the tale, the episodes are introduced, armour rings against armour, games are described, and sometimes a shield; while all the conduct of the passions, and all the mixture of well-conducted intrigue are entirely left out of the question.[66]

Another work with which Goldsmith's name is connected is *The Art of Poetry on a New Plan,*[67] which shows a similar irreverence for rules. In regard to rules of the epic, the statement is made that

some of the laws of poetry, as well as those of logic, are better dispensed with than observed; and we see that the good sense of the present age has so far abrogated the tyrannic ordinances of logic, that a man who reasons well may be heard, tho' he does not speak in mood and figure, or throw every argument into a syllogistic form.[68]

Two reviews of contemporary epics are a little less harsh. The author of an essay on *The Epigoniad* rejects the poem because it does not abide by the rules of Le Bossu and Addison.[69] And William Kenrick, reviewing *Fingal,* writes that genius may indeed rise above rules, but at the same time it is necessary to compare any new work with standards in its field.[70] The rules of Aristotle, he argues, were formed by *a posteriori* rather than *a priori* methods. Here again, of course, is the apology for the rules; nature and Homer being the same, Aristotle formed his rules on the practice of Homer.

[64] *Works,* ed. Peter Cunningham (London, 1854), II, 12.

[65] For the identification of Goldsmith as the author, see R. S. Crane, " A Neglected Mid-Eighteenth-Century Plea for Originality and Its Author," *Philological Quarterly,* XIII (1934), 21-29.

[66] *Critical Review,* 1st ser., IX (1760), 13.

[67] See Elizabeth Eaton Kent, *Goldsmith and his Booksellers* (Ithaca, New York, 1933), p. 64.

[68] *The Art of Poetry on a New Plan* (London, 1762), II, 371.

[69] *A Critical Essay on the Epigoniad* (Edinburgh, 1757), pp. 12-13.

[70] *Monthly Review,* 1st ser., XXVI (1762), 41. For the identification of the reviewer, see Benjamin Christie Nangle, *The Monthly Review: First Series, 1749-1789* (Oxford, 1934), p. 103.

With this defense of the rules may be compared several outright repudiations of them.   Laurence Sterne had no love at all for them or critics.   He represents the criticism of an epic as " taking the length, breadth, height, and depth of it . . . upon an exact scale of *Bossu's* " [71]   Of Apollo he asks only " one stroke of native humour, with a single spark of thy own fire along with it." [72]   Then Mercury can take the rules and go " to— no matter."

John Gordon feels approximately the same way, though he is a bit more dignified in his expression.   He writes: " But I know not, how it is; I never in my life, out of complaisance to a set of rules or terms of art, could affect to be delighted with what I neither felt, heard, saw, nor understood.   This is really the plain truth, despise me, as much as you please, for it." [73]   He is convinced that those who follow only rules and look not at nature will be misled, and he concludes that many " have bartered their senses for a few terms of art." [74]

Richard Hurd denounced the rules of epic as they had been promulgated in England.   He was especially irritated with English critics who followed the French vogue of crying down the Italian epics:

Sir W. Davenant open'd the way to this new sort of criticism in a very elaborate preface to Gondibert; and his philosophic friend, Mr. Hobbes, lent his best assistance towards establishing the credit of it.   These two fine Letters contain, indeed, the substance of whatever has been since written on the subject.   Succeeding wits and critics did no more than echo their language.   It grew into a sort of cant, with which Rymer, and the rest of that School, filled their flimsy essays and rambling prefaces.[75]

Hugh Blair and Edward Burnaby Green also showed doubt. Blair labels as pedants those who judge by rule rather than feeling: " For all the rules of genuine Criticism I have shewn to be ultimately founded on feeling; and Taste and Feeling are necessary to guide us in the application of these rules to every particular

[71] *The Life and Opinions of Tristram Shandy, Gentleman,* ed. Wilbur L. Cross (New York, 1904), II, 42.

[72] *Ibid.,* II, 43.

[73] *Occasional Thoughts on the Study and Character of Classical Authors* (London, 1762), pp. 89-90.

[74] *Ibid.,* p. 134.

[75] *Letters on Chivalry and Romance, with the Third Elizabethan Dialogue,* ed. Edith J. Morley (London, 1911), p. 131.

instance." [76] Greene, in the preface to his essay "Observations on the Sublime of Longinus," wrote that the ancients and moderns have done much to injure criticism: "The former, to speak literally, have, with ARISTOTLE, cramped the imagination within the trammels of rule; and the latter have by indulging a critical affectation, created elegance, but destroyed majesty." [77]

In 1782 William Hayley addressed a poetical epistle to Mason on the subject of epic poetry, in which he showed himself an implacable enemy of the accepted rules and rule-makers, especially Boileau and Le Bossu. Boileau, he says, had elegance and judgment, but his remarks on epic poetry might well have clipped the wings of Milton, if they had affected him. Le Bossu, on the other hand, studied Homer by system,

> And wisely tells us, that his Song arose
> As the good Parson's quiet Sermon grows. [78]

Not even Aristotle is exempt. Hayley believes that a good critic must have understanding, imagination, and sensibility; and he makes bold to say that Aristotle had only the first in abundance. [79] He is certain that no one critic is to be followed, and he writes to Mason

> Thou wilt not hold me arrogant or vain,
> If I advise the young poetic train
> To deem infallible no Critic's word. [80]

He calls upon Mason to help him that they may both free young poets from the bonds of rules, and allow the fancy to range. [81]

In the last decade of the century two other writers on the epic expressed their respect for certain rules. William Belsham was willing to accept Aristotle's rules, but he would have nothing of the regulation of epic theory which had been added to Aristotle's system. The rules of Aristotle, if followed properly, would produce a poem which would "be worthy not only of regard and attention, but of the highest admiration, as manifestly requiring, in order to its accomplishment, the most noble and ardent efforts of the human

---

[76] *Lectures on Rhetoric and Belles Lettres* (4th ed., London, 1790), I, 49.
[77] *Critical Essays* (London, 1770), p. ii.
[78] *An Essay on Epic Poetry* (London, 1782), p. 14.
[79] *Ibid.*, p. 132.   [80] *Ibid.*, p. 17.   [81] *Ibid.*, pp. 4-5.

faculties." [82]   Henry James Pye likewise defended Aristotle, but he was not blind in praising him. He declares that Aristotle cannot be expected to account for all the changes in science and art that have taken place since his day. If, however, one makes allowances for the inevitable changes, he will find that, after all, " Aristotle is not so great a blockhead as some take him to be who have never read him." [83]

There is no point in going into further detail, for the writers already noted give sufficient indication of the critical opinion during the second half of the century. As we might expect, there was a marked tendency to doubt the value of the rules. Even those who showed themselves friendly to them were careful to qualify their statements. Thus Joseph Warton could accept some of the rules for the epic, but he could also reject others as completely useless; and Belsham and Pye could praise the law of Aristotle only with qualification. Particularly noticeable is the emphasis on the historical point of view, a theory which stated that Spenser and Ariosto cannot be held accountable to rules which they did not pretend to follow. From 1750 to 1800, then, we see that restiveness which marked the critical attitude toward rules in the preceding fifty years turning into outright revolt.

From the critical opinions expressed during the century and a half just surveyed we may draw several conclusions. First, reason was a dominant force in the criticism of Hobbes and Davenant, and it continued powerful for at least a hundred years. But its application as a critical term varied. The reason which at first was employed to offset the effect of mere authority and rules later became a term to explain and justify rules. Critics of the epic came to feel that they were justified in invoking reason as an ally in defense of or attack on the rules. When used to justify the rules, reason was the logical, sensible opinion of the majority, who looked upon rules and found them good; when employed to attack, reason was the opinion of the individual who examined rules and found them unacceptable.

In the second place, we note that rules became more and more

[82] *Essays Philosophical and Moral, Historical and Literary* (London, 1799), II, 523.

[83] *A Commentary Illustrating the Poetic of Aristotle* (London, 1792), p. xiii.

popular with critics of heroic poetry, as the second half of the seventeenth century wore on. But we also see that this popularity definitely began to wane even during the first fifty years of the eighteenth century. During this period—the true classical period of English criticism—there was a constant questioning of the rules, as well as a constant justification of them. It is particularly significant that even those who most heartily approved of rules felt the necessity of defending them. Practically no writer accepted them casually, as beyond doubt. Finally, we notice that the last half of the eighteenth century showed a marked tendency on the part of the critics of the epic to reject rules altogether, a conclusion which, in view of the changes that were taking place in the literature of the time, is hardly startling.

University of California at Los Angeles.

W. K. WIMSATT, JR.

One Relation of Rhyme to Reason: Alexander Pope

from

THE MODERN LANGUAGE QUARTERLY

Volume V(1944), 323-38

Reprinted by permission of the Editors

ONE RELATION OF RHYME TO REASON
ALEXANDER POPE

By W. K. Wimsatt, Jr.

I

The view of rhyme which I wish to discuss in this essay has been formerly advanced but has never, I believe, been widely entertained. I am aware of statements of it by French prosodists[1] and of theoretical discussions by German aestheticians,[2] but to my knowledge the view has never been expounded in English and has never become a part of English literary theory[3] in the sense of being illustrated from English poetry. It is a view which is worth expounding because it relates to the more radical metaphysical problem of unity and diversity in art, or the universal and the concrete, a problem posed implicitly by Aristotle and still at the heart of metaphysical aesthetics. The last chapter of John Crowe Ransom's book *The New Criticism* is entitled "Wanted: An Ontological Critic";[4] and here with a stroke of brilliant candor he points out that poetry is a double performance in which the verse makes concessions to the sense and the sense to the verse. The poet does two things simultaneously as well as he can, and thus he produces a certain particularity or irrelevance of sense, and further a heterogeneity of structure by which the phonetic effect serves to give thickness or texture to the meaning. The total is a concreteness which makes the difference between poetry and science. In the discussion of verse, and more particularly of rhyme, which follows, I wish to develop the idea that verse gives to poetry a quality of the concrete and particular not merely in virtue of being a simultaneous and partly irrelevant performance, but in virtue of a studiously and accurately alogical character by which it imposes upon the meaning a counterpattern and acts as a fixative or preservative of the sensory

---

[1] Cf. notes 15 and 58.

[2] The most formal statement seems to be that of J. S. Schütze, *Versuch einer Theorie des Reimes nach Inhalt und Form* (Magdeburg, 1802). I have been unable to consult this work and owe my knowledge of it to a summary in Dr. Henry Lanz's *Physical Basis of Rime* (Stanford University, 1931), pp. 162-66. I have on the whole found Dr. Lanz's survey of rhyme theory of great assistance—though I disagree with his central thesis.

[3] Cf. Louis Untermeyer, "Rhyme and Its Reasons," *Sat. Rev. Lit.*, Aug. 6, 1932, pp. 30-31; "The Future of Rhyme," *Sat. Rev. Lit.*, Nov. 15, 1924, p. 278; Theodore Maynard, "The Reason for Rhyme," *Freeman*, VIII (1924), 469-70; E. E. Kellett, "Rhyme and Reason," *Spectator*, CXLV (1935), 544-45; J. W. Rankin, "Rime and Reason," *PMLA*, XLIV (1929), 997-1004. Cf. notes 5, 11, and 19.

[4] *The New Criticism* (Norfolk, Conn., 1941), pp. 294-330.

quality of words. In a very abstract way I suppose this is believed by almost every theorist. I wish to apply the theory in detail to English rhyme, especially to the neo-classic rhyme of Pope, and thus to bring out a basic relation of rhyme to reason or meaning. Traditional prosodists have discussed rhyme as a degree of likeness in word sounds and have catalogued its approximations, alliteration, assonance, slant rhyme, eye rhyme, analyzed rhyme, dissonance, and so forth. But about the meaning of rhyme words they have had little to say. At least one ought to point out that the meanings of two words composing a rhyme pair are usually quite different— and that they thus create a contrast which gives point to the likeness of sound[5] and which is characteristic of verse, where parallels of form do not, as in prose, support parallels of stated meaning, but run counter to meaning.

II

It would be only an exaggeration, not a distortion, of principle to say that the difference between prose and verse is the difference between homoeoteleuton and rhyme. "Non modo ad salutem ejus exstinguendam sed etiam gloriam per tales viros infringendam," says Cicero, and Quintilian quotes[6] it as an example of homoeoteleuton or like endings. Here the *-endam* and the *-endam* are alike, logically and legitimately alike; each has the same meaning, or is the same morpheme, and each supports the logic of the sentence by appearing in analogous places in the structure. Stylistic parallels[7] or forms of meaning of this and of other sorts seem to come fairly to the aid of logic; they are part of the normal framework of prose. The difference between these and rhyme in prose may be illustrated by the following examples from St. Augustine: "Lingua clamat, cor amat"; "Praecedat spes, ut sequatur res."[8] Here not only the endings but also the roots rhyme, and the result is an effect of alogicality, if not of excess and artificiality. It is not really to be expected that the roots should rhyme. The same may be said for all parallels of sound which do not inhere in some parallel meaning of the words themselves, but acquire their parallel merely through being placed in parallel structures. Such, for ex-

---

[5] *"Mice* most assuredly sounds like *mice,"* says a recent critic. "But, the ear asks, what of it?" (T. Walter Herbert, "Near-Rimes and Paraphones," *Sewanee Review,* XLV [1937], 437). Rather, one might say, the *mind* asks, what of it? Cf. note 58.

[6] *Pro Milone,* II, 5; *Institutio Oratoria,* IX, iii, 73 ff. Cf. Aristotle, *Rhetoric,* III, 9.

[7] I have discussed such parallels in my *Prose Style of Samuel Johnson* (New Haven, 1941), pp. 15-43.

[8] Richard C. Trench, *Sacred Latin Poetry* (London, 1864), p. 28 n. Cf. F. J. E. Raby, *A History of Secular Latin Poetry in the Middle Ages* (Oxford, 1934), I, 49. Cf. Quintilian on verbal resemblances (*op. cit.,* IX, iii, 73 ff.) ; *Ad Herennium* on the figure "similiter desinens."

ample, is the transverse alliteration of Lyly,[9] where the series of parallel consonants has logically nothing to do with the antithetic parallel of the words. Of somewhat the same character is the cursus or metrical ending.[10] And if a prose writer were to reënforce a pair of parallel or antithetic clauses by making each one an iambic pentameter, we should say that this was decidedly too much, that the metrical equality was hardly interesting unless it combined with a vein of logic that ran differently.

III

It is possible to point out examples, in balladry and in other primitive types of poetry, where the equalities of verse coincide with the parallels of meaning. Even in sophisticated poetry such as Tennyson's *In Memoriam* one may find some stanzas where a high degree of parallel is successful.[11] But on the whole the tendency of verse, or certainly that of English verse, has been the opposite. The smallest equalities, the feet, so many syllables, or so many time units, are superimposed upon the linear succession of ideas most often without any regard for the equalities of logic. Two successive iambs may be two words, or one word, or parts of two words, and so on. The larger units, the lines, also are measured without reference to logically parallel sections of sense. Even in heavily end-stopped verse, such as that in Shakespeare's early plays, the complete phrase of which each line is formed stands in oblique relation to the lines before and after. The lines do not parallel one another but spring ahead, one from another, diversely.

The more primitive and forthrightly emotional the poetry, as in balladry, the less it may demand the sensory resistance of verse non-parallel to logic. The more sophisticated and intellectualized the poetry, the more it will demand such resistance. The point is worth illustrating from the blank verse of *Paradise Lost*—one of the most artful verse forms in the range of English literature. An

---

[9] "Althoughe hetherto Euphues I have shrined thee in my heart for a trustie friende, I will shunne thee heerafter as a trothles foe" (*Euphues,* in *Works,* ed. R. Warwick Bond [Oxford, 1902], I, 233; cf. I, 123).

[10] Cf. Eduard Norden, *Die antike Kunstprosa* (Leipzig, 1898), II, 950-51.

[11] Cf. C. Alphonse Smith, *Repetition and Parallelism in English Verse* (New York, 1894); Charles F. Richardson, *A Study of English Rhyme* (Hanover, 1909), p. 16.

The parallels of Hebrew poetry are, of course, the outstanding exceptions to the generality which I propose, but in this connection I believe it ought to be observed that the lines and half lines of Hebrew poetry are not equal with the metrical exactitude of classical and modern European verse. The number of accents is the same, the number of syllables indeterminate, and the parallel of sense (as in looser English verse like Whitman's) plays an important rôle in strengthening the equality and pattern of the verse. Cf. W. O. E. Oesterley, *Ancient Hebrew Poems Metrically Translated* (New York, 1938), pp. 3-7; W. O. E. Oesterley and Theodore H. Robinson, *An Introduction to the Books of the Old Testament* (New York, 1934), pp. 140-45.

important phrase in Milton's own prescription for blank verse is "sense variously drawn out from one verse into another." This various drawing out he accomplishes for the most part by his ever various, subtly continuous, confused and tenuous syntax, by which the sense drips down from line to line and does not usually run parallel in any successive lines. But if it does run parallel, there will be certain careful and curious dislocations that prevent the lines from seeming to be the unit of logical measure.

> Abhorred *Styx*, the flood of deadly hate;
> Sad *Acheron* of sorrow, black and deep;
> *Cocytus,* named of lamentation loud
> Heard on the rueful stream; fierce *Phlegethon,*
> Whose waves of torrent fire inflame with rage.[12]

It is I who have italicized the names of the four infernal rivers. These are the four heads of the parallel—moving back toward the front of the line, from Styx to Cocytus, then leaping to the end with Phlegethon. The modifiers of the first two are of about the same length and place in the line; that of the third is longer and runs through two lines; that of the fourth fills just one line. Thus comes the sense of weaving back and forth, of intellect threading complexity, in place of a cool, simplifying triumph of classification.[13] The same handling of parallel can sometimes be seen in single lines.

> *Un*×re′spit×*ed′*, *un*×pit′*ied*×, *un*′re×*prieved′*
>
> *Un*×sha′ken×, *un*′se×duced′, *un*×ter′ri×fied′
>
> *Thou′* art′ my× fa′ther×, *thou′* my× au′thor×, *thou′*
> My being gavest me.[14]

The italicized syllables escape a prosaic parallel by falling in different metrical positions, now in thesis, now in arsis. The third "thou" is thrust out alone at the end of the line. The verse runs sinuously, intertwining with the sense and making a tension and resilience.

IV

We come then to rhyme, the subject of our argument. And first it must be admitted that in certain contexts a high degree of parallel in sense may be found even in rhyme. Even identical words may rhyme. In the *sestina,* for example, the same set of rhyme words is repeated in six different stanzas. But here the order changes and so does the relation of each rhyme word to the context. That is the

---

[12] *Paradise Lost,* II, 577-81.
[13] Cf. the morning *laudate* of Adam and Eve—recited in "holy rapture" and "various style" (*Paradise Lost,* V, 146-47, 192-99). This passage affords an instructive comparison with the King James version of Psalm cxlvii, 2-4, 8-10, where the Hebrew parallel of sense and rhythm is largely preserved.
[14] *Paradise Lost,* II, 185; V, 899; II, 864.

point of the *sestina*. Somewhat the same may be said for a refrain when it does not rhyme with any other line of the context. In the broadest sense, difference of meaning in rhyme words includes difference of syntax. In fact, words have no character as rhymes until they become points in a syntactic succession. And rhyme words (even identical ones) can scarcely appear in a context without showing some difference of meaning. The point of this essay is therefore not to prove that rhyme words must exhibit difference of meaning,[15] but to discuss the value of the difference and to show how a greater degree of difference harmonizes with a certain type of verse structure.

Under certain conditions (much more common than the *sestina* or refrain mentioned above) the opportunity and the demand for difference of meaning in rhyme may be slight.

> Scogan, that knelest at the stremes hed
> Of grace, of alle honour and worthynesse,
> In th'ende of which strem I am dul as ded,
> Forgete in solitarie wildernesse,—
> Yet, Scogan, thenke on Tullius kyndenesse;
> Mynne thy frend, there it may fructifye!
> Far-wel, and loke thow never eft Love dyffye.[16]

The three identical "nesse" rhymes could be very flat, mere prosy homoeoteleuton, if the three words occurred in positions of nearly parallel logic or syntax. But Chaucer's sense, meandering like the stream through the stanza, makes no great demand upon these rhymes, and weak though they are, they are strong enough. Even in Chaucer's couplets the same continuity of sense through the verse may be discovered, and the same tendency in rhyming,[17] as we shall illustrate in the comparison which follows.

Pope is the English poet whose rhyming shows perhaps the clearest contrast to Chaucer's. Chaucer found, even in Middle English, a "skarsete" of rhyme.[18] There would come a day when an even greater scarcity of easy rhymes would create a challenge to the English poet and at the same time indicate one of his most subtle opportunities. In the course of three hundred years English lost many of its easy rhymes, stressed Germanic and Romance endings, y, ing, ere, esse, and able, age, al, aunce, aile, ain, esse,

---

[15] The most positive statement that I know is that of Théodore de Banville, *Petit Traité de Poésie Française* (Paris, 1894), pp. 75-76; "Vous ferez rimer ensemble, autant qu'il se pourra, des mots très-semblables entre eux comme SON, et très-différents entre eux comme SENS. Tâchez d'accoupler le moins possible un substantif avec un substantif. . . ."

[16] *Lenvoy de Chaucer a Scogan*, lines 43-49.

[17] Cf. the Rhyme Indexes of the Chaucer Society; Max Kaluza, *Chaucer und der Rosenroman* (Berlin, 1893), pp. 65-81; Edward P. Morton, "Chaucer's Identical Rimes," *MLN*, XVIII (1903), 73-74; Gustav Vockrodt, *Reimtechnik bei Chaucer als Mittel zur chronologischen Bestimmung seiner im Reimpaar geschriebenen Werke* (Halle, 1914), pp. 13, 26, 35-37.

[18] *Complaint of Venus*.

oun, ous, ure,[19] so that Pope perforce rhymed words differing more widely in meaning. The characteristics of Pope's couplet, as opposed to Chaucer's, are, of course, its closure or completeness,[20] its stronger tendency to parallel, and its epigrammatic, witty, intellectual point. One can hardly imagine such a couplet rhyming "wildernesse" and "kyndenesse," or "worthynesse" and "hethenesse," as Chaucer does in one couplet of the knight's portrait.

Most likely it is neither feasible nor even desirable to construct a scale of meaning differences to measure the cleverness of rhyme. The analysis which I intend is not in the main statistical. But an obvious, if rude, basis for classification is the part of speech. It may be said, broadly, that difference in meaning of rhyme words can be recognized in difference of parts of speech and in difference of functions of the same part of speech, and that both of these differences will be qualified by the degree of parallel or of oblique sense in the pair of rhyming lines. We may distinguish (I) lines of oblique relation having (a) rhymes of different parts of speech, (b) rhymes of the same part of speech; (II) lines of parallel relation having (a) rhymes of different parts of speech, (b) rhymes of the same part of speech. The tenor of the comparison which follows will be to suggest that Pope's rhymes are characterized by difference in parts of speech or in function of the same parts of speech, the difference in each case being accentuated by the tendency of his couplets to parallel structure.

Class Ia includes a large number of rhymes in both Pope and Chaucer, or indeed in any English poet, which statistically are rather neutral to our inquiry.

> Whan that Aprille with his shoures soote
> The droghte of March hath perced to the roote . . . .[21]

---

[19] Cf. Max Kaluza, *Englische Metrik in historischer Entwicklung* (Berlin, 1909), §§ 140, 149, pp. 162-64, 172-73. It is beyond the scope of this essay to consider the history of rhyme meaning-differences by languages and periods. That seems to me a field where research may yield some interesting results. Cf. Jakob Schipper, *A History of English Versification* (Oxford, 1910), p. 11; Norden, *op. cit.,* II, 825, 839-40; Kaluza, *op. cit.,* § 145, p. 168. In a limited sense rhyme apparently does originate in parallel of syntactic construction and identity of endings (cf. Norden, *op. cit.,* II, 819-24, 867-68; Lanz, *op. cit.,* pp. 127, 184), but certainly the step to the more difficult rhyming of roots and of words in non-parallel positions is the most important which rhyme takes in its development.

[20] The difference is far greater than is shown by the statistics of William E. Mead, *The Versification of Pope in its Relations to the Seventeenth Century* (Leipzig, 1889), pp. 31-33. Mead gives Chaucer's *Canterbury Prologue* a percentage of 10.7 unstopped lines against 5.41 for the *Rape of the Lock.* But he does not take into account the various degrees of end-stopping nor the difference between stopping the first line of a couplet and stopping the second. Cf. Friedrich Klee, *Das Enjambement bei Chaucer* (Halle, 1913), pp. 19-22, 33, and Table II; Mary A. Hill, "Rhetorical Balance in Chaucer's Poetry," *PMLA,* XLII (1927), 845-61.

[21] *Canterbury Prologue,* line 1.

Here the rhyme makes its contribution to difference of sense against equality of verse, but because the oblique phrases themselves make a fundamental contrast to the metrically equal lines, and the rhyming parts of speech are a function of the phrases, the rhyme is not likely to be felt as a special element of variation. There is a higher proportion of these rhymes in Chaucer than in Pope.[22] Class Ib also includes a higher proportion of rhymes in Chaucer than in Pope,[23] and for the same reason, that in general Chaucer relies for variation more on continuous sense and syntax than on rhyme. But in rhymes of Class Ib, since the rhyme words are the same part of speech, there is some opportunity for comparing the effect of the rhyme itself. Chaucer is apt to give us a dullish rhyme:

> Me thynketh it acordaunt to resoun
> To telle you al the condicioun. . . . [24]

Pope is apt to find some quaint minor contrast in length and quality of words:

> What guards the purity of melting maids,
> In courtly balls, and midnight masquerades?[25]

It is in Class IIa and Class IIb, however, that the rhyming of Pope is seen to best advantage. Because of the parallel in sense between the lines, the difference in parts of speech of rhymes in Class IIa is much more noticeable than in Class Ia. And not only are there more of these rhymes in Pope than in Chaucer,[26] but their effect is more pronounced in Pope because the parallel within the closed couplet of Pope is likely to be more intellectual and pointed. Chaucer will write:

> And everemoore he hadde a sovereyn prys;
> And though that he were worthy, he was wys.[27]

---

[22] I base my statement on a general impression which is borne out in a line-by-line analysis of four passages from each author: Chaucer (*Works,* ed. F. N. Robinson [Boston, 1933]), *Legend of Good Women,* Prologue F, lines 1-148; *Canterbury Prologue,* lines 1-148; *Knight's Tale,* Part II, first 148 lines, 1355-1502; *Nun's Priest's Tale,* first 148 lines, 2821-2968; Pope (*Complete Poetical Works,* ed. H. W. Boynton [Boston, 1903]), *Essay on Criticism,* I, 1-148; *Rape of the Lock,* I, 1-148; *Epistle to Dr. Arbuthnot,* lines 1-148; *Dunciad,* Book IV, lines 1-148.
The numbers for the first type of couplet described above, by passages, in the order named, are: Chaucer, 41, 23, 33, 34; Pope, 26, 24, 29, 27. (I should hardly expect another tabulator to arrive at exactly the same results.)
T. Walter Herbert's "The Grammar of Rimes," *Sewanee Review,* XLVIII (1940), 362-77, is a statistical investigation which seems to me to test not so much the rhyme as the line-ending. It would apply almost as well to blank verse. Franz Beschorner, *Verbale Reime bei Chaucer* (Halle, 1920), studies the number of finite verbs and infinitives used as rhymes by Chaucer. Unlike Mr. Herbert, he finds Chaucer's "Tendenz" in this direction "außerordentlich stark" (p. 1).
[23] The numbers are: Chaucer, 18, 15, 24, 16; Pope, 11, 10, 20, 8.
[24] *Canterbury Prologue,* line 37.
[25] *Rape of the Lock,* I, 71.
[26] The numbers are: Chaucer, 0, 13, 8, 11; Pope, 21, 22, 12, 22.
[27] *Canterbury Prologue,* line 67.

Similarly but more often Pope will write:

> The light coquettes in Sylphs aloft repair,
> And sport and flutter in the fields of air.[28]

Or he will write:

> Oft, when the world imagine women stray,
> The Sylphs thro' mystic mazes guide their way.

> When Florio speaks, what virgin could withstand,
> If gentle Damon did not squeeze her hand.[29]

In the last two examples the syntax is oblique but the sense is antithetic and hence parallel. It is a subtlety which is frequent in Pope (whose couplets, no matter what their syntax, tend to hover on the verge of parallel) but is rarely to be found in Chaucer. Here the structure of Pope's couplet forces more of the burden of variety on the rhyme.

In Class IIb one might expect to find that the parallel of general sense and of rhyming parts of speech would produce a quality of flatness, a sort of minimum rhyme such as we found in St. Augustine—"Lingua clamat, cor amat"—the first step beyond homoeoteleuton. One thing that prevents this and often lends the rhyme a value of variation is that through some irregularity or incompleteness of parallel the rhyming words have oblique functions. Thus Chaucer:

> No deyntee morsel passed thurgh hir throte;
> Hir diete was accordant to hir cote.[30]

And Pope:

> From each she nicely culls with curious toil,
> And decks the Goddess with the glitt'ring spoil.[31]

There are more of these couplets in Pope than in Chaucer,[32] and with Pope the rhyme difference is more likely to seem the result of some deft twist or trick.

> Some are bewilder'd in the maze of schools,
> And some made coxcombs Nature meant but fools.[33]

There is a kind of inversion (from pupils to schools and back to the pupils in a new light) which in some couplets appears more completely as chiasmus, an effect concerning which I shall have more to say.

---

[28] *Rape of the Lock,* I, 65.
[29] *Rape of the Lock,* I, 91, 97.
[30] *Nun's Priest's Tale,* line 2834.
[31] *Rape of the Lock,* I, 131.
[32] The numbers are: Chaucer, 5, 6, 5, 6; Pope, 9, 10, 9, 10.
[33] *Essay on Criticism,* I, 26.

The two types of rhyme difference which characterize Pope's poetry (that of different parts of speech and that of the same part of speech in different functions) are a complement, as I have suggested, of his tendency to a parallel of lines. To recognize this may affect our opinion about how deliberately or consciously Pope strove for difference of rhyme, but it should not diminish the impression which the actual difference of rhyme makes upon us. Such rhyme difference may be felt more clearly as a characteristic of Pope if we examine the rhymes in a passage where the parallel is somewhat like that which Chaucer at times employs. It is difficult to find passages of sustained parallel in Chaucer. The usual narrative movement of his couplets is from then to then to then, with the oblique forward movement of actions in a sequence. But in the character sketches of the *Canterbury Prologue* a kind of loose parallel often prevails for ten or twenty lines, as one feature of a pilgrim after another is enumerated. The sense is continuous, in that the couplets tend to be incomplete, but the lines are all members of a parallel bundle. A clear example may be seen in the yeoman's portrait.

And he was clad in cote and hood of grene.
A sheef of pecock arwes, bright and kene,
Under his belt he bar ful thriftily,
(Wel coude he dresse his takel yemanly:

.   .   .   .

Upon his arm he baar a gay bracer,
And by his syde a swerd and a bokeler,
And on that oother syde a gay daggere
Harneised wel and sharp as point of spere;
A Cristopher on his brest of silver sheene.
A horn he bar, the bawdryk was of grene.[84]

"Thriftily" and "yemanly," "bracer" and "bokeler," "sheene" and "grene," rhymes like these (aside even from the use of final syllables, "ly" and "er") I should call tame rhymes because the same parts of speech are used in closely parallel functions. To see the difference in this respect between Chaucer and Pope we may turn to the classic lines of another portrait:

Bless'd with each talent and each art to please,
And born to write, converse, and live with ease;
Should such a man, too fond to rule alone,
Bear, like the Turk, no brother near the throne;
View him with scornful, yet with jealous eyes,
And hate for arts that caus'd himself to rise;
Damn with faint praise, assent with civil leer,
And without sneering teach the rest to sneer;
Willing to wound, and yet afraid to strike,
Just hint a fault, and hesitate dislike;

[84] *Canterbury Prologue,* lines 103-116. Another clear example is the knight's portrait, lines 47-58.

> Alike reserv'd to blame or to commend,
> A tim'rous foe, and a suspicious friend; ... [35]

The parallel of lines is continuous, but the rhymes are always different parts of speech. The portrait continues:

> Dreading ev'n fools; by flatterers besieged,
> And so obliging that he ne'er obliged;
> Like *Cato,* give his little Senate laws,
> And sit attentive to his own applause.

Here the same parts of speech are rhymed, but one verb is passive, one active; one noun is plural, one singular. The functions are different, in each case what he does being set against what he receives.

It is to be noted that in the yeoman's portrait such rhymes as "grene" and "kene," "thriftily" and "yemanly" fall into Class IIb and are of the sort which we described above as minimum rhyme, only one step away from homoeoteleuton. Class IIb often escapes this extreme, as we saw, by some irregularity of parallel. But it is significant to add now that even when Pope does not escape the extreme he has resources of piquancy.[36] Here and there he will be guilty of a certain flatness:

> Each motion guides, and every nerve sustains,
> Itself unseen, but in th'effects remains.[37]

Very often, however, he conveys some nice contrast in the parallel.

> True wit is Nature to advantage dress'd,
> What oft was thought, but ne'er so well express'd.[38]

Here the two rhyme verbs are not merely parallel examples. One is literal, one is figurative, and in being matched with each other they express in brief the metaphor on which this classic critical doctrine is based, that to express is to dress.

> Th' adventurous Baron the bright locks admired;
> He saw, he wish'd, and to the prize aspired.[39]

Here the difference between "admired" and "aspired," the swift ascent of the Baron's aspiration, is precisely the point. In other parallel rhymes Pope finds an opportunity for brisk irony.

---

[35] *Epistle to Dr. Arbuthnot,* lines 195-206.
[36] Since examples within this sub-classification differ so widely, the numbers have little significance: Chaucer, 10, 17, 4, 6; Pope, 9, 8, 4, 7.
[37] *Essay on Criticism,* I, 78.
[38] *Essay on Criticism,* II, 97.
[39] *Rape of the Lock,* II, 29.

One speaks the glory of the British Queen,
And one describes a charming Indian screen.

Do thou, Crispissa, tend her fav'rite Lock;
Ariel himself shall be the guard of Shock.[40]

From "British Queen" to "Indian screen," from "Lock" to "Shock,"
here is the same bathos he more often puts into one line—"When
husbands, or when lapdogs breathe their last."[41]

V

But what I conceive to be the acme of variation occurs in a
construction to which I have already alluded, chiasmus. The basis
of chiasmus will be a high degree of parallel, often antithetic. The
rhyme may be of the same part of speech or of different parts.
If it is of the same part, the chiastic variation will be a special case
of the "schools"—"fools" rhyme already quoted, where a twist in
the meaning gives different functions to the rhyme words. If the
rhyme is of different parts, the variation will be a special case of
that already discussed, where different parts of speech rhyme in
parallel lines.

$\quad\quad\quad\quad\quad\quad$ 1 $\quad\quad$ 2
Whatever Nature has in worth denied
$\quad$ 2′ $\quad\quad\quad\quad\quad\quad\quad\quad\quad$ 1′
She gives in large recruits of needful Pride.[42]

$\quad\quad\quad\quad\quad\quad$ 1 $\quad\quad\quad\quad$ 2
Whether the nymph shall break Diana's law,
$\quad\quad\quad\quad$ 2′ $\quad\quad\quad$ 1′
Or some frail China jar receive a flaw.[43]

In the first line the breakage, then the fragile thing (the law); in
the second line another fragile thing (the jar) and then its breaking
(the flaw). The parallel is given a kind of roundness and completeness, and intellectual lines are softened into the concrete harmony
of "law" and "flaw."

$\quad\quad\quad\quad\quad\quad\quad\quad$ 1 $\quad\quad$ 2
What dire offence from am'rous causes springs,
$\quad\quad\quad\quad\quad$ 2′ $\quad\quad\quad$ 1′
What mighty contests rise from trivial things.[44]

$\quad\quad\quad\quad\quad\quad\quad\quad\quad\quad\quad$ 1 $\quad\quad$ 2
Love, Hope, and Joy, fair Pleasure's smiling train,
$\quad\quad\quad\quad\quad\quad$ 2′ $\quad\quad$ 1′
Hate, Fear, and Grief, the family of Pain. . . . [45]

---

[40] *Rape of the Lock*, III, 13; II, 115.
[41] *Rape of the Lock*, III, 158.
[42] *Essay on Criticism*, II, 5.
[43] *Rape of the Lock*, II, 105.
[44] *Rape of the Lock*, I, 1.
[45] *Essay on Man*, II, 117.

> 1   2   1   2
> Fear to the statesman, rashness to the chief,
>   2'   1'   2'   1'
> To kings presumption, and to crowds belief.[46]
>
>   1   2
> Thus critics of less judgment than caprice,
>   2'   1'   1"   2"
> Curious, not knowing, not exact, but nice, . . .[47]

In the fourth example the antithesis is tripled, and the order being successively chiastic, returns upon itself, which is sufficient complication to make "caprice" and "nice" a surprise. Then one is an adjective and one a noun, and "caprice" has two syllables.[48]

The contemplation of chiastic rhyme, the most brilliant and complex of all the forms of rhyme variation, leads me to make a brief general remark upon the degree of Pope's reputation for rhyme. I have relied heavily upon examples of rhyme from Pope because he takes clearer advantage of the quality of difference in rhyme than other poets that I know. To that extent, and it seems to me a very important extent, he is one of the greatest English rhymers. Yet a critic of Pope's rhyme has spoken of "true" rhymes and "false" rhymes and "rimes to the eye" and has been concerned to discover that of 7874 rhymes in Pope 1027 are "false."[49] Another has approved of Pope's "correctness" in excluding polysyllables from his rhymes, but has found Pope's repeated use of the same rhyme words "monotonous in a high degree and a very serious artistic defect." The same critic has actually spoken of Pope's "poverty of rhyme."[50] One of the purposes of my argument is to cut the ground from under such judgments as far as they are value judgments. They can spring only from a very limited view of rhyme as a kind of phonetic harmony, to be described and appraised in terms of phonetic accuracy, complexity, and variety—in other words, from a failure to connect rhyme with reason.

In more recent years Robert K. Root has pointed out that Pope usually makes the rhyme fall on significant words and has added a caution to readers against overstressing the rhyme word.[51] Geoffrey Tillotson, in his progressive essay, *On the Poetry of Pope,* has recorded his impression that Pope prefers "a verb for at least one of the rime-words in a couplet" and that "a verb at the end

---

[46] *Essay on Man,* II, 243.

[47] *Essay on Criticism,* II, 85.

[48] For three exquisite examples of chiasmus from three other poets, see the rhyme of "dust" and "lust" in Andrew Marvell's "Coy Mistress," "thrush" and "bush" in Christina Rossetti's "Spring Quiet," and the double chiasmic rhyme of "leaping" and "sleeping," "laid" and "fade" in A. E. Housman's "With rue my heart is laden."

[49] L. Mary. McLean, "The Riming System of Alexander Pope," *PMLA,* VI (1891), 134-60.

[50] Mead, *op. cit.,* pp. 48, 140.

[51] Robert K. Root, *The Poetical Career of Alexander Pope* (Princeton, 1938), p. 37.

of the first line is often followed by its object in the next line."[52] These are glances in the right direction. Mr. Tillotson's remark is clearly one that I may quote in support of my own analysis of Pope's rhyme.

In this essay I have not pretended to explain all the rhetorical values that may be found in rhyme or in Pope's rhyme. Nevertheless, the principle on which I am intent is one that concerns rhyme as a fusion of sound and sense; and, as it is a broad principle, it is rather a starting place for many analyses than the conclusion of any one. In the examples already quoted from Pope I have shown several modes of its operation. In my next section I shall suggest another or obverse aspect of the whole.

VI

We have so far considered rhyme as it makes variation against the parallels of verse. If we think now of the meaning of the words as the basis of comparison, thus beginning with variation or difference, we can discuss the sameness of the rhyme sound as a binding force. Rhyme is commonly recognized as a binder in verse structure. But where there is need for binding there must be some difference or separation between the things to be bound. If they are already close together, it is supererogatory to emphasize this by the maneuver of rhyme. So we may say that the greater the difference in meaning between rhyme words the more marked and the more appropriate will be the binding effect. Rhyme theorists have spoken of the "surprise" which is the pleasure of rhyme, and surely this surprise is not merely a matter of coming upon a similarity which one has not *previously* anticipated. It cannot be a matter of time. Even after the discovery, when the rhyme is known by heart and said backwards, the pleasurable surprise remains. It must depend on some incongruity or unlikelihood inherent in the coupling. It is a curious thing that "queen" should rhyme with "screen"; they are very unlike objects. But Pope has found a connection between them, has classified them as topics of chat, and then the parallel of sound comes to his aid as a humorous binder.[53] The principle is well illustrated in Pope's penchant for proper-name rhymes. What more illogical than that a proper name should rhyme with any thing? For its meaning is unique.

> Poor Cornus sees his frantic wife elope,
> And curses Wit and Poetry, and Pope.[54]

---

[52] Geoffrey Tillotson, *On the Poetry of Pope* (Oxford, 1938), p. 124.

[53] In this respect the relation between rhyme and alliteration may be readily seen. It is the very disparity of the words brought into one web of sense which gives virtue to the alliterative binding. "*Fed* with *soft Dedication* all *day* long" (*Epistle to Arbuthnot,* line 233). "*Through* pain up by the *roots* Thessalian *pines*" (*Paradise Lost,* II, 544).

[54] *Epistle to Arbuthnot,* line 25.

> Yet ne'er one sprig of laurel graced these ribalds,
> From slashing *Bentleys* down to piddling *Tibbalds*.[55]

> The hero William, and the martyr Charles,
> One knighted Blackmore, and one pension'd Quarles.[56]

"Elope" and "Pope" suggest there is some connection between the two; the joke is that we know very well there is not. Poor "Tibbald" was not a "ribald," nor did "Charles" pension "Quarles," but we are well on the way to believing both things; the rhyme at least is a *fait accompli*.

The most extreme examples of this kind of humor are the extravagant double or triple rhymes of a Butler, a Swift, a Byron, or a Browning. One stanza from Byron will do.

> He was a Turk, the colour of mahogany;
> And Laura saw him, and at first was glad,
> Because the Turks so much admire philogyny,
> Although their usage of their wives is sad;
> 'Tis said they use no better than a dog any
> Poor woman, whom they purchase like a pad:
> They have a number, though they ne'er exhibit 'em,
> Four wives by law, and concubines "ad libitum."[57]

If Byron had rhymed "philogyny" and "misognyny," it would not be very funny, for one expects these two words to sound alike; they are formed alike from the Greek and make the end words of a very natural antithesis. They are mere homoeoteleuton. "Mahogany" makes a comic rhyme with "philogyny" because of the wide disparity in meaning between the words. Mahogany, the Spanish name of a reddish hardwood, is not a likely companion for the learned Greek abstraction, but once an ingenious affinity in meaning is established, the rhyme sounds a triple surprise of ratification. Then comes "dog any," and difference of meaning in rhyme has proceeded to the point of disintegration and mad abandon. Rhymes of this sort are not distant relations of the pun and the "mixt Wit" which Addison defined as consisting "partly in the Resemblance of Ideas, and partly in the Resemblance of Words."[58] I mean that what convinces us that "dog any" belongs in this stanza is not so much its inevitable or appropriate meaning as the fact that it does rhyme.

---

[55] *Epistle to Arbuthnot*, line 163.
[56] *Epistle to Augustus*, line 386.
[57] *Beppo*, stanza LXX.
[58] *Spectator*, No. 62. For the relation of rhyme to pun see Léon Bellanger, *Études Historiques et Philologiques sur la Rime Française* (Angers, 1876), pp. 1-26, on the early sixteenth-century rhyming school of Molinet and Crétin. For identical rhyme (*reicher Reim, rime riche*) in Middle English, see Max Kaluza, *op. cit.*, §§ 144-49, pp. 167-73; Jakob Schipper, *op. cit.*, p. 273. Cf. Lowell's *Fable for Critics* (*Works* [Boston, 1910], X, 16, 29).

VII

"Rime," says Henry Lanz, "is one of those irrational satellites that revolve around reason. It is concerned not with the meaning of verse but only with its form, which is emotional. It lies within the plane of the a-logical cross-section of verse."[59] It is within the scope of my argument to grant the alogical character of rhyme, or rather to insist on it, but at the same time to insist that the alogical character by itself has little, if any, aesthetic value. The music of spoken words in itself is meagre, so meagre in comparison to the music of song or instrument as to be hardly worth discussion. It has become a platitude of criticism to point out that verses composed of meaningless words afford no pleasure of any kind and can scarcely be called rhythmical—let them even be rhymed. The mere return to the vowel tonic (the chord or tone cluster characteristic of a vowel[60]) will produce not emotion but boredom. The art of words is an intellectual art, and the emotions of poetry are simultaneous with conceptions and largely induced through the medium of conceptions. In literary art only the wedding of the alogical with the logical gives the former an aesthetic value. The words of a rhyme, with their curious harmony of sound and distinction of sense, are an amalgam of the sensory and the logical, or an arrest and precipitation of the logical in sensory form; they are the ikon in which the idea is caught. Rhyme and other verse elements save the physical quality of words—intellectualized and made transparent by daily prose usage.[61] But without the intellectual element there is nothing to save and no reason why the physical element of words need be asserted. "Many a man," says Dr. Lanz at the close of his book, "was cruelly put to death for a 'daring rhyme.'" And he regards it as a "triumph of modern science that, instead of marveling at the mystery of this force, we can 'dissect it as a corpse.'"[62] There is more truth than malice in my adding that men are cruelly put to death not for melodies but for ideas, and that it is only when reduced to a purely "physical basis" that rhyme becomes a "corpse."

> When Adam dalf and Eve span,
> Who was then a gentilman?[63]

If there is something daring in this rhyme of John Ball's, it is certainly not in the return to the overtone of 1840 vibrations per

---

[59] Henry Lanz, *The Physical Basis of Rime, An Essay on the Aesthetics of Sound* (Stanford University, 1931), p. 293.
[60] Lanz, *op. cit.*, pp. 10-13.
[61] Cf. G. W. F. Hegel, *The Philosophy of Fine Art,* trans. F. P. B. Osmaston (London, 1920), IV, 7-10, 84, 90-91, Part III, Subsection III, chap. iii.
[62] Lanz, *op. cit.*, p. 342.
[63] Lanz, *op. cit.*, pp. 121, 342.

second characteristic of ǎ [ae],[64] but in the ironic jostle by which plebeian "span" gives a lesson in human values to aristocratic "gentilman."

Yale University

---

[64] Lanz, *op. cit.*, pp. 18, 20, 22, 243.

H. BUNKER WRIGHT

and

HENRY C. MONTGOMERY

The Art Collection of a Virtuoso

in Eighteenth Century England

Condensed from

THE ART BULLETIN

Volume XXVII(1945), 195-204

Reprinted by permission of the Editors

THE ART COLLECTION OF A VIRTUOSO
IN EIGHTEENTH CENTURY ENGLAND

H. BUNKER WRIGHT and HENRY C. MONTGOMERY

"The Italians," wrote John Dryden, "call a man a virtuoso, who loves the noble arts, and is a critic in them."[1] The term has had many other meanings, but in England in the early eighteenth century it was often used in this sense.[2] The virtuoso was an informed amateur in the arts rather than a specialist, one who collected works of art with discrimination rather than a creative artist. The professional became a virtuoso only when he possessed an interest in the arts outside his own field and displayed something of a "universal genius." This was an ideal appropriate to the Augustan Age, a period when Englishmen were attempting to develop a national culture comparable to that of ancient Rome. The spirit of the times was exemplified by the poet who studied painting, the architect who produced plays, and the painter who composed a ballet or edited Paradise Lost.[3] Although some pretenders to the title of virtuoso were hardly more than ridiculous dilettanti, it was most accurately applied to the true connoisseur.

England had need of such men in those days. Interest in
art, which had not been encouraged during the Puritan period,
was just beginning to revive. There had been no great patrons
of art since the time of Charles I and the second Earl of
Arundel.[4] Jonathan Richardson, who was both a painter and a
virtuoso, in 1719 bewailed the fact that "so few here in England
have considered that to be a good connoisseur is fit to be part
of the education of a gentleman, that there are so few lovers of
Painting; not merely for furniture, or for ostentation, or as
it represents their friends or themselves; but as it is an art
capable of entertaining, and adorning their minds...."[5] To promote such an attitude Richardson wrote a series of essays arguing not only the personal benefits to be derived, but also the
advantages to the nation:

> If our nobility, and gentry were lovers of
> Painting, and connoisseurs, a much greater
> treasure of pictures, drawings, and antiques
> would be brought in, which would contribute
> abundantly to the raising, and meliorating
> our taste, as well as to the improvement of
> our artists.[6]
>
> Thus a thing as yet unheard of, and whose
> very name (to our dishonour) has at present
> an uncouth sound may come to be eminent in
> the world, I mean the English school of
> Painting.[7]

Undoubtedly, as Richardson predicted, the intelligent patronage of connoisseurs did contribute to the development of English art. It is fortunate, therefore, that manuscripts which have recently come to light now make it possible to describe in some detail the artistic interests and the art collection of one of these virtuosi--Matthew Prior, poet and diplomatist.

While Jonathan Richardson was writing his <u>Discourse</u> <u>on</u> <u>the</u> <u>Dignity</u>, <u>Certainty</u>, <u>Pleasure</u>, <u>and</u> <u>Advantage</u> <u>of</u> <u>the</u> <u>Science</u> <u>of</u> <u>a</u> <u>Connoisseur</u>, he discussed the subject with Prior as one who "every body will readily acknowledge was very proper to be advised with on this, or a much greater occasion."[8] Richardson adopted Prior's recommendation that this science should be called "connoissance" and in his text proudly announced his indebtedness, as he put it, out of vanity in himself as well as in justice to his friend.[9]

Like Richardson, Prior thought that an acquaintance with the arts should be part of the equipment of a gentleman. In his "Heads for a Treatise upon Learning," which is Baconian in tone as well as in scope, he wrote:

> Besides the Serious Study which is to be the general exercise and employment of your life, and without being Master of which You can never make any great figure in the World You should be pretty well Versed in some more Pleasing and if I may so express it, some Secundary Science.

This You will find convenient it will take
idle Hours from your hand when alone, and
have a proper use in Company, a double one
if You are in any public Station, for it
will hinder the Curious pressing upon you
as to more solemn matter, and enable You
without appearing Ignorant or ill bred to
turn the Discourse to what may at once conceal your Secret and entertain your Company.
  Amongst these Arts of a Mechanical Consideration I reckon Architecture, Sculpture,
Painting, Gardening &ca.
  The Choice of these must be determined by
the bent of every Mans own Mind, and without such an inclination or what we call a
Genius he will make a very little Progress
in these or any of those Sciences which tho
Supported and improved by Judgmt are founded upon imagination. These Arts I say at
once Instruct and amuse, help Men that have
Estates to employ them agreably, and to
oblige those who have not, and may yet participate of another Mans pleasure; and add
at the same time to it; For there is no Man
that does any thing of this kind but is
pleased to show it, and no Man that understands it but is obliged to him for the
Communication; besides the Company wch the
Exercise of these Arts bring a Man into is
as well Honorable as agreable, Their Studies
are mixed with other Arts, and the conversation they must have met with before they can
have arrived to any Perfection in their own
Art must needs have rendered them in a
great Measure Scholars and Gentlemen.[10]

This utilitarian argument does not represent Prior's whole

attitude toward the arts. It may be that his knowledge of paint-

ing and architecture had been of practical value to him as min-

ister to the court of Louis XIV, and originally he may have been

prompted by a desire to emulate the noblemen whom he wished to

have as friends. It was not, however, for ostentation that he

devoted himself to "connoissance" in the years of his retirement
from political life, when he was no longer motivated by ambition.
At that time he numbered among his most intimate friends some
kindred spirits whom he called his virtuosi. They gathered occasionally at his house in Duke Street, Westminster, not for
formal discourse or deliberate self-improvement, but for the
pleasure of informal conversation over the bottle. The easy
familiarity of the meetings must have increased both the brilliance and the sincerity of the ideas that were exchanged, for
the men who attended were not mere dilettanti. They included
the painters Sir James Thornhill, John Wootton, and Michael Dahl,
and such eminent men in other fields as Humfrey Wanley, antiquary
and bibliophile; Charles Christian Reisen, gem cutter; Charles
Bridgman, landscape gardener; and James Gibbs, the architect.[11]

We have no clear evidence that Prior ever tried to practice
any of the graphic arts himself. He speaks vaguely of "contriving"
ornamental initials for the 1718 folio edition of his Poems on
Several Occasions,[12] and he may possibly have painted the murals
that have recently been discovered at St. John's College, Cambridge, in a room that he might have occupied in the early years
of his fellowship. These sketchy allegorical panels have been
attributed to Prior because they seem related to Dryden's The
Hind and the Panther, which Prior and his friend Charles Montagu
travestied in The Country-Mouse and the City-Mouse.[13]

It is certain, however, that Prior was a student of art, if not a painter. Among his manuscripts there are extensive notes on Colors and on Columns,[14] and one of the fragments shows a sophisticated appreciation:

> It is not enough to have Eyes, You must
> have understanding also, and in proportion
> to that understanding the pleasure you have
> from seeing the picture is augmented.
> If any man views the Copernican System upon
> paper he takes notice only of so many Circles
> that compose one great Scroll, as he appre-
> hends it more distinctly he will more particu-
> larly admire it, and when he is Master of it,
> He will wonder how it came into the Wit of
> Man to invent it; The like in Painting, an
> ignorant Person sees Men, Women or Animals,
> Buildings or Landscapes, and contents himself
> by thinking these things thus painted resemble
> what he has seen in the World. As he remarks
> more difference in these Representations, he
> begins to reflect how far one Painter exceeds
> another, and as he grows up to a fuller
> knowledge, and examines more studiously the
> beauties of the design, the disposition, and
> the colouring, he falls into admiration that
> it should be in the Wit or power of Man to
> draw these lights and shades forth from a flat
> ground, and to raise a little Creation from a
> poor piece of wood or an extended canvas.[15]

Prior even became capable of "discriminating between hands" with some confidence. For instance, he wrote to his friend Edward Lord Harley in 1719 describing in the following terms two pictures that he had seen at Dr. Freind's:

> ...One is of a good hand, Flemish -- I think
> one of the Van Halst -- but it is only a
> portrait of a soldier to the waist, not quite
> half-length; the other is a small piece of a
> Madonna and a Christo Infantulo -- I believe
> it to be of Carlo Maratte, but by no means his
> best manner.[16]

Prior was a patron of artists, not only in his friendship
with them and in his sponsorship of such men as Hugh Howard and
Charles Jervas, but also through the conventional practice of
commissioning portraits from them. Some of these paintings were
memorials of friends; others were of himself. There are over
two dozen portraits of Prior now extant; some of these are, of
course, copies, but he is known to have sat for at least seven
artists, including the most eminent of that age.[17]

Like most virtuosi, Prior was a collector in many fields.
He was naturally most active in accumulating a large library,
but he displayed the diversity of his interest by collecting
antique bronzes, jewels and trinkets, coins and medals, prints
and drawings, and in addition, the paintings and sculptures with
which we are here concerned.[18] It is not surprising that Prior's
house was nicknamed "Matt's Palace," for it was regally adorned
with works of art. There were pictures in every room except the
servants' quarters. The drawing room and the adjoining "closet"
were a veritable private gallery, with almost a hundred pictures
covering their walls.

It was, to be sure, not a large collection by modern standard
nor were the pictures in it great masterpieces. It was, however,
an admirable accomplishment for a man who had inherited neither
pictures nor wealth. For the very reason that it was the work
of one individual whose limited means forced him to choose carefully, it was more indicative of the taste of a virtuoso than the
collections of the nobility, in part inherited, in part purchased

by agents who had been given cartes blanches. We may suppose that
not all the paintings that Prior might have desired were available,
and that many of those that were, were beyond his means. Nevertheless, the pictures that hung on his walls did represent works that
were admired by an English gentleman who during the reigns of
William and Anne had associated with the cultured people of London,
The Hague, Paris, and Versailles.

Under the circumstances, it is remarkable that so many painters of the first rank were represented in the collection, even if
only by minor paintings, works of doubtful authenticity, or copies.
The copies were often by reputable craftsmen, and they probably
served well the purposes of a virtuoso, although they would have
disappointed a speculator. Prior did not hesitate to acknowledge
that a picture was a copy if he knew it to be so. If he had more
copies than he realized or was in error in some of his attributions,
that is not to be wondered at considering the state of contemporary
scholarship on this subject. Many of his pictures he did not try
to ascribe to any artist.

Prior's collection had breadth and variety. The Dutch-Flemish school of painting was most adequately represented. The
Italian school came next, and then the French and the English,
with a sprinkling of others. There was every type of subject:
still life, genre, architecture, landscapes, seascapes, historical
subjects, religious and mythological subjects, and portraits. The
pictures in the last two categories were the most numerous:
about a fourth of the collection had religious and mythological
subjects, and more than a third consisted of portraits. This

preponderance of portraits was normal. The Dutch-Flemish school, which Prior favored, specialized in portraits, and an "old head" could be purchased for less than a large canvas by the same hand. Furthermore, portraiture was the one branch of art in which the English had achieved eminence, indeed, according to Richardson's boast, had "excelled all the world."[19]

There was naturally another reason for the number of portraits owned by Prior: they were mementos of people whom he knew. Not having an illustrious ancestry to commemorate, as many other collectors did, Prior substituted pictures that would indicate the heights to which he himself had ascended: the monarchs he had served, the noblemen who had been his patrons, and himself as a plenipotentiary. And to memorialize the friendships of his private life he had portraits of the men -- and women -- with whom he had been most intimate. Much of the pleasure that Prior took in his pictures must have been of a personal nature. He was not only familiar with many of the subjects; he was also acquainted with almost all of the contemporary artists who were represented in the collection.[20]

Prior may have begun collecting paintings while he was in Holland as secretary to the English embassy at The Hague, 1690-1697. It is certain that he made some acquisitions while in Paris during 1698 and 1699, and the collection probably continued to grow during the twelve succeeding years, which he spent in England. A number of his pictures seem to have been acquired between 1711 and 1715, when he was again in Paris. When the

change of ministry that followed the death of Queen Anne occasioned his recall, Prior did not bring back all of the pictures he
had with him. A score of them were left with Robert Arbuthnot,
a brother of Dr. John Arbuthnot and a merchant located in Rouen,
to be remitted to England in small lots at irregular intervals.[21]
Since Prior in recording the receipt of these expressed their
value in livres, it may be inferred that they were purchased in
France. In 1718, while these paintings were still abroad, Prior
listed forty-five of the pictures catalogued below as being "at
home." It appears, therefore, that he owned about half of the
collection at that time and acquired the rest between 1718 and
his death on September 18, 1721.

More specific information can be given about the history
of individual items subsequent to Prior's death. In his will,
drafted five weeks before his decease, Prior made some arrange-
ments for their disposal. His bust by Coysevox was to be placed
on his monument in Westminster Abbey.[22] His portrait by Belle
and the Earl of Jersey's by Rigaud were bequeathed to St. John's
College, Cambridge, his alma mater. Lady Henrietta Harley was
given the picture of Queen Elizabeth; and her daughter Margaret,
a miniature of himself by Boit. His friend Edward Lord Harley
was to receive the bust of Flora by Girardon and any six pictures
he might choose,[23] and was given the right to purchase any of the
remainder at the appraisers' valuation.[24] Harley bought seventy-
two items under this arrangement. After his daughter's marriage
to the second Duke of Portland, a number of these were taken to

Welbeck Abbey, where eleven of them are still preserved.[25]
During the settlement of Prior's estate, a few of the portraits
were given to the subjects or their families.[26] The remainder of
the collection was sold, probably to some London dealer, for a
public sale was precluded by the executors' desire that the effects be disposed of in a private manner.[27]

Information concerning both the history of the collection
and its composition is derived chiefly from the following
documents:

A. PRIOR'S LIST (Prior Papers, Longleat, Vol. XXI, extra sheets
    bound into the end of the volume).[28]

    In 1718, Prior dictated to his secretary, Adrian Drift, this
    list of the pictures then in his house, setting a valuation
    upon each one. In July 1719, February 1721, and July 1721,
    when Prior received shipments of the pictures he had left
    in France with Robert Arbuthnot, he added these to the list,
    stating their value in livres.

B. INVENTORY of pictures owned by Prior at the time of his death
    (Records of Prior's Executors, Welbeck, Vol. I, fols. 16v-18).[29]

    In 1721, soon after Prior's death, this complete room-by-
    room inventory of the pictures was made by Adrian Drift, who
    was co-executor with Edward Lord Harley.

C. PICTURES CHOSEN BY HARLEY as part of bequest (Ibid., fol. 68).

    From the Inventory, Lord Harley chose six pictures in ful-
    fillment of the provisions of Prior's will. When these were
    delivered, together with the items specifically willed to
    members of the Harley family, Drift made this separate list
    of them.

D. APPRAISAL of Prior's pictures (Ibid., fols. 46-46v).

    After the pictures that were bequeathed to Lord Harley and
    others had been removed from the collection, the professional
    appraisers, John Sanderson and Arthur Calcott, with the
    special assistance of J. Peters, set a value on each of the
    remaining items. In this list, the items were given in a new
    order and many of the descriptions were defective. The ap-
    praisals were astonishingly low even for that age, as both
    Drift and Harley agreed.[30]

E. PICTURES BOUGHT BY HARLEY (<u>Ibid</u>., fols. 72-72v).

From the Appraisal list, Lord Harley chose those pictures that he wished to buy. Drift then made this separate list of his purchases, following the order and numbering used by the appraisers, but expanding the entries sufficiently so that they may be identified with descriptions in the Inventory.

F. COMPARISON of the Appraisal of the pictures bought by Harley with the Valuation given in Prior's List (<u>Ibid</u>., Vol. II, fol. 20*, and another copy, <u>Ibid</u>., fol. 35).

In 1726, Drift submitted to Lord Harley this new list of these pictures with parallel columns giving "appraisers' valuation," "prime cost," and the difference between them. This helps to identify some of these items with the descriptions in Prior's List.

G. PICTURES SOLD BY THE COUNTESS OF OXFORD (<u>Catalogue of the Pictures belonging to His Grace the Duke of Portland, K.G., at Welbeck Abbey</u>..., compiled by Richard W. Goulding, Cambridge, The University Press, 1936, pp. xxxii-xxxiv).

This copy of Drift's list of the pictures acquired by Harley, with notes added to indicate their later history, identifies several items sold by Harley's widow when his collection was dispersed in 1742.

H. PICTURES THAT WERE AT WELBECK at one time but cannot now be located (<u>Ibid</u>., pp. xvii-xx, xxxii-xxxiv).

A list of the items that were mentioned in the Welbeck Catalogue of 1747 but have since disappeared. In each case there is given the date of the latest record of the picture's presence in the Duke of Portland's collection.

I. PICTURES NOW AT WELBECK (<u>Ibid</u>., Nos. 14, 15, 61, 97, 122, 161, 227, 237, 282, 444, 445, 854).

Each of the pictures from Prior's collection that is now at Welbeck Abbey is described in detail. Its history is given in full and copies of it are listed.

The catalogue that follows is the result of careful collation of all these documents. Because the lists do not always agree and some entries are incomplete or obviously erroneous, perfect correlation is impossible. We have therefore based this catalogue on the Inventory of 1721 as the most complete account of the items owned by Prior at his death. Whenever an item can be identified in the other lists, we have used any supplementary information that they supply. In our ascriptions of the pictures now at Welbeck Abbey we follow the printed catalogue of that collection. In all other cases, the ascriptions of the eighteenth century lists have been allowed to stand, although the artists' names are here given in the form generally used today. Whenever the lists describe a picture as being "after Titian" or "after Holbein," etc., we have repeated the phrase without comment. We have also followed the manuscripts in the use of such descriptive terms as "Large," "Head," "Half length" even though these may be inexact. For the sake of convenience in reference, the items have been rearranged alphabetically according to artist and have been renumbered.[31]

THE PRIOR COLLECTION

ALBANI, FRANCESCO
    1. Venus and Cupid. Small.
    2. Charity.
AMBERGER, CHRISTOPHE
    3. A Physician. Small, half length, on board.
BELLE, ALEXIS SIMON
    4. Matthew Prior. Half length.
    5. Simon Harcourt. Half length.
    6. Abbé François Gaultier. Three quarters length.
BLOEMAERT, ABRAHAM
    7. The Golden Age. On copper. Engraved with the date 1604,
        "Bloemaert Inventor. Nicola de Bruin Sculptor."
BOGDANI, JAKOB
    8. Peaches and Birds.
    9. Peaches and Plums.
BONZI, PIETRO PAOLO (called Il Gobbo de' Carracci)
    10. Pomegranates, Grapes, Quinces, etc.
BOURDON, SÉBASTIEN
    11. Europa.
    12. The Judgment of Paris.
CANY, JEAN BAPTISTE DE
    13. Bernard de Porto-Moriso, General of the Capuchins.
        Head and shoulders, oval, pastel on paper. Signed.
CHÉRON, LOUIS
    14. Our Saviour and the Woman of Samaria.
COMBES, PETER
    15. Landscape.
    16. A Hawk. After Holbein.
COYSEVOX, ANTOINE
    17. Bust of Matthew Prior. Marble.
    18. Original Mask of Louis XV.
    19. Bust of Louis XV.
    20. A Madonna in Profile.   )Marble bas-reliefs in
    21. Marius, the Younger, in Profile.) oval marble frames.
DAHL, MICHAEL
    22. Self-Portrait.
    23. Barton the Messenger. Head.
DIEST, ADRIAN VAN
    24. Schievling (? Scheveningen) on the Seaside near the Hague.
DIXON, JOHN
    25. Descent from the Cross. Water colors, after Van Dyck.
DOBSON, WILLIAM
    26. Charles I on a Dun Horse. After Van Dyck.
DOMENICHINO, ZAMPIERI
    27. Head of an Old Woman. Oval, in distemper, framed.

DOU (DOW), GERARD
    28. Two Boys and a Bird. Small.
    29. Head of a Girl. Small.
FLORIS, FRANZ DE VRIENDT
    30. Assumption of the Virgin, Our Saviour on her lap. Small.
FRANCESCHI, PAOLO
    31. Landscape. Small.
FRANCKEN, FRANS, THE YOUNGER
    32. The Golden Age. On Copper. Stamped 1608, signed.
FURINI, FRANCESCO
    33. Lucretia.
GENTILESCHI, ARTEMISA LOMI or ORAZIO LOMIDE
    34. Venus and Cupid Kissing. "Big as the life."
GHEERAEDTS, MARCUS, THE ELDER
    35. Queen Elizabeth. Small, whole length. Signed.[32]
GIRARDON, FRANÇOIS
    36. Bust of Flora. On a marble pedestal.
HELST, BARTHOLOMEUS VAN DER
    37. Family Group. Large.
HOLBEIN, HANS
    38. Head of an Old Man. Small.
    39. Head of an Old Woman. Small.
HOWARD, HUGH
    40. Anne Durham portrayed as Flora.[33]
JERVAS, CHARLES
    41. Matthew Prior. Head and shoulders. In crayons, framed.
    42. Adrian Drift.
    43. Alexander Pope.
    44. St. Catherine.
    45. A Madonna. In crayons, framed.
JERVAS, CHARLES, AND PETER COMBES
    46. Matthew Prior.
KABLE, ADRIAAN VAN DER
    47. A Seaport with Two Figures.
KNELLER, SIR GODFREY
    48. Queen Anne. Three quarters length, in oval.
    49. William III in his Robes. Half length.
    50. John Dryden. Half length.
    51. Charles Sackville, sixth Earl of Dorset. In his robes, half length.
    52. Lady Mary Villiers. Three quarters length, oval.
    53. Artemisa.
LE CLERC, DAVID (or) SÉBASTIEN
    54. Madonna and Child. Needlework, framed, after Van Dyck.
LEMPUT, REMI VAN
    55. Diana and Acteon. After Titian.
    56. Two Little Boys Kissing. After Andrea del Sarto.
LE NAIN
    57. A Peasant Family.
LENS, BERNARD
    58. Parrots. Miniature in water colors, framed.

LORRAIN, CLAUDE (GELLÉE)
  59. A Seaport.
MARATTA, CARLO
  60. Diana and Acteon. After Titian.
MOLA, PIER FRANCISCO
  61. Venus Sleeping.
MOMPER, JOOST, AND JAN BRUEGHEL, THE ELDER
  62. Landscape.
MONOYER, JEAN BAPTISTE (Called Baptiste)
  63. A Basket of Flowers.)
  64. A Basket of Flowers.) Small, companion pieces.
MURILLO, BARTOLOMÉ ESTEBAN
  65. Head of an Old Woman.
NETSCHER, GASPAR
  66. A Venetian Lady. Small, half length. After Titian.
PENNI, LUCA
  67. The Virgin with Our Saviour. Small.
POELENBURGH, CORNELIUS VAN
  68. Ulysses and Minerva.
POURBUS, FRANÇOIS, THE YOUNGER (?)
  69. Elizabeth of France. Head and shoulders, small.
POURBUS, PIETER J.[34]
  70. Charles IX of France. Small head, in a ruff.
POUSSIN, NICHOLAS, AND PIERRE LE MAIRE
  71. Moses Found in the Water. Large.
  72. Cleobis and Biton.
REMBRANDT VAN RIJN
  73. Head of an Old Man. Small.
  74. Head of an Old Woman. Small.
  75. King David at Prayers.
RENI, GUIDO
  76. A Madonna. Two hands showing.
RICHARDSON, JONATHAN, THE ELDER
  77. Elizabeth Cox. Head.
RIGAUD, HYACINTHE
  78. William Bentinck, first Earl of Portland. Half length.
  79. Edward Villiers, first Earl of Jersey. Half length.
  80. Matthew Prior. Half length.[35]
ROTTENHAMMER, JACOB
  81. Mars and Venus. Small.
RUBENS, SIR PETER PAUL
  82. A Dutch Boy in a Cloak. Half length, on board.
  83. Head of an Old Man.
  84. Heads of Two Old Men.
RYCKAERT, DAVID III
  85. Boors Playing at Cards. Large.
SAVERY, ROELANDT JAKOBSZ
  86. Landscape with Cattle. Small.
  87. Landscape with Birds.

SNYDER, FRANS
 88. A Boy and a Girl Blowing Soap Bubbles.
 89. The Same Boy and Girl with Parrot and Fruit.
 90. Partridges and Fruit. Large.
STEENWYCK, HENDRIK VAN, THE YOUNGER
 91. St. Peter in Prison, Delivered by an Angel. Large.
TENIERS, DAVID
 92. A Boor and His Wife by a Fire.
TINTORETTO
 93. Head of Titian. Small.
TITIAN
 94. Head of a Venetian Lady.
VAN DYCK, SIR ANTHONY
 95. Gaston, Duke of Orleans. Small.
 96. A Man Reading.
VELDE, WILLEM VAN DE, THE ELDER
 97. A Sea Piece -- a Calm.
 98. A Sea Piece -- a Breeze.
 99. A Sea Piece -- a Storm.
VERELST, SIMON
 100. A Flower Piece. Large.[36]
VERONESE, PAUL
 101. Christ with His Disciples and Mary Magdalen. A small ske
VERRIO, ANTONIO
 102. Our Saviour's Last Supper.
VIVIANI, OTTAVIO, AND MICHELANGELO CERQUOZZI
 103. Roman Ruins. Large.
WOTTON, JOHN
 104. A Landscape. Small.
ARTISTS UNKNOWN
 105. Alexander III and Frederick I at Venice, 1177.
  After Tintoretto.
 106. Leo X and Cardinals, posed with Christ at Supper.
  After Tintoretto.
 107. Charles V and Clement VII at Bologna, 1532.
  A long picture, after Tintoretto.
 108. Henry III Entering Venice, 1574. After Tintoretto.
 109. The Virgin with Our Saviour.
 110. The Three Graces. After Guido (Reni?).
 111. Venus and Adonis. A fine sketch.
 112. Erasmus. Head, on a deal board, in imitation of a print.
 113. Head of a Man in a Cap, called Quintin Mesius
  (Quentin Metsys?).
 114. A Jerusalem Pilgrim, called Christopher Amberax of
  Neuremberg.
 115. Richard Shelton. Three quarters length, in oval.
 116. Head of a Man in a Ruff.
 117. Cicero. A small marble bust.
 118. A Boy Singing.
 119. A Young Italian. Head and shoulders. Signed VC, 1639.
 120. Portrait of a Foreign Nobleman. Half length.
  After Tintoretto.

121. An Italian Philosopher. Head.
122. Head of a Woman. Very small, black frame and glass.
123. Head of a Woman Singing. Small.
124. A Man Telling Money.
125. Head of an Old Man in a Ruff.
126. A Landscape. Small.
127. A Landscape. Small.
128. A Landscape. Small oval, in an octagon frame.
129.) Two pictures of Birds, Butterflies, Insects, etc.
130.)   Mother-of-pearl inlay on black marble, small.
131. Italian Fruit in a China Dish, on a Carpet.
132. Herrings, a Jug, Onions, etc.
133. Fishes. Large.
134.)
to) Seven Prints and Drawings. Small.[37]
140.)

MIAMI UNIVERSITY
Oxford, Ohio

NOTES

1. John Dryden, "Observations on The Art of Painting of...
u Fresnoy," Works, ed. Scott and Saintsbury, London, 1892,
VII, p. 444.
2. The term was also used during this period to denote a
abbler in natural history and experimental philosophy. This
ype was frequently satirized, as in Butler's Characters and
hadwell's The Virtuoso.
3. For example, Alexander Pope, Sir John Vanbrugh, Sir James
hornhill, and Jonathan Richardson.
4. The most detailed and comprehensive study of a seventeenth
entury collector is Mary F. S. Hervey's The Life, Correspondence,
nd Collections of Thomas Howard, Earl of Arundel, Cambridge,
he University Press, 1921.
5. Jonathan Richardson, "A Discourse on the Dignity, Certainty,
leasure, and Advantage of the Science of a Connoisseur," Works,
ondon, 1792, p. 173.
6. Ibid., p. 196.
7. Ibid., p. 194.
8. Ibid., p. 198.
9. Ibid., p. 199.
10. Matthew Prior, Dialogues of the Dead and Other Works in
rose and Verse, Cambridge, The University Press, 1907, p. 187.
rior did not publish this essay. The manuscript from which it
as since been printed is obviously not in a finished state.

11. MSS. of the Marquis of Bath, Historical Manuscripts Commission, 1904-8, III, pp. 482-83, 487-88, 498-99.

12. Prior to Swift, May 29, 1718, The Correspondence of Jonathan Swift, ed. F. E. Ball, London, 1910-14, III, pp. 8-9.

13. C. W. Previté-Orton, "The Wall-paintings in K, Second Court," The Eagle (A magazine supported by members of St. John's College, Cambridge), XLIV, 1924, pp. 1-9.

14. Prior Papers, Longleat, XXIX, fols. 73-87.

15. Dialogues of the Dead, p. 404.

16. MSS. of the Marquis of Bath, III, p. 476.

17. The best account of all the portraits of Prior is to be found in the Catalogue of the Pictures belonging to his Grace the Duke of Portland, K.G., at Welbeck Abbey, 17 Hill Street, London, and Langwell House, Compiled by Richard W. Goulding, Cambridge, The University Press, 1936, pp. 90, 177-8, 285, 382-3. The portrayals of Prior in his own collection are Nos. 4, 17, 41, 46, 80.

18. The prints and drawings (appraised at over £250) were kept in portfolios and bound volumes with the rest of the books; they will therefore be dealt with in a forthcoming study of Prior's library. The collections of jewels and trinkets, coins and medals were not extensive. The bronzes were disposed of before Prior's death.

19. Jonathan Richardson, "The Theory of Painting," Works, p. 20.

20. The portraits of acquaintances in Prior's collection include Nos. 5, 6, 18, 19, 22, 23, 40, 42, 43, 48, 49, 51, 52, 77, 78, 79, 115. Artists represented in the collection with whom Prior was acquainted include Belle, Chéron, Combes, Coysevox, Dahl, Howard, Jervas, Kneller, Richardson, Rigaud, Wotton.

21. MSS. of the Marquis of Bath, III, pp. 463, 468-9; Records of Prior's Executors, Welbeck, I, fols. 92, 101v, 108.

22. The monument itself was erected from designs by James Gibbs.

23. The six pictures chosen by Harley are Nos. 59, 71, 72, 76, 94, 106.

24. The Will of Matthew Prior, Probate Registry, Somerset House.

25. The paintings preserved at Welbeck are Nos. 7, 13, 26, 32, 41, 69, 80, 91, 114, 118, 119. Two of Prior's bequests, the portrait of Queen Elizabeth (No. 35) and the miniature that Boit made of the Rigaud portrait of the poet (No. 80) are also at Welbeck

26. The portraits returned to the subjects or their families are Nos. 5, 40, 42, 52, 77.

27. Records of Prior's Executors, I, fol. 185.

28. This and other unpublished materials from the Prior Papers preserved at Longleat are here used with the kind permission of the Marquis of Bath.

29. This and other materials from the unpublished Records of Prior's Executors which are preserved at Welbeck Abbey are here used with the kind permission of the Duke of Portland.

30. Records of Prior's Executors, II, fol. 29. Paintings ascribed to Tintoretto, Veronese, Rembrandt and Van Dyck were

appraised at 5s. to 15s., paintings by Rubens and Kneller at Ł1. 5s. to Ł5. The item given the highest valuation was the copper work by Bloemaert, appraised at Ł10. The total value of the collection after the bequests were removed was estimated at Ł228. 6s.

31. The original form of this study, as published in The Art Bulletin, XXVII, 1945, pp. 195-204, includes further details concerning the documents listed above. It also contains much additional material under each entry in the catalogue which follows. Wherever possible, it gives information concerning Prior's relation to the subject or the artist, discrepancies in attribution, the valuation at different dates, the history of the painting, and its present location. Some of the works are described more fully.

32. Prior believed that this famous painting was the work of Pieter J. Pourbus, and it is so ascribed in his will and in all the manuscript lists, perhaps through confusion with No. 69. The authority for the present ascription is the Catalogue of the Pictures....at Welbeck.

33. For the identification of the subject of this portrait, see H. B. Wright, "Matthew Prior's Cloe and Lisetta," Modern Philology, XXXVI, 1938, pp. 9-15. Two of Prior's poems refer to this picture: "To Mr. Howard" and "Venus Mistaken".

34. See note 32 on the ascription of No. 35 to Pourbus.

35. It was from this portrait that Charles Boit made the enamel miniature that Prior bequeathed to Lady Margaret Harley.

36. Prior wrote a poem on "A Flower, Painted by Simon Varelst".

37. These prints and drawings are included in the catalogue because they were the only ones hanging on the walls of Prior's house. Concerning the others that he owned, see note 18.

ARTHUR ELLICOTT CASE

The facts of Arthur Case's life show him to have had an
unusually successful career that was cut short on the eve of still
greater distinction. He was born in Trenton, New Jersey, April 11,
1894, the second of three children of Charles Blackwell and Florenc
N. (Case) Case. After attending the State Model School at Trenton
from 1901 to 1910, he entered Yale, graduating in 1914. As an
undergraduate he acted in the productions of the Dramatic Association and was an editor of the Yale Record, for which he wrote light
verse of high excellence. He was a member of Beta Theta Pi. From
Yale he went to Harvard Law School. Upon his graduation in 1917,
he was associated with the law firm of Rawle and Henderson in
Philadelphia. Late in 1918 he enlisted as a private in the Chemica
Warfare Service, U. S. Army. Later promoted to 1st Lieutenant, he
was stationed in Washington, D.C. In 1919 he returned to his law
firm until the spring of 1920. By this time he had become convinced that he had chosen an uncongenial profession. Accordingly
he turned to literature, which had always strongly attracted him,
and in the fall of 1920 entered the Yale Graduate School, getting
his Ph.D. in 1923. In the same year he was appointed Instructor
in English at Yale and, by offering a graduate seminar in the
early 18th century, at once began to work in the field of his particular interest. At Yale he served as Instructor from 1923 to 19
and as Assistant Professor from 1926 to 1930. In 1930 he was call
to Northwestern University as Professor of English, where he taugh

until his death on January 19, 1946.

On June 16, 1927, he married Grace R. Lewis. He had two sons, Richard S. and Daniel F. Case, who are in the Yale classes of 1953 and 1955 respectively.

His principal publications were: A Bibliography of English Poetical Miscellanies (1521-1750), Printed for the Bibliographical Society at the University Press, Oxford, 1935; Four Essays on Gulliver's Travels, Princeton University Press, 1945. As editor: All's Well that Ends Well, Yale University Press, 1926; Gulliver's Travels, Nelson, 1938; British Drama from Dryden to Sheridan (with G. H. Nettleton), Houghton, Mifflin, 1939.

To speak at length about Arthur Case's character and personality would be inappropriate for a volume of this kind and would, under any circumstances, have been distasteful to him. He was a man of unaffected modesty, whose reticence and complete self-control masked both sensitivity and tenderness. Some things, however, can and should be said. His ethical standards were inflexibly high but were unobtrusive. His seriousness of purpose never interfered with his constant enjoyment of life. His keenness of mind was no more conspicuous in his scholarship than in his wit. He was always busy, alert, and interested. He was always having fun. The range of his interests was remarkable; music, the drama, all sorts of games athletic and otherwise, genealogy, and type-setting were some of them. But he was not a dilettante; he was a solid citizen active in the concerns of his church, his community, and his country. To everyone his kindliness and charm were evident. In the case of his intimates respect and affection for him went hand in hand.

Theodore Banks

A CHECKLIST OF THE WRITINGS OF ARTHUR E. CASE

Prepared by Arthur Mizener

1. BOOKS

William Shakespeare, All's Well That Ends Well, edited by Arthur E. Case, The Yale Shakespeare, New Haven, The Yale University Press, MCMXXVI

Arthur E. Case, A Bibliography of English Poetical Miscellanies, 1521-1750, Oxford, Printed for the Bibliographical Society at the University Press, 1935

British Dramatists from Dryden to Sheridan, edited by George Nettleton and Arthur E. Case, Boston and New York, Houghton Mifflin Company, 1937

Jonathan Swift, Gulliver's Travels, edited with notes and commentary by Arthur E. Case, New York, Thomas Nelson Sons, 1938

Arthur E. Case, Four Essays on Gulliver's Travels, Princeton, Princeton University Press, 1945

2. ARTICLES

"Some New Poems by Pope?" The London Mercury, X (1924), 614-23.
"The New Poems of Pope," The London Mercury, XI (1925), 411-412.
"Pope and Mary Chandler," The Review of English Studies, II (1926), 343-344, 346.
"Some Stage Directions in All's Well That Ends Well, Modern Language Notes, XLII (1927), 79-83.
"Notes on the Bibliography of Pope," Modern Philology, XXIV (1927), 297-313.
"Aaron Hill and Thomson's Sophonisba," Modern Language Notes, XLII (1927), 175-76.
"The Model for Pope's Verses To the Author of a Poem Entitled 'Successio,'" Modern Language Notes, XLIII (1928), 429-39.
"Pope, Addison, and the Atticus lines," Modern Philology, XXXIII (1935), 187-93.
"New Attributions to Pope," Modern Philology, XXXIV (1937), 305-13
"Discussion (of "New Attributions to Pope")," Modern Philology, XXXV (1937), 187-91.
"The Game of Ombre in The Rape of the Lock," Studies in English, Department of English, The University of Texas, 1944, Austin, University of Texas, 1945, 191-96.
"Swift and Sir William Temple -- a Conjecture," Modern Language Notes, LX (1945), 259-65.
"Swift's Supposed Ingratitude Toward His Uncle: A Surmise," Pope and His Contemporaries: Essays Presented to George Sherburn, Oxford, The Clarendon Press, 1949, 129-34.

ARTHUR E. CASE

New Attributions to Pope

review of 'Pope's Own Miscellany', London, 1935; edited by

Norman Ault)

from

MODERN PHILOLOGY

Volume XXXIV(1937), 305-13

****

NORMAN AULT

New Attributions to Pope (a reply)

from

MODERN PHILOLOGY

Volume XXXV(1937), 179-87

****

ARTHUR E. CASE

(a reply)

from

MODERN PHILOLOGY

Volume XXXV(1937), 187-91

REVIEW ARTICLE

NEW ATTRIBUTIONS TO POPE[1]

THE volume here under consideration is an edition of a rare miscellany which first appeared in 1717 as *Poems on several occasions*. Mr. Ault's introduction is chiefly taken up with the discussion of Pope's editorial connection with the book, and with arguments to support the attribution of all but five of its forty-two anonymous poems to Pope. Since, as Mr. Ault points out, it was I who first called attention to the miscellany, asserted that Pope was its editor, and ascribed to him fifteen of these anonymous poems,[2] it seems to be incumbent upon me to review Mr. Ault's conclusions.

On many things Mr. Ault and I are in complete agreement. He accepts and supplements my argument that Pope's editorship is indicated by the large number of his friends among the contributors, by his own contributions, and by the frequency with which his work is praised in the miscellany. Mr. Ault further agrees with my ascription of fifteen of the anonymous poems to Pope, though he demurs at my reasons in one or two instances. Finally, he adopts my suggestion that various puzzling references to the miscellany in the later eighteenth and the twentieth centuries are due to the confusion of the book with Fenton's poems, which were issued by the same publisher in the same year. The striking difference between my conclusions and those of Mr. Ault is that he ascribes to Pope twenty-two additional poems, resting his case chiefly on parallels of thought and diction in these poems and in the acknowledged works of Pope.

To be convincing, parallels should be, like Sam Weller's knowledge of London, "extensive and peculiar." And even when a number of such parallels have been assembled, one must inquire whether their presence can be explained in any other way than by the assumption of common authorship. Have the parallels a common source in the work of a third writer? Are they, if they occur in a translation, directly derived from the text translated? Can they be explained as borrowings by or from the author to whom it is desired to ascribe them? Lastly, and very pertinently in the present case, can they be the result of editorial emendation?

Several of Mr. Ault's parallels fail when they are subjected to the tests suggested by the first two questions. "Smit with . . . . ," at the beginning of the line "Smit with thy lays, we join'd the Sylvan throng," is obviously an

---

[1] *Pope's own miscellany*, ed. Norman Ault (London: Nonesuch Press, 1935). Pp. xcvii + 165.

[2] *London mercury*, X (1924), 614–23, and XI (1925), 411, 412. Four of these fifteen were already included in the canon.

305

echo of Milton's "Smit with the love of sacred song" (*PL*, III, 29). And if one requires a source for such a passage as

> Now of her thoughts thou art the constant theme,
> By day her whole desire, at night her dream, ...

surely Dryden's

> Aeneas is my thoughts' perpetual theme,
> Their daily longing and their nightly dream, ...
>
> [*Dido to Aeneas*, ll. 27–28]

s closer than any of the parallels in Pope's works cited by Mr. Ault. In discussing the translation of an epigram from Claudian Mr. Ault notes a "conception of coldness being preserved amidst and in spite of surrounding heat, literally and metaphorically," and he finds the same conception in a passage from Pope's *Iliad*. In both instances the concept is present in the original passage from which the translation was made. Of another set of parallels Mr. Ault says:

> . . . . they state a moral problem which seems to have been almost an obsession with Pope, for not only has he treated it at full length in *Eloisa to Abelard*, but has summarized it again and again in such lines as:
>
> > Is it, in heav'n, a crime to love too well?
> >
> > [*Unfortunate Lady*, 6]
> >
> > Too soon they taught me 'twas no sin to love.
> >
> > [*Eloisa to Abelard*, 68]
> >
> > Alas, alas, that ever Love was sin!
> >
> > [*Wife of Bath*, 324]

The last two of these three quotations are derived directly from the originals which Pope was paraphrasing at the time—the last, in fact, is copied verbatim from its source.

But the largest number of the parallels which I find unconvincing fail because they do not pass the tests of extensiveness and peculiarity. Generally speaking, the less extensive the phrase, the more necessary it becomes that its components should themselves be unusual: single words, in fact, must be almost *hapax legomena* to carry any weight, and even then they must be suspect if there is a possibility of direct quotation by the second user. Since it is obviously impracticable to discuss all Mr. Ault's suggested parallels in an article such as this, I have selected several which seem to me to be representative, beginning with single words and passing to more extended examples.

The appearance in two anonymous poems of the word "unperforming," which Mr. Ault has found once in Pope's correspondence and also in an unspecified place or places in his acknowledged verse, does not seem to me to carry much weight. The *OED* shows Dryden using the word in one of his well-known poems, and Watts employing it in his *Horae lyricae* (1706) in the very same way (his phrase is "unperforming promises") as it is used in the poems we are considering. Again, Mr. Ault finds that in two of the anonymous poems there are lines beginning "Sure . . . ." or "And sure . . . ," in which the word "sure" is used adverbially. He regards these lines as evidential because he has found some fifty lines in Pope's acknowledged verse which begin in a similar way. In other words, this supposedly characteristic opening is employed by Pope less frequently than once in a thousand lines. On the other hand, it occurs twice in Gay's *Shepherd's week*, a poem of less than nine hundred lines. Three of the poems in the miscellany begin, "See how . . . ."; one of these is certainly the work of Pope, and Mr. Ault offers the opening as evidence of common authorship. But Mr. W. N. H. Harding's index of songbooks[3] lists over fifty songs published between 1650 and 1715 which begin in this manner. Again, Mr. Ault submits the phrases "unerring eyes" and "the glories of her eyes" as peculiar to Pope. The first of these may be found in Vanbrugh's "To a lady more cruel than fair." Of the second it may be observed that the connection of glory with a lady's eyes is one of the most hackneyed of Augustan commonplaces. It appears four times, for example, within fifty pages of the sixth volume of the 1716 edition of Dryden's miscellany,[4] and the exact phrase relied upon by Mr. Ault occurs in Sackville's "Oh, why did e'er my thoughts aspire" (1684), and as "the glories of your eyes" in a piece in the second edition of *Female poems* . . . . *by Ephelia* (1682). Doubtless these are not the only instances. Lastly, to give one more example, Mr. Ault cites the locution "peculiar care," which he has found seven times in the acknowledged works of Pope, twice preceded by "God's" and once by "Heav'n's." Even these three-word combinations, I imagine, will not sound unfamiliar to the readers of Augustan verse; at all events, in reading through the first half of the sixth volume of the 1716 edition of Dryden's miscellany I found "God's peculiar care" on page 123 and "Heav'n's peculiar care" on page 190.

In examining the diction of the poem which he is most anxious to prove Pope's, Mr. Ault employs an unusual extension of the argument from parallels:

First, then, as to vocabulary: there being no complete concordance to Pope's works in existence (for E. Abbott's compilation excludes the 'Homer' and other translations and poems amounting to considerably more than half the verse, besides the whole of the prose), it is impossible to say offhand that such and such a word was, or was not, used by Pope. A protracted search, however, enables me to state that every word in this lengthy panegyric occurs also in Pope's works, with the possible exception of 'banter' and 'swerve,' and these, too, I believe I encountered somewhere in the prose and forgot at the moment to note. Admittedly the majority of the words, together with these two, belong to the poetic diction of the period. Nevertheless, every writer has, within the contemporary usage, his own characteristic range, which in addition, frequently contains a few expressions more

[3] In MS, in the possession of its compiler in Chicago.
[4] Pp. 233, 236, 246, and 282.

or less peculiar to himself. If, therefore, this poem were written by another person, we should legitimately expect him to employ in the course of fifty-five lines of verse a larger proportion of words outside Pope's vocabulary than might be represented by these two questionable, and not at all uncommon, aliens. For which reason, and also because most of the words recur again and again in Pope's poems, we cannot avoid the conclusion that, so far as vocabulary is concerned, his authorship of the piece is not only possible but probable.

In order to test the value of this method of determining authorship I applied it to another and considerably longer poem in the miscellany—an elegy upon Thomas Rowe. In Abbott's concordance alone I found all but five of the words employed ("uncertain," "engagement," "resemblance," "impression," "elegance"); the last three of these I discovered, without a protracted search, in the postscript to the *Odyssey*, and in the interval between the writing of this review and its printing, I have come upon the remaining two words in Pope's early correspondence. We have, then, a poem of ninety-seven lines, every word of which occurs somewhere in Pope's works, to oppose to a poem of fifty-five lines containing two "questionable" words. The longer poem was written by Thomas Rowe's wife, Elizabeth Singer. Further comment on the value of the "vocabulary test" seems unnecessary.

Mr. Ault does not, of course, confine himself to the argument from parallels in dealing with the anonymous poems, but in many instances his supplementary arguments leave me still unconvinced. The technical terms concerning painting which appear in "On a picture of Mrs. Catherine L——," for example, do not seem to me uncharacteristic of either Gay or Prior, to mention only two contemporaries of Pope who were interested in art. And the ten reasons offered by Mr. Ault to show that Pope wrote "The old gentry" suggest to me an equal number of adequate replies. I should like, however, to pass to the consideration of a series of seven poems which occupies pages 108–16 of Mr. Ault's reprint of the miscellany. In attributing these poems to Pope, Mr. Ault ignores some significant internal evidence which is, in my opinion, extremely damaging to his case. One of these poems is addressed to "the Ld. L——n," whom Mr. Ault identifies (quite rightly, I think) as Lord Lansdown. The poem deals with a cruel mistress named Aurelia; its first four stanzas read:

> Where L——n woud'st thou have me go?
>   To whom shou'd I complain?
> You've seen the eyes that cause my woe,
>   And know her hearts disdain.

> Thy Muse (and all confess her power)
>   Cou'd scarce the Mother move,
> Tho' oft she watcht th' unguarded hour
>   To soften her to love.

Will the severer Daughter's ear
  Then listen to my lyre?
Or deign the wretched youth to hear
  She only cou'd inspire?

Yet my *Aurelia!* do not boast
  Thy fated lover's lot;
In thine, thy mother's charms are lost,
  Her triumphs all forgot. . . . .

The plain implication of these lines is that Aurelia is the daughter of Lansdown's famous cruel mistress, Myra. The last two stanzas of the poem indicate that Aurelia was not engaged to be married. A subsequent poem in the series, "The King's box to Aurelia," must be dated 1714 or later, if the king referred to is George I. And the poem immediately following this gives still more information about Aurelia:

In her own isle the Goddess lay,
Fenc'd from the sun's severer ray; . . . .

How blest the world, how eas'd of care,
Had but her Isle detain'd her there,
Thousands and thousands had been free,
That sigh and languish now with me.

With me, their fable once, they prove
Companions now in hapless love . . . .

And yet I warn'd them of their fate,
Shew'd 'em what wounds her eyes create,
Describ'd her arm'd at every part,
And caution'd 'em to shun the dart. . . . .

The statement that Aurelia was "fenc'd from the sun's severer ray" in "her own Isle" suggests that the isle was Ireland. If this is so, the meaning of the foregoing lines is that their author met Aurelia in Ireland, that he returned to England and warned the English of the power of her charms, and that she herself has now come to England, where her triumphs are proving the poet a true prophet. This interpretation seems to be entirely consistent with such facts as I have been able to discover about the two daughters of Lansdown's Myra, who in real life was Frances Brudenell. The elder daughter, born in 1694, was the posthumous child of the second Earl of Newburgh, whom she succeeded as Countess in her own right. The younger daughter was Dorothea Bellew, born, in 1696, of Myra's marriage with Lord Bellew, an Irish peer. I have not been able to determine which of the two daughters (if either) was Aurelia, or when either of them visited England. The elder was married in 1713, the younger in 1717, but as the poems need not all have been written at the same time these dates do not help us much. Neither does the fact that

Lansdown is addressed by his title (acquired in 1712), since the substitution in the verse of "Lansdown" for the family name "Granville" would have been the simplest of editorial emendations. The reference to "the king" is some ground for conjecture that at least one of the poems was composed as late as 1714. But in any event it is unlikely, having due regard for the ages of Myra's daughters, that any of the poems was written before 1710. This fact would dispose of Mr. Ault's identification of this series of poems as the products of Pope's "childhood" of which the poet speaks in his letter to Cromwell on August 21, 1710.[5] Moreover, there does not appear to be any record of an acquaintance, let alone an affair of the heart, between Pope and either of the suggested Aurelias, though such an acquaintance, if it ever existed, must have come about during the period following Pope's entrance into the world of literary London, where such a matter would certainly have excited comment. Finally, if I am right in my conjecture that the author of this series of poems had met Aurelia in Ireland, then he cannot possibly have been Pope.

Before entering upon the examination of one last poem I should like to discuss a general argument advanced by Mr. Ault: that it is inconceivable that Pope would have printed in this miscellany of his anything written by another poet who had either stolen his phrases or imitated his style, and that he would have hotly resented as plagiarisms parallels appearing in anyone else's verse. In making this generalization Mr. Ault is perhaps thinking of Pope's attacks on James Moore-Smythe for his use in *The rival modes* of six lines by Pope. These lines, however, were appropriated before Pope had published them. That Pope was complaisant about imitations of and borrowings from his published verse is made clear by his inclusion in the 1717 miscellany of Broome's paraphrase of the forty-third chapter of Ecclesiasticus, which is plainly modeled upon Pope's *Messiah*, and which contains recognizable echoes of that poem and of others by Pope. I quote some of the most obvious:

> The everlasting mountains melt away   [l. 11]
> Rocks fall to dust, and mountains melt away
>   [*Messiah*, l. 106]
>
> Pours o'er the world a flood of radiant light   [l. 16]
> And on the sightless eyeball pour the day
>   [*Messiah*, l. 40]
>
> The fragrant infants [flowers] paint th' enamel'd vales   [l. 25]
> Here blushing Flora paints th' enamell'd ground
>   [*Windsor Forest*, l. 38]
>
> Oft waves on waves in solid mountains rise,
> And *Alpes* of ice invade the wondring skies   [ll. 89–90]
>
> New scenes unfold, and worlds on worlds arise   [l. 128]
> Hills peep o'er hills, and Alps on Alps arise!
>   [*Essay on criticism*, II, 132]

---

[5] As a matter of fact, the letter clearly identifies these "childhood" poems as the imitations of Waller.

When the seas rage, and loud the ocean roars,
And foamy billows lash the sounding shores: [ll. 97–98]

But when loud surges lash the sounding shore,
The hoarse, rough verse should like the torrent roar.

[*Essay on criticism*, II, 168–69]

Broome's attempt to imitate Pope's style throughout the poem is, in fact, so marked that one wonders if it may not have been one of the factors which led Pope to invite his collaboration in the translating of Homer. Certainly the appearance of Broome's paraphrase in this miscellany disposes of the suggestion that Pope would not countenance imitations of his manner or borrowings from his published works.

With this introduction let me turn to the examination of "To Mr. Pope on his translation of Homer." Mr. Ault lays particular emphasis upon his ascription of this poem to Pope, because he regards it as the fundamental cause of Pope's concealment of his connection with the miscellany. I may say at once that I should be quite willing to assent to a suggestion that Pope *might* have written this poem, although I must confess that, if it were proved that he did write it, the fact would not "throw a deepening shade on his character" in my estimation, as it would in Mr. Ault's. The practice of puffing was too general in the eighteenth century to carry any serious moral stigma. I am quite ready to agree that the man who had already written the fortieth number of the *Guardian* might well have repeated his performance, although I think he would have done a better job than this particular eulogy. Mr. Ault, too, finds the poem below Pope's standards, but he explains this falling-off as the result of Pope's attempt to conceal his own style. This is also the explanation advanced for the scarcity of parallels in the poem—a scarcity which Mr. Ault endeavors to counterbalance by an examination of the vocabulary of the poem as a whole. I have already discussed the fallacy (as I see it) underlying this argument. I should like in this instance to apply another test to Mr. Ault's methods of proof. I should like to see whether it is not possible, using means adopted by Mr. Ault, to make an equally good case for some person other than Pope as the author of the eulogy. If this can be done, then Pope's authorship has certainly not been definitely established.

John Hughes, in 1714, addressed complimentary verses to Pope on the occasion of the proposals for the translation of the *Iliad*. In Hughes's poem we find the line, "Crown'd on thy Windsor's plains with early bays," which suggests the second line of the anonymous poem we are considering, "Sung Windsor's forests, and her flow'ry plains." I have not the familiarity with the works of Hughes which would be necessary if I were to make an exhaustive search for parallels, but I have gone through his poems rapidly with an eye open merely for those phrases in the anonymous poem which Mr. Ault cites as characteristic of Pope. The first of these is "Sure" (or "And sure" or "But sure") used adverbially at the beginning of a line—a locution which I have previously discussed. One line of the anonymous eulogy begins thus; I have noted four similar lines in the work of Hughes. Another line of the eulogy begins, "You, only you. . . . ." Mr. Ault finds, in the range of Pope's verse, fourteen lines beginning in some such way (e.g., "Thou, only thou . . . ." and "Death, only death . . . ."), and he has not encountered similar openings elsewhere. Hughes has "Gain, pow'rful gain . . . ." and "Now, e'en now . . . ." to indicate that the device of repetition for emphasis was not foreign to his style. I have not found the phrase "Smit with . . . ." (which, as I have pointed out, is an echo of Milton, not of Pope) in Hughes's acknowledged poems, but it would be quite natural for him to use it, as he was one of the most enthusiastic Augustan admirers of Milton.[6]

It need hardly be pointed out that the pedestrian character of the eulogy, which is an obstacle to its attribution to Pope, is rather helpful than otherwise to anyone who ascribes it to Hughes. But there is a much more striking argument in favor of Hughes. Pope, in editing the miscellany, tended toward a policy of grouping poems by a common author. The eulogy we are examining was printed between "The old gentry" (which Mr. Ault assigns to Pope, but which I believe to have been written by Prior) and "To a lady with the tragedy of Cato," which is printed anonymously, but which was written, as Mr. Ault points out, by John Hughes. Mr. Ault offers no explanation of the suppression of Hughes's name, but it is now easy to suggest a plausible one. Hughes was a member of the group at Button's, which depended upon Addison for the distribution of Whig patronage. He would not have liked to appear publicly as an admirer of Pope's *Homer* after the Pope-Tickell imbroglio, even if he mitigated his offense by flattering Addison in the next breath. The safest course, naturally, would have been to avoid having his name connected with either eulogy by allowing both to be printed anonymously.

I hope that no one will conclude from all this that I believe Hughes has been proved the author of "To Mr. Pope." I merely wish to record as forcibly as I can my conviction that no sound conclusions on questions of authorship can be reached by these means.

Perhaps it will be well for me, in closing, to state my present beliefs about the authorship of the anonymous poems in the miscellany. I consider that the twelve poems beginning with the imitations of Waller are definitely proved to be Pope's because, as I said in 1924, they are printed as compositions by the same hand, and Pope later printed two of them as his own.[7] I feel that I

---

[6] These are the phrases which Mr. Ault selects as "most striking." He adds two other groups of parallels which I have not bothered to search for. The first set consists of references by the author to the particular poems of Pope which he is praising—references which, as Mr. Ault admits, would have been natural if the eulogist had been someone else than Pope. The other set of parallels consists of four "approximations of word or idea" added as a sort of makeweight.

[7] Despite Mr. Ault's disagreement, I must adhere to my original statement that these twelve poems are printed as the work of one hand. The group begins with the heading, "Verses in imitation of Waller. By a youth of thirteen." Six poems follow without further

should qualify my original positive ascription to Pope of the translation from Maynard; however, the unusual phrasing of the subtitle ("In English *for* Sir W. Trumbull"), the juxtaposition of this poem with another which Pope wrote and permitted Trumbull to appropriate, and the other circumstances set forth in my article, make the attribution extremely plausible. Mr. Ault seems to me to make an equally good, if not a better case for Pope's authorship of "The monster of Ragusa," from evidence contained in the correspondence of Pope and Swift. Aside from this I think Mr. Ault makes his best cases for the pastoral, "Palaemon," and for the group of four poems near the end of the miscellany, beginning with the lines on the statue of Cleopatra. Here he cites the only parallels which I regard as really significant; it is interesting to compare them with those he adduces elsewhere. I should be even more deeply impressed than I am by his arguments about these five poems were it not for Pope's habit of emending freely the verses of friends or acquaintances which were submitted to him—a habit which Mr. Ault stresses, apparently without realizing the extent to which it jeopardizes his contentions in general. Were it not for this habit I should regard as conclusive the parallel between "Palaemon" and a manuscript passage in "Winter" which Pope never published. As it is, I think that these poems must for the present be classified as possibly by Pope. I cannot feel that anything has been proved with regard to the remaining poems which Mr. Ault attributes for the first time to Pope. I should like to believe that some of them are Pope's, but the better they are, the less likely it seems to me that Pope, if he had written them, would have excluded them from his collected poems of 1717 or of later years. Some of them suggest, more or less strongly, that they may have been the work of this or that poet other than Pope. The problems they raise call for further study. We should be grateful to Mr. Ault for making them generally accessible, and for saying all that could be said, on the grounds of internal evidence, in favor of Pope's authorship.

ARTHUR E. CASE

Northwestern University

---

indication of authorship. Next comes a heading, "Verses in imitation of Cowley. By the same hand." Five poems follow: "Weeping," "Presenting a lark," "The river," "The fourth ode of Catullus. Paraphrased in the manner of Cowley," and "Catullus. Ad peninsulam Sirmionem." As in the case of the imitations of Waller, there is no additional indication of the authorship of the individual poems. Last comes the twelfth poem of the group: "Lydia imitated from the lyric of Corn. Gallus. By the same hand." I can see but one reasonable interpretation of these facts.

It should perhaps be stated that the indentations of the titles in the table of contents, as printed by Mr. Ault, appear to be editorial emendations based upon his own theories; at all events, the indentations do not appear in any of the three original copies of the miscellany which I have examined.

DISCUSSION

NEW ATTRIBUTIONS TO POPE

To the Editor of MODERN PHILOLOGY

SIR:

The ingenious, if misleading, review article, entitled "New attributions to Pope," by Professor A. E. Case, in your February issue cannot, in the interests of Pope scholarship, be passed over in silence. May I therefore, as the editor of the work criticized, *Pope's own miscellany*, be allowed the courtesy of your columns for a brief general comment and some illustrative correction of detail?

In the course of the arguments for Pope's authorship of a number of anonymous poems which he himself inserted in his 1717 miscellany, *Poems on several occasions*, I naturally put forward every kind of relevant evidence available; and this evidence inevitably included the witness furnished by parallel passages in his acknowledged works—for Pope is perhaps unique among poets in the extent to which he repeated himself both in thought and phrase. Mr. Case, however, devoted the greater part of his nine-page review to a discussion of a relatively small number of these parallel passages; and, although he casually remarks somewhere that I do not confine myself to the argument from parallels, he has in effect completely ignored the rest of the evidence I adduced. By such means, and by choosing the less striking parallels, one from this case and one from that, and considering them in isolation, he has presented to the unsuspecting reader a gross caricature of the arguments for Pope's authorship of the various poems—arguments which many students of the poet and the period, including scholars of international repute, have found, in the great majority of cases entirely convincing, and in the others only a little less so.

Two or three examples of Mr. Case's methods may be cited. Of the very first parallel which he discusses, namely, the locution "Smit with . . . ." (which begins the line, "Smit with thy lays, we join'd the Sylvan throng" in an anonymous panegyric of Pope), he says—twice over, indeed—that the phrase "is obviously an echo of Milton's 'Smit with the love of sacred song' (*PL*, III, 29)," and "not of Pope"; and so dismisses it as evidence. Later, when arguing that Hughes might have written the panegyric as easily as Pope, he says that, although he had failed to find the phrase in Hughes's works, "it would be quite natural for him to use it, as he was one of the most enthusiastic Augustan admirers of Milton"; but he omits to mention both that Milton used this locution once, and once only, throughout all his works, and that Pope used it frequently, having, as I have shown, at least seven lines

179

which begin "Smit with . . . .," a number of others beginning "And smit with . . . .," and yet others where the phrase occurs elsewhere in the line. Whether Milton originated the phrase or not, whether Pope borrowed it from him or not, are alike beside the point, which is, of course, the use of the phrase in the early eighteenth century; and until Professor Case can either show that the phrase was in general use about 1717 or point to another poet of that date who employed the phrase as frequently as Pope, its appearance in this anonymous poem in this miscellany which Pope edited, and in which he included a number of poems unquestionably written by himself but never acknowledged, suggests at least the possibility of his authorship.

For most people, perhaps, the possibility would seem to become something like a probability when in the same panegyric we find other phrases just as characteristic of Pope's usage: such, for example, as the emphatic repetition "You, only you . . . ." at the beginning of the line, "You, only you! the fierce Maeonian steed | Mount with success . . . . "—an opening of which Pope was fond enough to employ at least ten times ("You, only you . . . .," "Thou, only thou . . . .," "He, only he . . . . ," "I, only I . . . .," being some of his variations) but which Mr. Case has not been able to find anyone else using at that time. He is consequently reduced to suggesting that Hughes's "Now, e'en now . . . ." and "Gain, pow'rful gain . . . ." are just as good parallels for his particular argument.

One other locution in this same poem may be mentioned, if only for the sake of Mr. Case's mathematics, namely, the adverbial use of "Sure" at the beginning of a line. Pope may almost be said to have employed this habitually, seeing that it appears thus in his acknowledged poems nearly fifty times, which is in marked contrast to its use by other poets; for I have not been able to find it more than twice in all Prior's works, for example, and Professor Case has noted only four instances of its use by Hughes and two by Gay. Of the latter, however, Mr. Case seems inclined to make the most, for he compares these two of Gay's with Pope's approximate fifty thus:

In other words, this supposedly characteristic opening is employed by Pope less frequently than once in a thousand lines. On the other hand, it occurs twice in Gay's *Shepherd's week*, a poem of less than nine hundred lines.

But, as he omits to say that it does not occur at all in *Wine, Rural sports, The fan, Trivia*, or the translations from Ovid (to name the rest of Gay's longer poems down to 1717), which together amount to practically three thousand five hundred lines, his mathematical demonstration is apparently not to be taken any more seriously than his other arguments.

Although these three parallels constitute only a fraction of the various evidence which, as I have shown, points to Pope as the author of the poem; yet the existence of most of this evidence is not even hinted at in Professor Case's enterprising endeavor "to make an equally good case for some person other than Pope as the author of the eulogy"—an attempt which may be judged by his three references to Hughes noted above, for they form the larger, though perhaps not the most astonishing, part of his hypothetical case for that poet's authorship.

Professor Case makes similar play with much the same result with what he calls a "vocabulary test." I had pointed out, as a preliminary to my discussion of the above-mentioned panegyric, that all the words it contained (with, possibly, two trifling exceptions) are present in Pope's works; and, on the ground that, within the contemporary usage, a writer has his own characteristic range, had concluded with the modest statement that, so far as the vocabulary of the piece could testify, Pope's authorship of the eulogy was probable. In answer to this, Professor Case points to a longer poem in the same miscellany (Mrs. Singer's elegy on her husband), of which he says "every word occurs somewhere in Pope's works"; and then remarks: "Further comment . . . . seems unnecessary." Once again he has ignored the relevant facts, namely, that while all the words in the panegyric which Pope has been shown to have used were (with the possible exception of "dross," which I cannot find him employing before 1732) in use by him at the date of its publication, if not earlier, there are, on the other hand, at least nine words in Mrs. Singer's poem, which—according to Abbott's concordance—Pope did not begin to use until from fifteen to twenty years later.

Another example, this time of Professor Case's lapse of memory, is seen in the brief note with which he alludes to and dismisses another set of parallels, thus:

In discussing the translation of an epigram from Claudian Mr. Ault notes a "conception of coldness being preserved amidst and in spite of surrounding heat literally and metaphorically," and he finds the same conception in a passage from Pope's *Iliad*. In both instances the concept is present in the original passage from which the translation was made.

What are the facts? I wrote: "The conception [as above] was rather a favourite with Pope"; and proceeded to prove it by quoting in addition two other instances of Pope's use of this idea chosen from several which are to be found in his *original* work. In short, I cited three specific parallels to the thought in the anonymous couplet, two of them being from Pope's original poems; and Mr. Case, as shown above, not only has forgotten to mention them but also never thought to allude to the rest of the evidence—evidence which, incidentally, helps to make this one of the most probable attributions among the shorter anonymous pieces.

But enough has probably been said to show that Mr. Case is not pleased with my use of parallel passages; and that may explain why his numerous criticisms of them—with two, or possibly three, exceptions—are each, in fact or in effect, a misrepresentation of the arguments and evidence put forward in *Pope's own miscellany* in support of the new attributions. And, did space (and patience) allow, the fact that they are misrepresentations could be proved, as easily as the foregoing examples, by a simple statement of the whole truth in each case. Lastly, of these parallels it may be remarked that by far the larger number (which, oddly enough, coincide with the closest or most distinctive of them) were not quoted at all by Mr. Case; and also that the weight of their evidence was consistently ignored by him, until, in his final summary, he attempted to explain them away as Pope's editorial emendations—to which point I return later. In the meantime Professor Case's ingenious hypothesis concerning the "Aurelia" love-poems (which consist of the first two and last two of a group of seven anonymous poems all written "By the same Hand") deserves a word of comment.

The biographical value of the conventional love-poetry of the late seventeenth and early eighteenth centuries is extraordinarily small, and the interpretation of its hyperbolical language into matters of fact and history hazardous in the extreme. Consequently, "the plain implication," which Professor Case sees in various lines in the Aurelia love-poems, may to other people seem neither so obvious nor so reliable as he supposes—especially when it is realized that more than one lady is addressed in this group of poems. Thus, in the lines in which Lansdown is apparently invoked ("Thy Muse . . . . | Could scarce the Mother move"), Mr. Case's identification of "the Mother" with one of Lansdown's two "Myras," the Countess of Newburgh, has nothing more to support it than can be read into the seven words above quoted. For not only were there two "Myras" whom Lansdown's Muse sought to move—platonically or otherwise—but there was also a Flavia living "in the north" with whom his Muse was concerned at one time, and another lady at (we hope) another time, to whom, under the name of Clarinda, he likewise wrote a series of love-poems, besides a number of other ladies, named and unnamed, who were amorously addressed in one or more poems—all of which exercise of his Muse, being quite in the mode, does not in this present year of grace add to one's confidence in Mr. Case's "plain implication." Similarly, in the poem beginning "In her own isle the Goddess lay," in which the Venus fable is obviously conflated with the poet's obviously feigned experience, there is no ground for supposing that the line just quoted contains a genuine topographical reference, either to Ireland or any other isle. Nevertheless, it is on these two highly doubtful inferences that the Professor proceeds to build up his case by methods which not only allow erroneous dating but also permit an assumption in one sentence to be referred to, and argued from, as "this fact" in the next; so that at length he is enabled to reach the conjecture that the author of these poems had met Aurelia in Ireland, and therefore "he cannot possibly be Pope." (Incidentally, in the course of his argument he asserts that one of the Aurelia poems, *The King's box to Aurelia*, "must be dated 1714 or later, if the king referred to is George I." But the truth is that not even an approximate date can be deduced from the use of the word "King" in this connection, for either of two reasons: first, because in 1717, the third year of George I's reign, when this poem was first printed, it would have been absurd to retain the old style and call it "the Queen's Box," supposing that was how it had been originally written; and second, because the usage, "the King's Box," may simply have been due to the persistence of the habit of the previous century—exactly in the same way that many people continued to speak of "the King's English" right to the end of Elizabeth's reign—of which, "Abusing of God's patience and the King's English" in *Merry wives of Windsor* [1598], and "clipst the Kinge's Englyshe" in *Satiromastix* [1601], are sufficient examples at the moment.)

But Professor Case's hypothesis, even were it convincing, raises more difficulties than it solves; for the author remains still to seek; and it completely fails to explain the mutually corroborating evidence of the seven poems—very far from negligible in its cumulative effect—which points to Pope's authorship. For all the foregoing reasons, therefore, and because the poems composing the "Aurelia" group were written to more than one lady, they still appear to me to be exercises in the fashionable mode by the youthful Pope, equally with those other juvenile poems he addressed to other ladies, to Serenissa, Celia, Lydia, and Delia—imitations not only of Waller but of other poets— which, not foreseeing Mr. Case's meticulous criticisms, he used later when referring to them to lump together as the compositions of his youth.

The last argument advanced by Mr. Case against these new attributions is derived from the fact that Pope himself edited the miscellany in which they are found. Thus, although Mr. Case admits himself "deeply impressed" by the evidence I have adduced for what he calls my "best cases," he is reluctant to accept their attribution to Pope, because (he says) Pope had a "habit of emending freely the verses of friends or acquaintances which were submitted to him—a habit which Mr. Ault stresses, apparently without realizing the extent to which it jeopardizes his contentions in general." Noting, in passing, that, so far from my stressing it, or even calling it a habit, the only thing of the sort to which I had occasion to allude was the "correction" of Wycherley's poems undertaken by Pope years before at Wycherley's request; it is obvious that the snag in Mr. Case's statement lies in the words "which were submitted to him"; for the question immediately arises: "Submitted to him as a friend? or as an editor?" Mr. Case makes no distinction, but there are grounds for believing Pope made one. Of course Pope and his poetical friends indulged in the normal give-and-take criticisms and corrections of each other's work usual in close literary circles: there is plenty of evidence to show that he submitted his verse to his friends and embodied in it their suggestions and corrections, and also that he corrected theirs in like manner. But the fact of that friendly exchange of service in no way jeopardizes my contentions—unless, of course, Mr. Case is prepared to be consistent and maintain that everybody's works were written by somebody else—or possibly, a syndicate. Editorship and friendship are different matters; and it is highly improbable that, when Pope was compiling this miscellany, he forgot in which capacity he was acting, and was as free with his emendations as, on Professor Case's hypothesis, he must have been to account for the numerous parallels to his work in it. His letters (e.g., to Parnell [1717], and to Broome, December 6, 1715) seem to show that he did not—at this period, at least—correct his friends' verses unsolicited or without permission; and, if we are to judge from the one surviving piece of direct evidence (which, unfortunately, I did not unearth until after the book was published), Pope was decidedly more reticent as an editor than as a friend.

Among the "Homer MSS" in the British Museum is the manuscript of Lady Winchilsea's poem *To Mr. Pope* corrected for the press by Pope himself for inclusion in this miscellany. His autograph corrections (which were carried out by the printer) are as follows: line 3, "ventrous Poet" substituted for "Alexander"; lines 21–24 (*i.e.*, st. 6) entirely deleted; and line 30, "you sung" substituted for "that's gone." There is no other tampering with the text, none of his characteristic expressions introduced, no echo of his own work inserted. Such is the testimony of an actual specimen of Pope's editorial emendations for this particular miscellany; and there is not the slightest ground for supposing that the anonymous poems represent a·different treatment. If, then, these numerous parallels, many of them couplets, which bear witness to his hand, were not late editorial interpolations, they must have been there originally, and the only reasonable explanation of their original presence is that Pope wrote the poems in which they appear.

Naturally enough, perhaps, Professor Case wants to have the argument both ways. Thus, although, as we have seen, he ascribes the Pope parallels in the anonymous poems to the intervention of Pope's editorial pen, yet, to confute one of my arguments, he roundly asserts that the Pope parallels which he finds in a poem by Broome on another page (it will be noticed that Mr. Case is not so critical of his own cited parallels as of mine!) are Broome's imitations of Pope; and from this assertion he goes on to another, namely, that their presence "in this miscellany disposes of the suggestion that Pope would not countenance imitations of his manner or borrowings from his published works." But this time it looks as though Mr. Case has contrived to be wrong both ways; for there is no evidence at all to show that Pope inserted the parallels in the anonymous pieces; and there is indisputable evidence that he actually promised to emend Broome's contributions to this miscellany (as Professor Case should have remembered, seeing that he himself quoted it in his original article in the *London mercury*), namely, the sentence in the abovementioned letter to Broome, as follows: "Your own verses, and those of your friend, I shall commit to Mr. Lintot, and take what liberties you allow me with yours." It is therefore a practical certainty that Pope himself, and not Broome, was responsible for the parallels cited by Professor Case. Thus, even if his arguments had not themselves been mutually destructive, they are found on examination to have no foundation in fact. One other point may be noted: Pope's letter would also seem effectually to dispose of Mr. Case's hopeful conjecture that it was the success of these "imitations of Pope" by Broome which in part "led Pope to invite his collaboration in the translating of Homer."

A last specimen of Professor Case's critical methods is seen in the following comment: "The ten reasons offered by Mr. Ault to show that Pope wrote *The old gentry* suggest to me an equal number of adequate replies." He says nothing further, and thus leaves a doubt whether they would have been any more adequate than the rest of his article. Refusing to be intimidated by such gestures, I cannot better conclude these remarks than by printing for the first time a new piece of manuscript evidence which indirectly strengthens the attribution to Pope thus so airily dismissed. It should be first stated, perhaps, that an eight-line version of *The old gentry* (from a French epigram of the same length, entitled *Sur la noblesse*, by de Coulanges) appeared anonymously in this miscellany; and that twenty-two years later a poem of the same title, with an almost identical first stanza, a more or less approximate second stanza, and three new stanzas neither in the French nor the 1717 version, was included in Drift's collection of Prior's posthumous works, 1739. The evidence and arguments for the extreme probability of Pope's authorship of the earlier short version occupied several pages in *Pope's own miscellany*, and obviously cannot be repeated here. But I concluded by saying that Prior probably first encountered the theme, not in the French, but in the short English version when it was reprinted by Pope in 1720, and that "his poem was his momentary reaction to it, meant as a half-whimsical, half-serious embroidery of its subject rather than an appropriation of its lines. We cannot even be certain that he ever intended to print it." Shortly after the publication of that inference, Mr. Francis Needham very kindly sent me a careful transcript of Prior's first draft of his additions to *The old gentry*, which had recently been discovered by him in the Duke of Portland's library at Welbeck Abbey. The writing is in Prior's autograph and is scribbled on the backs of two sheets of memoranda, a folio leaf [A] and a quarto [B]. The draft runs as follows:

[A]

> his rustic pains
> Each when ~~his~~ pains begun
>
> ~~To merit~~ pleaded equal right
> To merit
>
> Twas only who left off at Noon
>
> ~~And~~ Or who went on to work till
> Night

                    better books We cast
Our Eye We must allow
that those are happiest who last
Took their hands frō the plow
~~alass~~ Yet still
~~but Each alass~~ his honʳ owns
          others
To favor and affection
By Nature We are Edoms sons
and sons of Anstis by Election

Kenoul, three hundred years have
                              rowld
since thy forefathers held the
                              plow
When this shall be in story told
Add, that my Kindred do so now

          how greatly is he fed
~~and~~ Independᵗ Eats his bread
~~who~~ the Man   getts
          in   great
                    and Eats
His bread in independᵗ state
               [B]
The Man who by his labor getts
His bread, ~~above all titles great~~
                    in independᵗ state

Himself can fix or change his fate

but Coronetts we owe to crowns
and favors to a Courts affection
By Nature We are Adams sons
and sons of Anstis by Election

Kenoul 8 hundred years—

The remarkable thing about this draft is that it omits the first quatrain which Prior took over almost verbatim from the 1717 version, and starts with the second, where his unquestioned work begins with a real divergence from its English precursor and the French original, after which it continues for another three stanzas with matter found nowhere else. In other words, all the work that is indubitably Prior's appears here in the process of composition; and as Mr. Needham is of opinion—from the various memoranda jotted down on the other side of the papers—that the draft was written in 1720, or early in 1721, his discovery would seem to support my earlier suggestion (based on other evidence) that Prior designedly adopted the first four lines of this anonymous epigram from the French as a theme for variations which he then proceeded to develop in his own way.

NORMAN AULT

Oxford

Mr. Case replies:

It was inevitable that Mr. Ault should consider the parallels which I commented upon the weakest of those that he suggested. I can only repeat that they seem to me a fair sample of those that he offered, always excepting the group which I spoke of near the end of my review as being much more cogent than the rest. I could not (and did not pretend to) discuss all of Mr. Ault's parallels, either in considering the epigram from Claudian or elsewhere.

Numerous instances of the use of the phrase "Smit with . . . ." by eighteenth-century authors will be found in Appendix A of *The influence of Milton on English poetry*, by R. D. Havens.

Mr. Ault seems to misapprehend the point of my remarks concerning the use of "Sure." I did not say and do not think that it is characteristic of Gay, or even more common in his works than in those of Pope. My argument is two-headed: (a) the locution does not seem to me to be very characteristic of Pope; (b) even if it were, its occurrence twice in *The shepherd's week* shows that it may by chance appear more frequently in a single poem by another author than it does generally in Pope's works, and that therefore it can hardly be relied upon as evidence of authorship.

I am a little uncertain whether Mr. Ault thinks that I take my "hypothetical case" for John Hughes seriously. Lest there should be any misunderstanding, let me say again that I do not think that it raises the slightest presumption in favor of Hughes.

I regret that I could not anticipate Mr. Ault's extension of his "vocabulary test." He now urges that Pope had used, *before July, 1717*, all but three of the words employed in "To Mr. Pope," of which one ("dross") occurs in his works in 1732 (the remaining two, "banter" and "swerve," never appear, so far as has been ascertained). On the other hand, Mr. Ault states that there are at least nine words in Mrs. Singer's poem which, "according to Abbott's concordance," were not used by Pope before 1717. Had Mr. Ault looked beyond the concordance (as he must have done in the case of "To Mr. Pope"), he could have reduced this list to two—"ecstasy," which Pope used at least as early as 1723, and "elegance," which is to be found in the postscript to the *Odyssey* (1726).[1] Both of these words may occur somewhere in the early correspondence which I have not examined, but it hardly seems worth while to make an exhaustive search for them. The plain truth is that neither of the poems in question contains a word that was not perfectly familiar to every contemporary versifier.

There can be little doubt, it seems to me, that the public of 1717 would have identified Aurelia's mother as the Countess of Newburgh on the strength of the lines I quoted: Lansdown's passion for Myra, as well as the lady's real name, were already well known. Undoubtedly, as Mr. Ault says, the most important poem in the "Aurelia" group is based on the Venus legend, but a poet who draws upon a conventional fable commonly selects those features of it which approximate the actual facts he is celebrating. The hypothesis I outlined is, of course, only a hypothesis, but it seems to me sufficiently plausible to require further investigation. I do not regard very seriously the objection that my theory "leaves the author still to seek."

Mr. Ault's references to Pope's editorial emendations appear on pages lxxix, lxxxv, and lxxxix of his introduction; if he does not think that they "stress Pope's habit," I gladly withdraw the phrase. The habit was a fact, nevertheless: Pope altered the verses of Wycherley, Addison, Broome, and Parnell, among others, and if we may believe his statement in the "Epistle to Dr. Arbuthnot," he was importuned to perform the same service for complete strangers:

> The piece, you think, is incorrect? Why, take it!
> I'm all submission: what you'd have it, make it.

As for the suggestion that Pope would have been somewhat chary of correcting the work of contributors who were not his friends, I can only ask: If the anonymous poems in question were not written by Pope, what is more likely than that they were written by some of his friends, as were all five of the anonymous pieces which Mr. Ault ascribes to authors other than Pope?

Naturally, as Mr. Ault says, I like to have the argument both ways when I can. He is attempting to establish Pope's authorship of certain poems, and argues, in part, from parallels: my objection is that these may be explained either by the real author's having imitated Pope or by Pope's having inserted

---

[1] The words from Mrs. Singer's poem which do not appear in the concordance, and the places where they may be found in Pope's writings, are as follows: "active," "impression," "harmony," "resemblance," "circumstance" (*Iliad*, preface, pars. 9, 12, 15, 26, 34); "anguish," "distract," "unstained," "engagement," "clay," "regardless" (*Iliad* i. 48 and 253, ii. 58 and 405, vii. 115, xii. 363); "uncertain" (first letter to Caryll, Jr.); "concerned" (letter to Martha Blount, June 3, 1715); "Providence" (letter to Lady Mary Wortley Montagu, February 3, 1716/17). Several of these words, of course, occur more than once.

emendations. Mr. Ault seems to think that in any given poem only one of these possibilities could operate; in any event, having noted that Pope undertook to correct Broome's verses, he concludes, "It is therefore a practical certainty that Pope himself, and not Broome, was responsible for the parallels cited by Professor Case." I confess myself unable to follow this reasoning.

Finally, I should like to discuss Mr. Ault's objection that I confined my review to an attack upon his parallels, ignoring his other arguments, and that I "airily dismissed" his examination of "The old gentry." It seems to me that he has a real grievance here. In the original draft of my review I dealt with the matter of parallels at length, since this was the one test which Mr. Ault employed in all cases. I also examined all his arguments for Pope's authorship of one poem, in order to show the kind of supplementary evidence he adduced. The poem I chose for this purpose was "The old gentry." When the editor of *Modern philology* requested me to shorten my article I did so by striking out my discussion of this single poem and substituting the sentence of which Mr. Ault complains. Upon re-reading that sentence I cannot but confess that it has a cavalier air which I sincerely regret. I can only apologize for it and subjoin here the suppressed passage. Unfortunately this compels me once more to summarize Mr. Ault's arguments—a service which no author likes to have performed for him by another. I have done my best, but I hope that those who are interested in this controversy will, in justice to Mr. Ault, read his own statement of his case, on pages liv–lx of his introduction.

In allotting to Pope the eight-line epigram, "The old gentry, out of French," Mr. Ault employs several arguments. The difficulty in this case is that a longer and presumably later version of the poem, clearly written with knowledge of the shorter translation, appears in Prior's posthumous works. Mr. Ault assumes that the longer version is Prior's and he confirms that assumption in a letter to *TLS* (December 7, 1935) in which he reports the existence at Longleat of a MS version that omits the first four lines, which closely parallel the corresponding lines of the shorter form. Mr. Ault's arguments in favor of Pope's authorship of the short poem are given below in condensed form; in each instance I have added my own comment.

a) The poem is a close translation of the original, neat, concise, polished in workmanship, and of general application, and therefore definitely more characteristic of Pope's manner than of Prior's.

What one makes of this depends on one's estimate of Prior's ability as an epigrammatist. If Mr. Ault means that the verses are too neat, polished, and concise to have been written by Prior, I doubt whether he will find many people to agree with him.

b) Prior does not elsewhere work over and weaken one of his authentic, previously printed poems.

The easiest answer to this is a reference to Prior's series of epigrams on a lady's eyebrow. We do not know whether he arranged them in the order of their composition or in what he considered a climactic order, but the third epigram is clearly the least effective; and certainly we have here sufficient evidence that Prior was willing to write variations upon one of his own themes. There are, it may be added, other examples of this practice in his works.

c) The epigram, complete and perfect in its way, was in existence by July, 1717, yet Prior did not include it in his collected poems of 1718 (published in March, 1719), which contained verses of less merit.

This argument, upon examination, works rather against Mr. Ault's case than for it. It might be altered to read: The epigram, complete and perfect in its way, was in existence by July, 1717, yet Pope did not claim it in Lintott's miscellany (1720 ed.), or publish it in any collected edition of his works, which contain verses of less merit. This behavior is more remarkable in the case of Pope, who seldom failed to claim really good work he had written, unless he feared it might reflect upon him in some way. Prior, on the contrary, was notoriously careless about his own compositions, and omitted from his 1718 volume many pieces of more inherent worth than this epigram.

d) In spite of the epigram's having been printed at least eight times before the longer version appeared, and having thus become known to friends and contemporaries of Prior, his name was never associated with it.

Like the foregoing argument, this applies to Pope with even more force than it does to Prior.

e) Pope would not have suppressed Prior's name in connection with the epigram through jealousy, since he ascribed to Prior all three poems which the latter contributed to Lintott's miscellany of 1712, which may have been edited by Pope.

In 1712 Prior's name attached to a poem would have been an excellent advertisement. In July, 1717, Prior was under arrest on the charge of Jacobite plotting. Pope was very anxious at this time to avoid any suspicion of his being connected with Jacobites or Jacobitism: this fact alone would have supplied a reason for suppressing Prior's name.

f) The epigram appears in a group of Pope's poems in the miscellany.

The validity of this argument depends upon one's agreement that the poems surrounding the epigram were written by Pope.

g) Pope never claimed, explicitly or implicitly, a poem written by another person.

Pope does not here claim, explicitly or implicitly, that he is the author of the epigram.

h) The second line of the epigram begins with "Sure," a locution often used by Pope, but seldom by Prior, who deliberately deleted it in the longer version of the poem. The contraction "ith'" appears in Pope's works, but has not been noted in those of Prior, who eliminated this expression also from the longer poem.

The parallels in diction offered here are among the weakest put forward by Mr. Ault. The evidential value of "Sure," used adverbially, has already been discussed.[2] If Prior does not use "ith,' " he shows that he does not shun this sort of contraction by using "oth' " in "The dove." The disappearance of the two words from the longer version is the result of the alteration of the meter and the complete re-writing of the second quatrain.

i) There is another epigram translated from the French by both Pope and Prior: in that case the latter failed to mention his French original, while the former confessed his source: this procedure is paralleled in the present instance.

Setting aside the question of Pope's authorship of the "poet-fool" epigram, let us go straight to the implication behind this argument, viz., that Prior was likely to conceal the fact that he was translating, and that Pope was not. The inaccuracy of this generalization will appear if one examines the titles of all the poems in Prior's authorized edition of 1718. Pope, it may be added, was at least once caught up for not mentioning that he was translating: see his correspondence with Henry Cromwell about Voiture's *Où vous savez.*

j) The Longleat MS, in which Prior begins his longer poem without writing down his slightly altered version of the first four lines of the epigram, is evidence that he was improvising on a theme by another writer. (Mr. Ault advances this argument in his article in *TLS* and elaborates it above.)

The MS is of value only in showing that the shorter version preceded the longer. If Prior had been recasting his own verse, he would have been quite as likely to omit the first four lines of the epigram as he would have been had he been borrowing from Pope.

ARTHUR E. CASE

Northwestern University

[2] See the original review.